Peloubet's

NIV Bible Study Companion
2003–2004

*Based on the International Bible Lessons
for Christian Teaching Uniform Series*

James Reapsome

*130th Annual Volume
Founded by Francis N. Peloubet*

Cook Communications Ministries
Colorado Springs, Colorado/Paris, Ontario

Peloubet's NIV Bible Study Companion

© 2003 Cook Communications Ministries,
4050 Lee Vance View, Colorado Springs, CO
80918, U.S.A. All rights reserved. Printed
in U.S.A. May not be reproduced without
permission. Lessons based on International
Sunday School Lessons: the International
Bible Lessons for Christian Teaching,
© 1998 by the Committee on the Uniform
Series.

Editor: Daniel Lioy, Ph.D

Editorial Manager: Douglas C. Schmidt

Cover Design by Jeffrey P. Barnes

Cover photography © 1998 by Dan Stultz

ISBN: 0-7814-3813-6

Faith Faces the World

Lessons for Life

Jesus Fulfills His Mission (Passion Narratives)

Hold Fast to the Faith

Use Peloubet's with Materials
from These Publishers

Sunday school materials from the following denominations and publishers follow International Sunday School Lesson outlines (sometimes known as Uniform Series). Because *Peloubet's NIV Bible Study Companion* follows the same outlines, you can use *Peloubet's* as an excellent teacher resource to supplement the materials from these publishing houses.

NONDENOMINATIONAL:

David C. Cook Bible-In-Life: *Adult*

Echoes Literature: *Adult*

Standard Publishing: *Adult*

Urban Ministries

DENOMINATIONAL:

Advent Christian General Conference: *Adult*

American Baptist *(Judson Press): Adult*

United Holy Church of America: *Adult*

Church of God in Christ *(Church of God in Christ Publishing House): Adult*

Church of Christ Holiness: *Adult*

Church of God *(Warner Press): Adult*

Church of God by Faith: *Adult*

National Baptist Convention of America *(Boyd): All ages*

National Primitive Baptist Convention: *Adult*

Progressive National Baptist Convention: *Adult*

Presbyterian Church *(U.S.A.) (Bible Discovery Series—Presbyterian Publishing House or P.R.E.M.): Adult*

Southern Baptist *(Baptist Sunday School Board): All ages*

Union Gospel Press: *All ages*

United Holy Church of America: *Adult*

United Methodist *(Cokesbury): All ages*

Faith Faces the World

Trials and Temptations

DEVOTIONAL READING

2 Corinthians 4:5-11

DAILY BIBLE READINGS

Monday September 1
2 *Corinthians 4:5-10*
Persecuted, but Not Forsaken

Tuesday September 2
2 *Corinthians 4:11-15*
Facing Death for Christ's Sake

Wednesday September 3
2 *Corinthians 6:3-10*
A Great Endurance

Thursday September 4
1 Peter 4:12-19 Suffering That Glorifies God

Friday September 5
James 1:1-8 Faith Must Be Tested

Saturday September 6
James 1:9-12 A Crown Awaits One Who Endures

Sunday September 7
James 1:13-18 Temptations Come from Our Desires

Scripture

Background Scripture: *James 1:1-18*
Scripture Lesson: *James 1:1-8, 12-18*
Key Verses: *Consider it pure joy, my brothers, whenever you face trials of many kinds, because you know that the testing of your faith develops perseverance.* James 1:2-3.
Scripture Lesson for Children: *Luke 5:1-11*
Key Verse for Children: *Then Jesus said to Simon, "Don't be afraid; from now on you will catch men."* Luke 5:10.

Lesson Aim

To encourage resistance to temptations and perseverance through trials in order to mature spiritually.

Lesson Setting

Time: *The early 60s of the first century* A.D.
Place: *Jerusalem*

Lesson Outline

Trials and Temptations

   I. Greetings: James 1:1
  II. Dealing with Hardship: James 1:2-8
      A. *Experiencing Joy: vs. 2*
      B. *Experiencing Spiritual Growth: vss. 3-4*
      C. *Receiving Wisdom from God: vss. 5-6*
      D. *Remaining Singleminded: vss. 7-8*
 III. Resisting Temptation: James 1:12-18
      A. *Blessing from God: vs. 12*
      B. *Temptation from Evil Desires: vss. 13-14*
      C. *Evil Actions Leading to Death: vss. 15-16*
      D. *Experiencing God's Goodness: vss. 17-18*

Introduction for Adults

Topic: *Endurance in God's Strength*

A woman fell under an oncoming commuter train and was trapped under the first car. Paramedics came to her rescue, but were frustrated because they could not ease her from under the train. They told the engineer not to move the train. Then they inserted an inflatable airlift bag under the 50-ton car and slowly raised it six inches to release her.

God's strength comes to our rescue like that time and again. We feel crushed under our heavy burdens and no one seems to be able to help us. But when we cry to God, He lifts the burden and releases us to find joy and peace.

Beyond our immediate release, God also guarantees us a crown of life. We are the firstfruits of His creation and He will not allow us to go under.

Introduction for Youth

Topic: *Facing Ups and Downs*

A wise Christian once told a student who was worried about his doubts that he should consider the ocean surf. The waves rise and fall. The troughs are times of doubt, while the crests are times of vital faith. But all the time the waves march inexorably toward the shore. The troughs do not prevent the water from moving ahead.

Walking by faith, in the midst of trials and doubts, is like that. We have to trust the unseen hand that drives the waves to drive us also to our crown of life. God knows when we are in the pits and when we are on the mountaintops. Wherever we are, and whatever our circumstances, we keep on trusting Him. God is a generous giver of all good gifts. By faith we take His gifts and march through the storms triumphantly.

Concepts for Children

Topic: *Peter's Call to Discipleship*

1. Peter was a commercial fisherman who obeyed Jesus.
2. Jesus gave Peter and his friends an enormous catch.
3. Peter admitted to Jesus that he was a sinner.
4. Jesus told Peter that he was going to be bringing in people.
5. Peter, James, and John left everything to follow Jesus.
6. When we obey Jesus, He calls us to help other people and to spread the Gospel to others.

Lesson Commentary

I. GREETINGS: JAMES 1:1

A. Our Trials: vss. 1-2

James, a servant of God and of the Lord Jesus Christ, To the twelve tribes scattered among the nations: Greetings.

There are two main views regarding when the Letter of James was written. One group of scholars thinks the letter was penned between A.D. 60 and 70 and represents Jewish and Hellenistic influences. A second group thinks the letter was written no later than A.D. 60 and probably before A.D. 50. This view seems to be the most plausible for four reasons.

First, as the early church maintained, the human author was James, the half-brother of Jesus and a leader in the Jerusalem congregation (Acts 15:13; 21:18; Gal. 2:9). According to ancient church historians, James was martyred during the years before the outbreak of the Jewish war of A.D. 66–70. Second, the letter is distinctively Jewish in character, as seen in the importance it places on the law (Jas. 1:25; 2:8-12; 4:11-12).

Third, there is no mention of the debate and struggle that arose in the early church over Gentile circumcision (Acts 15:1). Fourth, the letter reflects a simple church government whose theology is unadorned by sophisticated rhetoric. For instance, church leaders are called "teachers" (Jas. 3:1) and "elders" (5:14); and the gathering place of the church is called a "meeting" (2:2), which can be more literally rendered "synagogue."

An examination of the Letter of James suggests it was written for several reasons. The Lord, through the human author, sought to expose hypocritical practices, to urge believers to be uncompromisingly obedient to the Word of God, and to encourage them to let their real faith produce authentic deeds of righteousness.

James 1:1 indicates that the epistle was from James, who declared himself to be a "servant of God." The Greek term rendered "servant" does not bear the connotation of a free individual helping someone else; rather, the word refers to one person who sold himself into slavery to another person. In this case, James gave himself fully to the Lord in Christian service.

The background for the concept of being the Lord's servant is to be found in the Old Testament. For a Jew this notion did not connote travail, but rather honor and privilege. At times the concept was used of national Israel (Isa. 43:10), but was especially associated with famous Old Testament personalities, including such great men as Moses (Josh. 14:7), David (Ps. 89:3), and Elijah (2 Kings 10:10).

The letter was directed to "the twelve tribes scattered among the nations" (Jas. 1:1). This suggests the epistle was a circular letter that was sent from one congregation to another, with no specific geographical destination in mind. More than likely, the original readership was Jewish believers who had been forced to live outside of Palestine. This may have been as a result of the martyrdom of Stephen (Acts

7:59-60; about A.D. 34). Another possibility is that the scattering was due to the persecution initiated by Herod Agrippa I (Acts 12:1-5; about A.D. 44).

Most of the recipients seem to have been destitute and suffering from oppression. Evidently some of the Jewish Christians had been imprisoned and deprived of their possessions and livelihoods. Under such conditions, some of them struggled with worldliness, fought among themselves, favored the rich over the poor, and wavered in their commitment for one another.

II. Dealing with Hardship: James 1:2-8

A. Experiencing Joy: vs. 2

Consider it pure joy, my brothers, whenever you face trials of many kinds.

In referring to his readers as "brothers" (Jas. 1:2), James wanted them to know that he identified with their plight. As believers who were scattered because of persecution, they had demonstrated the extent of their commitment to Christ.

James urged his readers to regard the various trials they encountered as opportunities for "joy." The word translated "consider" refers to serious contemplation. In the case of hardship, rather than respond with anger, believers were to make a conscious effort to consider their circumstance as an occasion for spiritual growth.

B. Experiencing Spiritual Growth: vss. 3-4

Because you know that the testing of your faith develops perseverance. Perseverance must finish its work so that you may be mature and complete, not lacking anything.

The reason for such a response to hardship is that, when our faith is put to the test, it "develops perseverance" (Jas. 1:3). The idea is that through difficulties believers learn how to endure. In fact, God uses the distresses of life to cause our patience to grow.

It would be natural for believers to fight this difficult process. Perhaps that is why James urged his readers to let "perseverance . . . finish its work" (vs. 4). The idea is that believers should submit, rather than resist, the outworking of God's will for their lives, especially when it came to spiritual maturity. If Christians learned to endure the hardships they faced, their patience would become more fully developed; also, as believers grew stronger in character, their maturing demeanor would enable them to face whatever circumstance they encountered.

C. Receiving Wisdom from God: vss. 5-6

If any of you lacks wisdom, he should ask God, who gives generously to all without finding fault, and it will be given to him. But when he asks, he must believe and not doubt, because he who doubts is like a wave of the sea, blown and tossed by the wind.

Perhaps in enduring life's tough times, James's readers found themselves in situations where they were forced to make difficult decisions. They possibly had to make judgments about circumstances concerning which they had little insight. In these predicaments, they desperately needed wisdom.

Throughout the Book of Proverbs, readers are directed to get wisdom, to pursue it, and to acquire it by observing life's object lessons. Certainly there is much wisdom to be gained by being alert; but in James 1:5-8, the focus is on the need for wisdom beyond the readers' ability to attain.

All true wisdom belongs to God, and that is exactly where James directed his readers to go for it. James did not instruct anyone to inquire about the wisest and most experienced believers (though it can be helpful to seek the insight of such people); instead, he invited every believer to "ask God" (vs. 5). They could come directly to the Lord in prayer and petition Him for wisdom.

Christians need not fear that God will resent their requests for wisdom. The reason is that He "gives generously to all." They also did not have to fret that the Lord will scold them for wanting insight in knowing His will, for He does not find "fault."

There is one condition, however, on receiving God's gift of wisdom. As verse 6 reveals, one who asks must "believe and not doubt." In other words, believers need to have confidence in God's willingness and ability to grant the wisdom requested. There is no room for doubt. The doubting person is compared to a wave moving around by the force of the prevailing winds and having no direction of its own.

D. Remaining Singleminded: vss. 7-8

That man should not think he will receive anything from the Lord; he is a double-minded man, unstable in all he does.

James wanted his fellow Christians to realize that God cannot bless doubt and unbelief (Jas. 1:7). The divine intent was not necessarily to free believers from a troubling situation, but rather to give them insight on how to learn from their difficulties.

In order for spiritual growth to occur, beleaguered Christians needed to remain singleminded in their trust in and devotion to God. When believers cultivated a steadfast confidence in the Lord's control of their situation, He would replace their uncertainty with assurance.

Given what James said in verse 8, we can infer that some of his readers were indecisive about how to handle their hardships. Perhaps at one moment they felt like doing one thing, and then later they sensed the need to do something completely different. It is no wonder that confusion and frustration prevailed.

The solution, of course, was to redirect one's faith to God. When we set our confidence on Him, rather than ourselves, others, or the things of this world, inner strife and conflict will subside and we will regain our spiritual composure.

III. RESISTING TEMPTATION: JAMES 1:12-18

A. Blessing from God: vs. 12

Blessed is the man who perseveres under trial, because when he has stood the test, he will receive the crown of life that God has promised to those who love him.

In James 1:12 we find a beatitude of comfort when we face trials: "Blessed is the man who perseveres under trial." We please God and show ourselves to be His spiritual children when we patiently endure testing. Moreover, God promises to reward with an eternal "crown of life" those who love and serve Him despite life's obstacles. This metaphor draws upon a customary practice in ancient times. Athletes who won a contest were rewarded with a garland of flowers as a sign of victory.

B. Temptation from Evil Desires: vss. 13-14

When tempted, no one should say, "God is tempting me." For God cannot be tempted by evil, nor does he tempt anyone; but each one is tempted when, by his own evil desire, he is dragged away and enticed.

In light of what James said, the options were clear. Faith in the Lord and obedience to His will held the promise of eternal joy and blessing, whereas doubt and disobedience resulted in eternal sorrow and disappointment.

James urged his readers to reject the second option and avoid blaming God for the temptations they experienced (Jas. 1:13). James explained that the urge to do wrong did not originate with the Lord. Because He is infinitely holy, He neither was enticed by sin nor did He entice people to sin.

Thus, the origin of temptations lay elsewhere; for example, James noted in verse 14 that the lure of our "own desire" is a prime source of sinful enticements. These evil desires ensnare us and drag us off (in a metaphorical sense) to do what is displeasing to God.

C. Evil Actions Leading to Death: vss. 15-16

Then, after desire has conceived, it gives birth to sin; and sin, when it is full-grown, gives birth to death. Don't be deceived, my dear brothers.

Some think of sin as having a certain level of spontaneity; however, the comparison James made to physical conception and birth suggests that disobeying God is just as much a *process* as it is an *act* (Jas. 1:15). Thus, the process begins when evil desires tempt us to do wrong. When we cave in to the allure of sin, we engage in evil actions; and "sin, when it is full-grown," leads to physical death.

It is tragic that, rather than the believer pressing on to spiritual maturity, he or she, in yielding to temptation, allows sin to reach a state of full growth or development. It is no wonder that James urged his readers not to "be deceived" (vs. 16), or led astray, by incorrect thinking. They could avoid being misled by not blaming God for their sin.

D. Experiencing God's Goodness: vss. 17-18

Every good and perfect gift is from above, coming down from the Father of the heavenly lights, who does not change like shifting shadows. He chose to give us birth through the word of truth, that we might be a kind of firstfruits of all he created.

The Lord, rather than being the source of evil, is the source of every "good and perfect gift" (Jas. 1:17). In describing God as "the Father of the heavenly lights,"

James was affirming the biblical truth that the Lord created all things, including the sun, moon, and stars. Even the luminaries of heaven cast shifting shadows, but there is no "change" with God. His goodness is unvarying, which is a reassuring truth in a world filled with evil.

One way God gave expression to His goodness was in regenerating us by means of "the word of truth" (vs. 18), that is, Scripture. The reference to "firstfruits" means we are an initial spiritual crop that precedes the full eternal harvest to come; in other words, we are a foretaste of all will who trust in Christ for salvation.

Discussion Questions

1. What might have been some of the trials facing the believers to whom James was writing?
2. Why is it important to look to God for wisdom in handling life's difficulties?
3. Why does God insist that believers not doubt Him?
4. Why is it easy for some people to blame God for their difficulties?
5. How do immorality and spiritual wickedness prevent God's Word from taking root in our lives?

Contemporary Application

How should we handle temptations when they come to us? First, we must recognize that these trials are tests. The Lord allows them to come upon us to make our faith strong. Enduring temptation is not automatic. We must be tried by adversity.

A good athlete knows that physical stamina comes only when he or she endures a daily and rigorous training program. The pain and frustration of demanding exercises in the present are overshadowed by the joys of victory in the future. Likewise, James wanted believers to look at the results of their trials and tribulations.

Second, we must cope correctly with trials. Temptations in themselves are powerless. The devil cannot make us do anything. As was the case with Job, Satan can come against us in many ways; yet God sets the limits in which Satan can operate. We never lose the power to choose between right and wrong. Although these trials would ensnare us, God offers victory through the power of the indwelling Christ. Thus, temptation must be handled with the resources God supplies.

Third, we should endeavor to grow in grace (2 Pet. 3:18). Spiritually mature persons are not born that way; neither do these individuals reach a maturity level overnight. Growth necessitates that we endure over a period of time and overcome whatever obstacles in our way. Spiritual growth also requires that we be faithful to our task. God can use regular times of prayer, Bible study, and Christian fellowship to help us become stronger in Him.

Faith and Action

DEVOTIONAL READING

Matthew 7:21-27

DAILY BIBLE READINGS

Monday September 8
Luke 6:43-49 A Good Heart Produces Good

Tuesday September 9
James 1:19-25 Act on the Word

Wednesday September 10
James 1:26—2:4 Live Out Pure Religion

Thursday September 11
James 2:5-13 Do Not Show Favoritism

Friday September 12
James 2:14-18 Faith and Works Go Together

Saturday September 13
James 5:7-12 Live with Patience

Sunday September 14
James 5:13-20 Pray for One Another

Scripture

Background Scripture: *James 1:19—2:26; 5:7-20*
Scripture Lesson: *James 1:22-27; 2:8-9, 14-17; 5:13-16*
Key Verse: *Do not merely listen to the word, and so deceive yourselves. Do what it says.* James 1:22.
Scripture Lesson for Children: *Mark 9:2-8*
Key Verse for Children: *"This is my Son, whom I love. Listen to him!"* Mark 9:7.

Lesson Aim

To consider the ways we can live out our faith through Christian action.

Lesson Setting

Time: *The early 60s of the first century* A.D.
Place: *Jerusalem*

Lesson Outline

Faith and Action

  I. Heeding God's Word: James 1:22-27
    A. *The Importance of Obeying God's Word: vs. 22*
    B. *The Folly of Disobedience: vss. 23-24*
    C. *The Promise of Divine Blessing: vs. 25*
    D. *The Measure of True Religion: vss. 26-27*
  II. Cultivating a Vibrant Faith: James 2:8-9, 14-17
    A. *The Peril of Favoritism: vss. 8-9*
    B. *The Peril of an Inactive Faith: vs. 14*
    C. *The Folly of an Ambivalent Faith: vss. 15-16*
    D. *The Value of an Active Faith: vs. 17*
  III. Praying in Faith: James 5:13-16

Introduction for Adults

Topic: *Faith Means Action!*

When we walk into our health clubs, we check our file folders. After finishing our workouts, we mark what we have done. We want to see how we measure up to our trainer's expectations.

James is like that workout checklist. He is our spiritual trainer, pushing us to new levels of strength and competence. If we want to see how we are doing as Christians, we go to James. He tells us exactly what to do and what not to do.

The health club's workout checklist is meant for living people. It won't do the dead any good. It's too late for them. In a similar way, James wanted to be sure his readers were alive spiritually. His list is a life-and-death list. Read it to find out how you stand.

Introduction for Youth

Topic: *Faith Equals Action!*

One of life's cruelest lessons is that words can be meaningless. Parents say they love their kids, but fail to spend time with them. Coaches promise to give you an opportunity to play football, but forget you are warming the bench. Conductors promise you a solo part, but you never get it. "I'll help you," your teacher declares, but disappears. "I love you," your girlfriend gushes, and then goes out with another guy.

In many cases, that's what our words mean to God. We say we believe in Him. We say that Jesus is our Savior. But we find it hard to do what Jesus wants us to do. It's painfully hard to keep our word.

James tells us to stop being phonies. If we really are alive in Christ, we will do what He says, no matter how risky or embarrassing. It's dangerous to put our faith into action.

Concepts for Children

Topic: *Peter Learned That Jesus Was God's Son*

1. Jesus gave Peter, James, and John an opportunity to see His change of appearance.
2. Jesus' followers heard the Father declare that Jesus is His Son.
3. God told Jesus' followers to obey His Son.
4. The Bible clearly reveals who Jesus is and what He does for us.
5. By faith we trust the power of Jesus to help us.
6. We can confidently tell others who Jesus is.

Lesson Commentary

I. HEEDING GOD'S WORD: JAMES 1:22-27

A. The Importance of Obeying God's Word: vs. 22

Do not merely listen to the word, and so deceive yourselves. Do what it says.

In the Olivet Discourse, Jesus talked about those who claimed to be pious but were spurious in their assertions. The determining factor was their willingness to minister to the hungry and homeless (Matt. 25:41-46).

A similar emphasis can be found in the Letter of James. Here we find true religion being defined in terms of helping orphans and widows (1:17), and doing good deeds for others (2:18). Such an emphasis corresponds to the admonition found in 1 John 3:18.

As James continued writing to his beleaguered friends in the faith, he underscored the necessity of heeding Scripture (Jas. 1:22). Too often, especially in trying circumstances, it is easy to listen passively to the teaching of God's Word, but then fail to apply it to one's life.

James recognized this problem and urged his readers both to listen to God's Word and obey what it had to say. Otherwise, if they opted to "merely listen," they were deceiving themselves. In the end, God is pleased when believers allow every part of their lives to be transformed by Scripture.

B. The Folly of Disobedience: vss. 23-24

Anyone who listens to the word but does not do what it says is like a man who looks at his face in a mirror and, after looking at himself, goes away and immediately forgets what he looks like.

James used an analogy from everyday life to illustrate his point. He referred to a "mirror" (Jas. 1:23), which, in ancient times, would have been made from gold, silver, or bronze. Such metals, when polished, provided an imperfect reflection of one's image.

Imagine someone looking carefully at himself in a mirror and seeing that he was disheveled. If he then did nothing, he would have missed an important opportunity to improve his appearance.

In a sense, the Word of God is like a mirror that reflects back to us what we are really like. If we catch a glimpse of our sinful selves but refuse to do anything about it, we are operating foolishly, not wisely (vs. 24). The goal is to listen to and obey Scripture, for only in that way will we see our lives transformed by God's Word.

C. The Promise of Divine Blessing: vs. 25

But the man who looks intently into the perfect law that gives freedom, and continues to do this, not forgetting what he has heard, but doing it—he will be blessed in what he does.

James referred to Scripture as "the perfect law that gives freedom" (Jas. 1:25). This statement reminds us that God's Word is infallible and authoritative. When we heed its injunctions, it leads to spiritual freedom, not bondage.

The focus of verse 25 is on remembering what Scripture teaches and taking prompt, appropriate, and corrective action. When, under the power of the Spirit, we allow biblical truth to reshape our desires, thoughts, and actions, we experience God's blessings. Perhaps the greatest blessing is experiencing genuine freedom from sin.

D. The Measure of True Religion: vss. 26-27

If anyone considers himself religious and yet does not keep a tight rein on his tongue, he deceives himself and his religion is worthless. Religion that God our Father accepts as pure and faultless is this: to look after orphans and widows in their distress and to keep oneself from being polluted by the world.

Christlike love is a key aspect of God's "perfect law" (Jas. 1:25). The compassionate believer strives to please God, grow in holiness, and love others unconditionally.

In many ways the process starts with our "tongue" (vs. 26); in other words, what we say and how we say it indicates how genuine is our "religious" inclination. "Religion that God our Father accepts as pure" (vs. 27) is more than public routines and rituals. Those who think otherwise, James declared, were deceiving themselves and practicing a "worthless" (vs. 26) religion.

Ultimately, our "God our Father" (vs. 27) is the one who determines how pure and spotless our "religion" truly is. James, in mentioning the "orphans and widows" (who were among the most vulnerable people in ancient times), stressed that acts of kindness and compassion to them greatly pleased God. Also, believers refusing to be corrupted by "the world" met with divine approval.

Here we see that the practice of our faith should affect every aspect of our existence. In short, God wants us to be characterized by holy lives and loving service. While rites and rituals have their place, they are inadequate substitutes for a vibrant faith characterized by humility and sacrifice.

II. CULTIVATING A VIBRANT FAITH: JAMES 2:8-9, 14-17

A. The Peril of Favoritism: vss. 8-9

If you really keep the royal law found in Scripture, "Love your neighbor as yourself," you are doing right. But if you show favoritism, you sin and are convicted by the law as lawbreakers.

Evidently most of the recipients of this letter were poor and suffering from oppression imposed by their fellow Jews, among whom they were living. It may be that some of these Jewish Christians had been imprisoned and deprived of their possessions and livelihoods.

Under such conditions, these believers fell into the clutches of worldliness, fought among themselves, favored the rich over the poor, and lost their original love for one another. In James 2, we find the vexing problems of prejudice against the poor and partiality toward the wealthy being addressed. James made it clear that these vices contradicted "the royal law" (vs. 8), as expressed in Leviticus 19:18, to love others as much as we love ourselves.

Jesus made reference to this same verse in Matthew 22:39. When the command to love others is joined with the command to love God (vs. 37), we fulfill "all the Law and the Prophets" (vs. 40).

The original readers of James' epistle were not guilty of loving themselves too little, but rather of loving themselves too much. Such self-centeredness prevented them from reaching out to the poor with the compassion of Christ. Instead, these believers treated the rich (the elite of society) better than the poor (the outcasts of society).

James revealed that such favoritism was "sin" (Jas. 2:9), for it transgressed a fundamental commandment of Scripture (Lev. 19:15; Deut. 1:17; 16:19). Rather than pay special attention to the rich, the readership of James' letter were urged to help the impoverished among them, even if the recipients of such charity could never repay the kindness.

B. The Peril of an Inactive Faith: vs. 14

What good is it, my brothers, if a man claims to have faith but has no deeds? Can such faith save him?

"Faith" is a key word in the Epistle of James. "Faith" primarily refers to a person's belief or trust in God. The term is also used in the New Testament to refer to the body of truths held by followers of Christ. This second use became increasingly prevalent as church leaders and scholars defended the truth of the faith against the attacks of false teachers.

Faith can be understood as having four recognizable elements. First is *cognition*, an awareness of the facts; second is *comprehension*, an understanding of the facts; third is *conviction*, an acceptance of the facts; and fourth is *commitment*, trust in a trustworthy object.

Evidently some among the readership of this letter boasted about their "faith," (Jas. 2:14), but failed to demonstrate it through loving acts to the disadvantaged. For James, faith in Christ expressed itself in displays of charity toward the needy.

The idea is not that people are saved by doing good works; rather, the reality of their faith is proven by living uprightly and ministering to the disadvantaged. In the absence of these two factors, claims to faith are suspect. Genuine faith that leads to salvation obeys the scriptural injunction to love others unstintingly.

C. The Folly of an Ambivalent Faith: vss. 15-16

Suppose a brother or sister is without clothes and daily food. If one of you says to him, "Go, I wish you well; keep warm and well fed," but does nothing about his physical needs, what good is it?

James targeted those who voiced empty platitudes but did nothing to help the disadvantaged. In this case, those in need required food and clothing (Jas. 2:15). If the religious individual merely left the destitute with a pious greeting, it did the latter person no good (vs. 16).

The more charitable response is to join meaningful deeds with well-intentioned words. For instance, the well-off believer can be a source of divine blessing by helping to clothe the naked and feed the hungry. This can be done either directly or through a Christian relief agency.

D. The Value of an Active Faith: vs. 17

In the same way, faith by itself, if it is not accompanied by action, is dead.

The focus here is on a broad concept of intellectual assent versus genuine belief. The former is "dead" (Jas. 2:17) and useless, being devoid of charitable acts. An active faith, however, is vibrant, being characterized by compassion and concern for others.

James wanted to move his readers from an atrophied and lackluster faith to one that was robust and growing. That is why he stressed the necessity of faith in Christ expressing itself by means of good "deeds" (vs. 18). When such faith is planted in the soil of kind acts, it has an opportunity to thrive.

II. PRAYING IN FAITH: JAMES 5:13-16

Is any one of you in trouble? He should pray. Is anyone happy? Let him sing songs of praise. Is any one of you sick? He should call the elders of the church to pray over him and anoint him with oil in the name of the Lord. And the prayer offered in faith will make the sick person well; the Lord will raise him up. If he has sinned, he will be forgiven. Therefore confess your sins to each other and pray for each other so that you may be healed. The prayer of a righteous man is powerful and effective.

Deeds of faith include more than compassionate care of the needy. Prayer, praise, and confession are important acts of faith (Jas. 5:13-16). Prayer is the response of faith to suffering (vs. 13), and songs of praise is the response of faith to pleasant circumstances of life.

One of the most common forms of suffering people encounter is sickness. Faith should prompt believers to appeal to the elders of the church to pray for them while anointing them with olive oil. Faith should prompt the elders to pray for them in the "name of the Lord" (vs. 14). The prayer offered in faith will "make the sick person well" (vs. 15). That is a general principle, to which there are many exceptions.

The Lord will also "raise . . . up" the sick person. God may use medicine as a means. He may also respond to prayer. In either case, God gets the glory for healing the ailing believer.

Sometimes sin is involved in sickness. Prayers for forgiveness of confessed sins always avail. Therefore, James exhorted his readers to confess their sins to one another and to pray for one another (vs. 16). Confession and prayer extends beyond the elders to involve the entire church, that is, to one another.

Healing probably has spiritual as well as physical overtones in verse 16. The "righteous" is a group of people synonymous with those of active faith. Their prayers of faith possess spiritual power and produce tangible effects.

Discussion Questions

1. How is it possible for believers to hear or read God's Word but not heed its injunctions?
2. What does it mean to "love your neighbor as yourself" (Jas. 2:8)?
3. Why do believers sometimes fall into the trap of paying special attention to the rich, and how can they avoid it?
4. What is the difference between faith that is genuine and faith that is spurious?
5. Why are believers sometimes content to sympathize with those in need rather than help them overcome their problems?

Contemporary Application

I have several acquaintances who have shared that they would like to write a book. I try to encourage them by saying, "Work up an outline and then write one or two sample chapters. Next, start sending the entire manuscript to book publishers." Usually they are amazed to learn that they do not need to write an entire nonfiction book before they sell it to a publishing house.

The typical response is, "That does not sound too hard." Later, however, when I inquire about their book project, the answer is always the same: "I have not gotten around to it yet."

What went wrong? These would-be authors were not willing to sit down and actually manuscript anything; yet, if they had made the effort to write their thoughts down, their words could have touched countless lives.

This serves as an illustration of James's contention to believers. It is almost as if he were saying, "You call yourselves Christians? Unless there is evidence of your faith in the way you act, I question the truth of your claim. You may believe there is a God who saves, but has He touched your behavior as well as your mind?"

Apple trees produce apples, orange trees produce oranges, bankers invest money, and Christians are known by their good works. The good news is that, as long as we have breath, even the unfruitful can choose to change, opening themselves up to bearing the fruit of God's good works.

Our hands, feet, backs, and pocketbooks are some of the means by which we can help our fellow Christians. These sorts of resources enable us to comfort those in sorrow, accompany those who are lonely, and contribute to those in dire financial straits. People can see by our actions that our faith is real and vibrant.

In order for us to respond to the needs of others, we must first be aware of those needs. Sadly, too many believers are so caught up in their own feelings about their faith that they have lost the art of observation. By opening our eyes—and hearts—to the needs of others, we show that the God we serve also cares about them.

Faith and Wisdom

DEVOTIONAL READING

Colossians 1:3-14

DAILY BIBLE READINGS

Monday September 15
Proverbs 2:1-5 Search for Wisdom

Tuesday September 16
Proverbs 2:6-11 God Gives Wisdom

Wednesday September 17
Ephesians 5:11-17 Be Careful to Live Wisely

Thursday September 18
Colossians 1:9-14 A Prayer for Wisdom

Friday September 19
James 3:1-6 Keep the Tongue in Check

Saturday September 20
James 3:7-12 Bless and Do Not Curse

Sunday September 21
James 3:13-18 Godly Wisdom is Pure

Scripture

Background Scripture: *James 3*
Scripture Lesson: *James 3*
Key Verse: *Who is wise and understanding among you? Let him show it by his good life, by deeds done in the humility that comes from wisdom.* James 3:13.
Scripture Lesson for Children: *John 13:2b-10a, 12-15*
Key Verse for Children: *After that, he poured water into a basin and began to wash his disciples' feet.* John 13:5.

Lesson Aim

To prepare our minds and hearts to respond to others with godly wisdom and verbal self-control.

Lesson Setting

Time: *The early 60s of the first century* A.D.
Place: *Jerusalem*

Lesson Outline

Faith and Wisdom

I. The Tongue Personified: James 3:1-12
  A. *The Gravity of Teaching: vs. 1*
  B. *The Importance of Controlling the Tongue: vs. 2*
  C. *The Point Illustrated: vss. 3-4*
  D. *The Power of the Tongue: vss. 5-6*
  E. *The Potential of the Tongue: vss. 7-8*
  F. *The Inconsistency of the Tongue: vss. 9-12*

II. The True Source of Wisdom: James 3:13-18
  A. *The Truly Wise Person: vs. 13*
  B. *The Worldly Wise Person: vss. 14-15*
  C. *The Outcome of Worldly Wisdom: vs. 16*
  D. *The Harvest of Divine Wisdom: vss. 17-18*

Introduction for Adults

Topic: *Living Wisely*

Virtually every day we have to choose between earthly and heavenly wisdom. Our culture presses us to follow prevailing ideas and habits, even though these are contrary to God's will. Choosing God's wisdom means believing that He is holy, wise, and good. It means believing He knows what is best for us.

Yes, we sometimes make mistakes and fail to follow God's will. We think we know what is best for us better than God does. James explained that envy and ambition often lead us to make unwise choices. The devil wins another round when we do so.

Finding God's wisdom comes from faithful prayer, worship, fellowship, and study of Scripture. God does not publish His wisdom in huge neon signs. When we walk closely with the Lord, we sense Him directing us down the right path.

Introduction for Youth

Topic: *Watch Your Tongue!*

How many times a day do we have to watch our tongues? Perhaps it's while sitting at breakfast, or while nagging our parents, or while picking on our siblings. It could be when we meet our friends and one of them decides to spread a false rumor or denigrate someone else.

It's no wonder David asked God to set a guard over his mouth (Ps. 141:3). Each day we have to ask God to control our tongues. When we are tempted to join the fun of running someone down, we have to ask God to help us say something positive.

God can use us to turn curses into blessings, especially if we are courageous enough to use our tongues as instruments of righteousness and truth. Our walk with Jesus will be strengthened as we trust Him for this courage.

Concepts for Children

Topic: *Jesus Washed His Disciples' Feet*

1. Jesus' followers met with Him for the Passover meal.
2. No one did the customary foot washing, so Jesus did it.
3. Jesus showed humility and self-control, because He knew His future.
4. Humble service for others strengthens our faith and blesses others.
5. Even small tasks are important to Jesus.
6. We can pray for opportunities to serve one another.

Lesson Commentary

I. THE TONGUE PERSONIFIED: JAMES 3:1-12

A. The Gravity of Teaching: vs. 1

Not many of you should presume to be teachers, my brothers, because you know that we who teach will be judged more strictly.

Perhaps Bible teachers are some of the most admired people in the church. Those who explain the meaning of Scripture to others in formal settings come across as being more knowledgeable than and perhaps even a notch above other Christians.

As we consider James 3:1, however, we are forced to reassess this notion. We discover that knowing divine truth is not necessarily the same as living it. Put another way, it is one thing to have an intellectual grasp of the Bible, but it is quite another matter to practice what it teaches.

Perhaps that is why James issued a warning to Christians. While it is noble to aspire to a teaching ministry, we should also be ready to "receive greater condemnation." Expressed differently, God will evaluate our lives more strictly based on our increased awareness of the truth and influence over the lives of others.

B. The Importance of Controlling the Tongue: vs. 2

We all stumble in many ways. If anyone is never at fault in what he says, he is a perfect man, able to keep his whole body in check.

A primary way to convey the truth of God's Word is by means of the tongue. Perhaps this is why Bible teachers are known for their love of conversation. It is a natural way to implant biblical principles to others.

The downside, of course, is that a slip of the tongue can create a great offense, and the recipient of our harsh words may or may not forgive us. Perhaps this is why James emphasized the importance of controlling what we say. In fact, the person who can control his or her tongue shows a great deal of maturity in many areas of life (Jas. 3:2).

C. The Point Illustrated: vss. 3-4

When we put bits into the mouths of horses to make them obey us, we can turn the whole animal. Or take ships as an example. Although they are so large and are driven by strong winds, they are steered by a very small rudder wherever the pilot wants to go.

By now in our study of this letter, we have noticed the love James had for analogy. In 1:6, he referred to the doubtful mind being as unsettled as the waves of a storm-tossed sea. In verse 15, lust is described in terms of human conception. Then, in verses 23-24, James talked about obedience to Scripture in terms of someone gazing in a mirror.

Other examples, of course, could be cited. For instance, James illustrated his point about the controlled use of the tongue in speech by referring to the bit a rider places in the mouth of a horse to guide it (3:3). Similarly, the pilot of a ship can steer a huge sailing vessel by means of a relatively small rudder (vs. 4).

In the case of the horse, the animal might be strong and self-willed; nevertheless, the smaller, less powerful human can use a simple device to get the beast of burden to "obey" (vs. 3). In the case of a sea-going vessel, there are times when it is buffeted by "strong winds" (vs. 4); yet, even in these situations, the skipper can turn the craft about with a "very small rudder."

D. The Power of the Tongue: vss. 5-6

Likewise the tongue is a small part of the body, but it makes great boasts. Consider what a great forest is set on fire by a small spark. The tongue also is a fire, a world of evil among the parts of the body. It corrupts the whole person, sets the whole course of his life on fire, and is itself set on fire by hell.

The intent behind these two analogies is that the tongue functions in a similar way with respect to the individual. In this case, the focus is on the damage such a small member of the body can do. Despite the tongue's boastful claims, it can wreck untold havoc in the lives of its victims.

To further illustrate his point, James noted how a "small spark" (Jas. 3:5) can set an entire forest ablaze. In a sense, the tongue is like a flame of "fire" (vs. 6); in fact, it is a source of "evil." When the tongue goes unchecked, it spews forth wickedness that spiritually defiles "the whole person" as well as the entire direction of one's life.

This should not surprise us when we realize that the tongue is "set on fire by hell." The Greek word rendered "hell" is *Gehenna.* This is a transliteration of the Hebrew words *ge hinnom,* which mean "Valley of Hinnom."

This was the valley along the south side of Jerusalem. In Old Testament times, the spot was used for human sacrifices to the pagan god Molech (Jer. 7:31; 19:5-6; 32:35), and it came to be used as a place where human excrement and rubbish were disposed of and burned. In the intertestamental period, it came to be used symbolically as the place of divine punishment.

James, in making reference to "hell" (Jas. 3:6), was indicating that the tongue, when left uncontrolled, could become a tool for evil, rather than good. For instance, under the influence of the devil, people can say things that are quite destructive in nature.

E. The Potential of the Tongue: vss. 7-8

All kinds of animals, birds, reptiles and creatures of the sea are being tamed and have been tamed by man, but no man can tame the tongue. It is a restless evil, full of deadly poison.

People, left to their own devices, miserably fail to control their tongues. In fact, as James argued, it is easier to tame a wild beast through conditioning and punishment than human speech. Perhaps James had witnessed firsthand the destructive power of the tongue in the lives of believers. He described human speech as a "restless evil" (Jas. 3:8) or an unruly, incorrigible entity that is "full of deadly poison." It is no wonder he admonished in 1:19, "be quick to listen, slow to speak."

F. The Inconsistency of the Tongue: vss. 9-12

With the tongue we praise our Lord and Father, and with it we curse men, who have been made in God's likeness. Out of the same mouth come praise and cursing. My brothers, this should not be. Can both fresh water and salt water flow from the same spring? My brothers, can a fig tree bear olives, or a grapevine bear figs? Neither can a salt spring produce fresh water.

The human tongue—representing human speech—shows its deadly nature in its erratic and inconsistent behavior. It can strike at any time. One moment it blesses God; the next it curses a human made in God's image (Jas. 3:9). James despaired that the same mouth could spout blessings and cursings in almost the same breath. Such inconsistency does not occur in the natural world. A spring gives either fresh or brackish water, not one now and the other later. Fruit trees and vines bear their natural harvests, never unnatural ones. The tongue, by contrast, is perverse (vss. 10-12).

II. THE TRUE SOURCE OF WISDOM: JAMES 3:13-18

A. The Truly Wise Person: vs. 13

Who is wise and understanding among you? Let him show it by his good life, by deeds done in the humility that comes from wisdom.

The turbulent, churning evil associated with the improper use of the tongue was something James wanted believers to avoid. The solution was to humbly seek divine "wisdom" (Jas. 3:13).

Wisdom may be defined as the ability to handle matters skillfully, to exercise sound judgment, and to apply biblical truths to one's conduct. Divine wisdom guides the believer to live in an upright, virtuous, and well-pleasing manner. The wise person is committed to God, devoted to His will, and obedient to His Word.

There are numerous facets of wisdom worth considering. There is an intellectual dimension in which sublime truths are taught (Prov. 4:1) and an ethical dimension in which such virtues as righteousness, justice, and equity are commended (2:7; 8:20). Wisdom stresses the importance of revering God (1:7; 2:5) and caring for the needy (Jas. 1:26-27). Divine wisdom also reveals how one can lead a truly satisfying life (Prov. 2:10-21).

The Word of God strongly urges believers to embrace the wisdom of God (3:1-2) and forsake the folly of the world (9:13-18). The wise person enjoys a productive life, peace with the Lord, and spiritual joy (3:16-18). The foolish person, however, reaps sorrow, emptiness, and death (4:14-17).

The fruit of wisdom is far superior to gold and silver (8:19) and far more creative than anything humankind can produce (vss. 22-31). Those who appropriate the wisdom of Scripture are pleasing to the Lord, while those who reject it are condemned by Him (12:2).

It makes sense at this point to ask, "Who is wise and understanding among you?" (Jas. 3:13). After all, there are plenty of people these days who declare themselves to be experts. How can we tell the genuinely wise person from the pretenders?

From what has been said, perhaps the way one lives is a logical starting point for consideration. While anyone can claim to be wise, the truly judicious person seeks to live uprightly, remain humble, and exercise prudence in whatever he or she does. Authenticity, rather than pretense, undergirds such a life.

B. The Worldly Wise Person: vss. 14-15

But if you harbor bitter envy and selfish ambition in your hearts, do not boast about it or deny the truth. Such "wisdom" does not come down from heaven but is earthly, unspiritual, of the devil.

Against the backdrop of humility and graciousness that characterizes a truly wise person, it is easier to spot the cheap imitations. The worldly wise are characterized by bitterness, envy, and selfish ambition. The trail of deceit and strife they leave behind is nothing to boast about; in fact, it contradicts "the truth" (Jas. 3:14).

Verse 15 spotlights the real source of worldly wisdom. The jealously and selfishness it spawns originates from below, not "from heaven." Such wisdom is earthly, unspiritual, and demonic in character. In this light, we can appreciate more fully the emphasis being placed here on seeking divine wisdom.

C. The Outcome of Worldly Wisdom: vs. 16

For where you have envy and selfish ambition, there you find disorder and every evil practice.

Chaos and disorder follow in the wake of wisdom from below; also associated with it is "every evil practice" (Jas. 3:16). Who in their right mind would want such turmoil and cruelty to be promoted?

D. The Harvest of Divine Wisdom: vss. 17-18

But the wisdom that comes from heaven is first of all pure; then peace-loving, considerate, submissive, full of mercy and good fruit, impartial and sincere. Peacemakers who sow in peace raise a harvest of righteousness.

After being exposed to the unwholesome images associated with earthly wisdom, it is refreshing to learn more about heavenly wisdom. First of all divine prudence is known for its purity and clarity. Such, in turn, promotes tranquility and harmony, gentleness and humility (Jas. 3:17).

The wisdom from above is furthermore characterized by sensibility and kindness, mercifulness and charity, impartiality and sincerity. None of these virtues comes about immediately; rather, the Spirit cultivates them as believers yield to God's will.

The emphasis in verse 18 is on being peacemakers, rather than peace-breakers. James likens peace to seeds that the godly plant. The harvest is an abundance of righteousness, goodness, and justice. These graces are worth cultivating!

Discussion Questions

1. Why do you think James encouraged those who taught in the church to be careful about what they said with their tongues?

2. In what ways is being able to control one's tongue, or speech, an indication of spiritual maturity?

3. In what ways can an uncontrolled tongue bring great harm and sadness to oneself and others?

4. Why is earthly wisdom so prone to brag about how much it supposedly knows?

5. What is the fruit of godly wisdom, and why is it to be preferred over that of earthly wisdom?

Contemporary Application

Godly wisdom is not just meant for life-and-death situations. It should be a part of everyday living. For instance, imagine that a neighbor storms up to your front door. He is angry because he is certain your dog is responsible for tearing up his vegetable garden last night, and he is letting you know exactly what he thinks about you and your pet.

There is one mistake, however. Only two weeks earlier, you had to take your dog to the veterinarian to be put to sleep. The dog had been like a part of the family, and you are still sad about the loss.

Perhaps your first impulse would be to blast your rude, insensitive neighbor with some sharp retorts to his accusations; but should you follow your impulse? Your neighbor has finished his tirade, and now you have an opportunity to respond. What will you say?

On the surface, this situation may seem relatively insignificant; but what if this neighbor is not a Christian and knows that you are one? Our lives are filled with situations that offer opportunities to demonstrate our faith to others by what we say and do.

Such opportunities can come quickly. We never know how one of our responses might impact someone. A good or bad word at a critical time in someone's life may leave an indelible impression on his or her thinking about Christians and ultimately about the Savior. As God's ambassadors, we need His wisdom daily to guide our words and actions.

Faith and Attitudes

DEVOTIONAL READING

1 Peter 5:1-6

DAILY BIBLE READINGS

Monday September 22
Psalm 66:8-15 Praise and Offerings to God

Tuesday September 23
Psalm 66:16-20 God Hears a Sincere Heart

Wednesday September 24
James 5:1-6 Warning about Trusting Riches

Thursday September 25
1 Peter 5:1-6 Be Clothed in Humility

Friday September 26
James 4:1-6 God Gives Grace to the Humble

Saturday September 27
James 4:7-12 God Exalts the Humble

Sunday September 28
James 4:13-17 Get Rid of Arrogance

Scripture

Background Scripture: *James 4:1—5:6*
Scripture Lesson: *James 4:1-10, 13-17*
Key Verse: *Humble yourselves before the Lord, and he will lift you up.* James 4:10.
Scripture Lesson for Children: *Mark 14:32-42*
Key Verse for Children: *"Simon," he said to Peter, "are you asleep? Could you not watch for one hour?"* (Mark 14:37).

Lesson Aim

To recognize the importance of humility and proper motives in our pursuit of righteousness.

Lesson Setting

Time: *The early 60s of the first century* A.D.
Place: *Jerusalem*

Lesson Outline

Faith and Attitudes

   I. Pride Leading to Strife: James 4:1-10
      A. *The Strife Resulting from Selfish Desires: vs. 1*
      B. *The Futility of Envy and Greed: vss. 2-3*
      C. *The Folly of Friendship with the World: vs. 4*
      D. *The Concern and Care of God: vss. 5-6*
      E. *The Prudence of Submitting to God: vss. 7-8*
      F. *The Wisdom of Yielding to God: vss. 9-10*
  II. Warning Against Bragging: James 4:13-17
      A. *The Transitory Nature of Life: vss. 13-14*
      B. *The Importance of Submitting to God: vss. 15-16*
      C. *The Value of Doing What Is Right: vs. 17*

Introduction for Adults

Topic: *Humility Is Next to Godliness*

Charles Wesley, the hymn writer, captured the essence of James when he wrote, "A humble, lowly, contrite heart, believing, true and clean." The Bible consistently cautions against pride and encourages humility. Some people say that pride is the essence of sin. If so, then humility is the essence of godliness.

We have to confess that too often our pride overrides our humility. Each day seems to bring some opportunity to exalt ourselves and our ways of thinking and doing things. We show pride not just in positions and possessions, but also in our church traditions.

At the beginning of each day we should ask God to keep us humble; and at the end of each day we should confess our pride. Then, as James affirmed, we will receive more grace.

Introduction for Youth

Topic: *Tough Choices*

The father remembered well when his teenaged son John first encountered James 4:4. "How can this be?" he asked. "I like lots of things in the world. Does that make me God's enemy?"

The father tried to explain that being the world's "friend" means more than liking sports, music, fishing, good food, and a happy family. It means shaping your own values according to the world's standards. For example, if the world says it's okay to lie, steal, and cheat, then we part company with the world. When we cave in to the world, we choose to be God's enemy.

Of course, the world hates to make such choices. As Christians, who place God's will above everything else, we choose to follow Him, even if we lose some friends who do not.

Concepts for Children

Topic: *Jesus Prayed*

1. Jesus took His followers to a place called Gethsemane to be with Him while He prayed.
2. Jesus was so sad that He prayed to the Father in heaven about dying on the cross.
3. Jesus gave Himself completely to His Father's will.
4. Jesus asked His followers to stay alert and pray.
5. When things look sad for us, we can pray to the Lord.
6. We are thankful that Jesus obeyed the Father and made salvation possible for us.

Lesson Commentary

I. PRIDE LEADING TO STRIFE: JAMES 4:1-10

A. The Strife Resulting from Selfish Desires: vs. 1

What causes fights and quarrels among you? Don't they come from your desires that battle within you?

A popular slogan in recent years has been "peace through strength." James, however, might change that to "peace through humility." The reason is that sources of wars and fights are internal desires for pleasures. Our cravings, in turn, lead to friendship with the world and enmity toward God. Thus, peace in the world depends on peace with God, and that requires humility.

Recently, the world in which we live has become filled with reports of "fights and quarrels" (Jas. 4:1). The sad realization is that clashes also prevail in local congregations. This was just as true in the early church as it is today.

What is the source of these conflicts? James focused specifically on our evil and selfish desires for pleasure. These "battle" with the will of God and strive for dominance in the church. Unless the Lord's will is allowed to prevail, the presence of strife and conflict are bound to continue.

B. The Futility of Envy and Greed: vss. 2-3

You want something but don't get it. You kill and covet, but you cannot have what you want. You quarrel and fight. You do not have, because you do not ask God. When you ask, you do not receive, because you ask with wrong motives, that you may spend what you get on your pleasures.

Believers, in their shortsightedness, "covet" (Jas. 4:2) what they do not have, and thus resort to scheming and injustice to get it. The more envious they become, the more they try to obtain what others have through worldly, underhanded means.

Despite such efforts, the displays of jealously and greed among believers—both in the early church as well as in modern times—leads only to futility and frustration. The solution is to pray to God about these and other pressing matters.

Verse 3 targets one important facet of prayer, namely, our motives. This prompts a key question: Why are we petitioning God? If it is merely to gratify our selfish desires, then we are asking "with wrong motives," and will not see God answer our requests. The solution is to reorient our desires to match those of God.

C. The Folly of Friendship with the World: vs. 4

You adulterous people, don't you know that friendship with the world is hatred toward God? Anyone who chooses to be a friend of the world becomes an enemy of God.

The vices just described prevail in fallen human society. When they also appear among Christians, it is because believers have jettisoned loyalty to God for "friendship with the world" (Jas. 4:4).

James used strong language when he labeled compromising Christians as "adulterous people." The idea is that they had become spiritually unfaithful to God by embracing the values and aims of the world. The more believers turn their hearts away from God, the greater is their alienation from Him.

In the Sermon on the Mount, Jesus declared that believers cannot serve two masters. Their devotion is either to God or money (Matt. 6:24). James reflected this teaching when he declared that those who are a friend of the world also are the enemy of God. Nothing less than enmity can exist when one's aim is to enjoy the world rather than love and serve God.

D. The Concern and Care of God: vss. 5-6

Or do you think Scripture says without reason that the spirit he caused to live in us envies intensely? But he gives us more grace. That is why Scripture says: "God opposes the proud but gives grace to the humble."

James declared that the "spirit he caused to live in us envies intensely" (Jas. 4:5). Some take this as a reference to the individual human spirit. In this case, the jealous yearning refers to the covetous desires of people.

The more immediate context of verse 4, however, could suggest that, in verse 5, James was referring to the Holy Spirit. The idea, then, is that the Spirit, who dwells in us, cares for us deeply and longs for us to be faithful to the Lord. Thus, when we opt for friendship with the world, it provokes God to anger.

Sometimes when we talk about God's love, we misconstrue it to be merely static and willful in nature; but the previous interpretation suggests that there is also a strong affective dimension to God. He longs to be in relationship with us and is displeased when we stray from Him.

Thankfully, God in His "grace" (vs. 6) does not abandon us in our spiritual waywardness; instead, He is ready to shower us with His kindness to overcome our envy and greed. In fact, we need His strength to turn from the world and back to Him. As the quote from Proverbs 3:34 teaches, God opposes all who are proud, but manifests His grace to the humble.

E. The Prudence of Submitting to God: vss. 7-8

Submit yourselves, then, to God. Resist the devil, and he will flee from you. Come near to God and he will come near to you. Wash your hands, you sinners, and purify your hearts, you double-minded.

Humbly surrendering to God is the best way to get rid of strife and turmoil in the church. It is also the best way to combat the enticements of the devil. In fact, when we resist him (under the power of the Spirit), we win the victory over him as well as our own surly ways (Jas. 4:7).

The consistent emphasis here is on reorienting our minds and hearts to God. When we draw near to Him, He will draw near to us. To underscore this point, James used concepts from the Old Testament. In ancient Israel, the priests would wash their hands before approaching God (Exod. 30:19-21). This process of external cleansing symbolized the internal purification of the worshiper's thoughts, motives, and desires (Ps. 23:3-4; Jer. 4:4; 1 Tim. 1:5).

Thus, rather than remain soiled by the moral filth of sin, we are to "wash [our] hands" (Jas. 4:8), which often are the primary tool for sinning. Also, instead of dividing our allegiance between God and this world, we are to "purify [our] hearts," which is the seat of our affections and desires.

F. The Wisdom of Yielding to God: vss. 9-10

Grieve, mourn and wail. Change your laughter to mourning and your joy to gloom. Humble yourselves before the Lord, and he will lift you up.

Some people indulge in worldly pleasures and use laughter to distract them from such sobering issues as life and death, sin and judgment. The Christian, however, understands that before the joy of salvation can be fully appreciated, we must enter into the sorrow of repentance (Jas. 4:9).

Thus, the point of mourning and weeping is to express our grief over sin and our desire to enter into a relationship with God. He will not spurn the heart that is truly broken and contrite. In fact, He welcomes such displays of humility, for they reflect what He desires to see in the penitent. He even promises to "lift . . . up" (vs. 10), or honor, those who humble themselves in this way.

II. WARNING AGAINST BRAGGING: JAMES 4:13-17

A. The Transitory Nature of Life: vss. 13-14

Now listen, you who say, "Today or tomorrow we will go to this or that city, spend a year there, carry on business and make money." Why, you do not even know what will happen tomorrow. What is your life? You are a mist that appears for a little while and then vanishes.

The folly of envy and greed is that those characterized by them have forgotten about the transitory nature of life. They are blinded by their own desires to go here and there, and do this or that (Jas. 4:13).

The point is that we are shortsighted to make the pursuit of business an end in itself, rather than a means to glorify God. After all, our lives are like a "mist" (vs. 14) that appears for a short moment and then disappears. Since we do not know what will happen in the future, we should align all our aims and desires with the will of God.

B. The Importance of Submitting to God: vss. 15-16

Instead, you ought to say, "If it is the Lord's will, we will live and do this or that." As it is, you boast and brag. All such boasting is evil.

James was not advocating that we discontinue living because of the uncertainties of the future; rather, his desire was for us to submit our goals and dreams to God. Thus, when we make plans, we should do so in conjunction with what the Lord wants for us (Jas. 4:15). The opposite tendency, then, is filled with peril and characterized by folly. Ultimately, nothing eternally wholesome can come from a life characterized by arrogant self-sufficiency; instead, only "evil" (vs. 16)—such as frustration or failure—is the most that can be expected.

C. The Value of Doing What Is Right: vs. 17

Anyone, then, who knows the good he ought to do and doesn't do it, sins.

The Letter of James discusses at length the practical ways in which believers display the righteousness of God in their lives. For many Christians, though, the concept of righteousness might seem too abstract to understand. This difficulty is decreased as they grow in their appreciation of what it means to live in a holy, or morally pure, manner.

People are considered righteous when their personal behaviors are in harmony with God's will as it is revealed in Scripture. The righteous person willingly serves the Lord (Mal. 3:18), takes delight in Him (Ps. 33:1), and gives thanks to Him for His mercy and love (140:13). The righteous are blessed by God (5:12) and upheld by Him (37:17).

The righteous may experience hardships and trials in life, but God promises to help them through the difficulty (Ps. 34:19). No matter how severe their afflictions might be, the Lord will never forsake them (37:25) or allow them to fall (55:22). The prospect for the righteous is joy (Prov. 10:28) and the way of the Lord is their strength, or refuge (vs. 29). The Lord promises to be with them in their darkest moments (11:8) and to be a refuge for them in death (14:32).

In summary, James was urging his readers to leave whatever sinful path they might have been on, and to follow the path of uprightness. Otherwise, they would be sinning by refusing to do what they knew to be "good" (Jas. 4:17). Here we see that sins of omission (neglecting to do what is right) are just as inappropriate as sins of commission (opting to do what is wrong).

Discussion Questions

1. What was causing quarrels and fights among the recipients of James's letter?
2. What is meant by the phrase "friendship with the world" (Jas. 4:4)?
3. How can humbling ourselves before God enable us to resist the devil?
4. What are the benefits to the believer of being sorrowful and repentant of sin?
5. In what ways did the planning of the traders display worldliness rather than godliness?

Contemporary Application

James 4 teaches the necessity of humility in the Christian life. Because pride causes us to depend on ourselves rather than God, it takes us far from the path of righteousness. Humility, however, allows us to submit to God, enables us to resist the devil, and acknowledges the Lord's role in our future.

The type of humility that accords with righteousness in our lives is one that says, "Lord, I want what You want for my life." Such submission concedes that God knows what is best for our lives and keeps us from plunging ahead without consideration of God or what He may be trying to teach us.

Humility is essential for godliness because it alone gives us access to the necessary strength to resist the devil. God does not give this power to those who arrogantly rely on themselves, but only to those who acknowledge their inability to live the Christian life by themselves.

Along with pride, another stumbling block in the life of faith is improper motives. James said that the prayers of his readers were not being answered because they asked from their desire to be friends with the world.

Thus, even when we pray, we should question the motives behind our requests. God wants us to pray about everything and bring our requests before Him (Phil. 4:6). But how often do we find ourselves pleading for things with no thought of God's will or consideration of all the things for which we can give thanks?

Called to Be God's People

DEVOTIONAL READING

Leviticus 19:1-10

DAILY BIBLE READINGS

Monday September 29
Deuteronomy 7:6-11 God's Treasured Possession

Tuesday September 30
Leviticus 19:1-5 People Led by a Holy God

Wednesday October 1
1 Peter 1:1-7 New Birth into a Living Hope

Thursday October 2
1 Peter 1:8-12 People of a Glorious Joy

Friday October 3
1 Peter 1:13-21 Disciplined and Holy People

Saturday October 4
1 Peter 1:22—2:3 People Longing for Spiritual Milk

Sunday October 5
1 Peter 2:4-10 God's Own People

Scripture

Background Scripture: *1 Peter 1:1—2:10*
Scripture Lesson: *1 Peter 1:3-5, 13-21; 2:4-5, 9-10*
Key Verses: *Just as he who called you is holy, so be holy in all you do; for it is written: "Be holy, because I am holy."*
1 Peter 1:15-16.
Scripture Lesson for Children: *Mark 14:66-72*
Key Verse for Children : *[Peter] swore to them, "I don't know this man you're talking about."* Mark 14:71.

Lesson Aim

To discover ways to revive a vibrancy of hope in our lives, especially during trials.

Lesson Setting

Time: *The early 60s of the first century* A.D.
Place: *Rome*

Lesson Outline

Called to Be God's People
  I. The Hope of Salvation: 1 Peter 1:3-5
     A. *The Blessing of the New Birth: vs. 3*
     B. *The Assurance of the Promised Inheritance: vss. 4-5*
  II. The Call to Holy Living: 1 Peter 1:13-21
     A. *The Reality of Christ's Return: vs. 13*
     B. *The Admonition to Obey God: vs. 14*
     C. *The Exhortation to be Holy: vss. 15-16*
     D. *The Impartiality of God: vs. 17*
     E. *The Redemption Provided by Christ: vss. 18-19*
     F. *The Intent of the Father through His Son: vss. 20-21*
  III. The Call to Godly Service: 1 Peter 2:4-5, 9-10
     A. *The Believers' Place in God's Spiritual Temple: vss. 4-5*
     B. *The Believers' Status as God's People: vss. 9-10*

Introduction for Adults

Topic: *Called to New Life*

The young man had received his Ph.D. degree and then applied for teaching positions around the country. After an exhausting search, he was offered a position in a university in Canada. He, his wife, and their two children discovered what it meant to be called to a new life. It was a stressful challenge for them, but because they understood this offer to be God's call, they accepted it.

Peter's argument to his scattered Christian readers was something like that. Be assured of God's call in Christ. Look at what He has guaranteed you in Christ. Look at the price of your redemption. Look at your high calling to be a holy, royal priesthood. Then move out in hope, obedience, and faith.

Our call comes not once but many times in our lives. When we are assailed by doubts, troubles, fears, and depression, we must remember our call and trust the living God.

Introduction for Youth

Topic: *Called to Something Big*

What's the biggest thing we could be called to? President? Not many of us want that. Football or basketball star? Possibly. Movie, music, or television stardom? Perhaps. A good job and happy family? Yes. A holy, royal priesthood? What's that?

We have to dig deeply to understand Peter's imagery of God's high calling in Christ. Fundamentally, God does not call us to a vocation. He calls us to Himself, to be His faithful, trusting, hopeful, and holy child. Because He redeemed us with Christ's blood, He wants us to confess Him as Lord and testify about Him to others. That's a tough calling. It's something really big.

Concepts for Children

Topic: *Peter Denied Christ*

1. When Jesus was on trial, Peter denied knowing Him.
2. Jesus had foretold that Peter would deny Him.
3. Peter cried when he realized what he had done.
4. Later on, Jesus forgave Peter and gave him a job to do.
5. Many times we feel pressured to deny Jesus or at least to hide the fact that we believe in Him.
6. We should pray for boldness and courage to tell others about Jesus.

Lesson Commentary

I. THE HOPE OF SALVATION: 1 PETER 1:3-5

A. The Blessing of the New Birth: vs. 3

Praise be to the God and Father of our Lord Jesus Christ! In his great mercy he has given us new birth into a living hope through the resurrection of Jesus Christ from the dead,

Peter wrote to encourage persecuted and bewildered Christians and to exhort them to stand fast in their faith (1 Pet. 5:12). That is why the apostle repeatedly turned their thoughts to the glories of their eternal inheritance and instructed them about proper Christian behavior in the midst of unjust suffering. Although this letter was addressed originally to afflicted believers, its timeless truths apply to all suffering Christians.

The conduct Peter enjoined in his epistle was possible for those whose depraved lives had been reclaimed by the power of Christ. The Savior has redeemed believers (1:18-19); He upholds and guides them (1:8; 2:25); and He will eternally reward them (5:4). Jesus is both the reason for and the sustainer of the Christian life. Thus, believers can move forward along the path of faith, assured that joy and salvation are theirs in Christ.

After his epistolary greetings (1:1-2), Peter noted that the "God and Father of our Lord Jesus Christ" (vs. 3) deserved unending praise for making the new birth possible. God's "great mercy" was the reason He provided salvation, and Jesus' "resurrection . . . from the dead" was the basis for the "living hope" believers have of redemption.

B. The Assurance of the Promised Inheritance: vss. 4-5

And into an inheritance that can never perish, spoil or fade—kept in heaven for you, who through faith are shielded by God's power until the coming of the salvation that is ready to be revealed in the last time.

God was to be honored because of the priceless "inheritance" (1 Pet. 1:4) He had reserved "in heaven" for believers. This inheritance will never end, never be ruined or contaminated, and never disappear. In short, the Lord was committed to preserving our inheritance.

Peter also noted that the all-powerful God was just as committed to ensure that believers received their eternal inheritance. Right now we do not fully see or understand all that God, in His grace, has in store for us; but "in the last time" (vs. 5), when Jesus returns, what the Lord has planned will be made fully known to us.

II. THE CALL TO HOLY LIVING: 1 PETER 1:13-21

A. The Reality of Christ's Return: vs. 13

Therefore, prepare your minds for action; be self-controlled; set your hope fully on the grace to be given you when Jesus Christ is revealed.

Peter was urging Christians to live in anticipation of their future deliverance. The Savior's return will trigger a chain of events, including the judgment of the wicked

37

and the vindication of the upright. The Lord, in His "grace" (1 Pet. 1:13), will glorify believers and allow them to be with Him forever in heaven.

Peter urged his readers to "prepare your minds for action." This admonition draws upon the ancient practice of gathering up one's robes to move freely and quickly. In the case of believers, the apostle was stressing the importance of mental readiness. Rather than become distracted, Christians were to focus on God's future grace. Despite their turbulent circumstances, He could enable them to be sober-minded and steadfast.

B. The Admonition to Obey God: vs. 14

As obedient children, do not conform to the evil desires you had when you lived in ignorance.

The apostle urged his readers not to give in to their "evil desires" (1 Pet. 1:14), which they indulged when they did not know God. Through faith in Christ, they had come to know the Father and were His spiritual children. As such, they were to obey Him.

C. The Exhortation to be Holy: vss. 15-16

But just as he who called you is holy, so be holy in all you do; for it is written: "Be holy, because I am holy."

Before coming to Christ, the lives of believers were profane and vile; but now, as redeemed children of the heavenly King, they were to be "holy in all you do" (1 Pet. 1:15). In other words, every aspect of their lives was to be characterized by rectitude, purity, and integrity.

God is the one who called us to salvation, and He is characterized by holiness. The latter refers to the Lord being infinitely exalted and absolutely set apart from creation and sin. Put another way, He is morally pure and perfect in the most unsurpassed way.

We can never be as holy as God, but we should not let that prevent us from striving to be more holy in our lives; after all, we are part of God's family and expected to be holy (vs. 16). This moral standard is consistent with the teaching of the Old Testament (Lev. 11:44-45; 19:2; 20:7) and thus is an unchanging expectation for God's people, regardless of the era in which they live.

D. The Impartiality of God: vs. 17

Since you call on a Father who judges each man's work impartially, live your lives as strangers here in reverent fear.

The apostle reminded his readers that, as regenerate people, they called the one to whom they prayed "Father" (1 Pet. 1:17). The Lord, of course, is impartial in His evaluation of people. Even when it comes to His spiritual children, God has no favorites. He objectively judges or rewards according to "each man's work."

In light of this fair, impartial standard, Peter urged his readers to "live your lives as strangers here in reverent fear." The apostle's statement reminds us that we are temporary residents here on earth, and that heaven is our ultimate destination. Heaven is characterized by moral purity. Out of reverence for our Father in heaven, we should seek to be holy.

E. The Redemption Provided by Christ: vss. 18-19

For you know that it was not with perishable things such as silver or gold that you were redeemed from the empty way of life handed down to you from your forefathers, but with the precious blood of Christ, a lamb without blemish or defect.

Peter had noted two reasons why we should be holy. First, God is morally pure; and second, He fairly judges our inner attitudes and external actions. Now the apostle mentioned a third reason for us to pursue holiness, namely, our redemption through the blood of Christ.

The Greek verb translated "redeemed" (1 Pet. 1:18) was used to refer to the offering of money to secure the freedom of a prisoner of war or a slave. In our case, before coming to Christ in faith, we were slaves to sin and under the curse of the law. We had adopted a futile way of life that our ancestors passed down to us.

It was God's eternal desire to rescue us from this empty existence; however, the ransom He paid to Himself was not in the form of "silver and gold," which are "perishable." Instead, the Lord freed us through "the precious blood of Christ" (vs. 19).

Peter compared Jesus to an unblemished and spotless sacrificial lamb (Exod. 12:3-6; Lev. 23:12; Num. 6:14; 28:3). The apostle was stressing that Jesus was our substitute; in other words, He died in our place so that we might be saved (John 1:29).

F. The Intent of the Father through His Son: vss. 20-21

He was chosen before the creation of the world, but was revealed in these last times for your sake. Through him you believe in God, who raised him from the dead and glorified him, and so your faith and hope are in God.

The Father's plan to provide redemption through His Son was foreordained "before the creation of the world" (1 Pet. 1:20). This means that, in eternity past, God already knew that Christ would be sacrificed on the cross to make salvation possible.

At the divinely appointed time, the Father revealed the Son to the world through the Son's incarnation. The divine intent was to redeem the lost through faith in the Son. In fact, God "raised him from the dead" (vs. 21) and gave Him great glory so that our "faith and hope might be in God."

III. THE CALL TO GODLY SERVICE: 1 PETER 2:4-5, 9-10

A. The Believers' Place in God's Spiritual Temple: vss. 4-5

As you come to him, the living Stone—rejected by men but chosen by God and precious to him— you also, like living stones, are being built into a spiritual house to be a holy priesthood, offering spiritual sacrifices acceptable to God through Jesus Christ.

In light of our heavenly hope and holy calling, it makes sense that we are also summoned to godly service. Peter addressed this issue by referring to God's spiritual temple.

In this case, Jesus is *the* "living Stone" (1 Pet. 2:4) and believers are subordinate "living stones" (vs. 5) who come to Him in faith and enjoy intimate fellowship with Him. People, both past and present, have rejected Jesus; but Peter called believers to unite with Christ in faithful service in God's "spiritual house."

The Father, of course, chose the Son, who is "precious" (vs. 4) to Him. Also, God has chosen believers to be a "holy priesthood" (vs. 5). They offer up "spiritual sacrifices," which Christ has made acceptable to God. Perhaps Peter was referring to such good works as praising God, nurturing believers, and evangelizing the lost.

B. The Believers' Status as God's People: vss. 9-10

But you are a chosen people, a royal priesthood, a holy nation, a people belonging to God, that you may declare the praises of him who called you out of darkness into his wonderful light. Once you were not a people, but now you are the people of God; once you had not received mercy, but now you have received mercy.

Peter, by making use of Old Testament terms and concepts, said believers are God's "chosen" (1 Pet. 2:9) people, a group of royal priests, and His "holy nation." These statements indicate the special status believers have as ministers of Christ in the kingdom of God.

Peter noted that it was God who called the redeemed out of the darkness of sin and into the marvelous light of His salvation. He has made those who were once not His people "the people of God" (vs. 10). Previously they were strangers to God's mercy, but now they have received mercy (Hos. 1:6, 9-10; 2:23) The proper response is for believers to tell others about God's wonderful grace.

Discussion Questions

1. What does it mean to be born again?
2. How is it possible for believers to be holy when they struggle with sin?
3. Why did God ransom us from our sins through Christ?
4. What is the significance of Jesus' resurrection for believers?
5. What does it mean to be a living stone in God's spiritual temple?

Contemporary Application

We have firsthand, written accounts of the Gospel; thus, the message of salvation is not as mysterious to us as it was to the prophets (1 Pet. 1:10-12). Nevertheless, it also may not be as special to us as it was to Peter's first readers. Much time has passed since that hope was first realized; thus, we sometimes become dulled to the spiritual reality that eternal life begins here and now. This leaves us without the hope we need to get through life's trials.

Hope helps us because it tells us that the present is not all there is. Being targeted for ridicule by someone at work, being ignored by family members, or losing someone close to us are crises; but they are not crises in which there is no comfort from God. Trials may cause others to look down on us, but with God no disappointment is final.

This is why hope helps us put trials in the appropriate perspective. We expect trials to occur and we expect them to hurt; but with hope, we do not expect to be devastated by them. We can develop a mindset of determination in which we can endure anything because we know the future that is coming is better than anything we have known before.

How can we can look beyond today and stay open to unknown factors? It is because we have learned that God often uses trials to refine us. We may even be thankful someday for how the trial has transformed us.

Be a Good Example

DEVOTIONAL READING

Galatians 5:16-25

DAILY BIBLE READINGS

Monday October 6
Romans 12:9-18 Be Zealous in Serving God

Tuesday October 7
1 Peter 2:11-17 Conduct Yourselves Honorably

Wednesday October 8
1 Peter 3:8-12 Don't Repay Evil for Evil

Thursday October 9
1 Peter 3:13-22 Be Ready with a Gentle Defense

Friday October 10
1 Peter 4:1-6 Live by the Will of God

Saturday October 11
1 Peter 4:7-11 Maintain Love for One Another

Sunday October 12
1 Peter 5:7-14 Keep Alert, Resist the Devil

Scripture

Background Scripture: *1 Peter 2:11—5:14*
Scripture Lesson: *1 Peter 2:11-12; 3:13-17; 4:7-11; 5:8-10*
Key Verse: *Live such good lives among the pagans that, though they accuse you of doing wrong, they may see your good deeds and glorify God on the day he visits us.* 1 Peter 2:12.
Scripture Lesson for Children: *John 21:1-13*
Key Verse for Children: *Then the disciple whom Jesus loved said to Peter, "It is the Lord!"* (John 21:7).

Lesson Aim

To choose better ways to deal with suffering.

Lesson Setting

Time: *The early 60s of the first century* A.D.
Place: *Rome*

Lesson Outline

Be a Good Example

   I. Living for God Despite Suffering:
     1 Peter 2:11-12; 3:13-17
     A. *Shunning Evil Desires: 2:11*
     B. *Behaving Honorably: vs. 12*
     C. *Experiencing God's Blessing: 3:13-14*
     D. *Giving a Ready Response: vss. 15-16*
     E. *Suffering for the Right Reason: vs. 17*

  II. Serving Believers Despite Suffering:
     1 Peter 4:7-11; 5:8-10
     A. *Being Serious about Prayer: 4:7*
     B. *Showing Love and Hospitality: vss. 8-9*
     C. *Making Use of Spiritual Gifts: vss. 10-11*
     D. *Resisting the Devil: 5:8-9*
     E. *Anticipating Eternal Glory: vs. 10*

Introduction for Adults

Topic: *Be a Good Example*

The owner of a downtown office building looked squarely at his prospective tenants and said, "I cannot lie to you, because I am a Christian." Without fanfare, he demonstrated what it means to be a good example. He was ready with a clear statement about his faith and lifestyle.

How many times do we fail to do a kind deed or say a word about our faith because we fear possible repercussions? Yes, it is risky, but we know this is what we must do, even in the face of persecution. Generally, we are free of persecution. Therefore, our responsibility to be a good example is great. Opportunities abound.

We can pray and ask for God's wisdom, His words, and His strength. By faith we encounter an unbelieving world filled with people with many needs.

Introduction for Youth

Topic: *You Are an Example*

An important part of military training is learning how to represent your branch of service in the public's eye. Every drunken soldier or sailor tarnishes the reputation of all other service personnel. The same principle applies to Christians.

We are to excel in good deeds and charitable words and service, even when we are provoked and ridiculed. In certain social settings, this is an extremely difficult assignment. Sometimes we fail and the devil chalks up another victim.

Each day calls for commitment, courage, prayer, and faith. Jesus goes into spiritual battle with us. Only in His strength can we do what His Word tells us.

Concepts for Children

Topic: *Peter and Others Recognized Jesus*

1. After His resurrection, Jesus met His followers by the seashore.
2. The followers of Jesus had returned to fishing, which was their job before the Savior had called them to serve Him.
3. At Jesus' command, His followers caught many fish.
4. When Jesus spoke to His followers, they recognized Him.
5. Our faith rests in the fact that Jesus is alive and cares for us.
6. When we obey Jesus, we get to know Him better and love Him more deeply.

Lesson Commentary

I. LIVING FOR GOD DESPITE SUFFERING: 1 PETER 2:11-12; 3:13-17

A. Shunning Evil Desires: 2:11

Dear friends, I urge you, as aliens and strangers in the world, to abstain from sinful desires, which war against your soul.

Much of what Peter wrote in his first letter concerns being a good example in the midst of suffering. The concept of suffering in Scripture involves physical and mental pain and sorrow as well as affliction and agony brought on by a great variety of experiences.

While Scripture reveals that some suffering is the direct result of human sin, it is also presented as a divine tool for shaping Christlike character and testing faith (1 Pet. 1:6-7; 5:10). Even Jesus Himself is said to have been greatly influenced by suffering; for example, suffering perfected Him (Heb. 2:10) and taught Him obedience (5:8).

Other Scriptures say that suffering cements the believers' identification with Christ, especially as they experience persecution for His sake (Phil. 1:29; 2 Thess. 1:5). Paul even went so far as to say that suffering is inevitable for those who desire to live in a godly way and to follow Christ (2 Tim. 3:12). If our Lord suffered, we also can expect suffering for His sake.

Peter, while addressing his readers warmly as "Dear friends" (1 Pet. 2:11), reminded them that they were foreigners and aliens in this present life. While they lived on earth for a time, heaven would one day be their eternal home. It is a place characterized by righteousness, peace, and joy in the Spirit (Rom. 14:17).

When believers embrace these sorts of virtues, they are saying no to the "sinful desires" (1 Pet. 2:11) that battle daily with their souls. This fight is not just on a physical, temporal plane and solely against earthly foes; more importantly, it is a spiritual battle that is waged using the resources God has made available in Christ (Eph. 6:10-18).

B. Behaving Honorably: vs. 12

Live such good lives among the pagans that, though they accuse you of doing wrong, they may see your good deeds and glorify God on the day he visits us.

The desire to retaliate is the natural human reaction to ill treatment. Peter, however, urged Christians to respond differently "among the pagans" (1 Pet. 2:12). In other words, believers were to conduct themselves honorably.

Apparently some Christians were falsely accused of wrongdoing by the unsaved. Early church writings suggest these allegations included rebelling against the government, refusing to participate in emperor worship, and impeding social progress.

Regardless of the allegation, Peter reasoned that one's detractors would notice gracious conduct. Perhaps the antagonists might turn to God in faith and "glorify"

Him for the winsome testimony they observed. Otherwise, they would reap the visitation of God's judgment at the return of Christ.

C. Experiencing God's Blessing: 3:13-14

Who is going to harm you if you are eager to do good? But even if you should suffer for what is right, you are blessed. "Do not fear what they fear; do not be frightened."

Peter reasoned that, under normal circumstances, there was little likelihood that the unsaved would harm believers for their good conduct. The apostle, of course, did not rule out the possibility that Christians might experience persecution, even though they lived uprightly (1 Pet. 3:13).

In that case, Peter declared, "you are blessed" (vs. 14). This means God would honor believers with His love and grace. His abiding presence is the reason that Christians do not have to be afraid or worry, despite the threats made by adversaries (Isa.. 8:12-13).

D. Giving a Ready Response: vss. 15-16

But in your hearts set apart Christ as Lord. Always be prepared to give an answer to everyone who asks you to give the reason for the hope that you have. But do this with gentleness and respect, keeping a clear conscience, so that those who speak maliciously against your good behavior in Christ may be ashamed of their slander.

There are times when believers cannot avoid suffering for being zealous followers of Christ. Peter urged believers to "set apart Christ as Lord" (1 Pet. 3:15) in their hearts. The idea is that Christians should revere the Savior as the sovereign of their lives.

Peter also urged believers to be ready to respond to those who asked for a "reason of the hope that you have." Sometimes inquirers will be sufficiently objective and open-minded to welcome a cogent explanation of one's faith. Peter also envisioned more derogatory interrogations of believers.

In those situations, Christians needed to know what they believed and why they held to those doctrines. In addition, they had to be able to express their views "with gentleness and respect." This means their response was to be humble and deferential as well as thoughtful and scriptural.

The broad goal, then, was to maintain a "clear conscience" (vs. 16) regardless of what happened. Then, even when antagonists defamed believers as evildoers, the former would be "ashamed" when they saw the consistently Christlike conduct of the latter.

E. Suffering for the Right Reason: vs. 17

It is better, if it is God's will, to suffer for doing good than for doing evil.

No believers should relish the idea of suffering; but, as Peter noted, there are times when God permits believers to endure persecution. The apostle declared that it is better to suffer "for doing good" (1 Pet. 3:17) than to suffer for "doing evil."

II. SERVING BELIEVERS DESPITE SUFFERING: 1 PETER 4:7-11; 5:8-10

A. Being Serious about Prayer: 4:7

The end of all things is near. Therefore be clear minded and self-controlled so that you can pray.

Peter noted that God is moving history to an end, with closure occurring when Jesus returns. At that time, He will judge the wicked and vindicate the upright.

In light of the Lord's imminent return, Christians should shun all evil desires and remain "clear minded" (1 Pet. 4:7) in their disposition. Expressed another way, believers should be serious and earnest in their pursuit of holiness. They should also be vigilant and "self-controlled" in their prayers. Such involved worshiping God, confessing sin, and petitioning the Lord for personal needs and the needs of others.

B. Showing Love and Hospitality: vss. 8-9

Above all, love each other deeply, because love covers over a multitude of sins. Offer hospitality to one another without grumbling.

Rather than wallow in self-pity or indulge evil desires as a response to suffering, Christians were to "love each other deeply" (1 Pet. 4:8). Sacrifice and generosity characterize such love. For the good of others, it holds back nothing, just as an athlete would in a highly competitive race.

Peter quoted from Proverbs 10:12 to support his point and give it particular application. This verse teaches that, when believers respond in compassion and kindness to each other, they cover over "sins" (1 Pet. 4:8), or offenses, that would otherwise come between them. This type of love, rather than seeking to get even, makes forgiveness the catalyst for harmonious relationships.

In moments of suffering, when emotions are frayed and resources are spread thin, it is easy for believers to minimize their involvement with one another; but Peter urged them to do the opposite, that is, to be hospitable "to one another without grumbling" (vs. 9). Thus, even in difficult times, Christians were to be cheerful in the way in which they welcomed their fellow believers into their homes.

C. Making Use of Spiritual Gifts: vss. 10-11

Each one should use whatever gift he has received to serve others, faithfully administering God's grace in its various forms. If anyone speaks, he should do it as one speaking the very words of God. If anyone serves, he should do it with the strength God provides, so that in all things God may be praised through Jesus Christ. To him be the glory and the power for ever and ever. Amen.

First Peter 4:10-11 is one of several places in the New Testament where spiritual gifts are discussed. They may be defined as special abilities that God graciously gives so that believers might humbly serve one another. Spiritual gifts are not the same as natural talents, though God may give spiritual gifts that also make use of innate human abilities.

God wants believers to "faithfully" (vs. 10) administer their special abilities. In other words, they are stewards who are to manage well these evidences of God's "grace." Some have the gift of speaking, while others have the special ability to help others in extraordinary ways.

Regardless of what the spiritual gift might be, Christians are to exercise it diligently and with all the energy that God supplies. The goal is that God will "be praised through Jesus Christ" (vs. 11). Here we see that, when ministry is done in the Savior's power and authority, He receives honor.

D. Resisting the Devil: 5:8-9

Be self-controlled and alert. Your enemy the devil prowls around like a roaring lion looking for someone to devour. Resist him, standing firm in the faith, because you know that your brothers throughout the world are undergoing the same kind of sufferings.

Peter had been emphasizing the care and sovereignty of God for Christians. This truth, however, did not justify a naive and carefree approach to life. Instead, believers are to be on their guard and remain alert for attacks from their "enemy the devil" (1 Pet. 5:8). Thus, self-control, discipline, and vigilance are enjoined.

To underscore the nature of the threat, Peter compared the devil to a ravenous lion that prowled around in search for an unsuspecting victim to "devour." It was not a question of *if* an attack would occur, but rather *when.* Peter urged believers to stand "firm in the faith" (vs. 9) as they resisted the evil one.

The apostle reminded his readers that other believers "throughout the world" were experiencing similar "sufferings." The realization that other Christians were successfully resisting the devil should have encouraged the readers of Peter's letter to stand firm in their faith. We, too, should resist our avowed enemy, rather than succumb to his attacks.

E. Anticipating Eternal Glory: vs. 10

And the God of all grace, who called you to his eternal glory in Christ, after you have suffered a little while, will himself restore you and make you strong, firm and steadfast.

First Peter 5:10 reminds us that, while there might be afflictions in this life, they will end one day. We are assured that God, in His "grace," has called us to "eternal glory" through the Savior.

Thus, the hope of heaven gives us the strength to endure suffering for "a little while." Then, at the appointed time, God promises to mend and stabilize our broken lives. He will also strengthen us so that the foundation of our faith remains steadfast and immovable.

Discussion Questions

1. What does it mean for believers to live as strangers here on earth?
2. Why is it important for believers to remain respectful when they explain their Christian hope to antagonists of the faith?
3. What role does praying serve for believers in the midst of their unjust suffering?

4. How can believers serve one another in the midst of suffering?

5. How can suffering believers take a firm stand against the attacks of the devil?

Contemporary Application

Peter, who was well acquainted with suffering for Christ's sake, offered practical advice about surviving suffering and allowing it to deepen our relationship with Christ. Over and over the apostle emphasized the importance of taking the "high road," so to speak.

If the people in our neighborhood, for example, take advantage of us or accuse us of things we did not do, our first reaction might be to lash out at them. Who do they think they are to pick on us? What did we ever do to them?

We might secretly wonder if we should write an anonymous letter to everyone in the neighborhood, denouncing the antagonists. Almost as if Peter knew this, he urged believers instead to keep a clear conscience; rather than returning evil for evil, believers could pray for their enemies, and even love them.

When we are called upon to speak up about the situation or the reasons we behave as we do, we should convey gentleness and respect, emphasizing the hope God has put within us. We also know not to be shocked by this suffering. Just consider what Jesus went through during His trial.

In the world, aggression is seen as a strength, while humility connotes weakness. Despite how the world thinks about these matters, believers are to think and act differently. Being clothed with humility means seeing ourselves as God sees us and respecting others by loving them unconditionally. This remains true even in the midst of unjust suffering.

How will we survive and even rejoice now and then? We can take confidence that God will eventually win. The victory may not come immediately or dramatically; but the person who mistreated you will come to respect you, even though he or she may not say so. The truth will come out and God's glory will be evident in the situation, probably in some way you did not expect.

Grow in Faith

Scripture

Background Scripture: *2 Peter 1*
Scripture Lesson: *2 Peter 1:3-15*
Key Verse: *His divine power has given us everything we need for life and godliness through our knowledge of him who called us by his own glory and goodness.* 2 Peter 1:3.
Scripture Lesson for Children: *John 21:15b-19*
Key Verse for Children: *[Peter] said, "Lord, you know all things; you know that I love you"* (John 21:17).

Lesson Aim

To adopt a plan for spiritual growth and commit to following it.

Lesson Setting

Time: *Between A.D. 65–68*
Place: *Rome*

Lesson Outline

Grow in Faith

  I. Being Faithful and Fruitful: 2 Peter 1:3-11
     A. *Living in a Way that Pleases God: vss. 3-4*
     B. *Growing in Christian Virtues: vss. 5-6*
     C. *Cultivating Christlike Love: vs. 7*
     D. *Opting for Spiritual Growth and Productivity: vss. 8-9*
     E. *Validating the Reality of One's Salvation: vss. 10-11*
  II. Heeding Scripture: 2 Peter 1:12-15
     A. *Being Reminded of the Truth: vss. 12-13*
     B. *Making the Truth Clear: vss. 14-15*

Introduction for Adults

Topic: *Growing in Faith*

The original church was built more than 100 years ago in an affluent Midwestern suburb. It flourished and grew to some 900 members. Facilities were added to accommodate people and programs. But somewhere along the line the congregation stopped growing. Its numbers have dwindled to less than 100.

Such stories are not unusual. They testify to the fact that it's possible for entire congregations to stop growing, shrivel, and die. We can point to many reasons for this phenomena, including the possibility that individual members lost their vision for what God had called them to do.

All Christians must keep growing. That's why Peter's practical reminders are so important. We can become so easily sidetracked. Personality clashes sap our energies. We must keep adding qualities of spiritual power to ourselves and our churches.

Introduction for Youth

Topic: *Everything You Need*

The woman, whom I'll call Jane, flew off to see her family in a far-distant South American country. She was very meticulous about her preparations. She thought she had everything she needed. But when she arrived, she found that she had forgotten to pack one of her prescription medicines. She called home and her husband took care of the matter.

Our pride tells us that we have everything we need. But Peter would say that such an attitude is counterproductive. An attitude of pride prevents us from grasping all that God has done for us in Christ. Because we, as believers, share in His divine nature and His promises, we can claim His power and wisdom and be bold about our faith and godliness.

We thus have everything we need in Christ. God, in turn, has commissioned us to use His resources for His glory.

Concepts for Children

Topic: *Peter Told Jesus He Loved Him*

1. After His resurrection, Jesus met Peter and the other disciples.
2. Jesus singled out Peter for a special talk.
3. Three times Jesus asked Peter if he loved the Savior.
4. When Peter said that he did, Jesus gave him a special job.
5. Jesus loves us and gives us opportunities to say that we believe in Him.
6. When we sin, we should confess our wrongdoing to Jesus.
7. We should also thank God for helping us to overcome our sins.

Lesson Commentary

I. BEING FAITHFUL AND FRUITFUL: 2 PETER 1:3-11

A. Living in a Way that Pleases God: vss. 3-4

His divine power has given us everything we need for life and godliness through our knowledge of him who called us by his own glory and goodness. Through these he has given us his very great and precious promises, so that through them you may participate in the divine nature and escape the corruption in the world caused by evil desires.

The Letter of 2 Peter can be divided into three literary sections. In part one (1:1-21), the apostle discussed the importance of cultivating Christian character and being fruitful for the Lord. In part two (2:1-22), Peter wrote a scathing condemnation of false teachers. He especially sought to defeat their efforts to encourage Christians to rebel against the teachings of the Lord. Then, in part three (3:1-18), the apostle related the confidence believers can have in the return of Christ.

A study of 2 Peter suggests that it was the apostle's final writing before his imminent death. He may have sent the epistle to Gentile and Jewish Christians living in Asia Minor. When reports of their difficulties with false teachers had reached the apostle, who was possibly in Rome, he wrote this letter to encourage believers to be faithful and fruitful as Christians and heed the truth of Scripture.

The call to holiness that is so evident in 1 Peter also resonates strongly in 2 Peter. In 1:2, the apostle stressed getting know the Father and Son more and more. Then, in verse 3, Peter noted that, through our increased knowledge of the Lord, we become more responsive to His "divine power."

The emphasis here is on living a godly life. The apostle explained that our knowledge of the Savior and His provision of "divine power" make it possible for us to pursue "life and godliness." Further incentive can be found in the truth that the Lord has invited us to share in His own "glory and goodness."

Our focus, then, is not on acquiring the world's fame and fortune, for these are fleeting; rather, it is to live in a way that pleases God. The Lord has made this possible by bestowing on us "very great and precious promises" (vs. 4).

Perhaps the most profound promise is that we will "participate in the divine nature." The idea here is not that we will gradually become divine, but that we grow in a host of Christian virtues. The more we pursue holiness, the more we will shun our evil desires and the "corruption" of the world that it spawns.

B. Growing in Christian Virtues: vss. 5-6

For this very reason, make every effort to add to your faith goodness; and to goodness, knowledge; and to knowledge, self-control; and to self-control, perseverance; and to perseverance, godliness.

In light of all the spiritual provisions we have in Christ, we have everything we need to be faithful and fruitful in our lives. We start by making a maximum "effort" (2 Pet. 1:5) to appropriate our God-given blessings.

At the moment of salvation, Christians are made holy in a legal sense; in other words, we are declared righteous in God's eyes. That event is called *justification*. Then, throughout our lives, the Holy Spirit works to bring our moral condition into conformity with our legal status; in other words, He helps to make us actually holy. This process is called *sanctification*.

Sanctification is the work of God (1 Thess. 5:23); nevertheless, the Bible contains many exhortations for believers to do their part in becoming more holy (Phil. 2:12-13). "Faith" (2 Pet. 1:5) is the starting point, and to it we are to add "goodness." This is one of several moral excellencies that Peter mentioned. The idea is that, with unwavering trust in the Savior as our foundation, we press on in a disciplined way to cultivate integrity and rectitude in our lives.

Peter next mentioned "knowledge." While an objective understanding of revealed truth is included, the apostle also had in mind a practical application of that truth. When we heed the teachings of Scripture, it will lead to "self-control" (vs. 6). Peter was referring to a mastering of one's carnal desires.

Because believers know God and are empowered by Him, they are able to control their fleshly passions. In turn, they become more patient. They are less likely to be discouraged and succumb to temptation, and more likely to persevere in doing what is right. This ability to endure allows "godliness" to flourish. The believer becomes more reverent and devoted to the Lord, and less preoccupied with himself or herself.

C. Cultivating Christlike Love: vs. 7

And to godliness, brotherly kindness; and to brotherly kindness, love.

A heightened loyalty to God results in believers having increased "brotherly kindness" (2 Pet. 1:7). This mutual affection is displayed in serving one another, sharing with one another, and praying for one another. These activities, in turn, foster genuine "love." This form of compassion is not flustered by the personal cost of reaching out to others in need. This sincere love seeks the highest good of others for the glory of Christ.

D. Opting for Spiritual Growth and Productivity: vss. 8-9

For if you possess these qualities in increasing measure, they will keep you from being ineffective and unproductive in your knowledge of our Lord Jesus Christ. But if anyone does not have them, he is near-sighted and blind, and has forgotten that he has been cleansed from his past sins.

It would be erroneous to think that the virtues mentioned in 2 Peter 1:5-7 can be added in a mathematically precise, sequential fashion; rather, they are developed together and evidenced gradually over many years of walking with the Lord.

The goal, of course, is that these moral excellencies will be present in us in "increasing measure" (vs. 8). Their abundance indicates spiritual health in believers. Peter noted that, if we continue to grow in this way, we will become increasingly productive and fruitful, rather than "ineffective" and "unproductive," in our knowledge of the Savior.

We again see that knowing God is more than an intellectual exercise. It is intended to foster spiritual vitality. The other alternative is to fail to develop these graces, which results in spiritual loss. Peter declared that those opting for this are blinded and shortsighted, for they have failed to appreciate fully the cleansing and forgiveness from "past sins" (vs. 9) secured by Christ.

E. Validating the Reality of One's Salvation: vss. 10-11

Therefore, my brothers, be all the more eager to make your calling and election sure. For if you do these things, you will never fall, and you will receive a rich welcome into the eternal kingdom of our Lord and Savior Jesus Christ.

Peter was discussing two different mindsets. One is transfixed on the concerns of this present life, while the other is sensitive to eternal, spiritual realities. Though we live in the world, the things of God should be our supreme focus.

Thus, we are to make every effort to confirm our "calling and election" (2 Pet. 1:10). By remaining loyal to God and ministering to our fellow believers, we show that we truly "participate in the divine nature" (vs. 4), that we fully appreciate the atoning sacrifice of Christ, and that we value His "very great and precious promises" to us.

Such a consistent life-orientation indicates we will not succumb to doubt or despair concerning our spiritual status. Rather than "fall" (vs. 10), we will be assured of our salvation. This assurance also includes our eventual entrance into "the eternal kingdom" (vs. 11) of Christ. The Lord, in turn, will honor our life of faithful service with more abundant privileges in heaven.

II. HEEDING SCRIPTURE: 2 PETER 1:12-15

A. Being Reminded of the Truth: vss. 12-13

So I will always remind you of these things, even though you know them and are firmly established in the truth you now have. I think it is right to refresh your memory as long as I live in the tent of this body.

At times even mature believers can wane in their diligence to grow in Christ. This is especially true in moments of hardship. Peter, perhaps realizing this, was determined to remind his readers about the truths he had previously shared. The apostle's decision did not mean his readers were ignorant of the truth or had failed to stand firm in it. Peter's intention was to ensure they remained "firmly established" (2 Pet. 1:12) in the faith and diligent in applying it to their lives.

In some way, Peter had become increasingly aware of the short time he had left "in the tent of this body" (vs. 13). This is a metaphorical reference to his body being laid aside like a tent. John 21:18-19 records a statement Jesus made concerning the way in which Peter would die. Perhaps the apostle had this in mind as he approached the end of his life.

B. Making the Truth Clear: vss. 14-15

Because I know that I will soon put it aside, as our Lord Jesus Christ has made clear to me. And I will make every effort to see that after my departure you will always be able to remember these things.

Based on what Christ had revealed to Peter, he was certain his days on earth were drawing to a close (2. Pet. 1:14). Tradition says that, while the apostle was in Rome, the church there persuaded him to leave and avoid death during Nero's persecution (probably in A.D. 67 or 68). According to the early church father Jerome, Peter subsequently decided to return to Rome. The apostle was then incarcerated in the Mamertine prison and finally crucified.

We can certainly appreciate the strong desire Peter had to reinforce to his readers the teaching of Scripture. His goal was to make the truth clear so that they could more readily recall and apply it (vs. 15). The destructive teachings of spiritual frauds (2:1-4) made the apostle's task all the more imperative.

Discussion Questions

1. Why did Peter think it was important for believers to come to an intimate and full knowledge of Christ?
2. What is the connection between knowing Christ and growing in spiritual virtues?
3. In what sense are those who fail to develop these virtues spiritually blind?
4. What are some ways that believers can demonstrate the reality of their salvation in Christ?
5. Why did Peter compare his body to a tent, and what was he anticipating for himself?

Contemporary Application

Accepting Jesus as Savior is the beginning of a Christian's growth process. The Holy Spirit then works in our lives to produce the virtues listed in the Scripture lesson text.

The order of the virtues is not a sequence in time, as if stages of the Christian life were being described; rather, the qualities Peter enumerated were to occur simultaneously and lead to a well-rounded and productive Christian life.

While the Spirit makes it possible for us to grow and mature as believers, we must also cooperate with Him in the process. That is why Peter urged us to "make every effort" (2 Pet. 1:5) to cultivate the character qualities he listed in verses 5-7. Faith is the starting point, and the series of elements the apostle mentioned climax with love, which is the preeminent fruit of the Christian life.

From this we see that the church is not a playpen, but rather a construction area where the Spirit desires to work in the lives of Jesus' followers. Why, then, do the lives of many believers exhibit little growth? Why do many of us remain childish?

One reason is that selfishness saps the energy that God wants us to use for growth. We too often focus on satisfying ourselves rather than on pleasing the Lord. For instance, Paul was concerned that the Corinthians were still spiritual babies because they were fighting among themselves (1 Cor. 3:1-4).

Sadly, temper tantrums in Christian circles are still too common. Many of us are also spiritually lazy. Maturing in Christ looks too much like hard work. We might wonder, "What awful trials will the Lord send if I tell Him that I desire to grow?"

An initial step toward growth is admitting that we need God's help. We must look beyond our fear and selfishness. Since God has provided the Spirit to help us grow, we can become partners with Him to transform our lives and help us become more like Christ.

Thus, the virtues listed in our Scripture lesson text are the result of our working together with God. Each time we choose to obey the Lord and not to just please ourselves, the fruit becomes more abundant; and, as we strive to mature, God will do for us what we cannot do for ourselves.

Trust God's Promise

Scripture

Background Scripture: *2 Peter 3*

Scripture Lesson: *2 Peter 3:3-5, 7-15a, 17-18*

Key Verse: *So then, dear friends, since you are looking forward to this, make every effort to be found spotless, blameless and at peace with him. Bear in mind that our Lord's patience means salvation. 2 Peter 3:14-15.*

Scripture Lesson for Children: *Acts 2:14, 22b-24, 36-42*

Key Verse for Children: *Peter replied, "Repent and be baptized, every one of you, in the name of Jesus Christ for the forgiveness of your sins." Acts 2:38*

Lesson Aim

To strive to be holy as we anticipate Jesus' return.

Lesson Setting

Time: *Between A.D. 65–68*

Place: *Rome*

Lesson Outline

Trust God's Promise

   I. The Certainty of Christ's Return: 2 Peter 3:3-5, 7-10

      A. *Christ's Return Derided: vss. 3-4*

      B. *God's Active Presence Denied: vss. 5, 7*

      C. *God's Tarrying Explained: vss. 8-9*

      D. *God's Judgment Affirmed: vs. 10*

  II. The Way Believers Ought to Live: 2 Peter 3:11-15a, 17-18

      A. *Enjoining Holiness and Godliness: vs. 11*

      B. *Anticipating the Consummation of History: vss. 12-13*

      C. *Keeping Priorities Straight: vss. 14-15a*

      D. *Departing from Error: vss. 17-18*

Introduction for Adults

Topic: *Being Faithful to Promises*

The man seated next to a Christian on a cross-country airline flight said he was an agnostic (namely, someone who believes God is not able to be known). The believer pointed him to Christ's resurrection as reasonable grounds for faith.

The resurrection of Jesus is the foundation for all of God's promises. Because He rose from the dead, we can be sure that He is coming back. We can be sure that His promise to forgive our sins is true. We can be sure that He will be faithful to His words about judgment and a new heaven and earth.

Compared to our lack of commitment, God will not fail to keep His promises. The same command that created the universe will bring judgment to some and salvation to others. Critics and agnostics not withstanding, God's promises are true.

Introduction for Youth

Topic: *Live Patiently and Faithfully*

Patience and faith are demanded while we wait to get our driver's licenses. Will we ever reach the mandatory age? Will we pass the test? How much freedom will our parents give us?

Each stage of life brings similar challenges. In the big picture, all of life is a test of our patience and faith. Can we keep on trusting God? Will He really do what is best for us? Will He really watch over me?

Jesus wants us to trust and obey Him. We are motivated to do this because His promises to us will come true. We can take comfort in this truth even when life seems uncertain and overwhelming.

Concepts for Children

Topic: *Peter Preached at Pentecost*

1. God gave Peter great opportunities to proclaim the good news.
2. Many people believed what Peter declared and were saved.
3. Peter discovered that God could use him, as Jesus had promised.
4. God wants us to be faithful witnesses, like Peter was.
5. We may not talk to crowds of people, but we can study the Bible and pray with others.
6. Our love and friendship will give us the opportunity to tell others the good news about Jesus.

Lesson Commentary

I. The Certainty of Christ's Return: 2 Peter 3:3-5, 7-10

A. Christ's Return Derided: vss. 3-4

First of all, you must understand that in the last days scoffers will come, scoffing and following their own evil desires. They will say, "Where is this 'coming' he promised? Ever since our fathers died, everything goes on as it has since the beginning of creation."

The Letter of 2 Peter contains some of the strongest warnings in the New Testament regarding those who spread false teachings within the church. In the second chapter of his epistle, the apostle alerted believers to frauds who introduced destructive heresies into the church. Peter also noted that one result of this problem was immorality, which damaged the reputation of the church.

Evidently the doctrine of the false teachers appealed to the sensual desires of those who were unfamiliar with biblical truth. The frauds used unrealistic promises and inflated language to attract followers. These promises were the bait that left those who embraced them more enslaved to sin than they were before. Against the backdrop of these spurious pledges was God's unassailable promise of Christ's return.

In chapter 3, Peter focused on erroneous ideas the false teachers were spreading. Of foremost concern was the truth concerning "the last days" (vs. 3). This refers to the entire present age from the first to the second advent of the Messiah. The Bible is explicit in teaching that Jesus will return; yet, as we draw nearer to that event, "scoffers" will deride the truth.

Peter explained that detractors reject the truth of divine judgment so they can indulge "their own evil desires." Their rationale is that Jesus has yet to return, despite the promise of His coming (vs. 4). The scoffers also note that countless godly leaders have died (such as the Old Testament patriarchs) and the world remains unchanged since "the beginning of creation."

B. God's Active Presence Denied: vss. 5, 7

But they deliberately forget that long ago by God's word the heavens existed and the earth was formed out of water and by water. . . . By the same word the present heavens and earth are reserved for fire, being kept for the day of judgment and destruction of ungodly men.

The false teachers' desire to pursue carnal passions led them to deny the truth of divine retribution. In their minds, if God did exist, He was distant and uninvolved; and because the universe seemed stable and unchanging, the likelihood of a catastrophic judgment appeared dim.

Peter revealed that these denouncers had willfully chosen to "forget" (2 Pet. 3:5) the truth. For instance, they choose to overlook the fact that long ago God, at His command, made the heavens and the earth. Water was an integral part in forming the latter.

The apostle explained that God subsequently used a mighty flood to destroy life on earth (vs. 6); also, there is a "day of judgment" (vs. 7) coming in which God will command the heavens and earth to be consumed by "fire." At that time, the "ungodly" will go to "destruction."

Throughout history, scoffers have laughed at the notion that God created, sustains, and will one day judge the world and humankind; and at times so-called experts cite data they think either supports or denies these biblical truths. Ultimately, the teachings of God's Word must be accepted by faith.

C. God's Tarrying Explained: vss. 8-9

But do not forget this one thing, dear friends: With the Lord a day is like a thousand years, and a thousand years are like a day. The Lord is not slow in keeping his promise, as some understand slowness. He is patient with you, not wanting anyone to perish, but everyone to come to repentance.

Because we are finite, time-bound creatures, it is hard for us to comprehend the passage of one year, let alone a "thousand years" (2 Pet. 3:8). The Lord, however, is infinite and eternal; thus, He processes time far differently.

God's knowledge of time and eternity is instantaneous, simultaneous, exhaustive, and absolutely correct. He is always aware of everything that occurs, regardless of whether it is past, present, or future. Thus, for Him, one day is the same as a thousand years, and a thousand years is the same as one day.

The rational human mind strives to make sense of what appears to be a divine delay. Peter, perhaps sensing this, explained that the Lord was not being "slow" (vs. 9) in fulfilling the promise of His return. Despite what the religious frauds taught, Peter revealed that God was being patient for the sake of humankind.

It is true that the Lord will one day destroy the present heavens and earth and that the ungodly will perish with the devastation of creation; nevertheless, as Peter explained, God wants everyone to repent and is giving the lost as much time as possible to turn from their sins. The sobering truth is that, because sinners spurn the grace of God, they one day will experience His wrath.

D. God's Judgment Affirmed: vs. 10

But the day of the Lord will come like a thief. The heavens will disappear with a roar; the elements will be destroyed by fire, and the earth and everything in it will be laid bare.

Peter acknowledged that God has continued to forestall His judgment. The apostle, however, did not want anyone to conclude that there would be no divine retribution for wickedness. The reference to "day of the Lord" (2 Pet. 3:10) underscored that God will one day intervene in human affairs to reveal His glory and vindicate His name.

The time of judgment will occur as unexpectedly as the arrival of "a thief" in the night; and once it takes place, there is nothing to stop it. Then the heavens will disappear with "a roar." God will use intense heat to destroy everything in the universe, from the stars to the very elements of creation. Even the earth and all that is on it will be consumed by fire.

II. THE WAY BELIEVERS OUGHT TO LIVE: 2 PETER 3:11-15A, 17-18

A. Enjoining Holiness and Godliness: vs. 11

Since everything will be destroyed in this way, what kind of people ought you to be? You ought to live holy and godly lives.

Our awareness of the eventual end of all things should affect how we live in the present. While we should not ignore the concerns and responsibilities of this life, our ultimate focus should be living for God.

Peter reflected this sentiment when he exclaimed, "what kind of people ought you to be?" (2 Pet. 3:11). Even the greatest human works on this planet will be "destroyed" in the day of judgment. We thus should pursue lives characterized by holiness and godliness.

Expressed another way, we should invest our lives in that which is eternal, not that which will ultimately be destroyed. The starting point is for us to relate to God in an attitude of reverence. We then should seek to honor Him by forsaking sin and pursuing Christian virtues.

B. Anticipating the Consummation of History: vss. 12-13

As you look forward to the day of God and speed its coming. That day will bring about the destruction of the heavens by fire, and the elements will melt in the heat. But in keeping with his promise we are looking forward to a new heaven and a new earth, the home of righteousness.

The prospect of divine judgment might cause us to cringe in terror; instead, we should anticipate and eagerly desire the future "day of God" (2 Pet. 3:12) in which He will destroy His enemies and establish His kingdom.

God will first incinerate the sin-cursed universe; then He will replace the old order with "a new heaven and a new earth" (vs. 13). Here the Greek term rendered "new" does not just refer to time. It also refers to the fresh, pristine moral quality of the new creation. It will be characterized by "righteousness," and be a place where justice, equity, and peace abide.

C. Keeping Priorities Straight: vss. 14-15a

So then, dear friends, since you are looking forward to this, make every effort to be found spotless, blameless and at peace with him. Bear in mind that our Lord's patience means salvation.

Teaching about the end times should not become an all-consuming focus; rather, it should prompt us to be at "peace" (2 Pet. 3:14) with God. This is possible when we make every effort to be "found spotless, [and] blameless" in our lives. When we strive to be people of integrity, we will live above reproach.

Peter reiterated what he said in verse 9, namely, that God is delaying His judgment so that the lost might be saved. The apostle also stressed that the Lord's "patience" (vs. 15), or forbearance, can be an ongoing opportunity for believers to witness to the unsaved. Through a variety of evangelistic efforts, we can be used by God to bring sinners to repentance.

D. Departing from Error: vss. 17-18

Therefore, dear friends, since you already know this, be on your guard so that you may not be carried away by the error of lawless men and fall from your secure position. But grow in the grace and knowledge of our Lord and Savior Jesus Christ. To him be glory both now and forever! Amen.

As Peter neared the end of his life, he issued one final warning to his readers about the "error of lawless men" (2 Pet. 3:17). The latter peddled the idea that God is uninvolved in the world and will not judge sin one day. Peter's desire was that believers not be "carried away" in their thinking; otherwise, they could spiritually stumble and "fall."

The way to remain stable and steadfast was to "grow in grace" (vs. 18). This means believers were to appropriate fully the special kindness and favor that come from Christ. They were also to deepen their "knowledge" of the Savior. The focus here is on both a factual and personal understanding of the Lord.

Because Jesus is the source of all truth, there is no need for us to embrace doctrinal error. When we make knowing Him the supreme focus of our lives, we will bring Him unending "glory," honor, and praise.

Discussion Questions

1. Why would scoffers mock the truth of Christ's second coming?
2. In the day of judgment, what will God do to the existing heavens and earth?
3. Why has God chosen to delay the return of His Son?
4. As believers await the return of Christ, why should they diligently evangelize the lost?
5. How should believers live as they await the fulfillment of God's promise concerning Jesus' second coming?

Contemporary Application

Peter was deeply concerned about the false teachers who had crept into the infant churches and beguiled many weak-minded Christians into believing doctrines that distorted the Gospel. Peter wrote his second epistle to urge his fellow believers to beware of these frauds, who were headed to certain "destruction" (2 Pet. 3:7).

We must be resolute in denouncing any teaching that falsifies the person and work of Jesus Christ. If we remain silent when Jesus is said to be anything less than what He truly is, we permit dishonor to His name. That is something we can never do.

Peter was also concerned that believers were losing their eagerness for Jesus' return. In response, the apostle assured his readers that the Lord will keep His promise to come again. They thus were not to be dismayed that He had not yet returned.

Now, nearly two thousand years later, many Christians still think that Jesus' return will occur in the long-distant future. Most importantly, some do not anticipate His coming with excitement and longing. They, instead, occasionally pray about it and at times discuss it as a theological issue; but do we truly yearn for Jesus' second coming?

Since so much time has passed, and since many of us live quite comfortably, it is understandable that Jesus' return does not impact us as it should; yet, as Peter said, "with the Lord a day is like a thousand years" (vs. 8). To the Father, the Son's return is imminent, and so it should be to us as well.

We need to always look forward to Jesus' coming again because that thought will help us live godly lives. If we truly love the Lord, none of us want Jesus to return right when we are sinning; instead, we want Him to find us living holy lives. Then, at His return, He will say to us, "Well done, good and faithful servant!" (Matt. 25:21).

In light of these thoughts, what kind of fruit are we bearing in our witness? That question should lead us to spread the Gospel to those around us far more than we do now. Thus, as we yearn for Jesus' return, we should strive to be morally pure and fruitful in all we think, say, and do.

Enjoy Fellowship with God

Scripture

Background Scripture: *1 John 1:1—3:10*
Scripture Lesson: *1 John 1:5—2:6, 15-17, 29—3:1*
Key Verse: *If we walk in the light, as he is in the light, we have fellowship with one another, and the blood of Jesus, his Son, purifies us from all sin.* 1 John 1:7.
Scripture Lesson for Children: *Acts 3:1-11*
Key Verse for Children: *When all the people saw [the crippled beggar] walking and praising God, . . . they were filled with wonder and amazement.* Acts 3:9-10.

Lesson Aim

To explore how a relationship with Christ should be evident in everyday living.

Lesson Setting

Time: *Between A.D. 85–95*
Place: *Ephesus*

Lesson Outline

Enjoy Fellowship with God

   I. A Biblical View of Sin: 1 John 1:5—2:2
      A. *Living in Darkness: 1:5-6*
      B. *Living in the Light: vs. 7*
      C. *Confessing Our Sins: vss. 8-9*
      D. *Recognizing the Reality of Our Sin: vs. 10*
      E. *Relying on Our Advocate: 2:1-2*
  II. A Biblical View of Obedience: 1 John 2:3-6, 15-17, 29—3:1
      A. *Obeying God's Commandments: 2:3-4*
      B. *Following the Example of Christ: vss. 5-6*
      C. *Shunning this Evil World: vss. 15-16*
      D. *Doing the Will of God: vs. 17*
      E. *Living Uprightly as God's Children: 2:29—3:1*

Introduction for Adults

Topic: *Enjoy Fellowship*

Depending on where we live, we are required to take our automobiles for periodic inspections, either for mechanical worthiness or for emission controls. When our vehicles pass the inspection, we are free to enjoy all the privileges of driving these marvels of technology.

John's letter is something like that. He writes so that his readers can pass the test and enjoy the blessings of eternal life in Christ. That's why his epistle is so practical. He gives clear pass-fail grades. "If you do this, you pass. If not, you fail."

All of us need John's reminders, lest we get sucked into ungodly ways of thinking and behaving. Professing faith in Christ is supposed to make a difference. We cannot enjoy fellowship with God and with each other if we continue to fail God's tests.

Introduction for Youth

Topic: *Live in Light*

What's it like to live in the light? Have you ever entered a dark room or an abandoned apartment, turned on the light, and watched the cockroaches scurry away? Living in the light means we do not have to run away when God shines His Word on our lives. It means we welcome His inspections. According to John, it means living as Jesus did.

That's a tough assignment and sometimes we fail to make the grade. But Jesus forgives us when we confess our sins. He pardons our transgressions. That's why it's so important to stay close to Him, whatever our circumstances. Jesus not only tells us how to live, but also helps us to do it when we rely on Him.

Concepts for Children

Topic: *Peter Healed a Man*

1. God gave Peter the power to heal a crippled beggar.
2. Peter healed the man in the name of Jesus.
3. The people thanked God for this healing.
4. God uses Jesus' followers to bring help and comfort to others.
5. We can ask Jesus to give us courage and faith to help others.

Lesson Commentary

I. A BIBLICAL VIEW OF SIN: 1 JOHN 1:5—2:2

A. Living in Darkness: 1:5-6

This is the message we have heard from him and declare to you: God is light; in him there is no darkness at all. If we claim to have fellowship with him yet walk in the darkness, we lie and do not live by the truth.

Neither the Epistles of John nor the Gospel of John identify their author. Church fathers as early as Irenaeus in the second century attributed them to John the beloved disciple of Jesus, the son of Zebedee, and the brother of James. The earliest citations of John's works are found in writings from western Asia Minor around Ephesus where the apostle John ministered in the later years of his life. John's authorship of these books has been universally accepted into the modern era, and even many critical scholars find the evidence compelling.

First John reflects a date of composition late in the first century, probably between A.D. 85 and 95. John addressed his readers from the perspective of an elderly man, calling them "my dear children" (2:1). In 2 and 3 John, the apostle referred to himself as "the elder" (2 John 1; 3 John 1). The false teaching addressed in John's letters also reflects ideas characteristic of a later date rather than an earlier one in the apostolic period.

In John's day, Ephesus was an ancient city that prided itself as the cultural center of the province of Asia. That culture was thoroughly Hellenistic and included many forms of revived paganism that tried to bring together different strands of religious thought, old and new, eastern and western. John's letters reflect a struggle between the truth of God's Word and some heretical teachings within the churches around Ephesus that threatened to divide the congregations.

The proponents of the heretical teachings seem to have agreed that "God is light" (1 John 1:5). They accepted Christ as a heavenly being, but denied His humanity (4:2). They believed the Gospel freed them from the presence of sin (1:8). They assumed they were free from any further practice of sin (1:10). They did not make a connection between their belief and their behavior. They were neither gracious nor loving (3:14-17).

The frauds were involved in missionary activity to expand their sect (2 John 10). In fact, the new sect had been a part of the church around Ephesus. By the time John wrote his first letter, it had separated from the church and had begun rivaling it (1 John 2:19). The apostle summoned the members of the church to resist the sect that wanted to divorce faith and life. He stressed that one must walk in the light; one must live in love; and to abide in God is to obey His commands.

In the beginning of his first letter, John drew attention to his role as a witness who possessed the authority of experience and was competent to tell about what he had seen, heard, and touched (1:1-4). In writing this brief epistle, the apostle sought to reassure Christians in their faith (5:13).

It was noted earlier that one corrupt notion being taught by the frauds asserted that it did not matter how a person behaved as long as he or she had a spiritual relationship with God. John countered this lie by declaring that "God is light" (1:5). In other words, because the Lord is pure, holy, and totally free from the darkness of sin, those who claimed to be His people could not live in spiritual darkness and have fellowship with God at the same time.

In Scripture, light symbolizes both intellectual truth and moral purity, while darkness portrays the opposing qualities of error and evil. Both the Old and New Testaments equate light with the truth of the Word.

For instance, Psalm 119:105 says, "Your word is a lamp to my feet and a light for my path." Also, in 2 Corinthians 4:4, Paul said that the devil had blinded the eyes of unbelievers so that they could not see "the light of the gospel of the glory of Christ."

Paul (like John) used light to denote righteousness and used darkness to refer to evil behavior. For example, in Ephesians 5:9, the apostle said that the fruit of Christians—the children of light—consists of "all goodness, righteous and truth." Also, Christians should have "nothing to do with the fruitless deeds of darkness" (vs. 11).

Some of the false teachers John was combating were claiming to "have fellowship" (1 John 1:6) with God; in other words, they asserted they genuinely knew Him and intimately communed with Him. Their unseemly behavior, however, undercut their claims.

John wanted his readers to think about the contradiction the religious charlatans presented. They maintained they were communing with the one who is light; but they abided "in the darkness." Since God is also truth and can never lie, the claimants were being deceptive.

B. Living in the Light: vs. 7

But if we walk in the light, as he is in the light, we have fellowship with one another, and the blood of Jesus, his Son, purifies us from all sin.

John clarified what it meant to truly be living "in the light" (1 John 1:7) of God's presence. First, Jesus, the Son of God, abides in the light. Second, those who claim to be His followers abide by His teachings and have fellowship with Him as well as His followers. Third, they have allowed the shed blood of Christ to cleanse them "from all sin." In turn, they make every effort to shun deception, immorality, and iniquity.

The apostle's singular and plural uses of "sin" have prompted some to suggest that, in verse 7, John was referring to a state of sinfulness before conversion, and in verse 9 to sins committed after one became a Christian; however, the phrase "all sin" (vs. 7) is so inclusive that it could hardly be limited to pre-conversion misdeeds; also, the emphasis in this verse on walking in the light strongly suggests the Christian life (rather than one's life before conversion) is in view.

C. Confessing Our Sins: vss. 8-9

If we claim to be without sin, we deceive ourselves and the truth is not in us. If we confess our sins, he is faithful and just and will forgive us our sins and purify us from all unrighteousness.

Evidently some of the false teachers were claiming "to be without sin" (1 John 1:8). Expressed another way, they wanted others to believe they had no sin nature. Perhaps this was how they tried to excuse their wanton excesses.

John, however, would have none of this trickery. He exposed the frauds by declaring that they were self-deceived. The apostle also emphasized that the charlatans were devoid of "the truth." Because they had rejected Jesus' teachings, they refused to forsake their sin.

John undermined the false doctrine of the religious frauds by declaring that, in order to get right with God, we must first "confess our sins" (vs. 9). This means we are acknowledging both our sinful condition and our sinful deeds. We are also expressing a desire to see our lives radically turned around.

When we humbly seek God's mercy, He does not reject us; rather, as the one who is always "faithful and just," He forgives any and every sin we commit, whether past or present. The Lord also cleanses us from all the "unrighteousness" for which we are guilty.

John most likely was writing to those who had received redemption through faith in Christ. If so, they were already saved from eternal judgment and just needed forgiveness and cleansing from sins committed in the course of their Christian walk. Through the act of confession, they were able to make a fresh start with God on the basis of His mercy and pardon.

D. Recognizing the Reality of Our Sin: vs. 10

If we claim we have not sinned, we make him out to be a liar and his word has no place in our lives.

Evidently some of the charlatans admitted they had a sin nature; but they claimed to be innocent of ever committing any sin. This assertion, however, contradicted what the Lord had revealed in His Word. Thus, the false teachers were calling God "a liar" (1 John 1:10) and demonstrating that His message of truth was not in their hearts.

E. Relying on Our Advocate: 2:1-2

My dear children, I write this to you so that you will not sin. But if anybody does sin, we have one who speaks to the Father in our defense—Jesus Christ, the Righteous One. He is the atoning sacrifice for our sins, and not only for ours but also for the sins of the whole world.

John, as he addressed his readers with pastoral affection and concern, explained why he was writing. He wanted them to deal with their sin nature and sinful deeds. In fact, the apostle wanted them to forsake their sin altogether.

John, of course, knew how intractable sin can be for even the most seasoned believers. The apostle explained that, in those moments when believers sin, they can turn to "Jesus Christ, the Righteous One" (1 John 2:1) to be their advocate with "the Father." The Greek term rendered "one who speaks" implies that Jesus intercedes on our behalf. He can plead our case before the throne of God because He is completely upright.

Jesus won the right to be our Advocate by being the "atoning sacrifice" (vs. 2), or propitiation, "for our sins." "Atoning sacrifice" renders the Greek term *hilasmos*, which conveys the ideas of "turning aside divine wrath" and "cleansing from sin." The apostle was stressing that Jesus, at the cross, dealt with our sin in such a way that it no longer stands as a barrier to our open fellowship with God.

Jesus is not only the atoning sacrifice for our sins, but also for "the sins of the whole world." This truth should prompt us to tell others what Jesus has done for them. Though some might reject the good news, others might welcome it and be saved.

II. A BIBLICAL VIEW OF OBEDIENCE: 1 JOHN 2:3-6, 15-17, 29—3:1

A. Obeying God's Commandments: 2:3-4

We know that we have come to know him if we obey his commands. The man who says, "I know him," but does not do what he commands is a liar, and the truth is not in him.

The false teachers evidently were claiming to "know" (1 John 2:3) God; but their perverse lives indicated they were ignorant of Him. John declared that people truly know and belong to God when they "obey his commands." Submission to God's will, not insubordination, is the consistent testimony of their lives.

The converse is also true. Those who willfully and persistently violate God's "commands" (vs. 4) are lying when they claim to know God. In fact, "the truth" of God's Word is not in their hearts. In contrast, the regenerate know God intimately, as shown by their obedience to His commands.

B. Following the Example of Christ: vss. 5-6

But if anyone obeys his word, God's love is truly made complete in him. This is how we know we are in him: Whoever claims to live in him must walk as Jesus did.

Those who heed God's Word show that "God's love" (1 John 2:5) is "made complete" in them. The idea is that no aspect of His love is lacking in their lives. It manifests itself fully in all they think, say, and do.

These individuals also show that they have a genuine relationship with the Savior. After all, the Son obeyed the Father completely and loved Him perfectly. Jesus' disciples, by following His example, confirm their status of being truly born again (vs. 6).

C. Shunning this Evil World: vss. 15-16

Do not love the world or anything in the world. If anyone loves the world, the love of the Father is not in him. For everything in the world—the cravings of sinful man, the lust of his eyes and the boasting of what he has and does—comes not from the Father but from the world.

Evidently the false teachers had set their affections on the evil world system dominated by Satan. John declared that Jesus' followers do not have such a "love" (1 John 2:15) for the world. Conversely, those who make what the world offers the focal point of their lives are devoid of "the love of the Father."

Fallen human society can only offer three categories of "lust" (vs. 16): those of "sinful man" (sensual pleasure), of "his eyes" (materialism and greed), and of "the boasting of what he has and does" (human attainments and achievements). None of these originate from "the Father," but from "the world."

D. Doing the Will of God: vs. 17

The world and its desires pass away, but the man who does the will of God lives forever.

Ultimately, devotion to "the world" (1 John 2:17) is foolish from an eternal perspective, for fallen human society and all the evil it craves and produces are disappearing. In contrast, those who strive to obey God on a consistent basis show that they truly know and love Him. Because they are regenerate through faith in Christ, they "live forever."

E. Living Uprightly as God's Children: 2:29—3:1

If you know that he is righteous, you know that everyone who does what is right has been born of him. How great is the love the Father has lavished on us, that we should be called children of God! And that is what we are! The reason the world does not know us is that it did not know him.

The false teachers wanted others to think they were "born" (1 John 2:29) of God; but their unrighteous lifestyle indicated they were far from the Lord. John declared that the children of God make righteousness their constant pursuit, for their heavenly Father is righteous.

The false teachers, who belonged to "the world" (3:1), did not really know God, despite their claims. These frauds also did not genuinely know or understand His true children. The extent of the Father's love for the second group is evident by the fact that He allows them to be called His "children." Nothing the world offers can ever match this priceless gift.

Discussion Questions

1. What two kinds of people did John describe?
2. How can we deceive ourselves regarding sin in our lives?
3. What happens when we acknowledge our sins to God?
4. How is it possible for God, who is holy, to forgive us when we sin?
5. In what ways do the desires of the world contrast with those of the Father?

Contemporary Application

John's letter identifies three marks of a genuine relationship with Christ. One is walking in righteousness. Broadly speaking, this means upright living. If we want to be followers of Christ, we must be willing to live His lifestyle. That means changing any attitude or action not in keeping with the example Christ set for us.

A second mark of believers should be their obedience to God. Imagine that someone had been pretending to be your friend because that person felt obligated to or was trying to look good in front of others. If you became aware of this, the "friendship" would be meaningless.

We must not have that kind of relationship with God, namely, one characterized by legalistically obeying His commands. Our obedience, like Christ's, should come from our love for God, not from just doing what He says we should do. Then others will notice the joy we have in our relationship with the Lord.

A third mark is loving other believers. Jesus said, "By this all men will know that you are my disciples, if you love one another" (John 13:35). When Christians demonstrate sacrificial, not self-seeking, love toward each other, they stand out in our "me-first" world.

The priority of Christians becomes giving instead of taking. They are encouraging to each other instead of berating. That kind of love should show others the depth of our relationship with the Father through the Son.

Love One Another

DEVOTIONAL READING

1 Corinthians 13:1-13

DAILY BIBLE READINGS

Monday November 3
1 Corinthians 13:1-7 Love Believes, Hopes, Endures

Tuesday November 4
1 Corinthians 13:8-13 Love Never Ends

Wednesday November 5
1 John 3:11-17 Lay Down Your Life for Another

Thursday November 6
1 John 3:18-24 Love in Truth and Action

Friday November 7
1 John 4:1-7 Love Is from God

Saturday November 8
1 John 4:8-12 God Is Love

Sunday November 9
1 John 4:13-21 We Love Because God Loved Us

Scripture

Background Scripture: *1 John 3:11—4:21*
Scripture Lesson: *1 John 3:11, 14-16; 4:7-16*
Key Verse: *Dear friends, since God so loved us, we also ought to love one another.* 1 John 4:11.
Scripture Lesson for Children: *Acts 9:36-43*
Key Verse for Children: *[Peter] got down on his knees and prayed. . . . He said, "Tabitha, get up"* (Acts 9:40).

Lesson Aim

To examine the reality of God's love for us and express gratefulness for His compassion.

Lesson Setting

Time: *Between* A.D. *85–95*
Place: *Ephesus*

Lesson Outline

Love One Another

   I. Describing Real Love: 1 John 3:11, 14-16
      A. *Love Commanded: vs. 11*
      B. *Hatred Denounced: vss. 14-15*
      C. *Love Displayed: vs. 16*
  II. Showing Real Love: 1 John 4:7-16
      A. *Love and Hatred Contrasted: vss. 7-8*
      B. *God's Initiation of Love: vss. 9-10*
      C. *Love Enjoined: vss. 11-12*
      D. *God's Provision of the Spirit: vs. 13*
      E. *God's Provision of the Son: vss. 14-15*
      F. *God's Provision of Love: vs. 16*

Introduction for Adults

Topic: *Love One Another*

The Gospel's demand that we love one another is likely to be greeted with a big yawn. We've heard that before. What else is new?

We confront spiritual inertia on this point. We can name a few people who seem to excel in love, but in too many cases we live in isolation chambers.

If this diagnosis seems too negative, perhaps we could take an anonymous survey of people in our Sunday school classes and churches. We could find out (1) if people feel they receive love from fellow Christians, and (2) how they demonstrate love for one another.

Whatever the outcome, we have to seek the Holy Spirit's conviction to stir up obedience to our Christian duty to love one another.

Introduction for Youth

Topic: *A Love-Filled Life*

We like to sing, "They'll know we are Christians by our love," which is straight from the teaching of Jesus. But how much harder it is to practice the words. Any group of Christian adolescents is bound to include some who are not especially lovable. In fact, they may turn us off by their quirky behavior.

Yet we cannot dodge the hard commands of Jesus and John. To love is our inescapable imperative. Failure to do so negates our Christian profession. Perhaps we need to confess our bad attitudes and listless behavior. Out of our weakness we must ask Jesus to make us more loving toward others, including those who may turn us off.

Concepts for Children

Topic: *Peter Prayed for Dorcas*

1. The death of Dorcas deeply touched her community.
2. Peter was summoned to help.
3. God answered Peter's prayer and Dorcas came back to life.
4. Many people believed in the Lord.
5. We must be available to others in their time of need.
6. Even when it seems we can do nothing, we can pray for them.

Lesson Commentary

I. DESCRIBING REAL LOVE: 1 JOHN 3:11, 14-16

A. Love Commanded: vs. 11

This is the message you heard from the beginning: We should love one another.

When John wrote his letter, he was probably battling an emerging heresy known as Gnosticism. While its doctrines were not fully developed until the second or third centuries, enough of Gnoticism's ideas were around in the first century to alarm the apostle.

Basically, Gnosticism denied that Jesus could have been God in the flesh, for Gnosticism taught that all matter is evil. God, however, is wholly spirit, so He is good. Salvation is accomplished by escaping from the body rather than through faith in Christ.

John countered such false teachings by emphasizing that Jesus—who existed in eternity with the Father—became a real man with a flesh-and-blood body. Because John and the other apostles had seen, heard, and touched the "Word of life" (1 John 1:1), they were the ones competent to testify about Him, not the Gnostic teachers, who relied on mere philosophy rather than fact.

Another consistent teaching of 1 John is that God's children obey His commands and are compassionate toward other Christians (3:10). This truth was part of the eyewitness testimony regarding Jesus. One intent behind the gospel proclamation was to bring the hearers and readers of John's letter into fellowship with God and His apostolic representatives (1:3).

At the end of Jesus' earthly ministry, He commanded His followers to love each other in the same way He had loved them, namely, sacrificially and unselfishly (John 15:12-13, 17). John reiterated this same message, which his readers had "heard from the beginning" (1 John 3:11). Here we see that mutual compassion and kindness are foundational to living for Christ and promoting His cause in the world.

B. Hatred Denounced: vss. 14-15

We know that we have passed from death to life, because we love our brothers. Anyone who does not love remains in death. Anyone who hates his brother is a murderer, and you know that no murderer has eternal life in him.

The attitudes and actions of the false teachers prompted John's remarks. The frauds were characterized more by hatred than love. John stressed that love for our fellow believers was proof that we have passed from the realm of "death" (1 John 3:14) to "life." This meant that those who were truly regenerate demonstrated the reality of their salvation by acts of compassion and kindness to others.

The apostle then noted that those who did not love their "brother" (vs. 15) were still under the power of death. Their actions indicated they had not gone from death to life and that they were taking their cues from Satan, not the Savior. Jesus declared that the devil "was a murderer from the beginning" (John 8:44).

Perhaps this truth prompted John to stress that the one who hates other believers is really a "murderer" (1 John 3:15) at heart. The apostle was referring to people who abided in death and who made hatred, not love, the soil of their affections. It is not hard, then, to see how they did not have "eternal life" within them. In short, they had never experienced the new birth.

C. Love Displayed: vs. 16

This is how we know what love is: Jesus Christ laid down his life for us. And we ought to lay down our lives for our brothers.

The love of God was manifested in a real and tangible way when Jesus "laid down his life for us" (1 John 3:16). The virtues of sacrifice, commitment, and generosity are all evident in this display of compassion. It is the same sort of love that should exist among believers, namely, the willingness to "lay down our lives for our brothers."

II. SHOWING REAL LOVE: 1 JOHN 4:7-16

A. Love and Hatred Contrasted: vss. 7-8

Dear friends, let us love one another, for love comes from God. Everyone who loves has been born of God and knows God. Whoever does not love does not know God, because God is love.

The false teachers were focused more on themselves than on others, and this prompted them to be greedy and self-serving. John countered such an influence by urging his readers, whom he affectionately referred to as "Dear friends" (1 John 4:7), to "love one another." Such compassion is displayed in actions, not just words.

God is the source of this unselfish, giving form of love. Thus, when believers consistently loved their fellow Christians in this way, they demonstrated that they were "born of God" and knew Him. In other words, they were truly regenerate and had an intimate relationship with the Lord.

The converse is also true. Those who did "not love" (vs. 8) did not know the Lord, for "God is love." They did not have an intimate and experiential knowledge of God because their lives were characterized by hatred. Because they consistently failed to love others in an unselfish, sacrificial way, their claims to be regenerate were suspect.

John, in saying that "God is love," was not implying that "love is God." The apostle was referring to a quality of God's character, just as he was when he declared "God is light" (1:5). Thus, while God is characterized by love, this virtue does not fully describe every aspect of His being.

B. God's Initiation of Love: vss. 9-10

This is how God showed his love among us: He sent his one and only Son into the world that we might live through him. This is love: not that we loved God, but that he loved us and sent his Son as an atoning sacrifice for our sins.

John again stressed that real love is displayed in actions, not just in words. For example, the Father showed the extent of His love for humankind by sending "his one and only Son into the world" (1 John 4:9). Jesus came when we were "still powerless" (Rom. 5:6), "ungodly," and "sinners" (vs. 8). When He appeared in human form, He "made himself nothing" (Phil. 2:7).

This amazing display of love did not end with Jesus' incarnation. The Son, in accordance with the Father's will, "humbled himself" (vs. 8) further by dying on the cross. Jesus experienced death to the fullest (Heb. 2:9) so that "we might live through him" (1 John 4:9).

The initiator, then, was God, not us. He displayed real love for us by sending His Son to be the "atoning sacrifice for our sins" (vs. 10). The idea is that Jesus satisfied the demands of God's justice and wrath against sin. God made Christ, who had never sinned, "to be sin for us" (2 Cor. 5:21) so that "in him we might become the righteousness of God."

C. Love Enjoined: vss. 11-12

Dear friends, since God so loved us, we also ought to love one another. No one has ever seen God; but if we love one another, God lives in us and his love is made complete in us.

The proper Christian response to God's love is for us to "love one another" (1 John 4:11). This is not a mere sentiment, but a commitment to regularly display kindness and compassion to our fellow believers.

God dwells in light that is so glorious that it is "unapproachable" (1 Tim. 6:16). Understandably, no one has ever seen Him; but if we "love one another" (1 John 4:12), we show the world that God truly lives "in us." We also demonstrate that His "love is made complete in us." Expressed another way, divine love is truly growing and maturing in our hearts.

D. God's Provision of the Spirit: vs. 13

We know that we live in him and he in us, because he has given us of his Spirit.

Our mutual love for one another is a strong indication of our regenerate status. We also know that we are one with God, and He with us, by the provision of "his Spirit" (1 John 4:13). The Spirit, as the third member of the Trinity, permanently indwells believers, is characterized by "truth" (John 14:17), and guides Christians "into all truth" (16:13).

The Spirit also reassures believers that they are "God's children" (Rom. 8:16). He furthermore enables them to put off the "acts of the sinful nature" (Gal. 5:19) and manifest such "fruit" (vs. 22) as love, joy, and peace. From this information we see that the Father's provision of the Spirit is essential to our Christian life and growth.

E. God's Provision of the Son: vss. 14-15

And we have seen and testify that the Father has sent his Son to be the Savior of the world. If anyone acknowledges that Jesus is the Son of God, God lives in him and he in God.

Evidently some of the false teachers denied that Christ "has come in the flesh" (1 John 4:2). John thus reaffirmed the truth of Jesus' incarnation. The apostle declared that God the Father actually sent God the Son to earth as a human being "to be the Savior of the world" (vs. 14). This was necessary in order for Jesus to truly be "Immanuel" (Matt. 1:23), namely, "God with us."

Religious frauds were denying that Jesus is the "Son of God" (1 John 4:15). This phrase underscores the special and intimate relationship that exists between the first and second persons of the Trinity (Matt. 16:16; Luke 1:35; John 6:69). It additionally indicates that the Son is to be identified with the Father and considered fully and absolutely equal to Him. Those affirming this truth were assured that God abided in them and they "in God" (1 John 4:15).

F. God's Provision of Love: vs. 16

And so we know and rely on the love God has for us. God is love. Whoever lives in love lives in God, and God in him.

Jesus, the "exact representation" (Heb. 1:3) of God's "being" to humankind, was no fiction to John. The apostle had heard and seen the incarnate Son with his own eyes and touched Him with his own hands (1 John 1:1). John believed the truth concerning "the love God has for us" (4:16) in His Son.

Thus, the apostle again affirmed that "God is love." In turn, those who lived in the love of God were assured that they abided in God and that He abided in them. These children of God likewise consistently displayed His love to others in deeds of compassion and kindness.

Discussion Questions

1. How can believers show they have eternal life?
2. What characterizes real love?
3. What was unique about God's expression of love for us?
4. What evidences do believers have of the reality of God's life in us?
5. What does it mean when believers confess that Jesus is the Son of God?

Contemporary Application

"I love you but . . ." Here we find three beautiful words ruined by one small conjunction. We humans want to add conditions to our love, probably because we know, at some deep level, that the essence of love is self-sacrifice. The deeper the love, the more complete the quality of self-giving.

How do we know that God loves us completely? The extent of His love was ultimately revealed when Jesus willingly gave His life to reconcile us to God. We particularly experience God's love through the forgiveness of our sin and a restored relationship with Him through Christ. We also inherit the same privilege and responsibility of loving others.

As we examine God's love, we find three characteristics we will want to have.

First, God's love is not based on our being lovable or worthy of love. He reached out in love to us while we were still His enemies. In the same way, we can take the risk to reach out in love, even to people who seem unlovable or unloving.

Second, God held nothing back in giving what was precious to Him when He gave His Son to die for us. Because God's love dwells in us by His Spirit, we also can love others sacrificially and not just superficially. His Spirit helps us turn our focus away from where it normally is—on ourselves—and onto the needs and best interests of the people around us.

Third, God's love is not a onetime expression, but an ongoing commitment. His ongoing love for us equips us to live in love. Our love for other people allows them to discover the depth of God's love and sets them free to love in return.

In short, God demonstrated His love for us by sending His Son. It is only natural that, as His children, we will want to imitate His love in our compassion for others.

Live with Confidence

Scripture

Background Scripture: *1 John 5*
Scripture Lesson: *1 John 5:1-15*
Key Verse: *This is the testimony: God has given us eternal life, and this life is in his Son.* 1 John 5:11.
Scripture Lesson for Children: *Acts 10:1-8, 17-20, 28-33*
Key Verse for Children: *Then Peter began to speak: "I now realize how true it is that God does not show favoritism."* Acts 10:34.

Lesson Aim

To trust Christ alone for overcoming sinful influences.

Lesson Setting

Time: *Between A.D. 85–95*
Place: *Ephesus*

Lesson Outline

Live with Confidence

    I. Overcoming the World: 1 John 5:1-5
        A. *Belief Resulting in Love: vs. 1*
        B. *Obedience Confirming Love: vss. 2-3*
        C. *Belief Resulting in Victory: vss. 4-5*
   II. Affirming Jesus' Identity: 1 John 5:6-12
        A. *The Son Revealed: vs. 6*
        B. *The Sources of Testimony: vss. 7-8*
        C. *The Trustworthiness of the Testimony: vss. 9-10*
        D. *The Specifics of the Testimony: vss. 11-12*
  III. Being Assured of Eternal Life: 1 John 5:13-15
        A. *Salvation Affirmed: vs. 13*
        B. *Prayers Answered: vss. 14-15*

Introduction for Adults

Topic: *Live with Confidence*

Charlie parked in the same lot downtown every day and got to know the attendant. To spark some conversation, one day he asked the man if he had life. The attendant was puzzled and did not know what to say. Charlie told him what he meant by his question. Thereafter, all Charlie had to say was, "Joe, do you have life?" After several months, one morning Joe rushed up to him and exclaimed, "Charlie, I have life!"

The man had found new life in Christ. The believer was a new person and began to live with the same kind of assurance Charlie had. This believer is typical of people in all walks of life who every day are finding that the answer to worry and fear is eternal life in Christ.

Jesus gives us peace and hope. He also gives us courage to offer peace and hope to others. The Spirit moreover gives us the confidence we need to share our faith with people in need of salvation.

Introduction for Youth

Topic: *Confident Living*

Skydiving is filled with risk. Even after heeding all the safety instructions, it's easy to become apprehensive about what might go wrong. What if the parachute fails to open? Despite such misgivings, skydivers trust their instructors and their equipment. This gives them the confidence they need to leap into air and free fall their way to earth.

Jesus does not call all of us to be skydivers, but He does want us to trust in Him regardless of what He leads us to do. Many Christians will tell you that depending on the Savior in this way is far more exciting and satisfying than even jumping out of an airplane.

The Christian life includes many "jumps." In the final analysis, we take leaps of faith (namely, doing what Jesus desires) because we know He will take care of us; and our awareness of His care grows with each successful "jump." As we serve Him day in and day out, we grow stronger in our faith and our assurance of salvation.

Concepts for Children

Topic: *Peter Told Cornelius about God*

1. Cornelius was a person who wanted to serve God.
2. God heard the prayers of Cornelius and sent Peter to his house.
3. Peter told Cornelius the good news about Jesus, and Cornelius and his household became Christians.
4. God can help us tell others about Jesus.
5. We know God hears and answers the prayers of people seeking Him.
6. We can pray for our friends to come to faith in Jesus.

Lesson Commentary

I. OVERCOMING THE WORLD: 1 JOHN 5:1-5

A. Belief Resulting in Love: vs. 1

Everyone who believes that Jesus is the Christ is born of God, and everyone who loves the father loves his child as well.

At the end of the fourth Gospel, John stated his desire that his readers would "believe that Jesus is the Christ, the Son of God" (John 20:31). By putting their faith in the Messiah, they would "have life in his name." A similar emphasis can be found in this week's lesson.

In 1 John 5:1, for example, the apostle declared that all who believe Jesus is the Messiah are "born of God." Evidently some false teachers were denying that Jesus is the Christ. In response, John emphasized that affirming the messiahship of Jesus was evidence of being spiritually regenerated.

In addition, the new birth was evidenced by love for the Father as well as His other children. In the first century A.D., family members were closely affiliated under the father's position of authority. Thus, the family served as an example of the truth that anyone who loves God the Father will surely love His children. Similarly, we cannot love fellow believers without loving the Father in the process.

B. Obedience Confirming Love: vss. 2-3

This is how we know that we love the children of God: by loving God and carrying out his commands. This is love for God: to obey his commands. And his commands are not burdensome.

The false teachers claimed they loved "the children of God" (1 John 5:2), but their lives undermined their assertions. John declared that a genuine love for other believers is demonstrated by loving God and keeping "his commands."

The Christian triad of faith, love, and obedience resonate strongly in this letter. Faith moves beyond intellectual assent to unfettered loyalty to Christ; and genuine belief in the Son results in unconditional love for His followers as well as whole-hearted devotion to His Word. The growing presence of love and obedience, in turn, reassures believers that they are saved.

Thus, for John, it was impossible to separate "love for God" (vs. 3) and the keeping of "his commands." In this context, the apostle was speaking about a lifestyle of obedience to the Lord. Such was not burdensome to the Christian, for Jesus' "yoke is easy and [His] burden is light" (Matt. 11:30).

C. Belief Resulting in Victory: vss. 4-5

For everyone born of God overcomes the world. This is the victory that has overcome the world, even our faith. Who is it that overcomes the world? Only he who believes that Jesus is the Son of God.

The new birth is what makes all the difference. First, Christians no longer view obeying God as a burden to shoulder. Second, they have the indwelling Spirit to empower them to do what is right.

Our victory in Christ over the world's sinful pattern of life is another reason we are able to obey the Lord. Believing in the deity of Jesus opens the door for triumph over sin. Of course, the extent of our "victory" (1 John 5:4) depends on our willingness to embrace what is ours by faith.

The evil forces of the world cannot prevail against the believer whose confidence is in Messiah. Stated another way, our faith in Jesus as "the Son of God" (vs. 5) gives us access to the victory that He obtained while He was on the earth. Because of the triumph associated with His sacrificial death and resurrection, we can successfully battle our sinful impulses and obey God.

II. AFFIRMING JESUS' IDENTITY: 1 JOHN 5:6-12

A. The Son Revealed: vs. 6

This is the one who came by water and blood—Jesus Christ. He did not come by water only, but by water and blood. And it is the Spirit who testifies, because the Spirit is the truth.

The false teachers, in denying the true identity of Jesus, had failed to appreciate the central role that the Messiah served in the believers' life of victory. This is why John spent a considerable amount of time declaring that Jesus is both God and man.

There are various ways to understand 1 John 5:6. One group says that the "water" and "blood" refer to baptism and the Lord's Supper (respectively). A second group connects the passage with the spear thrust into the side of Jesus and the blood and water that came out of the wound (John 19:34-35). A third group finds a link to Christ's birth in the "water" (1 John 5:6) and to His death in the "blood."

The strongest view makes the water and the blood references to Christ's baptism and death. Support for this thought is found in the fact that Jesus began His earthly ministry with His baptism and He ended it with His crucifixion. The Spirit, who is characterized by "truth," affirms the veracity concerning the Father's revelation of the Son.

B. The Sources of Testimony: vss. 7-8

For there are three that testify: the Spirit, the water and the blood; and the three are in agreement.

The testimony of the triune God (1 John 5:7) is affirmed by the threefold testimony of "the Spirit, the water and the blood" (vs. 8). Deuteronomy 19:15 says two or three witnesses were necessary in a court of law. The idea is that no one could be convicted on the basis of a single testimony.

The water, the blood, and the Spirit together agree that Jesus is the Son of God, who came to earth in the flesh. The Spirit, in particular, opens our eyes to the historical witness of Christ. The Spirit helps us understand that Jesus was truly human and that He really died. When we accept the Spirit's testimony regarding the Messiah, we enter eternal life.

C. The Trustworthiness of the Testimony: vss. 9-10

We accept man's testimony, but God's testimony is greater because it is the testimony of God, which he has given about his Son. Anyone who believes in the Son of God has this testimony in his heart. Anyone who does not believe God has made him out to be a liar, because he has not believed the testimony God has given about his Son.

John noted that we readily "accept man's testimony" (1 John 5:9). How much more, then, should we accept "the testimony of God" concerning "his Son"? If the agreement of three witnesses on earth is sufficient to establish a case in a courtroom, then certainly the agreement of three with God as their source should be more than enough to establish the identity of Jesus.

John wanted us to accept the witness of the Spirit concerning Jesus. Whoever believes the evidence concerning "the Son of God" (vs. 10) has the Father's own witness in his or her heart. Here we see that faith itself is God's gift to the believer (Eph. 2:8).

Sadly, not all accept what God has testified concerning His Son. Those who reject the witness of the Father are actually calling Him a liar, for He has confirmed Jesus' identity. Thus, those stand opposed to what the Father has revealed about His Son do not have eternal life.

D. The Specifics of the Testimony: vss. 11-12

And this is the testimony: God has given us eternal life, and this life is in his Son. He who has the Son has life; he who does not have the Son of God does not have life.

So that there is no doubt concerning the testimony of the Father concerning His Son, John articulated it for his readers. God has made "eternal life" (1 John 5:11) available, not through esoteric knowledge or good works, but through faith "in his Son." The corollary is that faith in the Son leads to "life" (vs. 12), while rejection of the Son leads to death.

A familiar analogy is found in the Sermon on the Mount. The genuine followers of Christ, like the wise person who constructed his life on a foundation of bedrock (Matt. 7:24-25), trust in Jesus for salvation and build their life on the Savior's teaching. In contrast, the unregenerate, like the foolish person who constructed his house on sand (vss. 26-27), fabricate their life on mere opinions and good works. Eternal ruin, not salvation, results.

Matthew 7:13-14 reveal that the entrance into eternal life is narrow. In contrast, the entrance into eternal destruction is wide, and its pathway is broad and spacious. The road to eternal ruin is also convenient and acceptable to the unsaved. There are no obstacles or annoyances to discourage people from traveling down this path, and that is why so many enter through its gate.

Throughout life people are faced with many decisions. The most important one is that concerning eternal life. Will we choose the path of life or the path of ruin? Picking deliverance through faith in Christ is far wiser. Despite the conflicts believers might experience, God will bless them with His heavenly riches.

III. BEING ASSURED OF ETERNAL LIFE: 1 JOHN 5:13-15

A. Salvation Affirmed: vs. 13

I write these things to you who believe in the name of the Son of God so that you may know that you have eternal life.

Evidently some of the false teachers had already severed their ties with the community of faith (1 John 2:19). We can imagine the frauds claiming that only those who sided with them were truly saved. This undoubtedly would have shaken the confidence of Jesus' genuine followers concerning their status as believers.

John wanted his readers to be assured about their decision to "believe in the name of the Son of God" (1 John 5:13). Their faith in Jesus meant they truly had "eternal life." The apostle, of course, wanted them to continue to put their trust in Christ.

B. Prayers Answered: vss. 14-15

This is the confidence we have in approaching God: that if we ask anything according to his will, he hears us. And if we know that he hears us—whatever we ask—we know that we have what we asked of him.

Because of their personal relationship with Christ, believers can also be confident that the Father will listen when they pray. First John 5:14 is not a sweeping promise that we will get whatever we ask from God. The precondition for answered prayer is that we ask "according to his will." Also, the goal is to bring honor and glory to the Lord.

Through the ministry of the Spirit, Scripture, and other believers, we tend to know whether our desires line up with God's will. In those instances when they do, we are assured that the Lord is pleased with our requests and will answer our petitions (vs. 15); of course, we must be willing to receive the answer that He gives.

Discussion Questions

1. What prompted John to emphasize the importance of correct teaching and belief about Jesus?
2. How is faith in Jesus the key to overcoming sinful impulses?
3. What is the testimony concerning Christ?
4. What results when people refuse to believe in Christ?
5. What does it mean to have the Son?

Contemporary Application

John declared that our faith is the victory that overcomes the sinful influences of the world. In fact, no other agent or formula defeats the enticements we encounter. Only Jesus faced them all and overcame them. It is only when we acknowledge our helplessness and place our confidence in the sufficiency of Christ's victory that we experience victory over sin.

We may try other means, such as willpower, accountability, support groups, human thought or philosophy, rituals or routines, aversion techniques, or shame and guilt. We may even find that some of these things offer limited success in helping us curb certain behaviors or keep them in check temporarily.

It is only through faith in Christ, however, that we can be tuned in to His will. Trusting in Jesus enables our mind to comprehend His desires for us (as revealed in His Word); also, our actions can become joyful acts of worship.

If we are believing in and relying upon anything but Christ's victory to overcome sin, our efforts are doomed. It is a good idea, then, for us to examine our life periodically to be sure our faith is not misplaced (2 Cor. 13:5).

What a relief it is to know that the hard part of overcoming sinful influences has been done for us by Jesus' life, death, and resurrection. To remain in His victory, we need only to hold confidently to God's provision for us in Christ.

Remain Loyal

DEVOTIONAL READING

John 15:1-8

DAILY BIBLE READINGS

Monday November 17
  *Philippians 3:10-15 I Press
  On*

Tuesday November 18
  *Philippians 3:16-21 Hold
  Fast*

Wednesday November 19
  John 15:1-7 Abide in Christ

Thursday November 20
  2 John 1-6 Walk in Truth

Friday November 21
  *2 John 7-12 Be on Guard,
  Don't Lose Out*

Saturday November 22
  *3 John1-8 Be Faithful to the
  Truth*

Sunday November 23
  *3 John 9-15 Imitate What is
  Good*

Scripture

Background Scripture: *2 and 3 John*
Scripture Lesson: *2 John 4-9; 3 John 3-11*
Key Verse: *Dear friend, do not imitate what is evil but what
is good. Anyone who does what is good is from God. Anyone
who does what is evil has not seen God.* 3 John 11.
Scripture Lesson for Children: *Acts 12:6-17*
Key Verse for Children: *Peter . . . described how the Lord
had brought him out of prison.* Acts 12:17.

Lesson Aim

To follow the God-man, Jesus Christ (as revealed in
Scripture), not humanly invented notions about Him.

Lesson Setting

Time: *About A.D. 85–95*
Place: *Ephesus*

Lesson Outline

Remain Loyal

  I. Living in the Truth: 2 John 4-9
      A. *Obeying the Truth: vs. 4*
      B. *Loving One Another: vss. 5-6*
      C. *Recognizing False Teachers: vs. 7*
      D. *Adhering to the Truth: vss. 8-9*
  II. Caring for Itinerant Ministers: 3 John 3-11
      A. *Devotion to the Truth: vss. 3-4*
      B. *Reports of Christian Hospitality: vss. 5-6*
      C. *Befriending Fellow Believers: vss. 7-8*
      D. *Displays of Arrogance: vss. 9-10*
      E. *Doing What Is Right: vs. 11*

Introduction for Adults

Topic: *Remain Loyal*

Some of history's great battles were lost because troops deserted, in some cases to the enemy. The first American president, General George Washington, was plagued by deserters. Some of his soldiers got tired of the bitter struggle, left camp, and went home. The fight for independence evidently wasn't worth it to them.

Churches have also suffered losses from deserters and deceivers. In John's day this was a life and death issue. The tiny congregations had no resources other than the faithfulness of their members. Many wavered and reverted to paganism.

Perhaps today it's too easy to drop out. We think we won't be missed. We think there are others to take our place and do our work. But when that attitude takes over, our churches suffer and the individuals who leave often degenerate spiritually as well. We must remain loyal because we need each other.

Introduction for Youth

Topic: *Walk this Way*

The Christian life (or walk) can be boiled down to simple principles—obedience and love. As we grow in our intellectual understanding of our faith, we also grow in how to live our faith. But sometimes it works the other way around.

When we dare to live our faith in front of others, we find that our understanding grows as well. It turns out that we believe what we do as well as do what we believe.

A young man entered a university scared that he would lose his faith. He was determined to follow Jesus. After his first year, he told his Christian friend, "You know what? They threw me to the lions and I survived. Now I'm really convinced that my Christian faith is true."

Concepts for Children

Topic: *Peter Freed from Prison*

1. When Peter was in prison, Christians prayed for him.
2. We can pray for Christians who are imprisoned for their faith.
3. God delivered Peter from prison, but the Christians found this hard to believe.
4. God often does the unexpected and surprises us.
5. As we pray, we can think of ways that God might surprise us.
6. We can pray for our church leaders to be bold and courageous.

Lesson Commentary

I. LIVING IN THE TRUTH: 2 JOHN 4-9

A. Obeying the Truth: vs. 4

It has given me great joy to find some of your children walking in the truth, just as the Father commanded us.

Second and 3 John were written shortly after John's first letter. They respond to problems associated with the same false teaching the apostle addressed in 1 John. Second John anticipated the arrival of traveling false teachers at outlying churches around Ephesus and encouraged true believers to refuse hospitality to them. Third John was sent to a church in which key leaders resented and resisted the authority of the apostle John. John felt concern that such a church was ripe for heresy.

Second John was addressed to "the chosen lady and her children" (vs. 1) and concluded with greetings from the "children of your chosen sister" (vs. 13). Are the "chosen lady" (vs. 1) and her "sister" (vs. 13) women of stature in the church or symbols for two churches? Are the children physical offspring of literal women or spiritual offspring of the Gospel? The Greek word translated "lady" (vs. 1) is the feminine form of "lord." It's a formal title, not a mere synonym for "woman." This favors literal women of noble birth or character.

However, the letter is not a deeply personal note to an individual but a general exhortation meant for a group. In verses 1 through 7 and verse 13, all occurrences of the Greek pronoun rendered "you" are singular in number. In verses 8 through 12, all occurrences of "you" are plural. It seems probable that John was addressing a church and its members under the metaphor of a noblewoman and her offspring.

Apparently, "the chosen lady" (vs. 1) had opened her home somewhat indiscriminately to false teachers who had stopped on their way through the town where she lived. Perhaps John was concerned that the spiritual frauds would take advantage of this woman's kindness (vss. 10-11).

Before dealing with the issue, however, the apostle commended the woman's "children" (vs. 4) for obeying "the truth," which is a reference to the commandments of God, as recorded in His Word. These believers had made living in the truth a consistent part of their lives. Here we see that their relationship with God was authentic, and they manifested this through kind acts.

B. Loving One Another: vss. 5-6

And now, dear lady, I am not writing you a new command but one we have had from the beginning. I ask that we love one another. And this is love: that we walk in obedience to his commands. As you have heard from the beginning, his command is that you walk in love.

During Jesus' earthly ministry, He commanded His disciples to love one another (John 13:34-35). Thus, when John reiterated this injunction, he was not issuing a "new command" (2 John 5) but one that had existed all along.

The influence of false teachers threatened to undermine the ability of John's readers to love one another. The apostle urged them to remain obedient to God's commandments, the premier one of which was to be wholehearted in their love for God and for His people (vs. 6).

C. Recognizing False Teachers: vs. 7

Many deceivers, who do not acknowledge Jesus Christ as coming in the flesh, have gone out into the world. Any such person is the deceiver and the antichrist.

Whereas the Gospel of John was written to bring people to faith in Jesus Christ (20:30-31), the Johannine epistles seem more concerned with correcting a false belief about Christ that was spreading in the churches. For instance, 2 John 7 identified as deceivers those who did not confess the incarnation of the Messiah. From this emphasis, it can be assumed that the opponents held to the divinity of Christ but either denied or diminished the significance of His humanity.

This verse spotlights the source of the problem facing John's readers. A number of deceivers were purporting to be "apostles of Christ" (2 Cor. 11:13); but, like Satan, they were messengers of darkness, not angels "of light" (vs. 14).

The charlatans' wayward lives mirrored their twisted thinking concerning the Messiah. They consistently denied "Jesus Christ as coming in the flesh" (2 John 7). Their rejection of the Savior's incarnation meant they were archenemies of Christ. To deny the Messiah's true nature means one is an "antichrist."

John did not mean that each individual is to be identified as the Antichrist; rather, John was comparing these frauds to the arch-deceiver (Satan) and the Antichrist, since they were accomplishing the devil's work and preparing the way for the Antichrist.

D. Adhering to the Truth: vss. 8-9

Watch out that you do not lose what you have worked for, but that you may be rewarded fully. Anyone who runs ahead and does not continue in the teaching of Christ does not have God; whoever continues in the teaching has both the Father and the Son.

At stake for John and his readers was the fullness of the reward they would receive in heaven for all the good works they had done on earth. John thus warned his readers to take extra care in their adherence to the truth.

In order to "be rewarded fully" (2 John 8), believers needed to discern between truth from error and the religious frauds who peddled the latter. For instance, the work of God's people was undermined when false teachers were aided in any way (vss. 10-11). Thus it was imperative for Jesus' followers not to transgress "the teaching of Christ" (vs. 9).

Those who deterred from and refused to abide in the apostolic teaching concerning the Messiah did not abide in God. Conversely, those who embraced the truth about Christ had fellowship with "both the Father and the Son." Thus, to deny the teaching about the Son (in this case, His incarnation) is to deny the Father.

II. Caring for Itinerant Ministers: 3 John 3-11

A. Devotion to the Truth: vss. 3-4

It gave me great joy to have some brothers come and tell about your faithfulness to the truth and how you continue to walk in the truth. I have no greater joy than to hear that my children are walking in the truth.

Third John is populated with a cast of characters about whom nothing is known beyond what can be inferred from the letter: Gaius (3 John 1), Diotrephes (vs. 9), and Demetrius (vs. 12). Gaius was a common Roman name. Diotrephes and Demetrius were Greek names. Demetrius was more common because a series of kings of ancient Macedon had carried the name.

The apostle was overjoyed to learn from traveling ministers about Gaius remaining faithful to and abiding in "the truth" (vs. 3). John was referring to apostolic teaching, especially that concerning the Messiah. Nothing brought John "greater joy" (vs. 4) than to learn that his "children" were living in the truth. Most likely, Gaius was one of the apostle's spiritual children in the faith. Gaius not only affirmed what he had been taught but also consistently ordered his life around it.

B. Reports of Christian Hospitality: vss. 5-6

Dear friend, you are faithful in what you are doing for the brothers, even though they are strangers to you. They have told the church about your love. You will do well to send them on their way in a manner worthy of God.

The warmth of John's feelings for Gaius are evident in the words "Dear friend" (3 John 5). The apostle commended Gaius for his unstinting commitment to take care of "the brothers." These would have been traveling ministers who passed through from time to time.

In the first century A.D., there were no comfortable hotels or inns; thus, travelers were often accommodated in homes. In the case of itinerant Christian workers, members of local churches often gave them hospitality. Concerning Gaius, though the ministers who came to his home were "strangers," he consistently extended hospitality to them.

The "church"(vs. 6) to which John belonged had received reports from several itinerant ministers that Gaius had shown them "love." The apostle, being well aware of these expressions of kindness and friendship, encouraged Gaius to continue to send his visitors "on their way" in a manner pleasing to God and honoring to them.

C. Befriending Fellow Believers: vss. 7-8

It was for the sake of the Name that they went out, receiving no help from the pagans. We ought therefore to show hospitality to such men so that we may work together for the truth.

The traveling missionaries had gone out "for the sake of the Name" (3 John 7). This means they sought to bring glory to the Lord through the proclamation of the

Gospel. They decided in advance not to accept help from "the pagans," namely, unbelievers.

Thus it was imperative that other Christians do whatever they could to help itinerant ministers in their missionary endeavors. For instance, a believer such as Gaius could "show hospitality" (vs. 8) to these believers by welcoming them into his home and giving them food and lodging. In this way, he would be a partner with them in spreading the truth.

We are reminded of Jesus' words to the righteous recorded in Matthew 25:34-40. He commended them for their deeds of kindness; and when they asked Him when they did all the things He mentioned, Jesus responded, "whatever you did for one of the least of these brothers of mine, you did for me" (vs. 40).

D. Displays of Arrogance: vss. 9-10

I wrote to the church, but Diotrephes, who loves to be first, will have nothing to do with us. So if I come, I will call attention to what he is doing, gossiping maliciously about us. Not satisfied with that, he refuses to welcome the brothers. He also stops those who want to do so and puts them out of the church.

The statement "I wrote to the church" (3 John 9) indicates that John had penned a previous letter that no longer exists. Perhaps the apostle had asked believers in a particular congregation to show hospitality to some itinerant ministers.

Sadly, a prominent church leader named Diotrephes had refused to acknowledge John's apostolic authority. In fact, the former loved "to be first" among his peers. Diotrephes thus rejected John's requests to help traveling missionaries with the same sort of generosity Gaius had displayed.

When John had the opportunity to visit the congregation, he would expose the uncharitable deeds and malicious gossip of Diotrephes (vs. 10). The apostle specifically mentioned the latter's refusal to "welcome the brothers" and insistence that others also not receive them. If anyone defied the authority of Diotrephes, he expelled them from the church.

John's warning is similar to that Paul issued in 2 Corinthians 10:2. There the apostle expressed his desire not to be bold in confronting antagonists to his authority and ministry. Paul expressed himself more strongly in 13:2 when he declared, "I will not spare" them, namely, those who were self-centered, self-seeking, and self-promoting in their attitudes and actions.

E. Doing What Is Right: vs. 11

Dear friend, do not imitate what is evil but what is good. Anyone who does what is good is from God. Anyone who does what is evil has not seen God.

John expected far more from Gaius. The apostle urged him not to "imitate" (3 John 11) the "evil" example of Diotrephes; instead, Gaius was to emulate the example of those who did "good," such as Demetrius, who is mentioned in verse 12.

John reminded Gaius that believers demonstrated their regenerate status by their consistent practice of kind deeds. Conversely, those outside the faith showed by their unrelenting "evil" (vs. 11) ways that they had "not seen God." The Lord did not abide in them, indicating that they had never truly known Him.

Discussion Questions

1. What was it that filled John with joy concerning his readers?
2. How did John describe the religious frauds?
3. What news about Gaius gave the apostle great joy?
4. Who were the "strangers" (3 John 5) the apostle was talking about?
5. What did John urge Gaius to continue doing?

Contemporary Application

We find two applicational strands in this week's Scripture lesson text. The first concerns the issue of heresy. Bible scholars use this term to refer to religious opinions, teachings, or practices that conflict with accepted biblical truth or established beliefs and standards. The compromise in doctrine and conduct is intellectually justified as being appropriate and acceptable. From the perspective of Scripture, however, all deviations from the revealed truth of God (as found in His Word) are to be renounced as unbiblical.

Many heresies concern the person and work of Christ. For example, there are some who deny that Jesus is fully human and there are others who deny that He is fully divine. Heretics often pervert the truth of the Gospel by teaching that one has to add some sort of good work to the grace of God in order to be saved. Scripture exhorts all believers to do their part in combating false doctrine and in fighting for the Christian truths they hold sacred.

The second applicational strand concerns the biblical model of leadership. The dictatorial style practiced by Diotrephes (3 John 9) reflects the mindset of the world. It defines leadership as the ability to direct the thoughts and actions of others. People are supposedly good leaders if they can command the obedience, confidence, respect, and loyal cooperation of their subordinates. The emphasis is on the followers doing exactly what the leader demands (Mark 10:42; Luke 22:25).

The biblical model for leadership is quite different. If people want to be great leaders in the eyes of God, they must unsparingly serve others (Matt. 23:11; Mark 10:43-45; Luke 22:26). They must humbly set aside their desires and minister to the needs of others (John 13:12-15). Their goal is to shepherd the flock of God willingly, not because they are forced to do so (1 Pet. 5:2).

Devout Christian leaders make the Bible their guidebook and the holiness of God their life aim (1 Thess. 4:3; 2 Tim. 4:1-2). They seek to be an example to those whom they are spiritually leading and feeding (1 Pet. 5:3). Their ultimate goal is to please the "Chief Shepherd" (vs. 4), not themselves.

Maintain Steadfast Faith

DEVOTIONAL READING

Galatians 6:1-10

DAILY BIBLE READINGS

Monday November 24
Isaiah 26:1-6 The Steadfast Are Kept in Faith

Tuesday November 25
Isaiah 26:7-13 O Lord, We Wait for You

Wednesday November 26
Psalm 112:1-8 The Righteous Have Steady Hearts

Thursday November 27
Revelation 3:7-13 Keep My Word

Friday November 28
Galatians 6:1-10 Don't Give Up in Doing Right

Saturday November 29
Jude 1-13 Contend for the Faith

Sunday November 30
Jude 16-25 Build Up Your Faith

Scripture

Background Scripture: *Jude*
Scripture Lesson: *Jude 3-4, 8, 10, 12-13, 16-23*
Key Verse: *Keep yourselves in God's love as you wait for the mercy of our Lord Jesus Christ to bring you to eternal life. Be merciful to those who doubt.* Jude 21-22.
Scripture Lesson for Children: *Acts 15:6-12, 22-23, 28-31*
Key Verse for Children: *We believe it is through the grace of our Lord Jesus that we are saved.* Acts 15:11.

Lesson Aim

To explore ways we can build ourselves up in our Christian faith.

Lesson Setting

Time: *About A.D. 65*
Place: *Unknown*

Lesson Outline

Maintain Steadfast Faith

I. A Warning about Apostates: Jude 3-4, 8, 10, 12-13, 16
  A. *The Importance of Defending the Faith: vss. 3-4*
  B. *The Apostates' Defiant Attitude: vs. 8*
  C. *The Apostates' Decadent Lives: vs. 10*
  D. *The Apostates' Barren Deeds: vss. 12-13*
  E. *The Apostates' Haughty Disposition: vs. 16*

II. A Call to Faithfulness: Jude 17-23
  A. *The Warning of the Apostles: vss. 17-18*
  B. *The Divisiveness Caused by the Apostates: vs. 19*
  C. *The Importance of Devotion to God: vss. 20-21*
  D. *The Importance of Helping Others: vss. 22-23*

Introduction for Adults

Topic: *Maintain Steadfast Faith*

John's wife suffered from a brain tumor and the physicians gave her two months to live. The months dragged by and she grew less and less responsive. John lapsed into bitterness and despair. His wife lingered and gradually John began to recover. His outlook brightened. He knew that he had to keep his faith, no matter what. Eight months later his wife passed away.

For many Christians like John, keeping faith is a battle against overwhelming despair. For others, it's a battle against various religious and intellectual arguments. That's what it was like for John's son, who was convinced that the Christian faith held nothing for him. But he too gave Jesus a more serious look during his mother's illness.

Whatever our battlegrounds, faith in the truth of the Gospel is the issue. If we yield on this point, we have no hope for ourselves or for others.

Introduction for Youth

Topic: *Keep the Faith*

When Wilmer graduated from college, one of his professors expressed disappointment that he had not been able to shake what he called Wilmer's "Sunday school" faith. The academic had assumed that when Wilmer got a college education, he would outgrow his beliefs.

Wilmer, however, learned how to grow in and defend his faith, because in college he joined a Christian group and studied the Bible, prayed, and told other students about Jesus. When Wilmer's faith was attacked in class, he consulted the library shelf where the Christians had placed a number of scholarly books that held the Bible to be true and trustworthy.

Keeping the faith required hard work, perseverance, knowledge, and Christian fellowship. Wilmer knew he could not go through college in neutral as far as his faith was concerned. If he did not spiritually grow, he would lapse into indifference and unbelief. So, he took the offensive and won the battle.

Concepts for Children

Topic: *Peter Took a Stand*

1. Peter declared that we are saved by God's grace through faith.
2. Peter's stand required faith, knowledge, and courage.
3. Wrong ideas about salvation can harm us.
4. With patience and love we can encourage people to believe in Jesus.
5. Our faith is only as strong as our knowledge of the Bible.
6. When we are in doubt, it is wise for us to consult older believers.

Lesson Commentary

I. A WARNING ABOUT APOSTATES: JUDE 3-4, 8, 10, 12-13, 16

A. The Importance of Defending the Faith: vss. 3-4

Dear friends, although I was very eager to write to you about the salvation we share, I felt I had to write and urge you to contend for the faith that was once for all entrusted to the saints. For certain men whose condemnation was written about long ago have secretly slipped in among you. They are godless men, who change the grace of our God into a license for immorality and deny Jesus Christ our only Sovereign and Lord.

Jude was a younger brother of James, who wrote the epistle bearing his name. Both were half-brothers of Jesus (Matt. 13:55; Mark 6:3). Neither brother drew attention to his family tie to the Lord (Jas. 1:1; Jude 1). Both called themselves Jesus' servants.

Although Jude follows the letters of Peter and John in the New Testament, it precedes most or all of them in time of composition. Jude 4-18 and 2 Peter 2:1-22 are so similar that one relied directly on the other or both used a third source that no longer exists. Most New Testament scholars think Peter relied on Jude. If that is so, Jude had to be written long enough before Peter's death in the late A.D. 60s to have been recognized as authoritative. Assuming Jude precedes 2 Peter, it may have been written about A.D. 65.

Jude made extensive use of Old Testament allusions. This may indicate he wrote to an audience in Palestine. The false teachers Jude warned against seem to have interpreted the doctrine of salvation by grace to imply that carnal sins were acceptable or even desirable as stimulants for more grace (Jude 4). The false teachers John's epistles combated held false views about the full humanity and full deity of Christ. Jude's (and 2 Peter's) false teachers seem primarily to have tried to join the gracious Gospel of Christ to immorality.

Jude's original intent was to write to his dear friends in the faith about "the salvation we share" (Jude 3), and he was "very eager" to offer pastoral counsel. The presence of false teachers, however, prompted Jude to redirect his attention.

Spiritual frauds were threatening believers with a counterfeit gospel. The danger was so great that Jude exhorted his readers to "contend for the faith." This refers to the body of apostolic truth "that was once for all entrusted to the saints." God, in His grace, gave His inspired and infallible Word to His holy people, and they were to uphold and defend it against heretics.

Jude referred to the charlatans as "godless men" (vs. 4) who had crept in undetected among the fellowship of believers. The frauds purported that the "grace of our God" permitted people to live in a manner characterized by lewdness and immorality. The charlatans also denied the necessity of obeying Jesus Christ.

Long ago Scripture revealed that the impious were eternally marked out for "condemnation." Their decision to be unrestrained in their wickedness was the reason they faced this gloomy end. Thus, they bore full responsibility for their judgment.

B. The Apostates' Defiant Attitude: vs. 8

In the very same way, these dreamers pollute their own bodies, reject authority and slander celestial beings.

Jude called the false teachers wretched "dreamers" (Jude 8) possibly because they claimed to have inspired dreams and visions. This became the basis for them flaunting all forms of authority, whether civil or spiritual, and living immorally. They feared neither God nor people and even reviled "celestial beings."

C. The Apostates' Decadent Lives: vs. 10

Yet these men speak abusively against whatever they do not understand; and what things they do understand by instinct, like unreasoning animals—these are the very things that destroy them.

The false teachers not only were self-deluded and pretentious but also boorish, especially as they spoke "abusively against whatever they [did] not understand" (Jude 10). Put another way, their unregenerate state prevented them from comprehending eternal truths, especially those related to the things of the Spirit.

Jude compared the false teachers to "unreasoning animals" who operated by impulse and instinct. Despite their confidence about the things they asserted, the frauds had been corrupted in their own thinking. Consequently, their baseless and senseless actions would bring about their demise.

D. The Apostates' Barren Deeds: vss. 12-13

These men are blemishes at your love feasts, eating with you without the slightest qualm—shepherds who feed only themselves. They are clouds without rain, blown along by the wind; autumn trees, without fruit and uprooted—twice dead. They are wild waves of the sea, foaming up their shame; wandering stars, for whom blackest darkness has been reserved forever.

The Greek word rendered "blemishes" (Jude 12) can refer to moral spots or stains that marred the fabric of a church. "Blemishes" can also refer to hidden reefs that threatened to shipwreck the unsuspecting. Both meanings suggest the false teachers were shameless, selfish, and filthy minded. This was especially true during congregational "love feasts." These were fellowship meals that believers regularly held to celebrate God's love in Christ.

Jude described the barren deeds of the apostates as "clouds without rain" that were blown along by the wind but never brought any water to the arid land. The frauds were also like trees at harvest time with either withered "fruit" or no fruit at all. Though the apostates promised much, their lives were spiritually empty and only fit for uprooting, thus being "twice dead."

The "shame" (vs. 13) of the false teachers churned up like foam produced from the "wild waves of the sea." Expressed differently, the promises of the frauds brought chaos and disgrace. Their aimless and untrustworthy lives were comparable to "wandering stars" that brightly appeared for a moment but proved unreliable for charting a course. The everlasting "blackest darkness" associated with hell was their eternal end.

E. The Apostates' Haughty Disposition: vs. 16

These men are grumblers and faultfinders; they follow their own evil desires; they boast about themselves and flatter others for their own advantage.

The frauds were noted for their constant murmuring and complaining and for doing whatever their "evil desires" (Jude 16) dictated. Such arrogance also manifested itself in speech characterized by boasting. They were also brash enough to flatter people to gain an "advantage."

The godly, in contrast, seek to praise God and encourage His people. The righteous also shun evil desires and reach out to others in need; thus, rather than exploiting and manipulating people, believers make great sacrifices to proclaim the truth so that the lost might be saved.

II. A CALL TO FAITHFULNESS: JUDE 17-23

A. The Warning of the Apostles: vss. 17-18

But, dear friends, remember what the apostles of our Lord Jesus Christ foretold. They said to you, "In the last times there will be scoffers who will follow their own ungodly desires."

Numerous apostolic warnings appear in Scripture that, in coming generations, the church will be attacked by spiritual frauds. For instance, Paul referred to them as "savage wolves" (Acts 20:29); and Peter called them "false prophets" (2 Pet. 2:1) who taught "destructive heresies."

Jude urged his readers to "remember" (Jude 17) these and other declarations made by "the apostles of our Lord Jesus Christ." They specifically revealed that, in the era spanning the first and second comings of Christ, "scoffers" (vs. 18) will arise who will follow after "their own ungodly desires." The impious will scoff at divine revelation, flaunt divine authority, and indulge themselves in unrestrained wantonness.

B. The Divisiveness Caused by the Apostates: vs. 19

These are the men who divide you, who follow mere natural instincts and do not have the Spirit.

Jude wanted his readers to know that the false teachers had infiltrated their ranks and were dividing their congregations. The apostates had a worldly-minded disposition. They took their cues from Satan, not God. The frauds were unregenerate, for they did not have "the Spirit" (Jude 19) indwelling them.

C. The Importance of Devotion to God: vss. 20-21

But you, dear friends, build yourselves up in your most holy faith and pray in the Holy Spirit. Keep yourselves in God's love as you wait for the mercy of our Lord Jesus Christ to bring you to eternal life.

Christians were to respond by continually building their lives on the bedrock of their "most holy faith" (Jude 20). They were also to keep praying "in the Holy Spirit." The idea is that believers can only combat the threat posed by the false teachers in the power of the Spirit and the true teaching of God's Word.

In addition, Jude urged his readers to keep themselves grounded "in God's love" (vs. 21). With God's love as the anchor of their souls, believers could remain united in their faith and committed to one another. They were also to wait eagerly for "the mercy of our Lord Jesus Christ." This is a reference to the Savior's return, at which time believers will be resurrected, resulting in their full and final reception of "eternal life."

D. The Importance of Helping Others: vss. 22-23

Be merciful to those who doubt; snatch others from the fire and save them; to others show mercy, mixed with fear—hating even the clothing stained by corrupted flesh.

Among Jude's readers were those "who doubt" (Jude 22). This possibly refers to people who were genuinely wavering in their faith. These sincere doubters deserved mercy from Jesus' followers.

A second group appears to be those who were further entrenched in unbelief. Jude urged his readers to make every effort to "show mercy" (vs. 23) to them "with fear." God was able to make the witness of believers so persuasive that unbelievers could be snatched out of "the fire" of judgment.

A third group were the apostates, whose lives, like "clothing," were "stained," or defiled, by moral filth. Believers, while abhorring the depravity of the false teachers, were to show mercy on them. The adage of "hating the sin but loving the sinner" seems applicable here.

Paul, who was no stranger to religious frauds, solemnly urged Timothy to "preach the Word" (2 Tim. 4:2). Regardless of whether the time seemed favorable, he was to be persistent and patient to "correct, rebuke, and encourage." This command remained in effect even though some would "turn their ears away from the truth and turn aside to myths" (vs. 4). The minister of the Gospel was called to "endure hardship" (vs. 5) and "do the work of an evangelist."

What enables us to be "stand firm" (1 Cor. 15:58) and give ourselves "fully to the work of the Lord"? It is the promise that our "labor in the Lord is not in vain." Thus, in our moments of travail, we have the assurance of knowing that God will keep us from stumbling and present us "without fault and with great joy" (Jude 24) before God's "glorious presence."

Discussion Questions

1. What were some of the characteristics of the false teaching Jude warned about?
2. How did Jude graphically describe the false teachers?
3. What vices did Jude associate with the false teachers?
4. What actions did Jude recommend for believers to guard against false teaching?
5. What types of people did Jude think would need correction from false teaching?

Contemporary Application

Jude urged his fellow believers in Christ to grow in their spiritual maturity; but, at the same time, he knew they would have to contend with the evil that had crept into the churches. Despite the attempts of ungodly people to lead believers into immorality, apostasy, and division, Jude reminded the faithful that God will keep them from falling, especially as they continuously build up their faith in Christ.

The same types of temptations and problems that emerged in the churches in the first century still persist. That is why it is imperative that we obey Jude's exhortations, which include praying in the Holy Spirit, remaining in God's love, and showing mercy to others.

Here we see that a strong faith is an active faith; yet only Christ can give us the power to truly pray, love, and be compassionate and wise in our dealings with others. When we feel tempted to submit to fleshly desires, when we hear heretical teachings about Christ, or when we encounter conflict within the church, then we must immediately turn to Jesus for strength, wisdom, and encouragement.

It is also important that we build up one another in the Lord. No one should live in complete isolation from others. Since God intended for us to live in community, we need each other; and we need to help each other, especially as we strive together to be the people Christ wants us to be.

Lessons for Life

Samuel: A Child Dedicated to God

Scripture

Background Scripture: *1 Samuel 1:1—2:10;
Luke 1:46-55*

Scripture Lesson: *1 Samuel 1:20, 26-28; 2:1-8*

Key Verses: *"I prayed for this child, and the Lord has granted me what I asked of him. So now I give him to the Lord. For
his whole life he will be given over to the Lord."* 1 Samuel
1:27-28.

Scripture Lesson for Children: *1 Samuel 1:20, 26-28,
2:18-20*

Key Verse for Children: *So now I give him to the Lord. For
his whole life he will be given over to the Lord."* 1 Samuel
1:28.

Lesson Aim

To keep our promises to God.

Lesson Setting

Time: *1105 B.C.*

Place: *Shiloh and the hill country of Ephraim*

Lesson Outline

Samuel: A Child Dedicated to God

   I. Samuel's Birth: 1 Samuel 1:20

  II. Samuel's Dedication: 1 Samuel 1:26-28

      A. *Hannah's Answered Prayers: vss. 26-27*

      B. *Hannah's Sacrifice: vs. 28*

 III. Hannah's Prayer: 1 Samuel 2:1-8a

      A. *God Her Joy: vs. 1*

      B. *God Her Rock: vs. 2*

      C. *God Her Judge: vs. 3*

      D. *God Her Provider: vss. 4-5*

      E. *God Her Exalter: vss. 6-8*

Introduction for Adults

Topic: *Dedicating to God*

Catherine was nine years old when she first earned some money by helping a neighbor woman. Proudly Catherine brought home her pay. Then she said to her mother, "Now I can give my own money to God on Sunday." Sheer joy broke out when Catherine dropped her own money in the offering plate.

Dedicating everything to God requires sacrifice, but the rewards far surpass the pain. We are absolutely stunned by the liberation and peace we feel when we give our lives and everything we have to Him. Yet we continue to struggle with the pull of possessions, pride, and self-interest. These enemies of our souls never seem to let us alone.

Dedicating ourselves to God means doing so every day. Each day we let go of something that drags us into the world's values. Then God frees us to serve Him with joy.

Introduction for Youth

Topic: *I'm Yours, God*

Young people who enter the U.S. Marine Corps are left in no doubt about who owns them. They belong to the Corps 24 hours a day. There are no reservations and no retreats. This kind of military discipline produces stalwart fighters.

Our spiritual strength grows out of complete commitment to God. When we leave everything to Him, we are freed from countless needless worries and fears. Consider Eric Lidell, whose account is told in the film *Chariots of Fire*. He was an Olympic champion and a missionary to China. When he gave himself to God for missionary service, God freed him to run and win for His glory.

"I'm yours, God" sounds scary to us, and sometimes it is. But we can trust God to watch over us. He will not let us down.

Concepts for Children

Topic: *Samuel: A Child Dedicated to God*

1. Samuel was born in answer to his mother's prayers.
2. Hannah promised to give Samuel to the Lord, and she did.
3. Hannah thanked God in a prayer that gave Him all the praise.
4. Hannah's account reminds us that God cares about every detail of our lives.
5. When we feel sad about life, we can think about Hannah.
6. The faith Samuel noticed in Hannah, his mother, encouraged him to serve God.

Lesson Commentary

I. SAMUEL'S BIRTH: 1 SAMUEL 1:20

So in the course of time Hannah conceived and gave birth to a son. She named him Samuel, saying, "Because I asked the LORD for him."

"A Child Is Given" is a series of four lessons that focus on God's gift of a child as the means by which He spoke to people at various times to bring grace and redemption. These accounts are about God's work through the prophet Samuel, John the Baptist (the one who announced Messiah's coming), and Christ.

With respect to 1 Samuel, the first three chapters of the book establish the prophet's role as Israel's leader between the time of the Judges and the anointing of Saul as Israel's first king. Samuel was the last of the judges and the first of the prophets (Acts 3:24; 13:20). Scripture describes both Samuel's positive role and the priest Eli's failures (1 Sam. 2). God's Word also tells about Samuel's birth (chap. 1) and his divine call (chap. 3).

The Bible pays much attention to the births of people like Moses, Samuel, John the Baptist, and Jesus. Also, we find accounts about barren wives in Genesis 18:1-15; Judges 13:2-5; 1 Samuel 1, and Luke 1:5-17.

In 1 Samuel, we learn that in the town of Ramah (1:19) a man named Elkanah had two wives, Peninnah and Hannah. The former bore children, but Hannah was barren. In addition to her personal anguish, she was tormented and humiliated by Peninnah. Elkanah tried to mitigate Hannah's suffering by giving her a double portion of the meat of the sacrificial animal. But Hannah did not eat, showing her grief with many tears (1:2-8).

Finally, Hannah turned to God in prayer. Hannah promised God that, if He gave her a son, she would dedicate the child to the Lord. She prayed so persistently that the priest Eli thought she was drunk. However, she convinced him that she was pouring out her heart to the Lord and Eli dismissed her with his blessing (1:9-18).

Scripture simply says that God remembered Hannah and she became pregnant. Her unflinching faith was blessed by the birth of a son. She named him Samuel, which means "name of God," or possibly "heard by God" (vs. 20). Hannah also remembered God. She knew that He had heard and answered her persistent prayers. Once Hannah's request was granted, she did not forget that her child was born because of the Lord's gracious intervention.

II. SAMUEL'S DEDICATION: 1 SAMUEL 1:26-28

A. Hannah's Answered Prayers: vss. 26-27

And she said to him, "As surely as you live, my lord, I am the woman who stood here beside you praying to the LORD. I prayed for this child, and the LORD has granted me what I asked of him."

When the time for annual sacrifices at Shiloh came, Hannah did not go with Elkanah and his family. She asked if she might stay at home until Samuel was weaned (1 Sam. 1:21-22). (Hebrew mothers usually nursed their children two years and sometimes three years.) Then, when the time was ready, Hannah would leave Samuel at Shiloh (vs. 22). Shiloh was the religious center of Israel at that time, an honor later conferred upon Jerusalem.

After Samuel was weaned, Hannah kept her promise by taking the child and the required offerings to the house of the Lord. After the sacrifices were made, Hannah took Samuel to Eli the priest (vss. 23-25). Hannah reminded him of their previous encounter (vs. 26).

For added emphasis, Hannah pointed out that this was the exact spot where she had stood before. Hannah wanted Eli to know that God had answered her prayers (vs. 27). What a striking difference between their first and second meetings. Hannah had previously been ridiculed by Eli as a drunkard, but now she had the opportunity to give thanks to God for His faithfulness to her.

B. Hannah's Sacrifice: vs. 28

"So now I give him to the LORD. For his whole life he will be given over to the LORD." And he worshiped the LORD there.

Hannah fulfilled her vow, painful as it possibly was for her to give her young boy to the Lord (1 Sam. 1:28). This was a total sacrifice on Hannah's part, for she had made a lifetime commitment of her son to God.

Consider the powerful pulls on Hannah's emotions. After years of barrenness and harassment, she finally bore a son. She could easily have thought about keeping Samuel for herself. But in the end Hannah gave God's gift to her back to Him, thus modeling for all time what it means to surrender everything to God.

Scripture next points to the worship that followed Hannah's dedication of Samuel. Who worshiped? It is unlikely a reference to Elkanah. Eli is the strongest possibility. Some scholars, however, think it was Hannah herself, even though the masculine form of the Hebrew verb was used.

III. HANNAH'S PRAYER: 1 SAMUEL 2:1-8

A. God Her Joy: vs. 1

Then Hannah prayed and said: "My heart rejoices in the LORD; in the LORD my horn is lifted high. My mouth boasts over my enemies, for I delight in your deliverance."

Before we learn more about Samuel, we are treated to his mother's magnificent prayer (1 Sam. 2:1-10). She referred to God repeatedly in this ode of praise, clearly showing us that He was the focus of her song.

Hannah's hymn takes its place with those of Miriam, Deborah, and Mary, as well as those of Moses, David, Hezekiah, and other psalmists and prophets. These odes spring from incidents in the lives of God's people. As they recounted historical events, they praised God for His glory and kingdom.

God was Hannah's joy (vs. 1). After keeping her vow, she rejoiced in the Lord. She was not bitter at leaving Samuel behind. Hannah's sacrifice filled her heart with happiness, for God worked not only in Hannah's body but also in her soul and spirit. Hannah said that God had lifted high her "horn," which symbolizes strength (Pss. 75:4-5, 10; 92:10; 2 Sam. 22:3; Luke 1:69). We might say, "In the Lord I find my strength."

Hannah boasted in the good sense, for she attributed her victory to the Lord. Hannah had no enemies in the political sense, but she had faced persecution and ridicule at home and in the Lord's house. Our salvation is always and entirely of the Lord, so it is fitting to praise Him.

B. God Her Rock: vs. 2

"There is no one holy like the LORD; there is no one besides you; there is no Rock like our God."

Hannah's prayer revealed profound spiritual truth. She identified both the holiness and uniqueness of her God (1 Sam. 2:2). In Hannah's day, idolatry was rampant, even among God's people, so she was careful to emphasize His supremacy over all other gods.

Hannah chose a common metaphor for God: He was her rock. This word denoted strength, power, security, protection, and peace. There was no other entity to turn to except the one true God of Israel.

Perhaps Hannah was familiar with the song of Moses (Deut. 32: 4, 15, 18, 30-31, 37). "Rock" was even a name among Hebrew men: Zurishaddai ("my Rock is the Almighty") and Zuriel ("my Rock is God"; Num. 1:6; 3:35). The expression was a favorite of the psalmists, for it spoke so clearly about permanence and protection.

C. God Her Judge: vs. 3

"Do not keep talking so proudly or let your mouth speak such arrogance, for the LORD is a God who knows, and by him deeds are weighed."

Hannah started to make declarations of truth in her prayer, directing her remarks to the proud and arrogant. She warned them that God hears their speech, for He "is a God who knows" (1 Sam. 2:3). Hannah also reminded the wicked of the basic truth that God judges all deeds.

Perhaps Hannah had Peninnah in mind here, especially because of the accusations she had made against Hannah. Her main point was that we cannot escape God as our judge. This is a primary teaching of the entire Bible. Hannah's prayer reflected both high levels of personal intimacy with the Lord as well as a healthy respect for His character. In a good way Hannah combined joy with wholesome fear.

D. God Her Provider: vss. 4-5

"The bows of the warriors are broken, but those who stumbled are armed with strength. Those who were full hire themselves out for food, but those who were hungry hunger no more. She who was barren has borne seven children, but she who has had many sons pines away."

Hannah's prayer is filled with remarkable contrasts, concerning which her life was a prime example. Although she did not use the personal pronoun, we can clearly see references in 1 Samuel 2:4-5 to her life.

Hannah contrasted the weak and powerful, the full and hungry, and the barren and the mother with many sons. In each case, she noted striking reversals. It was not the armed warriors who were strong, but those who stumbled. It was not those who sold out for food who were full, but those who were hungry. It was not the mother with many children who was happy, but the mother who was barren. In each case, God provided for the weak, powerless, and downtrodden.

Here we see that God is the great reverser of fortunes. He stands the world on its head. The proud who think they are strong, full, and fruitful really are the weak, empty, and barren. Hannah's profound spiritual insights point us to the same truths stated by Christ and His apostles.

E. God Her Exalter: vss. 6-8

"The LORD brings death and makes alive; he brings down to the grave and raises up. The LORD sends poverty and wealth; he humbles and he exalts. He raises the poor from the dust and lifts the needy from the ash heap; he seats them with princes and has them inherit a throne of honor."

God was not only Hannah's provider, but also her exalter. Hannah's prayer in 1 Samuel 2:6-8 overflowed with remarkable contrasts to make this point. God "makes alive . . . raises up . . . he exalts . . . raises the poor [and] . . . lifts the needy." He alone gives them a "throne of honor." What could possibly surpass God's power, grace, and generosity?

Hannah's prayer grew out of the soil of her own experiences and those of her fellow people. Society in Israel reflected the huge gaps between the rich and the poor, and between the powerful and the exploited.

There is no indication that Hannah herself had lived in dire poverty, but she undoubtedly had seen it around her. Therefore, her prayer can be taken as a message of encouragement and hope to God's impoverished people everywhere. Whatever our situation, God can give us the strength to endure. Even death itself is no hindrance to God.

Hannah's prayer makes a powerful case for God's sovereignty. Boasting, arrogance, pride, and rebellion are thus rebuked. The Bible tells us about the pride of powerful rulers like Nebuchadnezzar. Scripture also tells about the domestic pride of Peninnah, just to let us know that we are all vulnerable to this sin.

The summit of the humiliation-exaltation theme is, of course, the account of our Savior. Paul declared that, though the Son humbled Himself to the point of death, the Father highly exalted Him (Phil. 2:6-11).

Discussion Questions

1. What were some of the factors that made life difficult for Hannah?
2. What was the significance of Hannah's choice of "Samuel" for her son's name?
3. After Samuel was weaned, what did Hannah do that proved her faithfulness to the Lord?

4. What important lessons had Hannah learned about God that she disclosed in her prayer?

5. How can we find great joy in keeping the promises we make to God?

Contemporary Application

Hannah's account resonates with us because she emerged from humiliation to triumph. But her account differs from the usual plot, for she gave away to God what she had so eagerly desired. Too often, when we get what we want from God, we forget what He expects from us.

For example, we know how easy it is to make promises to God under duress of illness, loss, or disappointment. We are so bereft of hope that we promise to do anything for God, if only He will heal us, spare us, or get us out of a jam.

Hannah rose above human fickleness, for she kept her promise. She said that, if God gave her a son, she would give him back to God. That's how young Samuel, one of Israel's great prophets, got started in his lifelong service for God.

None of us knows the wonderful things that God can accomplish in our lives when we give everything to Him, even what is dearest and best to us. Hannah's remarkable courage and faith prompts us to live for God in a similar manner.

John: The Forerunner of Jesus

Scripture

Background Scripture: *Luke 1:5-80*
Scripture Lesson: *Luke 1:67-80*
Key Verse: *And you, my child, will be called a prophet of the
Most High; for you will go on before the Lord to prepare the
way for him.* Luke 1:76.
Scripture Lesson for Children: *Luke 1:13-15a, 67, 76-80*
Key Verse for Children: Luke 1:76.

Lesson Aim

To develop faith to help others find the way to Jesus.

Lesson Setting

Time: *6–5 B.C.*
Place: *Hill country of Judea*

Lesson Outline

John: Forerunner of Jesus
  I. Zechariah's Praise of God: Luke 1:67-75
    A. *Freedom for God's People: vss. 67-68*
    B. *The Standard of Salvation: vs. 69*
    C. *The Prophetic Picture: vs. 70*
    D. *Safety and Security: vs. 71*
    E. *Faithful and Merciful: vss. 72-73*
    F. *Delivered to Serve: vss. 74-75*
  II. Zechariah's Prophecy of John: Luke 1:76-80
    A. *Preparation for the Messiah: vs. 76*
    B. *Knowledge of Salvation: vs. 77*
    C. *God's Mercy to All: vss. 78-79*
    D. *John's Early Years: vs. 80*

Introduction for Adults

Topic: *Preparing the Way*

John the Baptist's birth had a miraculous note to it, but before he prepared the way for Jesus, his godly parents—Zechariah and Elizabeth—prepared the way for him (in a manner of speaking). We don't find many details about John's home life recorded in Scripture. It was enough for Luke to tell us that John's parents were "upright in the sight of God, observing all the Lord's commandments and regulations blamelessly" (Luke 1:6). We also learn that John "grew and became strong in spirit" (vs. 80).

From this information we can see that John's faithful, praying parents spiritually prepared the way for John's ministry. They had followed God for many years before he was born, and they undoubtedly continued to do so while he grew up. They did everything for John that they were supposed to do. Empowered by the Holy Spirit, he went on to urge many people to repent.

God gives us many opportunities to prepare others spiritually—starting with our loved ones—to become the Lord's mighty servants.

Introduction for Youth

Topic: *A Leading Role*

The high school band drum majorette stepped into her leading role at the head of the parade. Not too far along, however, she lost a step. As a result, her baton struck the trombone player's slide and knocked his instrument out of commission. Leading roles are great opportunities to show what we can do, but if we are not careful, we can make some tragic mistakes.

God gave John the Baptist the lead part in preparing Israel to receive the Messiah. John did not fail, because he never boosted himself, but always pointed people to Jesus. John succeeded because of this.

Pointing others to Jesus is the hallmark of true spiritual leadership. If we want to play a leading role in God's plan, we must allow Jesus to have first place in our lives.

Concepts for Children

Topic: *John: A Child Dedicated to God*

1. The angel told Zechariah that he and Elizabeth would have a son.
2. Because Zechariah did not believe the angel, he remained unable to hear or speak until John was born.
3. John's parents were wise, godly people who believed God's promises to Israel.
4. Zechariah knew that his son would be faithful to God.
5. John was not afraid to tell others about Jesus.
6. We can depend on God to give us the strength to serve Him.

Lesson Commentary

I. Zechariah's Praise of God: Luke 1:67-75

A. Freedom for God's People: vss. 67-68

His father Zechariah was filled with the Holy Spirit and prophesied: "Praise be to the Lord, the God of Israel, because he has come and has redeemed his people."

The account concerning John the Baptist began with the visitation of "an angel of the Lord" (Luke 1:11) to "a priest named Zechariah" (vs. 5). In addition to being John's father, Zechariah was a priest dedicated to serving God in the temple in Jerusalem. In fact, he belonged to one of 24 classes of priests who served in the temple in Jerusalem.

Despite this distinction, Zechariah and his wife, Elizabeth, who "was also a descendant of Aaron" (vs. 5), "had no children" (vs. 7), which was a social stigma in ancient times. They were also "well along in years."

One day when Zechariah was serving in the temple in Jerusalem, the angel from God "appeared to him, standing at the right side of the altar of incense" (vs. 11). At first Zechariah was "gripped with fear" (vs. 12). The angel, after reassuring the elderly priest, declared that "Elizabeth will bear you a son" (vs. 13), whom the couple would "name John." Sadly, Zechariah doubted this promise (vs. 18). Consequently, he lost the ability to hear or speak until after John's birth (vs. 20).

Six months after Elizabeth conceived, "the angel Gabriel" (vs. 26) was sent by God to Nazareth, where the angel announced to "a virgin" (vs. 27) named Mary that she would conceive and bear a son, whom she would name "Jesus" (vs. 31). Mary's child would be called "the Son of the Most High" (vs. 32).

Mary was shocked to learn that she would bear a child, for she was still "a virgin" (vs. 34). Gabriel explained that "The Holy Spirit will come upon you, and the power of the Most High will overshadow you" (vs. 35). For this reason, Mary's child would be "holy" and "called the Son of God." This miraculous conception would occur, "For nothing is impossible with God" (vs. 37).

Since the angel had told Mary that her relative Elizabeth had also conceived "in her old age" (vs. 36), Mary quickly left Nazareth and traveled south to the home of Zechariah and Elizabeth. There Mary would share with them, in the form of a beautiful song (vss. 46-55), her good news. Mary stayed with Elizabeth for three months and then returned to her home (vs. 56).

When John was born (vs. 57), Elizabeth's relatives urged her to name the child Zechariah after his father (vs. 59). Apparently, Zechariah had somehow communicated to Elizabeth what "an angel" (vs. 11) had declared concerning the child's name (vs. 13). Elizabeth, in turn, told those with her what the child's name would be (vs. 60). They, however, insisted on asking Zechariah (vss. 62), who wrote on "a writing tablet" (vs. 63) that the name would be John. At that moment Zechariah was able to speak, and he gave glory to God (vs. 64). When the news spread (vs. 65), the question everyone asked was, "What then is this child going to be?" (vs. 66).

Verse 67 says that John's father, Zechariah, became "filled with the Holy Spirit" and began to prophesy. Whereas Zechariah's previous words expressed unbelief, his subsequent words were filled with praise. His previous words had expressed doubt, but his song was full of assurance and faith.

Zechariah's song closely followed the pattern of Old Testament prophecies about the coming Messiah. Also, Zechariah's poetry reveals that devout people of Israel prayed for and understood the significance of the messianic age.

Zechariah began with a common benediction: "Praise be to the Lord, the God of Israel" (vs. 68). Then Zechariah gave his reasons for his praise, amassing all the evidence he could remember about God. First, he praised God because He had turned His face toward His people and set them free.

God had broken into Zechariah's life in such a special way that he could not miss its significance. He equated his experience with God's redemptive purposes for His people. God's saving intervention was the theme of the Old Testament prophecies. They painted glorious pictures of the Messiah's reign over Israel. Zechariah had imbibed deeply of these prophecies. Nothing in his mind superseded his hope of God's coming to redeem His people through the Messiah.

The angel had told Zechariah what John's role would be. He would be filled with the Holy Spirit to bring Israel back to God. He would "make ready a people prepared for the Lord" (vs. 17). It's no wonder that Zechariah was excited about what God promised to do through John the Baptist.

B. The Standard of Salvation: vs. 69

"He has raised up a horn of salvation for us in the house of his servant David."

Zechariah thanked God because He had raised up a standard of salvation through David's line. The godly Jews knew that the promised Messiah would be a descendant of King David. Prophecies about the Messiah's Davidic ancestry abound in the Old Testament (2 Sam. 7:12; Ps. 89:3; Jer. 23:5; 33:14). During Jesus' time the people were astonished and asked, "Could this be the Son of David?" (Matt. 12:23). They knew that "the Christ will come from David's family" (John 7:42). Many cried "Hosanna to the Son of David" (Matt. 21:9) when He entered Jerusalem. Paul likewise declared that God's Son was "a descendant of David" (Rom. 1:3).

"Horn of salvation" (Luke 1:69) was a common ancient metaphor for power and strength. In the Old Testament, the "horn" also symbolized a destructive kind of power, for it pictured the horn of various wild animals (1 Kings 22:11; Ps. 22:21; 75:5; Dan. 8:5-7).

C. The Prophetic Picture: vs. 70

"(as he said through his holy prophets of long ago)"

Zechariah praised God because He had promised "long ago" (Luke 1:70) through the "holy prophets" to provide redemption through the Messiah. Zechariah now saw what had happened in the light of his understanding of the Old Testament.

D. Safety and Security: vs. 71

"Salvation from our enemies and from the hand of all who hate us—"

Zechariah was thankful, for God had promised "salvation from our enemies" (Luke 1:71). Because Israel had suffered so much at the hands of foreign invaders, relief from their oppressing circumstances was uppermost in the minds of God's people. In John's time, the Jews were ruled by the despised Romans. The Jews vented their ill will by periodically rebelling against their captors. In fact, in A.D. 70, the Romans completely obliterated Jerusalem and its temple.

The salvation God promised was not in terms of political deliverance. Rather, the Messiah would usher in a universal reign of peace and justice. It's true that at His first advent, He was rejected and crucified; yet, at His second advent, He will reign in great power and glory.

E. Faithful and Merciful: vss. 72-73

"To show mercy to our fathers and to remember his holy covenant, the oath he swore to our father Abraham."

Zechariah continued to emphasize that what had happened was consistent with all God promised to do for His people. Zechariah was especially thankful for God's "mercy" (Luke 1:72) and for remembering "his holy covenant." This was in keeping with "the oath he swore" (vs. 73) with Abraham, the patriarch.

F. Delivered to Serve: vss. 74-75

"To rescue us from the hand of our enemies, and to enable us to serve him without fear in holiness and righteousness before him all our days."

Zechariah was convinced God would "rescue" (Luke 1:74) His people "from the hand of [their] enemies" so that they could serve Him. Israel's service before God "without fear" was stamped with "holiness and righteousness" (vs. 75). Zechariah underscored here the character of the Messiah's reign and the purpose of His coming. His ultimate mission was to restore Israel's people to their God-given duty to be holy.

Holiness speaks of our relationship with God through faith in Jesus Christ, while righteousness has to do with how we respond to others. We are to serve God "all our days," striving to be consistent in our witness before the world.

II. ZECHARIAH'S PROPHECY OF JOHN: LUKE 1:76-80

A. Preparation for the Messiah: vs. 76

"And you, my child, will be called a prophet of the Most High; for you will go on before the Lord to prepare the way for him."

At this point Zechariah focused his attention on John. He would be a "prophet" (Luke 1:76) to prepare the way for Messiah. John was the forerunner who would tell Israel that the promised Messiah had arrived in the person of Jesus of Nazareth.

When the crowds heard John preach, they recognized that he was indeed a "prophet of the Most High." His task was not pleasant, because he was called to expose people's sins. Preparing the way for the Lord was rough business. It was like road building through mountains and valleys (Isa. 40:3-4).

B. Knowledge of Salvation: vs. 77

"To give his people the knowledge of salvation through the forgiveness of their sins."

God would use John to bring to "his people the knowledge of salvation through the forgiveness of their sins" (Luke 1:77). Most of the Jews had erroneous ideas about the kind of salvation the Messiah would bring. They thought it would be political, not spiritual, in nature. God sent John to teach them the true and correct understanding of spiritual deliverance, which is based on the forgiveness of sins.

C. God's Mercy to All: vss. 78-79

"Because of the tender mercy of our God, by which the rising sun will come to us from heaven to shine on those living in darkness and in the shadow of death, to guide our feet into the path of peace."

Zechariah's song acknowledged that John's life and ministry would be blessed by the "tender mercy of our God" (Luke 1:78). Such mercy would be like the dawning of a new day. The priest knew that he himself had received God's mercy, and he was overcome by the prospect of God's people being spiritually revived and restored under His merciful hand.

John's amazing birth and his preaching of righteousness would be considerable evidence that God had not forgotten His people. Like the "rising sun," God's mercy would bring light to people "living in darkness and in the shadow of death" (vs. 79). Like the rising sun, God's compassion would lead them "into the path of peace."

These beautiful words reflect the majesty and glory of Zechariah's proclamation. He was filled with praise because he knew that God was about to do something special for His people through John.

D. John's Early Years: vs. 80

And the child grew and became strong in spirit; and he lived in the desert until he appeared publicly to Israel.

At the conclusion of Zechariah's song, Luke the historian added a brief postscript about John. We learn two main facts about him. First, while growing up, he "became strong in spirit" (Luke 1:80). This indicates John imbibed his parents' strong faith, trust, and hope in the Lord. In fact, from birth John was filled with the Holy Spirit (vs. 15).

Second, John chose a life of seclusion "in the desert" (vs. 80). This was part of his spiritual preparation for his mission. He was focused on God and on His calling. When John began to preach, his desert lifestyle gave power and authenticity to his words (Matt. 3:1-6).

Discussion Questions

1. How was Zechariah able to prophesy words of hope and promise to the people?
2. Why was it important for Zechariah to emphasize that the Savior would be of the lineage of David?
3. What was the "holy covenant" (Luke 1:72) that God had made with His people?
4. What was the message John would proclaim to the people?
5. How can we become more willing to let God speak through us to communicate the good news of salvation to those in our sphere of influence?

Contemporary Application

"What then is this child going to be?" (Luke 1:66), the neighbors of Zechariah and Elizabeth wondered. John's parents probably wondered the same thing too, and so do parents today concerning their children. The angel had told Zechariah that his son would be used in a significant way by God, but at first he didn't believe the angel. Then, after John's birth, Zechariah proclaimed that his son would prepare Israel for the coming of the Messiah.

Would parents today be as excited about this prospect as Zechariah and Elizabeth were? Wouldn't parents today be happier if God told them their child was going to be a rich financier, university president, professional athlete, musician, or leader of a country? Wouldn't it be a let down to learn that your child was going to be a preacher who would lead many people to find forgiveness through faith in Christ?

Such mixed feelings spotlight our foremost priorities in life. What we seek for our loved ones, and all the things we give them, speak volumes about what we think is important. Isn't it ultimately better to be a humble and faithful servant of the Lord than to be rich, powerful, or famous in the eyes of the world? Zechariah and Elizabeth would say yes, and so should we.

Jesus: God with Us

Scripture

Background Scripture: *Matthew 1:18-25*
Scripture Lesson: *Matthew 1:18-25*
Key Verses: *"The virgin will be with child and will give birth to a son, and they will call him Immanuel"—which means, "God with us."* Matthew 1:23.
Scripture Lesson for Children: *Luke 2:22, 25-33, 36-38*
Key Verse for Children: *Joseph and Mary took [Jesus] to Jerusalem to present him to the Lord.* Luke 2:22.

Lesson Aim

To develop the kind of faith and obedience that Joseph and Mary had.

Lesson Setting

Time: *6–5 B.C.*
Place: *Nazareth of Galilee*

Lesson Outline

Jesus: God with Us

   I. Mary's Pregnancy: Matthew 1:18-19
      A. *Through the Holy Spirit: vs. 18*
      B. *Impending Divorce: vs. 19*
  II. The Angel's Message: Matthew 1:20-21
      A. *What to Do with Mary: vs. 20*
      B. *What to Name the Baby: vs. 21*
 III. Isaiah's Prophecy: Matthew 1:22-23
      A. *The Virginal Conception and Birth: vss. 22-23a*
      B. *God's Presence: vs. 23b*
 IV. Joseph's Obedience: Matthew 1:24-25
      A. *Marriage to Mary: vs. 24*
      B. *Chastity Until Birth: vs. 25a*
      C. *The Name of Jesus: vs. 25b*

Introduction for Adults

Topic: Believing God's Promise

How long can we hold on to a promise before we give up? From 1993 to 2001, three missionary wives clung to the hope that their missing husbands would be found alive. They weren't.

Eight years seems like a long time until we consider how long the God-fearing Jews held on to the Lord's promise of a Messiah. We can hardly appreciate the overwhelming joy they must have found at the news that God the Son came to earth as a human being, whom we know as Jesus.

How long can we cling to the hope of the Messiah's return? Do we find a renewed sense of hope concerning His return when we celebrate His first advent? We must keep His return in mind even while we thank the Father for the Son's birth.

Introduction for Youth

Topic: The Perfect Christmas Gift

The best-selling author Rick Bragg, who came from a poor family, wrote about the Christmas gift he received every year—boxes of underwear. That was it. The perfect gift for him was to be at home with his mother, brothers, aunts, uncles, and cousins. That was enough to make Rick happy.

We don't need a lot of stuff to make this a perfect Christmas. Even the perfect gifts wear out, break, turn to rust, get lost, or are stolen. We can't pin our hopes for happiness on any one gift, that is, except the gift of eternal life the Father gives us in His Son, Jesus Christ.

Christmas gives us an opportunity to identify what's really most important and valuable to us. Thank God for good friends—and even new underwear—but most of all for Jesus.

Concepts for Children

Topic: Jesus: A Child Dedicated to God

1. Mary and Joseph presented the infant Jesus to the Lord in the temple.
2. The parents heard Simeon praising God for sending Jesus to provide salvation for His people.
3. The parents were encouraged by Anna's words of faith.
4. Godly influences can help us to make the right choices.
5. God's Word gives us the wisdom and courage we need to obey Him.
6. Jesus was born, died for our sins, and rose again so that we might be saved.

Lesson Commentary

I. MARY'S PREGNANCY: MATTHEW 1:18-19

A. Through the Holy Spirit: vs. 18

This is how the birth of Jesus Christ came about: His mother Mary was pledged to be married to Joseph, but before they came together, she was found to be with child through the Holy Spirit.

Ancient Jewish writers, such as Matthew, believed that the best way to begin to tell the account of a person's life was to present his or her genealogy. Matthew thus began his Gospel with the statement, "A record of the genealogy of Jesus Christ, the son of David, the son of Abraham" (Matt. 1:1).

Verse 17 explains that Jesus' genealogy, as Matthew presented it, comprises three sections of 14 generations each. Not every ancestor of the Savior appears in the list; yet as the descendant of Abraham and David—two of Israel's most esteemed ancestors—Jesus unquestionably qualifies as the nation's Messiah. Matthew wanted to show that the progress of biblical history had reached its fulfillment with the coming of the Savior.

The incarnation of Jesus—namely, God the Son coming to earth as a human being—is the central event of the opening chapter of Matthew's Gospel. He related the account of Jesus' miraculous conception and birth in a simple but heart-gripping style. Reading 1:18-25 will reassure a believer that the writer of these words was totally convinced that every detail of Jesus' incarnation was factual. Matthew did not attempt to throw a veil of mystery around Jesus' birth. Certainly there is a great mystery involved in what took place in the humble home of a young woman in Nazareth; yet Matthew's faith in the utter truth of the event was such that there was no shadow of doubt in his words.

In verse 18, Matthew noted the way in which the "birth of Jesus Christ came about." Mary and Joseph decided to enter into a legally binding arrangement by becoming engaged. If Mary and Joseph were of the ages typical for marriage in their time and place, she was in her early teens and he was somewhat older.

Ancient Jewish marriages consisted of three steps. First, a man and a woman became engaged when their two families agreed to the arrangement. The second step came when a public announcement was made and the couple became betrothed. This formal agreement between couples was considered legally binding and could be broken only by death or divorce. The relationship could not be physically consummated until after the couple was married. This comprised the third and final step in the process.

We can only imagine what Joseph must have felt when Mary was "found to be with child." Joseph initially did not know that Mary's offspring was from "the Holy Spirit." According to Jewish law, if a woman broke the second step of the betrothal process by being intimate with another man, she faced serious consequences. The fiance had a right to divorce her, and the religious authorities could have the law-breakers stoned to death (Deut. 22:23-24).

B. Impending Divorce: vs. 19

Because Joseph her husband was a righteous man and did not want to expose her to public disgrace, he had in mind to divorce her quietly.

Mary's pregnancy presented Joseph with a terrible dilemma. What should he do, now that his intended bride had become pregnant? In New Testament times the death penalty was rarely if ever carried out for adultery. Thus, conventional wisdom would recommend that Joseph divorce Mary and expose her to shame. But if Joseph did this, Mary faced the prospect of poverty and shame for the rest of her life.

Matthew described Joseph as "a righteous man" (Matt. 1:19). This means he was characterized by prayer, faithful to God, and observant of His laws. Joseph probably also held deeply to the traditional messianic hopes and expectations. Joseph was a carpenter by trade. Scholars surmise that he passed away before Jesus began His public ministry.

Because Joseph was upright and virtuous, he did not want Mary to be publicly humiliated. Joseph thus decided that breaking their engagement privately would be in the best interests of all concerned. This could be effected by a simple certificate signed by two witnesses.

II. THE ANGEL'S MESSAGE: MATTHEW 1:20-21

A. What to Do with Mary: vs. 20

But after he had considered this, an angel of the Lord appeared to him in a dream and said, "Joseph son of David, do not be afraid to take Mary home as your wife, because what is conceived in her is from the Holy Spirit."

While Joseph wrestled with the issue of Mary's pregnancy and what to do about it, "an angel of the Lord appeared to him in a dream" (Matt. 1:20). Whereas the celestial being manifested himself to Joseph in a dream, Luke states that an angel "went to" (Luke 1:28) Mary, delivered his message, and "left her" (vs. 38). Angels are spirit beings created by God to serve Him and to function as His messengers (Heb. 1:14). In addition to good angels, there are also fallen ones. The latter are under Satan's control and do his bidding.

In Joseph's case, the angel addressed him as "son of David" (Matt. 1:20). Matthew's genealogy listed Joseph as a descendant of the royal house of David. Now Joseph must prove himself to be a true son of David, who would have faith to believe that the promise of a Messiah was about to be fulfilled.

The angel's message to Joseph removed all of his concerns. The angel's statement, "because what is conceived in her is from the Holy Spirit," explained in the clearest way the great mystery of the Incarnation. Notice that the angel did not attempt to discuss the scientific details of how the virginal conception of Jesus took place. This is the way of divine inspiration. Truths the human mind could never completely fathom are expressed in direct and completely adequate terms.

B. What to Name the Baby: vs. 21

"She will give birth to a son, and you are to give him the name Jesus, because he will save his people from their sins."

The angel gave Joseph some more good news. Mary would "give birth to a son" (Matt. 1:21). Incidentally, Zechariah had also been told that Elizabeth would bear him a son (Luke 1:13), and Abraham moreover learned that his wife Sarah would bear him a son (Gen. 17:19).

The angel told Joseph to name the child "Jesus" (Matt. 1:21). *Jesus* is the Greek form of *Joshua*, which means "the Lord saves." The name was appropriate, for Jesus "would save his people from their sins." We know from the rest of the New Testament that all people who trust in Christ are redeemed. He truly is the Savior of the world!

The angel made it clear from the outset that Jesus' main purpose in coming was redemptive. This incomparable fact is often overlooked at Christmas. We celebrate the Messiah's advent with great joy and praise, but sometimes we miss the significance of His birth. It primarily had to do with saving the lost from their sins. Therefore, the good news of Christ's death and resurrection was, in effect, announced before Jesus was ever born. He came to save us from our sins. That's why His birth is so special.

III. Isaiah's Prophecy: Matthew 1:22-23

A. The Virginal Conception and Birth: vss. 22-23a

All this took place to fulfill what the Lord had said through the prophet: "The virgin will be with child and will give birth to a son."

Matthew's Gospel has been called the bridge between the Old and New Testaments, for it helps us understand the relationship between the old and new covenants. By way of example, several times Matthew refers to some historical fact by making a statement similar to this: "Then what was said through the prophet Jeremiah was fulfilled" (2:17). This suggests to us that the birth, death, and resurrection of Christ fulfilled the Old Testament prophecies concerning God's plan for the salvation.

In the case of Jesus' virginal conception and birth, Isaiah foretold some 700 years before that this would occur (Matt. 1:22). Verse 23 specifically quotes Isaiah 7:14. Most likely it was at His virginal conception that the Son of God took upon Himself human nature. Following this unique, miraculous conception, the prenatal development of Jesus' human nature and birth took place in a normal way (Luke 2:6-7).

The Bible reveals that Jesus became a human being to fulfill Scripture (Matt. 5:17), seek and save what was lost (Luke 19:10), provide eternal life (John 3:17), put to death the misdeeds of people (Rom. 8:13), break the power of the devil (Heb. 2:14), free those who all their lives were held in slavery by their fear of death (vs. 15), and make atonement for the sins of people (vs. 17).

B. God's Presence: vs. 23b

"And they will call him Immanuel"—which means, "God with us."

The angel had told Joseph to name Mary's child "Jesus" (Matt. 1:21), for He would save people from their sins. In Isaiah's prophecy we have another name for Messiah, "Immanuel" (vs. 23). That name also possesses tremendous significance.

"God with us" means that the Lord had visited His people, after centuries of apparent silence with the closure of the Old Testament canon. God the Son was coming to earth in the person of Jesus of Nazareth. His intent was to dwell among the human race. Jesus' name thus emphasizes the crucial fact of His deity.

The Bible tells us that Jesus always existed with the Father (John 1:1-2). Moreover, Jesus explained that anyone who had seen Him had seen the Father (14:9). This information indicates that the eternal, glorious, and sovereign Lord humbled Himself by taking on human flesh.

IV. Joseph's Obedience: Matthew 1:24-25

A. Marriage to Mary: vs. 24

When Joseph woke up, he did what the angel of the Lord had commanded him and took Mary home as his wife.

Joseph had received instructions from the angel and then he carried them out promptly (Matt. 1:24). Did he ponder the implications of his marriage to Mary? Perhaps Joseph did, but there is no indication that he delayed taking action. Perhaps throwing conventional wisdom aside, Joseph faithfully followed the prescribed rules for betrothal and marriage. Out of devotion to the Lord, Joseph was willing to risk public ridicule and embarrassment.

B. Chastity Until Birth: vs. 25a

But he had no union with her until she gave birth to a son.

Traditional Jewish marriages included the agreement, or betrothal, between the parties and their families. Money was exchanged, and the marriage was ratified at a public ceremony. Normally the marriage was consummated on the first night of a seven-day celebration; but, while Joseph and Mary were officially married, he was not physically intimate with her until after Jesus was born (Matt. 1:25). Matthew did not reveal why Joseph and Mary remained chaste. Perhaps they concluded that chastity was the only appropriate response.

C. The Name of Jesus: vs. 25b

And he gave him the name Jesus.

Joseph named Mary's child "Jesus" (Matt. 1:25). Though people often break promises, God is faithful to keep His pledge (Heb. 6:13-17). He did so when, in a most unusual and unexpected way, He sent His Son, "Immanuel "(Matt. 1:23), to be "God with us."

Discussion Questions

1. How did the Jews view the engagement period between a man and woman?
2. How did Matthew discuss the miraculous conception of Jesus?
3. In what ways did Joseph demonstrate his upright character in the situation involving Mary?
4. How did Matthew link the virgin birth to the Old Testament?
5. How can Christians be involved in the fulfillment of God's promise to provide a Savior to redeem the lost from their sin?

Contemporary Application

We know all the characters in the Christmas pageant, but how well do we know their accounts? How well do we know what their obedience to God cost them?

Christmas would mean nothing without the faith, hope, courage, and obedience of Joseph and Mary. In the midst of the color, pageantry, and celebration of the holiday, it pays for us to take the time to reflect on those whom God used in the early years of Jesus' life.

We must also not forget the great salvation themes of the Christmas narrative. The real joy of the holiday is not in the receiving of presents. It is in finding God's forgiveness through faith in Christ, the greatest gift of all. If He does not take away our sins, we have nothing to celebrate. Also, no amount of celebration can make up for the darkness of the soul that falls on those who reject Jesus and His salvation.

Jesus Grew in God's Favor

Scripture

Background Scripture: *Luke 2:40-52*
Scripture Lesson: *Luke 2:40-52*
Key Verse: *And Jesus grew in wisdom and stature, and in
favor with God and men.* Luke 2:52.
Scripture Lesson for Children: *Luke 2:40-52*
Key Verse for Children: *And the child [Jesus] grew and
became strong; he was filled with wisdom, and the grace of
God was upon him.* Luke 2:40.

Lesson Aim

To help one another grow in favor with God and others.

Lesson Setting

Time: A.D. *7–8*
Place: *Nazareth and Jerusalem*

Lesson Outline

Jesus Grew in God's Favor
  I. Jesus' Childhood: Luke 2:40
  II. Jesus at Twelve: Luke 2:41-50
    A. *The Passover: vss. 41-42*
    B. *The Lost Boy: vss. 43-45*
    C. *Among the Teachers: vss. 46-47*
    D. *The Parents' Concern: vs. 48*
    E. *Jesus' Answer: vss. 49-50*
  III. Jesus' Youth: Luke 2:51-52
    A. *Jesus' Obedience: vs. 51*
    B. *Jesus' Growth: vs. 52*

Introduction for Adults

Topic: *Learning to Grow*

Adults are prone to forget what it was like to grow up. But when they get older and suffer the consequences of broken bones and strokes (for example), they have to learn basic skills all over again. Amazingly, they can recover many of these, but it can be a long, painful process that requires hours of repetitive exercises.

Growing spiritually is also tough. We cannot grow in Christlikeness without following the disciplines of the Spirit. Sitting in a church pew one hour a week is no substitute for studying God's Word, praying, and serving one another. Every day God gives us growth opportunities. If we fail to use them, we become stunted, unfruitful, and unhappy Christians.

Introduction for Youth

Topic: *Growing in Mind, Body, and Spirit*

The Marine Corps attracts recruits with images of youth who appear to be tall, bright, and tough. The implication is that by joining the Marines you will get tough mentally and physically. Many veterans testify that they also grew spiritually while serving in the armed forces.

God calls us to enlist in His kingdom service, and He desires to toughen us for spiritual warfare. In one sense, Jesus trained for 30 years before He began His earthly ministry. His training included hard work and study. Most of all, He remained faithful to God.

When we trust in Christ for salvation, He will do far more for us than any human organization can promise. He enables us to excel as believers when we follow the disciplines of the Spirit, which include sacrifice, prayer, and obedience (among other things).

Concepts for Children

Topic: *Jesus: Growing in God's Favor*

1. Jesus grew up in a humble family where obeying God was stressed.
2. Jesus studied in the synagogue and learned the Scriptures.
3. Jesus talked with His Bible teachers about important truths.
4. Even when Jesus was 12, He had a strong desire to obey God.
5. Throughout Jesus' childhood, He sought to follow God.
6. When we study and obey God's Word, He blesses us with His love and grace.

Lesson Commentary
I. Jesus' Childhood: Luke 2:40

And the child grew and became strong; he was filled with wisdom, and the grace of God was upon him.

The Scripture passage immediately preceding this week's lesson text is the account of Jesus' presentation to the Lord (Luke 2:22). According to Jewish custom, a woman who had given birth to a male child was unclean for seven days, or until the child was circumcised. For 33 days afterward, she was not allowed to touch any holy thing, or come into the sanctuary (Lev. 12:4). Then she had to come to the temple to be purified in the proper way. It was in connection with this ritual that Mary and Joseph brought Jesus to Jerusalem (Luke 2:22).

The Mosaic law also stipulated that every firstborn son had to be presented to the Lord and redeemed or bought back from Him for the price of five shekels (Num. 18:15-16). It was during this visit to the temple that Joseph, Mary, and Jesus met Simeon, who spoke prophetically about the Messiah (Luke 2:34-35). Then Anna, upon seeing Jesus, began to praise God and speak about the child to all who were looking for the redemption of Jerusalem (vs. 38). No doubt the meeting with Simeon and Anna was another one of those mysteries Mary "pondered . . . in her heart" (vs. 19).

Luke states that Joseph and Mary returned to Galilee, to their own town of Nazareth (vs. 39). Luke, however, neither mentioned the events recorded in Matthew 2 nor any specific event that may have happened until Jesus was 12 years old. We assume that Joseph and Mary had children of their own during this time, for the Scriptures mention four of Jesus' half-brothers, James, Joseph, Simon, Judas (Matt. 13:55), and Jesus' sisters (vs. 56).

During Jesus' childhood years, He physically matured and became strong. Moreover, He grew spiritually. He was "filled with wisdom" (Luke 2:40). Jesus' wisdom was more than mere intellectual knowledge. It included the ability to use the knowledge He acquired to the best advantage.

Luke also noted that "the grace of God" was upon Jesus. Because Jesus was human as well as divine, during His earthly life He depended on His heavenly Father for all things, just as we do. But Jesus was sinless, and God's favor upon Him was for reasons unique to His earthly life and ministry.

Much of Jesus' growth and development from infancy to adulthood is difficult for us to fathom. Perhaps this is because, as a human being, Jesus was completely unhindered by those sinful influences that affect all of us who are descendants of Adam. Jesus' body and spirit responded to His heavenly Father much as a bud drinks in the sunshine and rain and grows into a beautiful and perfect blossom.

We can only imagine what an unusual situation existed in Joseph's home during those years. Was there sibling rivalry? How did Mary and Joseph deal with such problems in the home? These are issues that Scripture does not address. Despite this, the Bible sheds much light on the way in which Jesus related to His heavenly Father during the early years of the Savior's life.

123

II. JESUS AT TWELVE: LUKE 2:41-50

A. The Passover: vss. 41-42

Every year his parents went to Jerusalem for the Feast of the Passover. When he was twelve years old, they went up to the Feast, according to the custom.

Jesus' visit to Jerusalem for Passover is the only account we have about Him between His birth and His baptism. Joseph and Mary, being faithful to God, kept the Passover celebration every year. Passover lasted for a week and was the highlight of the Jewish festival calendar. It was one of three annual feasts in Jerusalem that all Jews were expected to attend. It marked Israel's deliverance from Egypt.

When Jesus was "twelve years old" (Luke 2:42), He went with His parents "to Jerusalem for the Feast of the Passover" (vs. 41). About the age of 12, a Jewish boy such as Jesus became "a son of the (divine) law" (that is, a *bar mitzvah*). This meant the child pledged to learn and to obey the commandments of God. Similarly today, a Jewish boy spends his twelfth year studying the *Torah* (a Hebrew word normally translated "law") with rabbis and other Jewish scholars and teachers.

B. The Lost Boy: vss. 43-45

After the Feast was over, while his parents were returning home, the boy Jesus stayed behind in Jerusalem, but they were unaware of it. Thinking he was in their company, they traveled on for a day. Then they began looking for him among their relatives and friends. When they did not find him, they went back to Jerusalem to look for him.

Mary and Joseph remained in Jerusalem the full seven days and then started for home, but Jesus stayed behind (Luke 2:43). The parents traveled with many other pilgrims, but not necessarily as a family. The children typically walked together and older adults rode mules.

Not until they had walked a day's journey did Mary and Joseph realize that Jesus was not in their group. So the parents started to look for Jesus among their friends and relatives, but without success (vs. 44). The parents then turned around and went back to Jerusalem to find Jesus (vs. 45).

Luke did not blame either Jesus or His parents for what had happened. Perhaps from our standpoint we might assume that Jesus should have told His parents what He was doing. However, in God's plan, the unfolding events served to highlight Jesus' unusual spiritual giftedness.

We can well imagine Jesus' thrill and exuberance on His visit to Jerusalem and the temple. This was no ordinary event. Perhaps it was the most dramatic thing that had occurred thus far in His life. Jesus undoubtedly followed the inspiration of His heart and the unique genius that was His nature.

C. Among the Teachers: vss. 46-47

After three days they found him in the temple courts, sitting among the teachers, listening to them and asking them questions. Everyone who heard him was amazed at his understanding and his answers.

Mary and Joseph had traveled with the caravan one day north toward Galilee, and it required a day for them to return to Jerusalem. Then they spent a day searching throughout the city for Jesus. They finally found Him "in the temple courts" (Luke 2:46). Jesus was engaged in dialogue with the teachers of the law. Of course, this scene drew interested observers as well. They were "amazed at his understanding and his answers" (vs. 47).

It's quite possible that these sorts of discussions in the temple occurred on a daily basis. The opportunity to exchange questions and answers drew Jesus' interest. It was highly unusual for the scholars to invite a youth into their theological debates, but Jesus asked such intelligent questions that they included Him.

Luke did not record the content of these discussions. Perhaps they concerned matters of rabbinical history and traditions. If so, this would have been more like a gathering of legal experts talking about matters of interest. Jesus, of course, listened and asked questions respectfully. He was able to follow the various arguments and, surprisingly, was also able to answer challenging questions put to Him.

D. The Parents' Concern: vs. 48

When his parents saw him, they were astonished. His mother said to him, "Son, why have you treated us like this? Your father and I have been anxiously searching for you."

The religious experts were taken aback by Jesus' understanding of the law and His ability to answer interpretative questions regarding it. Mary and Joseph were also "astonished" (Luke 2:48), but for quite a different reason. At this point they weren't focusing on Jesus' ability to hold His own among the legal scholars of the day. Instead, Mary and Joseph were concerned for Jesus' well being.

Interestingly, when Jesus' parents found Him, it was Mary who addressed Him. There was surprise and frustration in Mary's words. This was the natural response of a mother who temporarily had lost her child. One fact we learn from this incident is that Joseph and Mary acted like normal parents and they loved their child deeply.

E. Jesus' Answer: vss. 49-50

"Why were you searching for me?" he asked. "Didn't you know I had to be in my Father's house?" But they did not understand what he was saying to them.

Jesus' answer showed that He had a clear understanding of the relationship between Himself and His Father. Throughout Jesus' public ministry, He referred to this relationship again and again. Jesus knew that He was one with His Father. For instance, Jesus' statement to Mary, "Didn't you know that I had to be in my Father's house?" (Luke 2:49), revealed that Jesus knew His life was on a divine schedule. Mary and Joseph, it turns out, did not understand what Jesus meant (vs. 50).

This is the first clue we find in the Gospels that Jesus was not just an ordinary child from Nazareth. His pilgrimage to Jerusalem was a divinely ordained mission.

— In fact, Jesus' response to God's call resulted in the Messiah engaging the highest level of learning in the Jewish nation.

Perhaps Mary was for the first time learning what Simeon had told her about her heart being pierced (vs. 35). Some see this event as the first step in that painful separation. Ultimately, Jesus' divinely appointed mission would lead to His death on the cross.

III. JESUS' YOUTH: LUKE 2:51-52

A. Jesus' Obedience: vs. 51

Then he went down to Nazareth with them and was obedient to them. But his mother treasured all these things in her heart.

Jesus returned to Nazareth with His parents (Luke 2:51). Luke noted that over the next 18 years Jesus "was obedient" to His parents. In every way He submitted to their will.

During Jesus' time growing up, He learned the carpenter's trade (Mark 6:3). We can safely assume that Jesus continued His religious studies in the prescribed Jewish fashion. We know that He kept the law perfectly, for He was without sin. He also observed the religious festivals and rituals of the Jews, for He said that He had come to fulfill the Mosaic law, not to break it (Matt. 5:17).

From Jesus' later activities and associations, we know that He was familiar with the local customs of farmers and other sorts of trades people. From this we see that Jesus saturated Himself in the ways of ordinary people. He knew their stories and their traditions. He also moved among them comfortably.

Luke 2:51 notes that Mary "treasured all these things in her heart." She was a godly woman of great faith and humility. As she watched her son grow into manhood, she recalled the words of the angel and the prophecy of Simeon. No doubt Mary also reflected on the messianic prophecies.

B. Jesus' Growth: vs. 52

And Jesus grew in wisdom and stature, and in favor with God and men.

In another concise statement, Luke noted that Jesus continued to develop spiritually, morally, and intellectually. Holiness and humility marked His life. In fact, "wisdom and stature" (Luke 2:52) indicate robust spiritual health. From this we see that Jesus wedded truth and conduct. He not only knew the truth, but also lived it.

These things were so true in Jesus' life that He "grew . . . in favor with God and men." What more could be said of anyone than that they pleased God and others? Clearly, Jesus' life bore the stamp of divine and human approval.

Discussion Questions

1. What is the difference between the way in which God's favor was manifested to Jesus and the way it is often shown to us?

2. How might Jesus have anticipated attending the Passover festival with His parents in Jerusalem?

3. In ancient times, what was the spiritual significance of a Jewish boy's twelfth birthday?

4. What caused the teachers of the law to be so impressed with the way Jesus responded to them?

5. What can parents learn from Jesus' childhood regarding the rearing of their own children?

Contemporary Application

Perhaps the best illustration of what life was like for Jesus as a boy is found in De La Tour's famous painting, "St. Joseph the Carpenter." It has caught the appreciation of many people. Here we see something of the warm relationship that must have existed between Joseph and Jesus. It's a refreshing scene, especially because most classical painters focused on the relationship between Mary and the infant Jesus.

Jesus did not live a pampered life on earth. For instance, carpentry in ancient times was a physically demanding occupation. Thus, as Jesus learned this trade from Joseph, the Savior developed a strong body in order to handle the demands of the trade.

It's important to note that the Messiah, at the age 12, was fully aware of His unique identity. He was also committed to obeying His heavenly Father. Jesus thus continued to honor His earthly parents by submitting to them. Moreover, after Jesus returned with them to their home in Nazareth, the Savior continued to grow physically toward adulthood.

Jesus' fellow townsfolk became increasingly aware of His dedication to God and desire to obey His commandments. It was also more and more evident that the grace of God was upon Jesus' life. Young people sometimes become impatient in their desire to break away from their home ties; but a loving Christian home atmosphere can help them develop the patience they need to wait for God's leading in their lives.

Integrity in the Midst of Suffering

DEVOTIONAL READING

Romans 8:18-25

DAILY BIBLE READINGS

Monday December 29
Romans 8:18-23 Compare Present Suffering with Future Glory

Tuesday December 30
Romans 8:24-28 All Things Work Together for Good

Wednesday December 31
Romans 8:29-33 God Is for Us

Thursday January 1
Romans 8:34-39 Nothing Can Separate Us from Christ's Love

Friday January 2
Job 1:1-5 Job Was Upright

Saturday January 3
Job 1:13-22 Job Kept Integrity in Suffering

Sunday January 4
Job 2:1-10 Job Would Not Curse God

Scripture

Background Scripture: *Job 1—2:10*
Scripture Lesson: *Job 2:1-10*
Key Verse: *"Shall we accept good from God, and not trouble?"* Job 2:10.
Scripture Lesson for Children: *Genesis 37:12-14, 17b-28*
Key Verse for Children: *[Joseph's brothers] sold him for twenty shekels of silver to the Ishmaelites, who took him to Egypt.* Genesis 37:28.

Lesson Aim

To maintain a strong faith in the midst of adversity.

Lesson Setting

Time: *During the second millennium B.C.*
Place: *The land of Uz, a large territory east of the Jordan River*

Lesson Outline

Integrity in the Midst of Suffering
   I. Satan's Mission: Job 2:1
  II. God's Challenge: Job 2:2-3
 III. Satan's Proposition: Job 2:4-5
 IV. God's Answer: Job 2:6
  V. Job's Suffering: Job 2:7-8
 VI. Job's Wife's Rebuke: Job 2:9
VII. Job's Faith: Job 2:10

Introduction for Adults

Topic: *Holding Firm in Suffering*

Ann was blind from birth. Everything she knew and accomplished in life she owed to her parents' sacrifice and dedication. When her mother fell ill, Ann was distraught. She had never seen her mother. She knew only her voice and touch.

For months Ann sat with her mother in a nursing home, holding her hands and talking to her. But her mother had lost her speech and could not respond. Nevertheless, Ann held on firmly every day, speaking words of comfort and hope.

In times of suffering we hold on to each other and especially to God. Even when God does not seem to reply to our cries, we keep trusting in Him. Faith drives us to prayer and worship every day. In the darkness, we keep pursuing the light by faith. We claim God's promise that nothing can separate us from His love (Rom. 8:31-39).

Introduction for Youth

Topic: *Holding Fast in Tough Times*

One of the basic therapies for strengthening hand, wrist, and arm muscles is the squeezing of a rubber ball tightly several times a day. At first we feel the tension and pain, but gradually our muscles respond and we are able to function normally. This exercise is prescribed after injuries or surgeries—incidents and events we would prefer to avoid. In cases like these, holding fast to a rubber ball is a discipline that produces results.

God sometimes takes us through tough times to strengthen our spiritual muscles (so to speak). He knows how flabby we get when we neglect our worship and obedience to His good and perfect will. But when He gets our attention, we respond with therapies that give us new love and zeal for Him.

Job's account tells us that it is possible to be faithful to God, even when hard times hit. We surmount our difficulties by Christ's indwelling power and presence.

Concepts for Children

Topic: *Joseph's Life Was Changed*

1. Joseph's brothers were watching their father's sheep when he sent Joseph to check on them.
2. When the brothers saw Joseph coming, they talked about killing him.
3. The brothers finally decided to strip Joseph of his robe and throw him into a pit.
4. After doing this, the brothers sold Joseph to a group of traders.
5. God sometimes allows us to experience unhappy things in life.
6. God wants us to serve Him by being fair and loving to others.

Lesson Commentary

I. SATAN'S MISSION: JOB 2:1

On another day the angels came to present themselves before the LORD, and Satan also came with them to present himself before him.

The question of Job's authorship had been debated for centuries, and no one has come up with evidence for his or her answer that satisfies everyone. The main reason for this uncertainty is that the Book of Job itself neglects to identify its author. In fact, the complexity of its language makes it difficult even to determine a specific period of time within which the book was written.

Bible critics tend to view Job as a work of fiction. Some conjecture an Israelite took a foreign epic and made it stylistically palatable for a Hebrew audience. Others suggest the book was pieced together by a number of people over an extended period of time.

In contrast to such critical theories, one long-held view maintains that Job was indeed a historical person, and that he wrote the book himself sometime after his ordeal. If this is the case, the account of an encounter between God and Satan in the prologue of the book could have come to Job only by divine revelation.

Another traditional view holds that, while Job was a historical person, someone else wrote his account. Some think the writer personally knew Job and made keen observations and carefully recorded the poetic speeches. Others suggest the writer lived some years after Job and put his account together in poetic form based on what he knew about the historical person. Whatever view is taken, it is evident that the author was both divinely inspired and possessed of poetic genius.

A number of interesting and illuminating facts about Job can be obtained from Scripture. The Bible reveals that he was a spiritually mature person (Job 1:1, 8; 2:3). He was also the father of many children (1:2; 42:13) and the owner of many herds (1:3; 42:12). Scripture portrays Job as a wealthy and influential man (1:3), a priest to his family (vs. 5), and a loving, wise husband (2:9). He was both a person of prominence in community affairs (29:7-11) and someone known for his benevolence (29:12-17; 31:32). In addition, Job was a wise leader (29:21-24) and a grower of crops (31:38-40).

Concerning when Job was written, there is no conclusive evidence that has been found. Some have suggested an early date because of the fact that the book makes no mention of the patriarchs, the twelve tribes of Israel, or Moses. This leads some to believe that the book was written in the time before Moses (about 1566–1446 B.C.). If so, then Job is the oldest book of the Bible. As such, it offers us insight into people's conceptions of God before they possessed written revelation.

Some Bible scholars propose much later dates for the writing of Job. Some say it was written during the reign of Solomon (970–930 B.C.), while others are far more general, saying it was written sometime between the times of Moses and Ezra. Whatever view is taken, the writer undoubtedly was a skillful poet from the covenant community. While the numerous details in Job indicate that the events occurred during the patriarchal era, the literary evidence suggests that the book was written sometime later during an era when wisdom flourished.

In the prologue to the book (chaps. 1—2), six short but key scenes set the stage for Job's debate with his friends and his ultimate encounter with God (described later). The first scene (1:1-5) gives some background information about Job's good character and his family.

Then, in scene 2 (vss. 6-12), we are told about Satan's first challenge to God, in which the devil obtained the Lord's permission to destroy Job's family and possessions. Satan sought to prove that Job would curse his Creator when signs of God's blessings on his life ceased occurring.

Scene 3 (vss. 13-22) records Job's first test and how this godly man stood firm and faithful to God even after losing his family and possessions. The fourth scene (2:1-6) divulges Satan's second challenge to God. Scene 5 (vss. 7-10) sets forth Job's second test, and scene 6 (vss. 11-13) recounts the arrival of Job's friends.

Concerning scene 4, it begins with the mention of "the angels" (2:1), which is more literally rendered "the sons of God." These heavenly beings are superior to humans in power and intelligence. According to the Book of Job, the angels periodically presented themselves before God, though we know little about the gatherings.

In the scenes of the celestial assembly, only one heavenly being, other than God Himself, is identified. This entity is referred to in Hebrew only by his title, which means "the adversary." In English he is called "Satan" (1:6; 2:1). This character is one of the "sons of God" who serve under and reports to the Lord.

The Hebrew word for "son" (*bar*) can refer not only to an immediate male offspring, but also to a member of an entire class or category. In Job, the phrase "sons of God" conveys the sense of "from God" or "made by God." The idea, then, is that angels (including Satan) are created beings who inhabit the supernatural realm.

II. GOD'S CHALLENGE: JOB 2:2-3

And the LORD said to Satan, "Where have you come from?" Satan answered the LORD, "From roaming through the earth and going back and forth in it." Then the LORD said to Satan, "Have you considered my servant Job? There is no one on earth like him; he is blameless and upright, a man who fears God and shuns evil. And he still maintains his integrity, though you incited me against him to ruin him without any reason."

The Lord asked Satan where he had been. The adversary, in response, stated he had been going all over "the earth" (Job 2:2). Here we see Satan functioning as a "celestial prosecuting attorney." He took it upon himself to bring charges and produce proofs against Job.

Satan offered no report of what he had done to Job or of Job's response to his actions. But God showed that He knew about what had transpired by reminding the evil one about Job's integrity. Verse 3 piles on one virtue after another in describing this person's rectitude, including "blameless" and "upright." The sense is that Job was distinguished among his peers. He not only revered God but also shunned evil, being a person of genuine virtue.

The phrase "you incited me" (vs. 3) does not suggest that God can be provoked into doing something against His will. The Lord was simply pointing out that Satan had challenged the reasons for Job's faithfulness to God, and the Lord had allowed Satan to test Job. As it turned out, the devil had inflicted great misery on Job "without any reason," since Job's faith had remained firm. Thus, even Satan's attempts to harm Job could not cause him to deter from the path of uprightness.

III. SATAN'S PROPOSITION: JOB 2:4-5

"Skin for skin!" Satan replied. "A man will give all he has for his own life. But stretch out your hand and strike his flesh and bones, and he will surely curse you to your face."

The adversary disagreed with God's evaluation of Job's integrity. Satan cynically retorted that Job, like anyone else, was willing to sacrifice his family's "skin" (Job 2:4) in order to save his own. Satan was implying that Job would do anything—even barter his own family away—to escape calamity.

Supposedly Job blessed God only because the Lord had blessed him. Thus the accuser insinuated that even Job's psalm of praise amidst his anguish was a sham. It was Job's clever way of putting everything into the bargain to stay alive. The devil argued that, if God permitted him to attack Job's own "flesh and bones" (vs. 5), then Job would give in and curse God.

Satan's attack was not so much against Job as it was against God Himself. It may even reflect the essence of the ongoing struggle between the devil and the forces of evil, on the one hand, and God and the forces of righteousness, on the other hand.

IV. GOD'S ANSWER: JOB 2:6

The LORD said to Satan, "Very well, then, he is in your hands; but you must spare his life."

God agreed to the plan Satan proposed. Nevertheless, while God permitted the devil to afflict Job's body, he could not take "his life" (Job 2:6). Here we see that God may allow evil in His world, but He does not allow it to take total control. He will permit it to spread only so far before He cuts it back. One day the Lord will do away with all sin and evil and those who promote it.

V. JOB'S SUFFERING: JOB 2:7-8

So Satan went out from the presence of the LORD and afflicted Job with painful sores from the soles of his feet to the top of his head. Then Job took a piece of broken pottery and scraped himself with it as he sat among the ashes.

Satan left "the presence of the Lord" (Job 2:7) and caused painful sores to break out all over Job's body—"from the soles of his feet to the top of his head." This apparently was some type of rare and terrible disease. Symptoms of the ailment included boil-like inflammations that caused ceaseless itching (vs. 8), excruciating bone decay (30:17), discolored and peeling skin, and high fevers (vs. 30). When Job could find a way to sleep during the intense pain and misery, he suffered horrible nightmares (7:13-14).

Job, a once significant figure in his community, ended up sitting on a heap of "ashes" (2:8) in sorrow. He proceeded to scrape himself with a potsherd because of the interminable itching. In ancient times sitting on an ash heap was a way for people to mourn their condition. Additionally, people in that day thought an ash mound had medicinal qualities that might promote the health of a person with Job's afflictions.

VI. JOB'S WIFE'S REBUKE: JOB 2:9

His wife said to him, "Are you still holding on to your integrity? Curse God and die!"

At this point in the account, Job's "wife" (Job 2:9) came onto the scene. Evidently she was the sole surviving family member. As she looked upon her husband in the midst of his suffering, she chided him for trying to maintain his "integrity" and urged him to blaspheme God and die. Perhaps Satan had thought ahead when bringing disaster upon Job's family. He spared Job's wife, evidently anticipating he could later use her to achieve his evil ends.

VII. JOB'S FAITH: JOB 2:10

He replied, "You are talking like a foolish woman. Shall we accept good from God, and not trouble?"
In all this, Job did not sin in what he said.

Job's response to his wife's suggestion should be seen not as insensitive or harsh. By calling her "foolish" (Job 2:10), he did not mean that she was ignorant, but that she was morally deficient and operating according to worldly wisdom, not divine wisdom.

In Job's way of thinking, it would have been irresponsible for him to accept God's blessings in the past and then slander God for the pain and anguish He allowed in the present. Thus Job refused to take his wife's advice. He maintained the same trust in God that he had evidenced after his first test (1:20-22). In this way, Job proved that God's confidence in him was well placed.

As we study Job, we will discover that the book is not so much about suffering as it is about God's sovereignty and wisdom. Unknown to Job, the true purpose of his ordeal was to demonstrate in the face of Satan's challenge that he could stand as a supreme display of God's saving might. By remaining faithful to God under such distressing circumstances, Job demonstrated that true wisdom is rooted in the wisdom of God.

Discussion Questions

1. What did Satan request as he came before God in heaven?
2. Why do you think God asked Satan whether he had considered Job?
3. How had Satan misjudged Job in the accusation the devil brought against him?

4. What was inappropriate about the remarks Job's wife made to him in the midst of his suffering?

5. What example did Job provide for God's people when they find themselves in the midst of unexpected and intense suffering?

Contemporary Application

"Why me, Lord?" is often the first question that pops into our minds when something bad happens to us. Job's account began with another question, "Why is Job serving God?" Satan implied that Job's faith was only as genuine as his wealth and family blessings. Even when Job had lost everything, Satan again accused him of being faithful because he enjoyed good health.

Job's circumstances drive us to question our motives for serving the Lord. It also forces us to reexamine the faulty proposition that faith and material blessings always go hand in hand.

After round one, Job worshiped the Lord. After round two, he refused to sin by cursing God. In this way Job set a high standard for all who profess to trust the Lord. We should ask ourselves how genuine our faith is when troubles arise.

Of course, we all waver because our faith is not static. We cannot lock it up in a safety deposit box. Our faith is stretched by troubles. Our faith is also strengthened by words of encouragement from others. We all need to hear words that tell us to keep on believing, no matter what.

Integrity in Seeking God

Scripture

Background Scripture: *Job 9:32-35; 13:20-24; 19:25-27; 23:10-12*

Scripture Lesson: *Job 9:32-35; 13:20-24; 19:25-27; 23:10-12*

Key Verse: *"I desire to speak to the Almighty and to argue my case with God."* Job 13:3.

Scripture Lesson for Children: *Genesis 40:8; 41:16-31*

Key Verse for Children: *"I cannot do it,"* Joseph replied to Pharaoh, *"but God will give Pharaoh the answer he desires."* Genesis 41:16.

Lesson Aim

To develop complete confidence in our walk with God.

Lesson Setting

Time: *During the second millennium* B.C.

Place: *The land of Uz, a large territory east of the Jordan River*

Lesson Outline

Integrity in Seeking God

  I. Job's Plea: Job 9:32-35
      A. *For an Arbitrator: vss. 32-33*
      B. *For Mercy: vss. 34-35*
  II. Job's Requests: Job 13:20-24
      A. *For Relief: vss. 20-21*
      B. *For a Summons: vss. 22-24*
  III. Job's Faith: Job 19:25-27
      A. *Job's Redeemer Lives: vs. 25*
      B. *Job Will See His Redeemer: vss. 26-27*
  IV. Job's Confidence: Job 23:10-12
      A. *In the Outcome: vs. 10*
      B. *In Job's Obedience: vss. 11-12*

Introduction for Adults

Topic: *Seeking God in Times of Trial*

An elderly man—not a believer—suffered a heart attack after a personal disaster. His Christian daughter appealed to him to repent. Could he not see God's hand in what had happened? Absolutely not, the man said. It was just bad luck.

Some people reach the point in their lives where God no longer figures in their thinking. How important it is for Christians to show by example that God is the only one who really counts. When we seek Him in times of trial, we set a powerful example for others to follow.

Many times a crisis of faith is a God-given opportunity for us to demonstrate what it means to follow Him and allow Jesus to carry our pain and loss. Paul said that one reason he had suffered was so that he might comfort others in their trials (2 Cor. 1:3-7). That is true for all Christians.

Introduction for Youth

Topic: *Stand by Me*

Community tragedies, especially when they involve children and youth, invariably draw people closer together. Outpourings of love and support for the suffering play a major role in personal and community recovery. Schools and businesses employ grief counselors.

When tragedies happen, we are forced to reflect on our faith. The big question always seems to be "Why?" We must avoid glib answers and admit limited knowledge. At the same time, we can confess our faith and hope in Christ. As we live for Him, others might be drawn to us.

Like Job, we must also develop strong disciplines of obedience to God and love for His Word. We can only be an effective witness for Christ in times of tragedy if we have a treasure of Scripture in our hearts.

Concepts for Children

Topic: *Joseph Sought God's Wisdom*

1. Joseph told two other prisoners that God is the one who helps people understand their dreams.
2. Joseph told the king of Egypt that God would help him to understand his dream.
3. God used Joseph to help Egypt's king learn what God was going to do.
4. Joseph said that God would bring seven years of plenty, which would be followed by seven years of hunger.
5. Joseph told Egypt's king that the seven years of hunger would be terrible.
6. We can ask God for wisdom when we face tough decisions.

Lesson Commentary

I. JOB'S PLEA: JOB 9:32-35

A. For an Arbitrator: vss. 32-33

"He is not a man like me that I might answer him, that we might confront each other in court. If only there were someone to arbitrate between us, to lay his hand upon us both."

After Job's first speech (Job 3), the book proceeds with three rounds of speeches. Each friend speaks in turn and is answered by Job. As the first round begins (4:1—14:22), Eliphaz the Temanite defended the traditional wisdom view of an orderly world (chaps. 4—5). Eliphaz maintained that, in this just and orderly world, righteousness is rewarded and wickedness is punished. Many proverbs express this notion (Prov. 10:3, 24, 27-28, 30). Eliphaz expressed this view as an attempt to comfort. In other words, Job's own fear of God should have been his hope (Job 4:6).

Job's second friend, Bildad the Shuhite, discarded all pretenses at offering comfort (chap. 8). His whole purpose was to defend the traditional wisdom teachings that had been passed from generation to generation. Job's experience of injustice was unimportant to Bildad, especially when compared with the time-honored teachings of "the former generations" (vs. 8) and "what their fathers learned."

Bildad took one step beyond the wisdom teaching that the righteous prosper and the wicked suffer. He turned the teaching around to conclude that Job's children must have been wicked since they died (vs. 4). In fact, if Job were really pure, he would also not be suffering (vs. 6). This reformulation of the teaching might seem logical, but it was unjustified. While biblical writings, such as those appearing in Proverbs, do teach that the wicked will suffer, they never permit the reverse reasoning that everyone who suffers is being punished for wickedness.

Job's third friend, Zophar the Naamathite, went the next step and flatly stated that Job deserved his suffering. In fact, Job was getting off easy (11:6). Much of Zophar's council asserts that God is too mysterious for Job, a mere mortal, to understand (vss. 7-8). While this was true, Zophar undercut the impact of his own argument by his confidence that he, also a mere mortal, was able to explain the ways of God to Job.

In some respects the Book of Job is a long answer to a pointed question: if God is the sovereign Lord of the universe, then why does He allow suffering to come to the godly and good fortune to the wicked? For Job, thinking about this question moved into a consideration of the nature of God. In the face of Job's multiple calamities, he was forced to examine the foundations of his faith and to scrutinize his concept of the Lord.

Thus Job found himself struggling with this issue as well as with his counselors' traditional answers to it. As we have noted, their primary view, as stated and discounted throughout the book, was that human suffering is a direct result of sin. They believed that God punishes the wicked in this life by sending affliction, and He rewards the righteous in this life by providing blessings.

Such a view, however, did nothing to clear up Job's perplexity, for he knew he was a righteous man and had done nothing to earn the suffering he was having to endure. In reality, Job was afflicted in numerous ways as a test of his faithfulness to the Lord; nevertheless, Job was oblivious to the fact that he was the object of that test—one God Himself had permitted after being challenged by Satan.

In the midst of Job's ordeal, he focused his attention on God, especially His immensity. Job realized that God is not a finite, mortal creature. Thus, it was impossible for Job to "answer" (9:32) God, as if the two were in some sort of legal dispute.

Because God is infinitely holy, it was impossible for Job, a fallen person, to confront God "in court." The idea is that Job could not put God on trial and expect to win his case. In light of this realization, Job longed for an arbitrator between them (vs. 33). The idea is one of a mediator who could bring together God and Job, render a just verdict, and thereby settle their dispute.

Some think the expression "lay his hand upon us both" comes from a custom of a judge putting his hands on the two disputing parties in order to show that he is taking them both under his jurisdiction. The expression can also be used for the provision of protection (Ps. 139:5). Job's problem, however, was that God represented the other party, in addition to being the arbiter in rendering a verdict.

B. For Mercy: vss. 34-35

"Someone to remove God's rod from me, so that his terror would frighten me no more. Then I would speak up without fear of him, but as it now stands with me, I cannot."

Job thought that if a suitable mediator could be found, this person could force God to "remove [His] rod" (Job 9:34) from Job. The "rod" is a symbol of God's power to decree whatever judgments and afflictions fall upon people. "Terror" refers to God's awesome majesty that overwhelmed and frightened Job. He envisioned himself no longer living in dread of God's punishment.

Thus, Job reasoned that, if God's rod were withdrawn, if the terror were removed, Job could speak up without "fear" (vs. 35). Of course, none of us can contend with God on our terms. We must come to Him in humility and freely receive the pardon He offers through the "one mediator between God and men" (1 Tim. 2:5), Jesus Christ.

II. JOB'S REQUESTS: JOB 13:20-24

A. For Relief: vss. 20-21

"Only grant me these two things, O God, and then I will not hide from you: Withdraw your hand far from me, and stop frightening me with your terrors."

Job asked God to grant him "two things" (Job 13:20) so that he would be able face the divine and enter into dispute with Him. First, Job wanted God to remove His "hand" (vs. 21) of punishment from him. Perhaps Job was feeling trapped or confined. Second, Job petitioned God to stop "frightening" him with His awesome presence.

B. For a Summons: vss. 22-24

"Then summon me and I will answer, or let me speak, and you reply. How many wrongs and sins have I committed? Show me my offense and my sin. Why do you hide your face and consider me your enemy?"

If God met these two preconditions, Job would respond to what God said, and God could respond to what Job said (Job 13:22). In essence, Job was calling for a court to convene in which he would be either the defendant or the prosecutor.

In verse 23, Job used three terms for misdeeds against God: "wrongs," which means to go astray or err; "sins," which means to miss the mark or the way; and "offense," which means to openly rebel. The terms all emphasize different kinds of transgressions and different degrees of obstinacy. Job was demanding that God bring up any sins Job was guilty of committing.

Job felt as if God was hiding His "face" (vs. 24). This was a metaphorical way to indicate the withdrawal of divine favor or the outpouring of His wrath (Pss. 27:9; 30:7; Isa. 54:8). There are times when God hides His face to make Himself aloof (Job 34:29). Tragically, Job concluded that God considered him an enemy.

III. Job's Faith: Job 19:25-27

A. Job's Redeemer Lives: vs. 25

"I know that my Redeemer lives, and that in the end he will stand upon the earth."

As Job reflected on his situation, he declared in faith that his "Redeemer" (Job 19:25) lived. The focus here is not on God as one's Savior; rather, Job was thinking of the Lord as his defender who would vindicate him of wrongdoing. Although Job sensed he was going to die, he was confident God would acquit him before his accusers.

Some understand "the end" to be a reference to the close of the age, while others say the original should be translated "as the Last." In this case, the reference is to God as "the first and . . . the last" (Isa. 44:6; 48:12). When both senses are retained, we learn that God is the one and only vindicator who will defend the cause of His people to end of history.

This truth is reinforced by the statement that God will "stand upon the earth" (Job 19:25). The idea is of God rising up to mete out justice or descending from heaven to bring justice to the world. Job evidently sensed that the vindication of the righteous would occur after he had died and returned to dust.

B. Job Will See His Redeemer: vss. 26-27

"And after my skin has been destroyed, yet in my flesh I will see God; I myself will see him with my own eyes—I, and not another. How my heart yearns within me!"

Job realized that his disease was destroying his body and that, after death, his "skin" (Job 19:26) would decay. Nevertheless, he was confident that in his flesh he would "see God." This means he would witness his vindication. Here we find Job's faith rising to an unparalleled level and anticipating the New Testament doctrine of the resurrection of the righteous.

So strong was Job's anticipation of an afterlife with God that he declared he would see God "with my own eyes" (vs. 27). In this face-to-face encounter with the divine, Job expected to be exonerated. The prospect felt so overwhelming to Job that he exclaimed, "How my heart yearns within me!"

IV. JOB'S CONFIDENCE: JOB 23:10-12

A. In the Outcome: vs. 10

"But he knows the way that I take; when he has tested me, I will come forth as gold."

As Job lamented his situation, he went on a mental journey of the geography surrounding him in order to search for God. Despite Job's efforts, he claimed he could not find the Lord (Job 23:8-9). It could be that the geographical terms Job used referred to points of the Hebrew compass.

Based on this assumption, and the possibility that Job lived in or near Edom (as many believe), then "east" (vs. 8) indicated the great Arabian Desert, with its trackless wastes and occasional oases. "West" pointed to Egypt on the Nile and the expansive Mediterranean Sea. "North" referred to the land of Canaan, the cedar forests of Lebanon, the upper Euphrates River, and the Taurus and Ararat mountain ranges, while "south" denoted the Gulf of Aqaba and the Red Sea.

As Job reflected on his relationship with God, he affirmed his confidence that God knew where he was going and what he was doing. Evidently Job sensed that God, for whatever reason, was testing him (vs. 10). Even in the midst of this process, Job was confident he would "come forth as gold" and be proclaimed innocent.

B. In Job's Obedience: vss. 11-12

My feet have closely followed his steps; I have kept to his way without turning aside. I have not departed from the commands of his lips; I have treasured the words of his mouth more than my daily bread.

Job's life of integrity was the basis for his confidence. He was certain he had remained along the path of moral rectitude. Even when enticed to turn aside from God, Job had "kept to his way" (Job 23:11). In other words, Job had never refused to follow any of God's "commands" (vs. 12).

Job greatly treasured the teachings of God, as recorded in His Word. In fact, Job valued God's law more than his "daily bread." This reminds us of the words of the psalmist, who declared that he had hidden God's Word in his heart to keep him from sinning against the Lord (Ps. 119:11). May this be the constant desire of our heart.

Discussion Questions

1. What were the barriers that Job felt were keeping him from coming before God?
2. Why did Job feel that he needed an arbitrator between him and God?

3. In what way did Job see God as his Redeemer?

4. What did Job feel would be the final outcome of the testings God had allowed in his life?

5. How do believers feel when they emerge from a very difficult experience with a clearer understanding of God's will for their life?

Contemporary Application

When calamity struck Job and his family, he and his three friends wrestled with the question of whether God was fair. His friends took the view that God was punishing him, that he must have done something wrong to deserve such evil. Job disagreed, not only because he felt certain of his own integrity, but also because the wicked actually seemed to prosper, not suffer (Job 12:6).

Most significantly, Job rejected the conventional view that the world is orderly and that everything is arranged according to just principles. His tragedy was not just, for his upright and virtuous life did not result in good fortune. He was a living testimony to the fact that tragic things can happen to godly people.

This realization, though, only brought Job back to the original question concerning God's fairness. If the wicked prosper, where is justice in the world? Job concluded that the seemingly easy life of the wicked was very temporary and that sooner or later it would all fall apart (27:13-23). Job maintained that, in the end, God would humble the proud, enable those with integrity to inherit their possessions, and thereby establish justice. Thus He is indeed fair (36:6; 37:23-24).

Integrity in Everyday Life

Scripture

Background Scripture: *Job 27:2-6; 31*
Scripture Lesson: *Job 27:2-5; 31:5-8, 13-15, 24-25, 28*
Key Verses: *"As long as I have life within me, the breath of God in my nostrils, my lips will not speak wickedness, and my tongue will utter no deceit."* Job 27:3-4.
Scripture Lesson for Children: *Genesis 41:33-41, 53-57*
Key Verses for Children: *Then Pharaoh said to Joseph, "Since God has made all this known to you, there is no one so discerning and wise as you. You shall be in charge of my palace."* Genesis 41:39-40.

Lesson Aim

To grow in moral stature with God and others.

Lesson Setting

Time: *During the second millennium B.C.*
Place: *The land of Uz, a large territory east of the Jordan River*

Lesson Outline

Integrity in Everyday Life
   I. Job's Commitment to Truth: Job 27:2-5
  II. Job's Commitment to Honesty: Job 31:5-8
 III. Job's Commitment to Justice: Job 31:13-15
 IV. Job's Commitment to God Alone: Job 31:24-25, 28

Introduction for Adults

Topic: *Maintaining Integrity in Daily Living*

One Sunday morning a new couple appeared at church. The greeter asked them how they had come to be there. They said, "We live across the street from the Smiths. For a year now we have been watching them every Sunday morning. Without fail, they get up and go to church. We decided we needed to follow their example."

This couple recognized spiritual integrity in the Smiths. Their account reminds us that Christians are being watched every day. We claim that Jesus has made us different. But do our lives validate our claim?

Sometimes going to church is the easy part. However, when we are under fire at work, following Jesus can be harder. Job was the kind of person who lived his faith in his home, business, and community. When our faith and integrity are clear for all to see, people will be drawn to our Savior.

Introduction for Youth

Topic: *Living with a Clear Conscience*

How does Job's integrity relate to the lives of teens? For one thing, teens know all about the pressures to participate in immoral behavior. Job knew about that, too, and he remained committed to a life of godliness and virtue.

Job was also committed to telling the truth. Perhaps he was never tempted to cheat on an exam, but he might have been tempted to lie in business deals. His honesty and rectitude were evident in the way he treated others fairly and humanely.

In the final analysis, Job's life was characterized by faith and obedience to God. He lived with a clear conscience because of it. He thus serves as a wonderful example for teens to consider.

Concepts for Children

Topic: *Joseph Became a Leader*

1. Pharaoh put Joseph in charge to deliver Egypt from famine.
2. Joseph's wise plan worked as he said it would.
3. Joseph recognized that his importance had come from the Lord.
4. God honored Joseph's faithfulness and delivered the country.
5. When we are faithful to God in worship and prayer, He gives us many opportunities to serve others.
6. God wants us, as Christians, to help the poor and hungry.

Lesson Commentary

I. JOB'S COMMITMENT TO TRUTH: JOB 27:2-5

"As surely as God lives, who has denied me justice, the Almighty, who has made me taste bitterness of soul, as long as I have life within me, the breath of God in my nostrils, my lips will not speak wickedness, and my tongue will utter no deceit. I will never admit you are in the right; till I die, I will not deny my integrity."

Job is one of the most highly praised literary works known to humankind. The beauty of the original in Hebrew may well put the book in a class by itself. Job includes such poetic genres as laments, hymns, proverbs, oracles, and legal disputations. This material is characterized by an economy of expression in which transitions are often omitted and the relationship of ideas is left for the reader to determine.

As for the structure of Job, it consists of a prose framework in the prologue (chaps. 1—2) and epilogue (42:7-17), in between which is the poetic body of the book (3:1—42:6). This central section consists of Job's opening lament (chap. 3) and closing discourse (chap. 27), in between which are three cycles of speeches. There is also an interlude on wisdom (chap. 28), which is then followed by several monologues (29:1—42:6).

Whereas the prologue and epilogue portray Job as a patient saint who righteously endured suffering, the dialogue-dispute section shows him as one who longed for fair treatment by God. This tension between the patient and impatient Job shows him to be a real person who struggled with his emotions and feelings.

Throughout the book, Job's friends maintained that God was punishing him for his sin, and Job responded by declaring his innocence. In fact, Job made a vow by the living God, which means Job was staking God's life on the credibility of his words (Job 27:2). Job then accused God of denying him "justice." Supposedly "the Almighty" did this by afflicting Job unfairly. The sufferer's ordeal, in turn, left his "soul" feeling embittered. Put another way, his entire life was vexed by anguish. Despite how Job felt, he refused to depart from the path of virtue. Job declared that he would remain upright in conduct as long as he lived. After all, he realized that "the breath of God in [his] nostrils" (vs. 3) came from the Lord.

Thus, in submission to God, his Creator, Job vowed that his lips would never "speak wickedness" (vs. 4). The implication is that Job would not communicate deceitful things, no matter how quiet or subtle; instead, he would only speak the truth. Despite the discouraging words of his friends, Job staunchly refused to concede they were correct in their accusations against him. Job was so convinced of his innocence that he vowed to affirm, not deny, his "integrity" (vs. 5) until he died.

II. JOB'S COMMITMENT TO HONESTY: JOB 31:5-8

"If I have walked in falsehood or my foot has hurried after deceit— let God weigh me in honest scales and he will know that I am blameless— if my steps have turned from the path, if my heart has been led by my eyes, or if my hands have been defiled, then may others eat what I have sown, and may my crops be uprooted."

Job's ordeal caused him to make a sweeping inventory of his inner life. One of the areas he evaluated was his attitude toward women and how he handled his own sexual desires (Job 31:1). He viewed lust as a serious moral failure (vs. 11) and claimed his innocence regarding this sin.

In stating his practice of avoiding lustful stares, Job used a term—rendered "girl" in verse 1—that was sometimes used of pagan goddesses. This is one fact that has led some to conclude that Job was, at least secondarily, swearing he did not participate in the worship of fertility goddesses. Such often involved lewd practices; thus Job would have been declaring his innocence of immorality as well as idolatry.

Job was so convinced of his innocence that he vowed to affirm, not deny, his integrity until he died integrity (vs. 5). Job's defensive posture is woven tightly into the fabric of chapter 31. In vivid terms, he sought to demonstrate his innocence once and for all by explaining how he had refrained from committing acts of wickedness and how he had performed deeds of righteousness.

For instance, in verse 5 he denied ever walking "in falsehood" and hurrying "after deceit." The verbs "walk" and "hasten" (referring in the verse to the foot) are used metaphorically for the manner of life Job lived. He was so convinced of his innocence that he invited God to "weigh" (vs. 6) him on the scales of justice. Job was confident God would find him to be a person of integrity.

Here Job was focusing on deceitful practices in business. For instance, in his day scales were sometimes adjusted to cheat people. Job insisted he had never committed such a crime.

Job's friends, however, were convinced he had strayed from "the path" (vs. 7) of rectitude. They accused him of lusting for what his "eyes" had seen and defiling his "hands" with untold other sins. In short, he allegedly had used every part of his body to disobey God.

Job, of course, believed he was innocent of such excesses, especially in the realm of business. Nevertheless, if there was any possibility he was incorrect in his assessment, he offered to have all his "crops" (vs. 8) harvested or uprooted by others. He felt this would be a suitable punishment.

III. Job's Commitment to Justice: Job 31:13-15

"If I have denied justice to my menservants and maidservants when they had a grievance against me, what will I do when God confronts me? What will I answer when called to account? Did not he who made me in the womb make them? Did not the same one form us both within our mothers?"

Job's next claims of purity were somewhat more public than his claims not to have lusted and been deceitful. Job 31:13-28 records the kind and thoughtful ways Job had treated others, as well as how he had shunned greed and idolatry. For Job's first example of ways he was considerate of others, he referred to his treatment of his servants. In the ancient world, the wealthy had male and female servants, and they would appeal to their masters when complaints or disputes arose. In Job's case, he felt he had handled the grievances of his servants justly (vs. 13).

In verse 14, the verb "confront" means "to challenge in judgment," while "called to account" refers to Gods intervention for blessing or cursing. The idea is that, if Job had been unfair to his servants, God would hold him responsible for his actions and punish him with calamity.

Job acknowledged that God created both him and his servants. In fact, before any of them were born, God had given them life. Since all of them were equal before their Maker, Job's servants deserved fair treatment from him (vs. 15). Proverbs 22:2 expresses a similar thought: "Rich and poor have this in common: The LORD is the Maker of them all."

Throughout history, human beings have had a hard time treating those at lower social or economic levels with the respect they deserve as fellow creations of God. Nevertheless, as Job said, doing so is a good and godly action. Our behavior and attitude toward those who serve us is one indication of the Holy Spirit working in our lives.

Before his troubles, Job had been an advocate for the poor (Job 29:12-17). But his enormous wealth and power in his community may have distanced him from their pain. Though he was aware of their plight, he had never experienced it for himself. Then a series of disasters struck, and suddenly Job was reduced to poverty. As a result, the poor were no longer just a class of people that needed help, but fellow sufferers with whom Job shared a common ordeal.

With a new perspective, Job began to identify with slaves who feared unjust treatment from their masters (31:13). And he now understood what widows and orphans felt when they were forced to go without food, clothing, and shelter while watching others live in luxury (vss. 16-21). In the midst of his plight, Job discovered a new sense of equality with the disadvantaged, as expressed in his rhetorical question, "Did not he who made me in the womb make them?" (vs. 15). Job realized that people are basically the same, and that possessions and power have nothing to do with their fundamental humanity.

IV. JOB'S COMMITMENT TO GOD ALONE: JOB 31:24-25, 28

"If I have put my trust in gold or said to pure gold, 'You are my security,' if I have rejoiced over my great wealth, the fortune my hands had gained, then these also would be sins to be judged, for I would have been unfaithful to God on high."

Job's kindness and consideration touched not only those within his household, but also those outside of it. It was his lifelong practice to take care of the needs of the poor, the widows, the orphans, and the inadequately clothed (Job 31:16-23). Throughout history people have put their trust in "gold" (vs. 24) and anchored their happiness to "wealth" (vs. 25). Job declared that he had never placed confidence in his riches or raised his possessions too high in importance. God, not gold, was the foundation of his hope.

Job also did not place any confidence in the objects worshiped by others in his day. In fact, he asserted he had not been tempted to commit idolatry (vss. 26-27).

In Deuteronomy 17:2-7, false worship of heavenly bodies was a capital offense. Job, however, was talking about just a momentary glance at the sun or moon and the brief lapse into a pagan thought. Even in this case, it was still sin.

Since kissing was part of idol worship (1 Kings 19:18; Hos. 13:2), some think the worshipers threw kisses at these celestial deities. Job swore that he had not gestured such kisses (Job 31:27). His oath reflects the popularity of both the sun and the moon deities in ancient Syria and Palestine.

Yareah is a moon god mentioned in Ugaritic ritual and mythological texts. Another mood god, Sin of Haran, was worshiped throughout Palestine, Syria, and Mesopotamia. The characteristic crescent moon with dangling tassels, which symbolized this deity, has been found on numerous inscriptions and stone slabs.

Shemesh was an important sun deity appearing in all ancient Near Eastern pantheons. In Ugarit, the goddess Shapshu (meaning "sun") was the mediator of divine judgment as proclaimed by the chief god El. In this case, Shapshu was depicted in an image, found from Egypt to Mesopotamia, of the sun as a god of justice.

If Job had been guilty of greed, which is a form of idolatry, as well as conventional idolatry, then he would have deserved punishment from "God on high" (vs. 28). Job reasoned that greed and idolatry were nothing less than unfaithfulness to God, who ruled from heaven.

In summary, Job had remained pure in his kind acts to friends, servants, and strangers, in his attitude toward money and possessions, and in his refusal to worship anyone or anything other than God. Perhaps Job's blameless status made his disastrous circumstances all the more confusing.

Discussion Questions

1. How did Job demonstrate that his personal integrity in his daily life was extremely important to him?
2. Despite the accusations of his friends, what did Job refuse to do?
3. What were the "honest scales" (Job 31:6) in which Job was willing to be weighed?
4. How did Job see himself in relation to the male and female slaves he owned and who served him?
5. What can we do to maintain our personal integrity in our everyday living?

Contemporary Application

Job's self-defense strikes at the heart of everything we do. He knew the perils of idolatry posed by wealth. Much of our culture is based on this kind of idolatry. Job said, in effect, "Watch out, lest your wealth draw you away from God." Job knew what Jesus knew: you cannot serve God and money (Matt. 6:24).

Job also cut the ground from under social hypocrisy. By his humane treatment of his servants he demonstrated the Christian principles of equality and justice. Yet much of the world—and parts of the church—continue to violate the dignity of some people.

We can take lessons from how Job conducted his business affairs. Temptations to cheat abound on every hand, because of the great pressure to succeed and get ahead. Job was wealthy, but he did not resort to false bookkeeping or illegal deals to gain his stature.

And what about truth? Christians, of all people, should be known for their integrity and truthfulness. Is our word really good? Do we keep our promises? Do we honor our appointments? Do we appear for social engagements we have made? In all these things our goal is that "God may be praised through Jesus Christ" (1 Pet. 4:11).

Integrity in God's Presence

Scripture

Background Scripture: *Job 38:1-7; 40:7-9; 42:1-6*
Scripture Lesson: *Job 38:1-7; 40:7-9; 42:1-6*
Key Verse: *"My ears had heard of you but now my eyes have
seen you. Therefore I despise myself and repent in dust and
ashes."* Job 42:5.
Scripture Lesson for Children: *Genesis 50:15-26*
Key Verses for Children: *"Don't be afraid. Am I in the
place of God? You intended to harm me, but God intended it
for good."* Genesis 50:19-20.

Lesson Aim

To respond in faithful obedience to God.

Lesson Setting

Time: *During the second millennium B.C.*
Place: *The land of Uz, a large territory east of the Jordan
River*

Lesson Outline

Integrity in God's Presence
   I. God's Creation Power: Job 38:1-7
       A. *Job's Ignorance: vss. 1-3*
       B. *The Earth's Foundations: vss. 4-7*
  II. God's Justice: Job 40:7-9
 III. Job's Confession: Job 42:1-6
       A. *Job's Lack of Understanding: vss. 1-3*
       B. *Job's Openness: vss. 4-5*
       C. *Job's Repentance: vs. 6*

Introduction for Adults

Topic: *Encountering God*

One of the first Russian cosmonauts sent back a report that he did not find God in space. His news supposedly buttressed atheism, which is the belief that there is no God. Atheism continues to thrive in the hearts of many people.

Christians, of course, reject the tenets of atheism. In fact, when believers examine the world, they see evidence of God's existence everywhere, especially His "eternal power and divine nature" (Rom. 1:20). Today some people do not give credit to God for what they see in creation. They reject this witness.

Christians also see the revelation of God in Scripture and especially in Christ. This is as it should be, for the "Son is the radiance of God's glory and the exact representation of his being" (Heb. 1:3). Thus, in the midst of our pain and suffering, we can turn to our "great high priest" (4:14) to "receive mercy and find grace to help us in our time of need" (vs. 16).

Introduction for Youth

Topic: *Standing before God*

From our first days at school we learn that, when we stand before the principal, we must account for our actions. This authority figure commands our respect and attention.

Job pestered God for an audience because he thought he had been treated unfairly. God finally spoke to him and reminded him who was in control. When Job looked around and saw God's mighty hand at work in creation, he was humbled and confessed his sins to God.

Job learned a hard lesson that often comes only through some pain. The Lord alone is God, and we answer to Him, not the other way around. Happy are those who are willing to submit to God in faith and obedience.

Concepts for Children

Topic: *Joseph Practiced Forgiveness*

1. After Jacob died, Joseph's brothers were afraid that he would be mean to them for what they had done to him earlier.
2. Joseph's brothers asked for his forgiveness.
3. Joseph forgave his brothers and showed them kindness.
4. Joseph remained in Egypt and died there when he was very old.
5. Just before his death, Joseph asked that his bones be buried in Palestine.
6. God wants us to forgive others and treat them kindly.

Lesson Commentary

I. GOD'S CREATION POWER: JOB 38:1-7

A. Job's Ignorance: vss. 1-3

Then the LORD answered Job out of the storm. He said: "Who is this that darkens my counsel with words without knowledge? Brace yourself like a man; I will question you, and you shall answer me."

Job had complained about God being silent and aloof in the midst of his distress. Finally, "the LORD answered" (Job 38:1); but He did not appear in a vision, but rather spoke to Job out of a "storm"—perhaps a whirlwind not unlike the one that had killed Job's children (1:18-19). The storm is a common accompaniment for a divine manifestation (Ezek. 1:4; Nah. 1:3; Zech. 9:14).

No indication is given that Job actually saw the Lord, only that he heard God's voice. We can imagine how taken aback Job must have been. He probably did not expect God to speak to him in such a direct manner. The Lord initiated His speech by reminding Job of how he had questioned God's sense of justice. Though Job never cursed God, he had reached a point during his ordeal when the Lord seemed to be his enemy rather than his protector and provider. God immediately set him straight, asking him a rhetorical question that proved Job did not understand the divine plan for ordering the universe.

Job had presumed to question God's wisdom and purpose, even though the sufferer could only do so in "words without knowledge" (Job 38:2). God thus told Job to "gird up now thy loins" (vs. 3. KJV), an idiom that refers to taking the hem of a long garment or robe and pulling it up between one's legs and tucking it into the front of one's belt. This permitted easier and free movement of the legs.

B. The Earth's Foundations: vss. 4-7

"Where were you when I laid the earth's foundation? Tell me, if you understand. Who marked off its dimensions? Surely you know! Who stretched a measuring line across it? On what were its footings set, or who laid its cornerstone— while the morning stars sang together and all the angels shouted for joy?"

All of God's rhetorical questions focused on His awesome power, which contrasted with Job's limited strength and understanding. This statement reminds us that God has inherent characteristics or qualities that distinguish Him from His creation. One of His attributes is called omniscience, a term that literally refers to "all knowledge."

Scripture teaches that God has unlimited awareness, understanding, and insight. In other words, His knowledge and grasp of all things is universal and complete. His awareness is instantaneous, exhaustive, and absolutely correct. Even though all things are eternally present in God's view, He still recognizes them as successive, finite events in time.

The Lord is aware of every thought people have and every action they perform (1 Chron. 28:9). He can objectively and fairly evaluate the actions of people because He knows everything (1 Sam. 2:3). All wisdom and counsel reside with

Him (Job 12:13), and His understanding has no limit (Ps. 147:5). There is nothing in the entire universe that is hidden from God's sight. Everything is exposed by His penetrating gaze (Heb. 4:13).

God's awareness of all things serves two purposes. First, everyone is accountable to the Lord for his or her actions. Thus no one will be able to do evil and get away with it. Second, God's omniscience reminds us that He is intimately aware of our circumstances. He not only sees our plight but also reaches out in love to care for us (Gen. 16:13).

God's first queries to Job dealt with the creation of the earth in terms of constructing a building (Job 38:4-7). In Bible times, architects often based their structures on a foundation of stones. God demanded that Job tell Him where he was when God laid "earth's foundation" (vs. 4, NIV).

For measuring, builders would use a cord marked off in lengths. God wanted Job to tell Him who had measured the earth's "dimensions" (vs. 5). Builders preferred to lay their foundations on a firm base, and they would often use a large stone in the corner to anchor the whole building. God asked Job about the earth's "footings" (vs. 6) and "cornerstone."

Job did not even exist when God had established the earth at Creation. Other entities, however, were present. Verse 7 mentions the "morning stars," which possibly refers to angels under the imagery of stars or it may poetically include all creation. The "angels" are literally the "sons of God." Both groups cheered the Lord on as He created.

The description of the creation and the natural world in the Book of Job is harmonious with the Creation account in Genesis. Both portray God as the author and architect of the universe. Out of nothing, He created the light and the darkness, the dry land and the sea, the birds and the animals.

The Creation account found in Genesis and affirmed in Job is vastly different from other creation accounts, such as an ancient story of creation found in a Babylonian epic. In this tale, many gods appear along with monsters who have poison flowing through their veins instead of blood. The gods and monsters attack and kill each other, and the formation of the universe begins when the god Marduk kills the monster Timat.

II. GOD'S JUSTICE: JOB 40:7-9

"Brace yourself like a man; I will question you, and you shall answer me. Would you discredit my justice? Would you condemn me to justify yourself? Do you have an arm like God's, and can your voice thunder like his?"

Beginning in Job 40:7, the Lord interrogated Job about the moral aspects of how God ran the universe. Once again He spoke to Job from the midst of the storm, and once again God told His servant to prepare himself for a divine interrogation.

In verse 8, the Lord asked whether Job was going to "discredit [His] justice." In other words, was Job trying to make himself appear innocent by accusing God of unfairness? Job had not gone so far as to curse God, but Job had certainly called into question God's integrity, especially for allowing Job to suffer for no apparent reason. It was one thing for Job to claim his own integrity, but it was another matter altogether to nullify God's righteousness in the process.

God answered His own questions with more questions (vss. 9-14), with each one portraying attributes of God. In an almost mocking tone, God sought to adjust Job's attitude by asking him whether he thought he had "an arm like God's" (vs. 9) and a voice of "thunder." Job would come to see that he had assumed the role of being God's critic, which was almost like making himself equal or superior to the Lord.

III. Job's Confession: Job 42:1-6

A. Job's Lack of Understanding: vss. 1-3

Then Job replied to the LORD: "I know that you can do all things; no plan of yours can be thwarted. You asked, 'Who is this that obscures my counsel without knowledge?' Surely I spoke of things I did not understand, things too wonderful for me to know."

When God had finished speaking, it was Job's turn to respond (Job 42:1). He replied simply, without trying to indulge in fancy rhetoric, that he understood the message of God's speeches. For instance, Job realized that God is all-powerful and that nothing could oppose His "plan" (vs. 2). Here we see that, in God's strong hands, all things—even justice for the suffering—will be worked out eventually.

God wanted to know why Job had questioned His wisdom when His servant knew so little about things. Job, in response, confessed that he had spoken in ignorance. In fact, he tried to grasp issues that were "too wonderful" (vs. 3) for him to comprehend.

Here we see that, as Job came to the end of his ordeal, he had a moment of insight. He now realized that God is all-powerful and all-wise in ways that are unimpeachable and unfathomable. Job's awareness was not merely intellectual in nature. More importantly, he felt a sense of wonder after having nothing less than an awe-inspiring encounter with the living God.

This point is clear from the language Job used to describe his response. After hearing from God, Job realized that he had talked about matters that were far beyond his ability "to know." The Hebrew word translated "know" implies more than a grasp of information. It suggests intimate knowledge of the sort that comes by personal experience. In essence, Job was admitting that his previous remarks were nothing more than nonsense, for he really did not grasp or fathom the mysterious ways of God.

B. Job's Openness: vss. 4-5

"You said, 'Listen now, and I will speak; I will question you, and you shall answer me.' My ears had heard of you but now my eyes have seen you."

Job repeated God's injunction for him to listen and respond to His questions (Job 42:4). Job then confessed that he previously only had an indirect and incomplete knowledge of the Lord. Now, in this encounter with the divine, Job had seen God with his own "eyes" (vs. 5). This does not mean Job had seen the Lord in a vision; rather, Job simply meant that this experience of God was real and personal.

C. Job's Repentance: vs. 6

"Therefore I despise myself and repent in dust and ashes."

Job concluded with the statement, "I despise myself" (Job 42:6). This means he abhorred what he had said. He admitted that, in comparison with God, his own knowledge, self-assessment, and arguments were nonsense.

Job also repented by sitting "in dust and ashes." The statement "I . . . repent" should not be taken to be regret for the host of sins Job's friends had accused him of committing. After all, Job was correct in his opinion that his miserable condition was not a result of his sin. Also, he had learned from God that life and suffering are far more complex and mysterious than he or his friends had ever imagined.

In speaking of repentance, Job did not use the Hebrew term *shub*, which means "to turn back" or "to return." Instead, he used the word *nacham*, which means "to be sorry" or "to console oneself." The idea is that Job threw away his pretensions to wisdom and expressed his remorse by sitting in "dust and ashes." He found comfort in the knowledge that his sufferings were all part of the purposes of God, even if Job could not comprehend those purposes with his finite mind.

It is interesting to note that the Lord never did answer all of Job's questions, most noticeably the question about why the innocent suffer. Instead, God simply disclosed Himself as the source and master of all creation. Apparently this was sufficient for Job, for in the presence of the divine, he bowed and accepted God's mystery (vss. 1-6).

At this point, the Lord reinstated Job's former glory. Perhaps more importantly, God vindicated Job. His three friends and their simplistic wisdom were routed and profound insights into true wisdom received God's approval (vs. 8). In the epilogue of the book (vss. 7-17), the Lord reversed Job's situation and restored his blessings.

Concerning Job's three friends, Eliphaz, Bildad, and Zophar were sincere in their remarks and also sincerely wrong. It's true that their speeches contain numerous accurate statements. Nevertheless, they did not speak about God in a completely accurate way as they interacted with Job.

The book does not detail how the comments of the three were deficient. We can only imagine how difficult it was for them to grapple with tough issues and find an explanation for Job's troubles. Perhaps his friends were just trying to sound authoritative, to be seen as wise and powerful men, rather than simply admitting they had no answers and then caring for Job in his pain and sorrow. Regardless of the motives behind the misstatements of the three, God found them unacceptable. He thus instructed them to have Job offer a sacrifice to atone for their sin of misrepresenting him (vss. 7-8).

It is worth noting that, throughout most of his ordeal, Job did not get much support from his three friends. That's why they are remembered more for their condemnation, rather than their comfort, of Job. Nevertheless, the three friends started out with good intentions, and some of their actions serve as a useful pattern for intervening in the midst of a friend's distress.

For instance, the three came as a group to be with their friend, and they agreed ahead of time that they should come to Job's aid. Also, they wanted to mourn with him and comfort him. When the three could not recognize Job in his disfigured body, they openly wept with him (Job 2:12).

Job's friends tore their robes in anguish for him, which was customary in that day. They gave him their silent presence for seven days and were willing just to be with him (vs. 13). The three also refrained from speaking until Job first began to share his heart with them. They even listened patiently to Job's lament and frustration (chap. 3).

Discussion Questions

1. Why do you think God chose to answer Job "out of the storm" (Job 38:1)?
2. What was God's purpose in confronting Job with questions about the creation?
3. In what ways had Job questioned God's fairness and integrity?
4. What happened in Job's relationship with God that caused Job to repent?
5. How is it possible for us to grow in our knowledge of God when tragedy strikes?

Contemporary Application

God's emergence out of a whirlwind gave Job an answer to all his questions: trust the Lord regardless of the present circumstances. For Job to achieve godly wisdom, he had to simply trust in the almighty, infinite Creator, whose wisdom and ways were far beyond what he could imagine. In the end, all Job's understanding, reason, and doubt had to give way to faith.

In addition to teaching about God's nature and human suffering, the experience of Job brings to light a number of other applicational truths, including the following: there are matters going on in heaven with God that believers know nothing about, yet these matters affect their lives; even the best effort at explaining the issues of life can be useless; God's people do suffer, and bad things happen all the time to good people, so one cannot judge a person's spirituality by his or her successes or painful circumstances; though God seems far away, perseverance in faith is a most noble virtue, for the Lord is good and believers can safely leave their life in His hands; believers in the midst of suffering should not abandon God, but rather draw near to Him, so that out of this fellowship can come His comfort, even if there is no explanation for the hardship; and suffering may be intense, but it will ultimately end for the righteous, and God will spiritually bless them in abundance.

A Time for All Things

DEVOTIONAL READING

Psalm 1:1-6

DAILY BIBLE READINGS

Monday January 26
Genesis 8:15-22 God's Promise of Seasons

Tuesday January 27
Psalm 90:1-6 Human Time as Nothing to God

Wednesday January 28
Psalm 90:7-12 Teach Us to Count Our Days

Thursday January 29
Psalm 90:13-17 Prosper the Work of Our Hands

Friday January 30
Psalm 1:1-6 The Righteous Prosper, the Wicked Perish

Saturday January 31
Ecclesiastes 3:1-8 A Season for Everything

Sunday February 1
Ecclesiastes 3:9-15 God's Gift of Work

Scripture

Background Scripture: *Ecclesiastes 3:1-15*
Scripture Lesson: *Ecclesiastes 3:1-15*
Key Verse: *There is a time for everything, and a season for every activity under heaven.* Ecclesiastes 3:1.
Scripture Lesson for Children: *Esther 2:5-10, 15-17*
Key Verse for Children: *The king was attracted to Esther more than to any of the other women, . . . and made her queen.* Esther 2:17.

Lesson Aim

To find hope in God in the midst of life's good and bad moments.

Lesson Setting

Time: *970–930 B.C.*
Place: *Jerusalem*

Lesson Outline

A Time for All Things

  I. The Human Perspective: Ecclesiastes 3:1-8
 II. The Divine Perspective: Ecclesiastes 3:9-15
    A. *God's Plan: vss. 9-11*
    B. *God's Gifts: vss.12-13*
    C. *God's Sovereignty: vss. 14-15*

Introduction for Adults

Topic: *The Seasons of Life*

"My family is a wreck and I don't know what to do about it," the elderly widow cried to her pastor. From the woman's emotional state she could only see those things in life that had gone wrong. The widow felt helpless to bring about any changes for the better.

When life seems overwhelming to us, we are prone to depression, fear, worry, and despair. This woman was a firm believer in Christ, but she had been overcome by harmful events. Solomon reminded us that life includes the good and the bad, life and death, peace and war, building and tearing down (to name a few things).

Ultimately, in tough times, we are driven to the roots of our faith. We can pray and ask God to restore us spiritually and refresh us mentally. By means of Scripture reading, prayer, worship, and Christian fellowship we can find hope and peace in life's most difficult seasons.

Introduction for Youth

Topic: *Feel the Rhythm*

"Get off that treadmill and do some real walking," Joe yelled to his friend in the health club. Treadmills are handy devices for exercise. But to many people life itself seems like a treadmill. It's just like putting one foot down after the other.

The Book of Ecclesiastes reminds us that there are rhythms to life. The only way we can navigate safely through these times and changes—over which we have no control—is to trust in God's control of events. At times this might feel hard for us to do, but it nevertheless can be done.

Thus, when teens feel as if life has become a treadmill for them, they need to refocus the eyes of their faith on the Lord. He can enable them to find joy, satisfaction, and peace in the midst of troubling circumstances. Ultimately, their spiritual and mental health comes from loving and obeying the Lord.

Concepts for Children

Topic: *Esther Became Queen*

1. Esther, the cousin of a man named Mordecai, was taken to the palace of a king named Ahasuerus.
2. Esther made a good impression on the person who was in charge of the young women in the king's palace.
3. Mordecai told Esther not to tell anyone she was a Jew.
4. The time came for Esther to be presented to the king.
5. The king fell in love with Esther and made her queen.
6. When God gives us opportunities and responsibilities, we should accept them in faith and prayer.

Lesson Commentary

I. THE HUMAN PERSPECTIVE: ECCLESIASTES 3:1-8

There is a time for everything, and a season for every activity under heaven: a time to be born and a time to die, a time to plant and a time to uproot, a time to kill and a time to heal, a time to tear down and a time to build, a time to weep and a time to laugh, a time to mourn and a time to dance, a time to scatter stones and a time to gather them, a time to embrace and a time to refrain, a time to search and a time to give up, a time to keep and a time to throw away, a time to tear and a time to mend, a time to be silent and a time to speak, a time to love and a time to hate, a time for war and a time for peace.

The Book of Ecclesiastes belongs to what we call "wisdom literature," which was popular in ancient times. The writers' points do not seem to follow a logical plan, progression, or outline. The reasoning is often circular and repetitive, rather than linear and sequential.

With respect to this week's lesson, the term "Ecclesiastes" is the Greek translation of a Hebrew word that means "the teacher," "the preacher," or "the leader of the assembly." Ecclesiastes is exceptionally contemporary because the author, who was most likely King Solomon (1:1, 12), faced the same sorts of issues we do today. He considered those who lived in a humanly-centered manner and declared it was empty, meaningless, and filled with frustration (vs. 2).

Solomon was eminently qualified to expound on this matter, for he enjoyed enormous wealth and power. He also had all the material possessions he wanted. His testimony shreds the modern idea that we can find happiness and success in earthly things.

Solomon revealed that, when God gives meaning and purpose to life, we do not end up in cynicism and despair. Instead, God gives satisfaction and pleasure in our work, food, homes, and families. The Lord intends us to find our satisfaction ultimately in Him, not in anything the world has to offer. This is the same message we find revealed in the New Testament.

Ecclesiastes reminds us that emptiness and futility encompass all of life (vss. 2-11). Also, a candid assessment of human activity reveals that there is nothing new. Even the lofty goal of searching for wisdom apart from God is futile (vs. 18). These truths are underscored by the recurring phrase "under the sun" (vss. 3, 9, 14). It stands for everything in the world looked at from a purely human viewpoint.

Such things as wealth, status, and pleasure, when pursued apart from God, fail to satisfy (2:1-11). In the case of Solomon, he tried everything imaginable. He denied himself nothing (vs. 10). He concluded that, while it is better to be wise than foolish (vs. 13), death is the great equalizer of us all (vs. 16).

Unlike his pagan counterparts, however, Solomon recognized the difference God makes in everyday matters (vss. 24-26). We learn that meaning in life comes from trusting in and obeying God. We find satisfaction in His good and perfect will.

Solomon thought about the rhythm of the seasons and of the repetitive cycles of life. He declared that this was part of God's beautiful handiwork (3:11). When

Solomon reflected on life, he saw everything falling into a predictable pattern: a time and season for everything (vs. 1). God has ordained a time for practically everything. Our responsibility, as His faithful people, is to seek the Lord's wisdom so that we may discern what activities go with what seasons.

In addition to noting the regularity of the world in which we live, Solomon spoke about creation with magnificent, utter simplicity, giving one of the finest descriptions in all of world literature. Verses 2-8 list many of the activities that there are under heaven. We find here 14 pairs of opposites, which stand for all the activities of life.

As we read Solomon's thoughts, we find ourselves agreeing with his remarkable conciseness and brilliance, which he expressed poetically. Happiness and sadness are the extremes of each pair of contrasted events. In some cases the Teacher began with the happy, positive event; in others, with the sad, negative event.

Solomon first mentioned birth and death, which are the fundamental issues of life (vs. 2). We celebrate the birth of babies and grieve the loss of loved ones. Probably nothing draws us closer to life's essence than births and deaths. With them we encounter the really big questions of life: Where did we come from and where are we going? Is there any meaning to life and death? Ultimately, these events should draw us closer to each other and to God.

Solomon next looked at such common activities as planting (vs. 2) and building (vs. 3). These are positive, helpful, and necessary events. Tragically, however, people in their wickedness also uproot and tear down. History records the rise and fall of great empires, structures, and businesses. Many of the greatest enterprises no longer exist and new ones have risen to take their place.

Such calamities as murders and wars can brutalize our lives. But even these terrible events can also bring out the best in people, especially when they give themselves to healing and comfort, such as offering medicine, food, and shelter to the needy.

Death, uprooting, killing, and tearing down produce weeping and mourning (vs. 4). Solomon counterbalanced these dire thoughts by reminding his readers about the many opportunities people find to laugh and dance. Human experience would be bleak indeed without laughter and recreation to restore our minds, hearts, and souls after we suffer grievous losses.

Solomon considered the best and worst in human relationships (vs. 5). On the positive side, he saw the values in friendship and gathering stones; on the negative side, he spoke of enmity and scattering stones. Gathering stones probably refers to making the roads clear for a friendly army. The enemy, on the other hand, ruined fields by throwing stones over them.

Solomon had vast possessions that occupied his thoughts (vs. 6). He excelled in gaining and keeping treasures of all kinds (2:8). At the same time, he learned that treasures do not last and we have to give them away. That's the down side of great wealth.

Our lives often are split by unhappy events when we are torn from friends, loved ones, and possessions (3:7). But we receive great healing, or mending, from others and from seeking God's comfort and peace. Much of life is spent mending broken bodies and broken relationships.

Solomon noted that it's always wise to know when to keep silent and when to speak. Sometimes our silence is cowardly; at other times our speech is unseemly and hurtful. This aspect of life—the harmful use of our tongues—receives considerable attention in the Book of James.

The final couplet (Eccl. 3:8) contrasted love and hatred and war and peace. Much of our lives are absorbed by these contrasting situations. We pray for love and peace, but find ourselves consumed by hatred and wars that spill over and deeply touch our lives. We find it hard to admit that war is an escalation of personal hatred, which we sometimes accommodate and make excuses for.

II. THE DIVINE PERSPECTIVE: ECCLESIASTES 3:9-15

A. God's Plan: vss. 9-11

What does the worker gain from his toil? I have seen the burden God has laid on men. He has made everything beautiful in its time. He has also set eternity in the hearts of men; yet they cannot fathom what God has done from beginning to end.

Ecclesiastes 3:9-11 includes Solomon's commentary on the preceding thoughts he expressed about life. He followed the same positive-negative, optimistic-pessimistic counterbalances. He spoke of the hope introduced in 2:24-26, and also of the sobering realities of life expressed in 1:2—2:23.

Solomon regarded life apart from God as a burden that profits nothing (3:9-10). Solomon also saw the opposite, namely, the beauty of life when it is submissive to God's will. Although Solomon was realistic about the dark side of life, he could also consider the joy and goodness provided by the Lord.

Solomon then contemplated the hearts of people and found that, despite their frail, time-bound existence, they have "eternity" (vs. 11) in their hearts. We spend at least some time contemplating how our lives fit into God's eternal perspective, and this sets us apart from the animals.

We are different from such creatures as ferrets and foxes because we attempt to understand—through philosophy, theology, science, and ideology—the full scope of life. This search for meaning only frustrates us, however, because in our finite minds and hearts, we constantly discover anew that the whole picture of life on our planet eludes us. As a result, we must live by faith, not by sight (2 Cor. 5:7).

B. God's Gifts: vss. 12-13

I know that there is nothing better for men than to be happy and do good while they live. That everyone may eat and drink, and find satisfaction in all his toil—this is the gift of God.

Solomon finally reflected on God's good gifts to people. The king implied by his comments in Ecclesiastes 3:1 that the positives mentioned in verses 2-8 come from

God. In verses 12-13, Solomon further underscored God's providential care in providing for human happiness.

The Teacher explained his belief that, even though humanity carries a heavy burden as it toils day in and day out, there is still much in life to enjoy. Apparently one of Solomon's greatest yearnings—both for himself and for others—was that people might "be happy and do good while they live" (vs. 12). He said that a great source of contentment in life can be found in eating, drinking, and performing satisfying work (vs. 13). How can one find real contentment in the common activities of life? It's by believing that such a daily activity—indeed, all of life itself—is a gift of God.

C. God's Sovereignty: Ecclesiastes 3:14-15

I know that everything God does will endure forever; nothing can be added to it and nothing taken from it. God does it so that men will revere him. Whatever is has already been, and what will be has been before; and God will call the past to account.

Solomon found peace in God's sovereignty. The Lord's work is settled "forever" (Eccl. 3:14). Nothing can change it, and no one can add to it or subtract from it. The creator God sustains lives according to His will and power.

The great blessing of reflecting on God's sovereignty comes when we worship the Lord. His eternal plan is intended to drive us to Him in worship, praise, reverence, adoration, and obedience. We do not live according to blind fate, but according to God's wise and loving plan. Thus, Christians are not fatalists, for they believe in a personal God.

God's work is unchangeable, and His plans will not fail. His works are effective and complete, and His actions are totally secure. Solomon saw the great need to revere such an awesome God (3:14; 5:7; 12:13).

In 3:15, Solomon noted that God oversees the changing seasons of life. Instead of falling into despair, we rejoice in hope, for we know the God who controls all things. On the one hand, we are accountable to Him for all that we think, say, and do in life. On the other hand, He will not overlook our lives of faith and eternally bless us for worshiping and serving Him.

Discussion Questions

1. What role does God take in the ordering of life's events?
2. What place does birth and death as well as happiness and pain have in the unfolding drama of life?
3. What benefit is there to laboring and toiling throughout one's life?
4. Why is it best to order the priorities of one's life around God's will and precepts?
5. How can we encourage our loved ones to make God the center of their life?

Contemporary Application

Ecclesiastes presents the reflections of a person who boldly faced the complex questions of life, only to conclude in the end that true meaning and joy come from

God. The human author prefaced his treatise with the statement "Meaningless! Meaningless!" (Eccl. 1:2). Indeed, he carried this sentiment throughout the book.

The answer to this cry of despair does not become clear until the book's conclusion, in which the writer declared that, to discover meaning and wisdom, people must "Fear God and keep his commandments" (12:13). In fact, everything in Ecclesiastes must be seen within the framework of these opening and closing statements. From this perspective the book proves to be a brilliant, inspired discourse that should encourage believers to work diligently toward a God-centered view of life.

The author of Ecclesiastes examined the things that human beings live for, including wisdom, pleasure, work, progress, and wealth; and yet, no matter what they attempt to attain in life, they all meet the same destiny—they die and are forgotten by others. In that way, the author did not try to hide the futility that people face. Indeed, he emphasized that all the goals of human beings have limitations—even wisdom. Thus it is useless for them to seek to master their own destiny.

There is, however, an underlying hope in the book. Although every human striving will eventually fail, God's purposes will never fail. Through the experience of one who seemed to have tried everything, the author concluded, based on his faith in the Lord, that God had ordered life according to His own purposes. Therefore, the best thing a person can do is to accept and enjoy life as God has given it.

A Time to Remember

DEVOTIONAL READING

Psalm 143:1-8

DAILY BIBLE READINGS

Monday February 2
Psalm 63:1-8 I Have Beheld Your Power and Glory

Tuesday February 3
Psalm 77:4-10 I Consider the Days of Old

Wednesday February 4
Psalm 77:11-15 I Will Remember Your Wonders

Thursday February 5
Psalm 143:1-8 I Think about All Your Deeds

Friday February 6
Ecclesiastes 11:1-5 God's Work is a Mystery

Saturday February 7
Ecclesiastes 11:6-10 Youth Is Fleeting

Sunday February 8
Ecclesiastes 12:1-8 Remember Your Creator

Scripture

Background Scripture: *Ecclesiastes 11:7—12:8*

Scripture Lesson: *Ecclesiastes 11:7—12:8*

Key Verse: *Remember your Creator in the days of your youth, before the days of trouble come.* Ecclesiastes 12:1.

Scripture Lesson for Children: *Esther 4:5-8, 13-16*

Key Verse for Children: *"When this is done, I will go to the king, even though it is against the law. And if I perish, I perish."* Esther 4:16.

Lesson Aim

To find the answer to life's changes in our faith in God.

Lesson Setting

Time: *970–930 B.C.*

Place: *Jerusalem*

Lesson Outline

A Time to Remember

   I. Enjoy Life: Ecclesiastes 11:7-10
     A. *Sunny and Dark Days: vss. 7-8*
     B. *Freedom and Judgment: vss. 9-10*
  II. Remember God: Ecclesiastes 12:1-8
     A. *The Best Time: vs. 1*
     B. *The Worst Time: vss. 2-5*
     C. *Before the End: vss. 6-7*
     D. *Conclusion: vs. 8*

Introduction for Adults

Topic: *Change Comes to All*

Solomon was not bashful about old age and death. He evidently enjoyed the days of his youth, but he made no efforts to minimize the signs of failing mental and physical health. We cannot read his description recorded in Ecclesiastes 12:1-8 without a twinge of sadness and even fear, for we know we cannot escape this same end.

More importantly, sometimes we try to ignore the warning signs of spiritual decline and death. Jesus told us quite plainly that our souls are priceless. We cannot give anything in exchange for them. Therefore, the best way to prepare for the inevitability of death is to make sure we have trusted in Christ for salvation. Without His forgiveness, we are eternally lost. But through faith in Him, we have eternal life and hope.

Introduction for Youth

Topic: *Now Is The Time*

As Christians, we want our lives to count for something. If we drink heavily at the well of worldly philosophy, however, we will be led to think that everything in life is relative and fleeting. We supposedly should live it up, knowing that there is no life after death. Such notions stand opposed to the teachings of God's Word, and thus are to be rejected. There is life after death, and the decisions we make now will have eternal ramifications.

If we want our lives to have everlasting significance, we must commit ourselves wholeheartedly to the cause of Christ. This includes not only trusting in Him for salvation but also willingly serving Him regardless of the circumstances. As Scripture reveals, faithful service to the Lord brings rich and everlasting blessings.

Concepts for Children

Topic: *Esther Showed Courage*

1. Esther was told about the order the king had signed for the destruction of the Jews.
2. Mordecai urged Esther to plead on behalf of her people in the presence of the king.
3. Mordecai warned Esther that she could not escape danger just because she was in the king's palace.
4. Mordecai suggested that God had placed Esther in the king's palace for this important time.
5. Esther asked Mordecai to have the people go without food for a period of time, especially as the queen prepared to risk her own life by going to the king.
6. We can thank God for friends who will stand with us when we face a difficult situation.

Lesson Commentary

I. ENJOY LIFE: ECCLESIASTES 11:7-10

A. Sunny and Dark Days: vss. 7-8

Light is sweet, and it pleases the eyes to see the sun. However many years a man may live, let him enjoy them all. But let him remember the days of darkness, for they will be many. Everything to come is meaningless.

Ecclesiastes 11 opens with more proverbs, some of these giving examples of how we need to prepare and act in order to realize the results we desire. Of course, room must always be left for failure even with the best preparations and actions. Risks abound in this uncertain world. But just as we raise a child not knowing how he or she was formed in the womb, so we are to seek to do God's will even though we don't understand His ways.

Solomon evidently realized that he was coming to the end of his words, for in the second half of chapter 11 he began to move into his closing statements. At this point in his teaching, he looked back to his youth at the beginning of his life and then ahead to old age at the end. He taught that young people should enjoy their lives while the light of the sun is still bright and "sweet" (vs. 7).

No one knows how long the sun's light will shine on his or her life; therefore, all people should seek to enjoy each day (vs. 8). We are not to live naively, however. We are to live with the mature awareness that into every life there comes darkness and death. For many, regrettably, this makes their lives seem meaningless. But for those whose lives are centered on God, this sobering knowledge will merely add depth to their living.

B. Freedom and Judgment: vss. 9-10

Be happy, young man, while you are young, and let your heart give you joy in the days of your youth. Follow the ways of your heart and whatever your eyes see, but know that for all these things God will bring you to judgment. So then, banish anxiety from your heart and cast off the troubles of your body, for youth and vigor are meaningless.

Based on what the Teacher had said thus far, his advice to young people was to "be happy" (Eccl. 11:9). In fact, he encouraged youthful members of his audience to be joyful and "follow the ways of your heart and whatever your eyes see."

Perhaps at first glance this advice might seem to be advocating hedonism (idolizing pleasure), or at least giving youth a license for immorality. But that was certainly not Solomon's intent. He tempered his advice with a sobering reminder: "Know that for all these things God will bring you to judgment." Expressed differently, young people are encouraged to be free and joyful as long as their behavior is within the context of moral responsibility.

As youths pursue their God-given freedom and joy, they are to put aside worries and anxiety and do away with "all the troubles of your body" (vs. 10). By God's grace, the young can enjoy life this way, because before they realize it, their youthfulness will be gone. In that sense, youth is meaningless, for it does not have lasting value. From this we can see that what we believe and how we behave make an eternal difference. Our goals in life should not be dictated by what the world thinks; rather, they should be based on the teachings of God's Word.

II. REMEMBER GOD: ECCLESIASTES 12:1-8

A. The Best Time: vs. 1

Remember your Creator in the days of your youth, before the days of trouble come and the years approach when you will say, "I find no pleasure in them"—

Perhaps the highlight of Solomon's advice to the young is to "remember your Creator" (Eccl. 12:1). Once again the Teacher did not want his audience to assume that freedom and joy could be equated with lawlessness and folly. Solomon's advice did not mean that they could forget their Creator. It meant that they were to combine freedom and joy with moral responsibility in order to make the most out of life.

Thus the Book of Ecclesiastes reminds young people today that the farther they move away from God, the farther away they move from the solutions to life's problems. Solomon would have had adolescents wake up to this truth while they are still young.

The Teacher went on to say that the onset of old age is an especially good reason why people need to remember their Creator while they are still young. Days of trouble are coming, Solomon promised, days when old age will make it more difficult to participate and find pleasure in life. Thus the Lord wants us to learn to live for Him early in life, to begin exercising our faith when we are young, so that we can give Him our best and enjoy all the wonders of living.

B. The Worst Time: vss. 2-5

Before the sun and the light and the moon and the stars grow dark, and the clouds return after the rain; when the keepers of the house tremble, and the strong men stoop, when the grinders cease because they are few, and those looking through the windows grow dim; when the doors to the street are closed and the sound of grinding fades; when men rise up at the sound of birds, but all their songs grow faint; when men are afraid of heights and of dangers in the streets; when the almond tree blossoms and the grasshopper drags himself along and desire no longer is stirred. Then man goes to his eternal home and mourners go about the streets.

Having made the transition from advice for the young to a portrayal of what our elderly years are like, the Teacher then elaborated, describing old age in some of the most beautiful and yet sorrowful poetry in literature (Eccl. 12:2-8). Not everyone in our age of modern medicine will experience the drastic loss of faculties described here, but the point is clear. In old age we are not what we used to be.

First, Solomon characterized old age as being like the clouds that return to darken the sky after it has rained. This darkness is in contrast to the light given off by the sun, moon, and stars (vs. 2). The next series of images (vss. 3-4) can be taken at two levels. On a more literal level, when old age comes, those who work as house servants are not as strong. Indeed, they become shaky and bent. Long time grinders of grain have to stop their work because their eyesight grows dim. Even the sleep of the elderly is not always peaceful. Though they close up their houses at night, their sleep does not last as long because they are awakened by the first song of the birds—and that despite the fact that their hearing has faded.

Some Bible interpreters believe these two verses were meant to be metaphorical, presenting images referring to the decay of old age. Thus the housekeepers are thought to refer to the arms and hands. The grinders represent teeth, and "those looking through the windows" (vs. 3) are the eyes. The "doors to the street" (vs. 4) refers to the loss of hearing, and the birds singing in the morning to an elderly person's faint voice.

Verse 5 presents two literal images followed by three metaphors from nature. The Teacher apparently considered the fear of heights and the fear of busy streets as natural fears of the elderly. "When the almond tree blossoms" most likely refers to when the hair of an old person turns white. Though the base of the petals on a blossoming bitter almond tree turn pink, the outer tips turn white, making the entire tree appear white. The comparison of old age to a grasshopper that drags itself along the group probably symbolizes the immobility of old age, when one is not able to move as quickly as before.

The Hebrew word translated "desire" refers literally to the caper berry, an obscure fruit thought in ancient times to stimulate sexual desire. The same word, however, was used in several references to an appetizer, perhaps suggesting that the desire mentioned here is for food. In either case, the image reflects an old person's declining appetites. When people reach this point in life, they are close to dying and going to their eternal home. Solomon made reference to mourners who wandered through the streets, wailing in grief for the person who had died.

C. Before the End: vss. 6-7

Remember him—before the silver cord is severed, or the golden bowl is broken; before the pitcher is shattered at the spring, or the wheel broken at the well, and the dust returns to the ground it came from, and the spirit returns to God who gave it.

Solomon urged his readers, before they reached an infirm point in their lives, to remember their Creator (Eccl. 12:6). Like the poetic images of verses 3 and 4, those recorded in verse 6 are interpreted in at least two ways. In either case, these images are impressions of total collapse. The silver wire from which the golden lamp hangs is snapped, and the lamp itself (representing life) is broken. The clay pitcher is smashed so that it can no longer carry the water of life. Even the wooden waterwheel that drew the water has been broken.

According to another interpretation, the silver cord is the human spine, while the lamp is the head. The pitcher is the heart, which will no longer carry life-giving blood, and the wheel represents the lungs (carrying air), the heart (carrying blood), or the organs of digestion.

Having used imagery to describe the inevitable death of people, Solomon then showed the ultimate results of the breakdown of the body. In death, the original components, or "the dust" (vs. 7), will return "to the ground it came from." At the same time, the spirit, or soul, "returns to God who gave it."

D. Conclusion: vs. 8

"Meaningless! Meaningless!" says the Teacher. "Everything is meaningless!"

All his talk about decline and death must have depressed the Teacher, for he cried "Meaningless! Meaningless!" (Eccl. 12:8), just as he had done at the beginning of his monologue (1:2). Nevertheless, there was still more for Solomon to say. Next, he would bring his address to a close by revealing the purpose of humanity.

Most of the Book of Ecclesiastes is a first-person recording of Solomon's own experiences and thoughts. Beginning in 12:9, however, the point of view shifts suddenly. Here the writer gave a positive recommendation about the teachings contained in this book. The recommendation tells us that, though the Teacher examined life skeptically, he was not a cynic or a hedonist. God was real to Solomon, despite his many questions, and he knew that God cared for His people and would fulfill His will in the end.

Solomon concluded his philosophical treatise by noting that, if we really want to know how to live in a world that is unjust and meaningless, we are compelled to "fear God and keep his commandments" (vs. 13). As a matter of fact, that is our entire duty. The reason to pursue this duty is that, despite the endless cycle of history, despite the evil and greed, despite even death, what we do in life does matter. We know this is true, for God cares enough to judge our every thought and action (vs. 14). Thus the foolish, vain, and wicked things we have done will come before God's eyes for judgment. But so also will the kind, good, and gentle acts we have done.

This, then, is how Solomon brought to an end his teaching about life. He had proven that, although human efforts seem to lack value, we should enjoy life in the fear of the Lord, whose first gift to us is life itself. We are reminded of Paul's corresponding statement of hope recorded in 1 Corinthians 15:58, "Always give yourselves fully to the work of the Lord, because you know that your labor in the Lord is not in vain."

Discussion Questions

1. Why did the Teacher urge his readers to rejoice in the years of life God gives?
2. Why does life sometimes seem so fleeting?
3. How did the writer depict the onslaught of old age?
4. What happens to one's body and spirit at death?
5. How can we be good stewards of the blessings in life we receive from God?

Contemporary Application

The years of life can be compared to the times of the day—the morning hours when the sun is bright and life seems exciting, the heat of the day when the pressures of living bear down, and the gathering shadows of the evening that point toward the sunset of life. The Teacher's advice was to take advantage of the years of one's youth and relish the blessings and enjoyment they bring. At the same time, we need to be aware that God will hold us accountable for the way in which we have conducted ourselves.

We learn from the writings of Solomon that the time will come when the things that seemed very important in the earlier years of life begin to lose their appeal. The natural weaknesses that accompany old age will demand increased attention. The eyes will grow dim, the ears will become hard of hearing, and the mere task of living will seem more and more like a burden. Remembering the joyful days of youth when the body was strong and the spirit was alive will lessen the heaviness of heart and enable us to grow old gracefully.

Despite the fact that so many things the Teacher said were sobering, he did not end his book with a fatalistic view of life. It's true that the physical body will inevitably return to the dust from which it was made; but the writer noted that death is not the end of one's existence. The spirit that enlivened one's physical body will return to God, who breathes life into every person.

A Time for Love

DEVOTIONAL READING

Jeremiah 31:1-5

DAILY BIBLE READINGS

Monday February 9
Psalm 18:1-6 I Love You, O Lord

Tuesday February 10
Deuteronomy 6:4-9 A Commandment to Love God

Wednesday February 11
John 15:8-12 Love Others as Christ Loves Us

Thursday February 12
John 15:13-17 No Greater Love

Friday February 13
Jeremiah 31:1-5 God's Everlasting Love

Saturday February 14
Song of Songs 2:8-13 A Song of Love

Sunday February 15
Song of Songs 7:10-12; 8:6-7 Love Is Strong as Death

Scripture

Background Scripture: *Song of Songs 2:8-13; 7:10-12; 8:6-7*

Scripture Lesson: *Song of Songs 2:8-13; 7:10-12; 8:6-7*

Key Verse: *Place me like a seal over your heart, like a seal on your arm; for love is as strong as death, its jealousy unyielding as the grave. It burns like blazing fire, like a mighty flame.* Song of Songs 8:6.

Scripture Lesson for Children: *Esther 5:3-8; 7:1-3*

Key Verse for Children: *"Grant me my life—this is my petition. And spare my people—this is my request."* Esther 7:3.

Lesson Aim

To discover and enjoy all the beauty of love in God's will.

Lesson Setting

Time: *970–930 B.C.*

Place: *Jerusalem*

Lesson Outline

A Time for Love

  I. Love Refreshed: Song of Songs 2:8-13
     A. *The Lover's Virtues: vss. 8-9a*
     B. *The Lover's Entreaties: vss. 9b-13*
  II. Love Fulfilled: Song of Songs 7:10-12
 III. Love Sealed: Song of Songs 8:6-7

Introduction for Adults

Topic: *The Joy and Wonder of Love*

Nowhere is the joy and wonder of love better described than in the Song of Songs. The poem's beauty, respect for God's gift of love and physical intimacy in marriage, and its honest descriptions in powerful images stand in sharp contrast to the way contemporary culture talks about such matters.

Sadly, too many marriages grow stale and flounder on the lack of genuine intimacy. We need to renew the wonder and joy of love in our marriage relationships. We need to talk frankly about these matters with our children, especially those who are junior and senior high students.

Song of Songs opens the door to a wide range of possibilities and applications. This simple yet dramatic love ballad can change us for the better and give us a new appreciation for God's gift of love.

Introduction for Youth

Topic: *What Does Love Have to Do with It?*

Teens will be especially drawn to the subject matter of the Song of Songs. Whereas the other songs of Solomon covered a broad range of themes, this poem is specifically about love. Young people are able to appreciate the way the ballad portrays love's subtlety and mystery, its beauty and pleasures, and its captivation and enchantment.

Teens will benefit from learning that the Song of Songs reveals the romantic feelings of a woman and a man. The ballad also portrays the power of love. In fact, in this poem the power of love is shown to rival the strength of death itself. Thus one of the main lessons for teens to learn from a study of this book is that God intends for powerful love to be a hallmark of a marital relationship.

Concepts for Children

Topic: *Esther Made a Wise Request*

1. The king welcomed Esther into his presence and asked what she wanted from him.
2. Esther, in response, invited the king and an official named Haman to a special meal Esther was preparing.
3. While the king and Haman were at the special meal, the king again asked Esther what she wanted from him.
4. Esther, in response, invited the king and Haman to another special meal and promised to give the king her request at that time.
5. At the second special meal, Esther asked the king to spare the lives of her people.
6. It requires courage and wisdom for us to serve God.

Lesson Commentary

I. Love Refreshed: Song of Songs 2:8-13

A. The Lover's Virtues: vss. 8-9

Listen! My lover! Look! Here he comes, leaping across the mountains, bounding over the hills. My lover is like a gazelle or a young stag.

The Song of Songs (sometimes called the Song of Solomon) is love poetry filled with similes and metaphors. The singers are the bride and bridegroom, the beloved and her lover. Their songs are interspersed with songs of their friends. Since God is not mentioned in the Song of Songs, we must think carefully about His place in courtship and marriage according to New Testament principles.

Some Bible commentators take this love ballad as a picture of the relationship between Christ and His bride, the church. As we read this poem, we can see some parallels. However, in this study, we are focusing our comments on the relationship between the lover and his beloved, which is celebrated in very explicit terms.

The bride was identified as a Shulammite (6:13), a dark-skinned country girl (1:6). She was brought to the palace to become the bride of King Solomon (vs. 4). We have no details about their courtship. Their songs began with her introduction to the court from which she celebrated his love and name. Their songs fit the character and customs of an ancient Middle Eastern wedding. Brides commonly were in their teens.

It will help if we try to catch the spirit of the occasion and contemplate the intimate dialogue between the bride and bridegroom. They described their love in the colorful imagery of King Solomon's time. In anticipation of their union, it was important for her to recall their young love. She celebrated her lover's physical and moral qualities.

The bride used many word pictures to describe their relationship (vss. 12-14). As a point of clarification, women wore small perfume pouches around their necks, and henna blossoms were thought to be the most beautiful flowers. As the two sang to each other, they rejoiced in the beauty that had attracted them to one another (vss. 15-17).

In chapter 2, we find the couple's first extended conversation. We note how much freer they were to express their feelings than during their first days at the palace. At this stage, their songs are relatively brief. After a concise interchange (vss. 1-2), the beloved gave an extended picture of her lover (vss. 3-7). She described the pleasures she enjoyed in his presence and expressed her needs and desires.

The bride sang about their pleasant country place on a gorgeous spring day and extolled her lover's virtues. She compared her lover to both a speedy gazelle and a powerful stag. She saw him leaping over the mountains, as it were. His youth and virility entranced her (vss. 8-9). In this poetic imagery we can see how the bride admired the groom's qualities. She was not ashamed to picture him in terms that reflected her own life in the country. For instance, gazelles and stags were highly regarded wild animals.

B. The Lover's Entreaties: vss. 9b-13

Look! There he stands behind our wall, gazing through the windows, peering through the lattice. My lover spoke and said to me, "Arise, my darling, my beautiful one, and come with me. See! The winter is past; the rains are over and gone. Flowers appear on the earth; the season of singing has come, the cooing of doves is heard in our land. The fig tree forms its early fruit; the blossoming vines spread their fragrance. Arise, come, my darling; my beautiful one, come with me."

The bride remembered how her lover had first approached her dwelling. She remembered his shyness, hiding behind her wall, then sneaking up to her house and looking into the windows for her. Perhaps he had first knocked on her door, and getting no response, he had decided to look for her because he was so eager to see her (S. of S. 2:9).

The bride recalled how the bridegroom had entreated her to come away with him (vs. 10). She described how he had wooed her. He had not only used words of endearment ("my darling"), but also emphasized their personal relationship ("come with me").

The bride remembered the bridegroom's words with deep appreciation. His words had attracted her, reminding us of the power of words in building lasting love relationships. Using words to express our love is an important skill to develop.

In this case, Solomon had entreated her with pictures of the lovely spring weather (vss. 11-13). Winter was over, bad weather was gone, and the flowers were blooming. Doves were cooing and the fig trees were pushing out their fragrant blossoms.

Is it true that in spring a young man's fancy turns to love? That's what the poets say, and Solomon made the most of it. The beauty of the land matched the beauty of their love. Of course, nature by itself cannot maintain love, but often it inspires love. We have to build our love on more than flowers, birds, and trees, but God in His wisdom and love uses these things to enhance our human relationships. He lifts our hearts with the glories of His creation.

II. LOVE FULFILLED: SONG OF SONGS 7:10-12

I belong to my lover, and his desire is for me. Come, my lover, let us go to the countryside, let us spend the night in the villages. Let us go early to the vineyards to see if the vines have budded, if their blossoms have opened, and if the pomegranates are in bloom—there I will give you my love.

The songs continued through a variety of settings and experiences. The bride sang about her longings for her lover, and in her dream she feared that she had lost him (S. of S. 3). How delighted she was when she awoke to the reality of her bridegroom's wedding procession.

We are allowed to share the bridegroom's song as he sings to his bride on their wedding night (chap. 4). He sang about her beauty and his passion for her. Then we encounter the songs of the beloved's distress because some distance has entered their relationship and she feared losing her husband (chap. 5). But the lovers found each other and once again rhapsodized about their love and passion (chap. 6).

Chapter 7 reminds us of Solomon's statement that there is "a time to embrace" (Eccl. 3:5). The couple's words reveal how much the lover and his beloved enjoyed the deeper levels of fulfilled physical intimacy. They sang openly—without blushing—about the pleasures they found in each other, but never in a lewd, depraved way.

The lover's sentiments began in Song of Songs 6:13 and concluded with 7:9, "and your mouth like the best wine." His beloved responded: "May the wine go straight to my lover, flowing gently over lips and teeth." The groom had discovered the wisdom of Proverbs 5:18: "May you rejoice in the wife of your youth."

The bride responded to her lover's affection and found joy in his desire for her (S. of S. 7:10). She realized that she could find satisfaction in his compassion for her. Earlier she had sung, "My lover is mine and I am his" (2:16), and "I am my lover's and my lover is mine" (6:3). These subtle differences indicate mutual commitment, not domination by one party over the other. Paul wrote, "The husband should fulfill his marital duty to his wife, and likewise the wife to her husband" (1 Cor. 7:3).

The bride loved the groom and vice versa. She acknowledged the beauty of his desire and saw nothing offensive in his approach to her. She invited him to join her in the villages of the countryside and to the blooming vineyards (S. of S. 7:11-12). This was her metaphor for his enjoyment of her body (4:16; 6:2-3).

To this point, the bridegroom had initiated their expressions of affection. This is the first time the bride had done so. In their growing love, she found the security to give him her tender invitation to enjoy her caresses.

The bride said the time for intimacy was right because the evidence in nature was present. "Mandrakes" (7:13) were ancient aphrodisiacs. The very air incited the wife to give herself to her husband. This remarkably candid and beautiful scene shows how their love had matured.

III. LOVE SEALED: SONG OF SONGS 8:6-7

Place me like a seal over your heart, like a seal on your arm; for love is as strong as death, its jealousy unyielding as the grave. It burns like blazing fire, like a mighty flame. Many waters cannot quench love; rivers cannot wash it away. If one were to give all the wealth of his house for love, it would be utterly scorned.

The love song of the bride and groom climaxes in Song of Songs 8:6-7, which is among the finest portrayals of affection ever written. These verses are part of a series of short reprises leading to the ballad's conclusion.

The bride asked her bridegroom to place her like a seal over his heart and arm (vs. 6). The seal was a legal sign of ownership. They were engraved in stone or metal. She wanted him to acknowledge openly that she belonged to him. His heart represented his emotions and his arm stood for his strength.

The bride used powerful figures of speech to define her love. It was "strong as death" (vs. 6). The Hebrew term can mean either an irresistible assailant or an immovable defense. In the words of 1 Corinthians 13:8, "Love never fails."

Love's "jealousy" (S. of S. 8:6) is as "unyielding as the grave." This is jealousy in the right sense, not the evil sense. It means her rightful claim of possession. "Death . . . grave" show that just as the grave does not yield the dead, so her bridegroom will not give up his bride.

Love burns with such power that not even rivers of water can quench it (vs. 7). No amount of money could purchase the kind of love the bride shared with her bridegroom. We cannot buy another person's love.

These verses show how the couple's understanding of love has matured. Their love was more than the temporal arousal of passion. Its depth superseded even the depth of their physical intimacy. Their affection would endure long after their passion's flames had subsided. Their unquenchable flame "always protects, always trusts, always hopes, always perseveres" (1 Cor. 13:7).

Discussion Questions

1. How did the Shulammite woman describe her suitor in Song of Songs 2:8-9?
2. What indications of mutual affection are evident from the statements recorded in 2:10-13?
3. How strong was the desire of the bride and groom for one another?
4. What did the bride think would quench the love she and her husband had for each other?
5. How can married couples keep the ardor of their affection vibrant throughout the years of marriage?

Contemporary Application

In the Song of Songs, Solomon painted a picture of true chivalry, especially as he described the manner in which the suitor approached the maiden whom he desired to court. He did not approach her presumptuously, but courteously asked whether he might spend time with her. Because of the way the Shulammite woman described Solomon's conduct, we can be sure that she was favorably impressed. They had passed through the winter of adjusting to each other. Now the cold winds and rain were gone and the springtime had arrived. It was time to move forward in the relationship.

Once the period of courtship was completed, friends of the bride and groom had shown their excitement and concern for the couple, and the marriage had taken place, it was time for the honeymoon. The hectic pace that accompanies courtship and preparations for marriage can be physically and emotionally exhausting for any newly wedded couple. They must spend time alone, getting to know each other. They do so in the midst of God's blessing on their lives.

It seems that with each passing generation, the marriage vows become less and less significant. The soaring divorce rate reflects the lack of seriousness with which the marriage vows are taken. In contrast, the young couple in our biblical poem are so deeply in love and consider their vows so seriously that they are convinced no amount of earthly wealth could replace it (S. of S. 8:7). The young woman wanted her beloved to let her be as a seal upon his heart (vs. 6), as if one would affix an official seal to a document. The strength of their relationship was in their love for one another. Not even the raging waters could extinguish their affection.

Whatever we think of the parallel made between the lovers of the Song of Songs and Christ and the church, we can receive the overarching applicational message of God's love in our own lives. In this ballad, the bride called the husband to lasting love and contentment. In the Book of Revelation, the Spirit and the bride called for anyone who is thirsty to come (22:17). We are the thirsty ones, and God calls us to respond to His invitation to love Him with all our heart, mind, and soul. If we respond by running to Him in faith, He will quench our thirst with everlasting life and blessings.

A Time for Courage

DEVOTIONAL READING

Psalm 27:1-8

DAILY BIBLE READINGS

Monday February 16
Acts 4:13-22 Council Sees Disciples' Boldness

Tuesday February 17
Acts 4:23-31 A Prayer for Boldness

Wednesday February 18
Psalm 27:1-8 Whom Shall I Fear?

Thursday February 19
Esther 3:1-6 Mordecai Will Not Bow

Friday February 20
Esther 4:1-5 Mordecai Grieves for His People

Saturday February 21
Esther 4:6-11 Esther Called Upon to Show Courage

Sunday February 22
Esther 4:12-17 Esther Prepares to Plead the Cause

Scripture

Background Scripture: *Esther 3—4*
Scripture Lesson: *Esther 3:2-3; 5-6a; 4:7-16*
Key Verse: *"I will go to the king, even though it is against the law. And if I perish, I perish."* Esther 4:16.
Scripture Lesson for Children: *Esther 8:1-5, 14-16*
Key Verse for Children: *In every province and in every city, . . . there was joy and gladness among the Jews, with feasting and celebrating.* Esther 8:17.

Lesson Aim

To find resources in God for the courage we need to serve Him faithfully.

Lesson Setting

Time: *486–465 B.C.*
Place: *Susa, capital of the Persian Empire*

Lesson Outline

A Time for Courage

   I. Haman's Plot: Esther 3:2-3, 5-6a
      A. Mordecai's Refusal: vss. 2-3
      B. Haman's Revenge: vss. 5-6a
  II. Mordecai's Challenge: Esther 4:7-16
      A. Mordecai's Request: vss. 7-8
      B. Esther's Answer: vss. 9-11
      C. Mordecai's Insistence: vss. 12-14
      D. Esther's Response: vss. 15-16

Introduction for Adults

Topic: *Courage to Risk All*

Adults are often concerned more with personal matters than with those of their neighbors. That is why this has been called the "me" generation. We are told that in order to get ahead in life, we must aggressively push ourselves forward—"No one is gong to look out for me but me."

This week's lesson indicates, however, that we should not ignore the concerns of others. Success is not defined in terms of making our own decisions, receiving no help from anyone else, and offering no help to others; rather, the biblical view of success is one of reaching out to others in need and putting them first before ourselves. After all, this reflects the way God has treated His people throughout history.

Introduction for Youth

Topic: *Stand Up!*

Harry thought he was the only Christian in his university class. One day an especially critical professor began to attack Christians and their beliefs. He asked whether anyone in his class believed what Christianity taught. Harry looked around when he gingerly raised his hand and was delighted to see another fellow raise his, too. They became good friends and mutual encouragers.

Neither one risked their lives by raising their hands, but they risked experiencing ridicule. Sometimes in high school and college that can be the hardest thing to take. Nevertheless, by taking a stand for our faith, we help others to consider their own faith or lack of it.

Generally, people respect Christians who make their beliefs clear with love and tact. And our fears of ridicule and persecution seldom materialize.

Concepts for Children

Topic: *Esther's Wisdom Was Rewarded*

1. King Ahasuerus gave Esther the property that once belonged to Haman.
2. The king gave Haman's special ring to Mordecai, and Esther placed Mordecai in charge of Haman's property.
3. Esther asked the king to put an end to the evil plan that Haman had made.
4. Esther asked the king to send a letter throughout the nation giving the Jews permission to protect themselves.
5. The Jews rejoiced when they received the good news contained in the letter.
6. God will remain with us even when life seems overwhelming.

Lesson Commentary

I. HAMAN'S PLOT: ESTHER 3:2-3, 5-6A

A. Mordecai's Refusal: vss. 2-3

All the royal officials at the king's gate knelt down and paid honor to Haman, for the king had commanded this concerning him. But Mordecai would not kneel down or pay him honor. Then the royal officials at the king's gate asked Mordecai, "Why do you disobey the king's command?"

Esther is the exciting account of a wicked plot to wipe out the entire Jewish community during the reign of the Persian King Xerxes (Ahasuerus). The book may be divided into three parts. The first section deals with the *plight* of the Jews (1:1—3:15). Through the course of events, enemies plot for the execution and extinction of the Jewish people.

The second section deals with the *plan* of the Jews (4:1—5:14). Through the intervention of Mordecai and Esther's appeal to the king, the deliverance of God's people is set in motion. The third section deals with the *preservation* of the Jews (6:1—10:3). Haman's plot is overturned and God's people are rescued from potential slaughter.

At the beginning of Esther, the Jews faced the threat of *doom*. At the end of the book they experienced the triumph associated with *deliverance*. In the midst of persecution there was impending ruin for the Jews. God, nevertheless, remained in control. He preserved His people by providing an incredible release from danger. Throughout all the events of the book, God miraculously displayed His care.

Concerning Xerxes, his empire stretched from what is now India through Persia (Iran), Turkey, the Middle East, across North Africa, and as far south as Sudan. The winter capital of the empire was in Susa, located about 150 miles east of Babylon.

During his reign, Xerxes gave a huge feast to climax a six-month display of his wealth and power. For some unknown reason Queen Vashti decided not to go along with his show and the king deposed her (chap. 1). Sometime later the king got around to finding a new queen. Esther was among the women to be chosen for the honor. Because she surpassed all of them, King Xerxes selected her to be his queen and threw a great banquet in her honor (chap. 2).

Esther had been raised by her uncle Mordecai, and he kept a close eye on her in the court. He had strictly admonished her not to reveal that she was a Jew (vss. 10, 20). One day Mordecai overheard a plot by two assassins against the king and he reported it to Esther, who told it to the king, attributing the information to her uncle (vss. 19-23).

After these events, Ahasuerus selected Haman to be the second most powerful official within the Persian Empire. He was an Agagite and possibly a descent of the Amalekites (3:1). The aim of the Amalekites was to annihilate the Jews, and Haman clearly shared this goal.

The king was so impressed with Haman that he commanded that all the servants who were at the "king's gate" (vs. 2) bow down and do obeisance (an attitude of respect or reverence) to Haman. Mordecai, however, refused to revere Haman. There was no justification for Mordecai's behavior based on the Mosaic law (in other words, misplaced worship; Exod. 20:4) or scriptural precedent (Gen. 23:7; 33:3; 44:14; 1 Sam. 24:8; 2 Sam. 14:4; 1 Kings 1:16). Perhaps Mordecai's disobedience was based on the hatred that existed between the Jews and the Amalekites.

Mordecai, motivated by a strong sense of patriotism, defied Haman because he was an enemy of God's people and ultimately a menace to their existence (Esth. 3:10; 7:6; 8:1; 9:10, 24, 26). The king's servants noticed Mordecai's belligerent conduct regarding Haman and asked him why he refused to obey "the king's command" (3:3). Undoubtedly, Mordecai could not bring himself to bow before one who was descended from the Amalekites, the bitter enemies of the Jews.

B. Haman's Revenge: vss. 5-6a

When Haman saw that Mordecai would not kneel down or pay him honor, he was enraged. Yet having learned who Mordecai's people were, he scorned the idea of killing only Mordecai.

When Mordecai's peers spoke to him "day after day" (3:4), he refused to listen to them. They finally told Haman about Mordecai's insubordination in an effort to determine whether this behavior was permissible or intolerable. When Haman verified what he had learned, he was "enraged" (vs. 5). Mordecai's actions threatened Haman's inflated ego. Thus he became obsessed with the determination to retaliate against Mordecai.

When Haman was told who "Mordecai's people were" (vs. 6), Haman spurned the idea that killing this rebel would be sufficient. Haman determined that all the Jews living within the Persian Empire had to die, perhaps as a fitting punishment for Mordecai's insolence. Haman's anger drove him to devise a scheme whereby all of the Jews in the Persian Empire would be exterminated.

In the twelfth year of King Ahasuerus (vs. 7), the court astrologers and magicians cast a lot for Haman to determine when to exterminate the Jews. The lot fell on the last month of the Jewish calendar, giving Haman about 11 months to establish and implement his plan. He next presented his case to the king, and the monarch readily agreed and issued the decree (vss. 8-13). The edict was then dispatched to all of the provinces giving orders to annihilate all of the Jews in one day (vss. 14-15).

II. MORDECAI'S CHALLENGE: ESTHER 4:7-16

A. Mordecai's Request: vss. 7-8

Mordecai told him everything that had happened to him, including the exact amount of money Haman had promised to pay into the royal treasury for the destruction of the Jews. He also gave him a copy of the text of the edict for their annihilation, which had been published in Susa, to show to Esther and explain it to her, and he told him to urge her to go into the king's presence to beg for mercy and plead with him for her people.

When Mordecai learned about the decree, he began to go through the city streets dressed in sackcloth and ashes (the clothing of mourning) and wept loudly (Esth.

4:1-3). Esther's maids told her what Mordecai was doing, and she sent one of her attendants to find out from him what was happening (vss. 4-6).

Mordecai then reviewed the details of all that had happened to him (vs. 7). He even stated the enormous sum of money that Haman would place in the royal treasury for those who helped massacre the Jews. Mordecai also gave the official a copy of the king's decree (vs. 8). Mordecai asked the queen to go into the king's presence and seek his favor and mercy concerning her fellow Jews.

B. Esther's Answer: vss. 9-11

Hathach went back and reported to Esther what Mordecai had said. Then she instructed him to say to Mordecai, "All the king's officials and the people of the royal provinces know that for any man or woman who approaches the king in the inner court without being summoned the king has but one law: that he be put to death. The only exception to this is for the king to extend the gold scepter to him and spare his life. But thirty days have passed since I was called to go to the king."

The official explained to Esther the situation and she in turn sent back a reply to Mordecai (Esth. 4:9-10). Esther reminded her uncle that her life would be placed in jeopardy if she did what he had requested. The king might execute her for trying to seek an interview with him without being specifically summoned.

The king would only spare Esther's life (in other words, clear her of guilt) if he held out his "gold scepter" (vs. 11) and granted her permission to see him. She reasoned that this possibility was remote, for the king had not summoned her into his presence for over "thirty days."

C. Mordecai's Insistence: vss. 12-14

When Esther's words were reported to Mordecai, he sent back this answer: "Do not think that because you are in the king's house you alone of all the Jews will escape. For if you remain silent at this time, relief and deliverance for the Jews will arise from another place, but you and your father's family will perish. And who knows but that you have come to royal position for such a time as this?"

"When Esther's words were reported to Mordecai" (Esth. 4:12), he would not take no for an answer. He did not deny that Esther would take a great risk in approaching the king. What she said was true, but the well being of the Jews was so serious that Mordecai insisted that she appeal to the king.

Mordecai gave two reasons. First, he told the queen that she would not escape death when the edict was carried out (vs. 13). Her Jewish background would be revealed and she would perish with the rest of them.

Mordecai was confident that the Jews would be delivered in some way, and when they were, Esther and her family would be taken anyway. Divine punishment would come if the queen disobeyed the Lord. "From another place" (vs. 14) implies that Mordecai had God's intervention in mind.

Second, Mordecai raised a question in Esther's mind. The uncle speculated that she had been made queen specifically to bring about the deliverance of her people. Mordecai did not directly give God credit for bringing Esther to the throne, but there is the strong assumption that the uncle had this in mind.

"And who knows" implies that Esther's position was ultimately due to divine providence. In other words, the highly unlikely possibility that she had been made queen was more than what people call good luck. Mordecai put two and two together and told Esther that she had been selected from all the women in the empire specifically to ensure the well being of her people.

Mordecai's words prompted Esther to think about why she was queen. In her case, much more was involved than satisfying the whims and pleasures of the king. Hers was a much larger responsibility. She thus decided to place herself at risk for the good of her people.

D. Esther's Response: vss. 15-16

Then Esther sent this reply to Mordecai: "Go, gather together all the Jews who are in Susa, and fast for me. Do not eat or drink for three days, night or day. I and my maids will fast as you do. When this is done, I will go to the king, even though it is against the law. And if I perish, I perish."

Mordecai's persistence paid off. Esther reconsidered her options and courageously decided to see King Xerxes. However, before the queen did so, she asked for the help of all the Jews in Susa. She called for a three-day fast, and she and her maids would do the same (Esth. 4:15).

Fasting was the traditional Jewish way of asking for God's help in times of national crisis. Esther thus followed a long line of leaders who had called God's people to fasting and prayer. Normally, fasts lasted from sunrise to sunset, but Esther called for a much longer one.

After this time of fasting, Esther would break with Persian regulations by requesting an audience with the king. She resigned herself to the possibility of losing her life over this decision (vs. 16). Esther's attendants notified Mordecai, and he responded by heeding the queen's instructions (vs. 17).

Esther's reply was a sterling display of devotion to God and commitment to His people. Her bravery was also a demonstration of living trust in the Lord, especially at a critical time for the Jewish people.

Discussion Questions

1. Who were the servants at the king's gate in Susa?
2. Why do you think the king's servants asked Mordecai again and again for the reason he refused to bow down before Haman?
3. What was it that intensified Haman's vindictive attitude toward Mordecai?
4. What do you think Mordecai said to Esther that made her determine to approach the king, unbidden, on behalf of her people?
5. How did you feel at times in your life when you needed God's strength and courage to face issues and circumstances, even when others misunderstood you?

Contemporary Application

Courage has been defined as an attitude of facing and dealing with anything recognized as dangerous, difficult, or painful instead of withdrawing from it. All of us face problems and situations in life that require courage in one degree or another. Occasionally we must face extremely challenging situations alone. Sometimes the issue is controversial, and friends and loved ones may discourage us or be critical of what we feel we must do. God often wanted those whom He chose to perform difficult tasks for Him to be courageous. He promised them He would be with them and provide the required strength at the moment of their need.

As in the case of Mordecai and the apostles of Jesus, a time may come when our spiritual convictions force us to choose between obeying a humanly constructed law or the law of God. Of course, such a stand does not permit us becoming violent. Nevertheless, as with Mordecai, a firm stand for what we believe is the proper thing to do may result in others harming us. This possibility is especially strong in places where Christianity is despised. We should thank God daily for the religious freedoms we enjoy in our country.

As we have seen from this week's lesson, hatred is a devastating emotion, for when it festers within us, it becomes increasingly difficult to control. Often hatred has deep roots that may lie dormant for a long time before they produce their deadly fruit. Such was the case with Haman. His hatred for the Jews was ignited when he learned that Mordecai, who refused to bow before him, was a Jew. Misunderstandings, unresolved, can develop into hostilities that lay the groundwork for a simmering hatred. Hatred can drive us to do unreasonable and irrational things. Such a pattern was obvious in the downhill path Haman took as his hatred for Mordecai and the Jews exploded.

Mordecai's courageous refusal to bow before Haman no doubt was reflected in the attitude of Esther, whose life was influenced by her godly uncle. Godly parents and relatives can be role models of courage before their children. These character traits are absorbed in subtle and progressive ways. Esther's respect for Mordecai was such that she was willing to risk her life and throw herself at the mercy of the king. God honored her act of courage and it saved her people from annihilation. The results of our acts of courage may not be as dramatic, but they can accomplish much for the glory of God and for the blessing of others.

A Time to Celebrate

DEVOTIONAL READING

Psalm 98:1-9

DAILY BIBLE READINGS

Monday February 23
*Psalm 146:1-9 The Lord
Sets the Prisoners Free*

Tuesday February 24
*Psalm 147:1-5 A Song of
Praise Is Fitting*

Wednesday February 25
*Psalm 147:6-11 Sing to God
with Thanksgiving*

Thursday February 26
*Psalm 147:12-20 Praise
Your God, O Zion!*

Friday February 27
*Psalm 98:1-9 God Has
Brought Victory*

Saturday February 28
*Esther 8:1-8 Esther Saves the
Jews*

Sunday February 29
*Esther 9:18-23 The Jews
Celebrate Their Deliverance*

Scripture

Background Scripture: *Esther 8—9*
Scripture Lesson: *Esther 8:3-8; 9:18-23*
Key Verse: *For the Jews it was a time of happiness and joy,
gladness and honor.* Esther 8:16.
Scripture Lesson for Children: *Esther 9:18-22, 27-28, 32*
Key Verse for Children: *The Jews in Susa, however, had
assembled . . . and made it a day of feasting and joy.*
Esther 9:18.

Lesson Aim

To learn how to celebrate the goodness of the Lord.

Lesson Setting

Time: *486–465 B.C.*
Place: *Susa, capital of the Persian Empire*

Lesson Outline

A Time to Celebrate
  I. Esther's Plea: Esther 8:3-8
     A. *Esther's Approach: vss. 3-4*
     B. *Esther's Case: vss. 5-6*
     C. *The King's Answer: vss. 7-8*
  II. The Jews' Celebration: Esther 9:18-23
     A. *Nationwide Feasting: vss. 18-19*
     B. *The Annual Celebration: vss. 20-23*

Introduction for Adults

Topic: *Feasting and Sharing*

> When faced with an irresolvable problem, believers can choose either to panic or rely on God. The first option leads to anxiety and failure, whereas the second option leads to peace and joy, even if the problem is not resolved.
>
> This week we will see the potential catastrophe facing God's people and how He brought them through this crisis. We will learn that when we put our trust in the Lord, He enables us to triumph even in the midst of difficult circumstances.

Introduction for Youth

Topic: *Let's Party!*

> We, like all people, need love, comfort, and security. God often meets these needs when we unselfishly serve Him and His people. When we reach out to others with the love of God, we are blessed with love in return. And when we show to others that we truly care about them, we are showered with their gratitude.
>
> In order for these things to happen, we must look beyond our desires to the needs of others around us. With God's help and sustaining presence, we can do so.

Concepts for Children

Topic: *Esther's People Celebrated and Gave Thanks*

1. The Jews in Susa set aside a number of days for feasting and gladness.
2. Mordecai sent out a letter telling the Jews to set aside two days to celebrate their relief from their enemies.
3. These two days became a longstanding custom among the Jews.
4. This time of celebration was called Purim.
5. Queen Esther's command made the Feast of Purim an official celebration among the Jews for generations to come.
6. By our joy and happiness in the Father we can encourage others to put their faith in His Son.

Lesson Commentary

I. ESTHER'S PLEA: ESTHER 8:3-8

A. Esther's Approach: vss. 3-4

Esther again pleaded with the king, falling at his feet and weeping. She begged him to put an end to the evil plan of Haman the Agagite, which he had devised against the Jews. Then the king extended the gold scepter to Esther and she arose and stood before him.

As we enter this week's lesson, Haman's plans to exterminate the Jews seemed to be progressing as planned. There was a reversal of fortunes, however, when the king honored Mordecai and ordered Haman to be hanged on the gallows he intended for Mordecai's execution.

Especially noteworthy is the information contained in Esther 7. While Xerxes and Haman were dining with Esther, the king again asked her what she wanted from him. The queen implored Xerxes to spare her life and that of her people, explaining that they had been bartered away (by means of the bribe Haman offered) to be slaughtered. She would not have bothered the king if the Jews had been sold as slaves (vss. 1-4).

When Xerxes asked who would do such a thing, Esther fingered Haman. Filled with rage, the king went into the palace garden. In the monarch's absence, Haman kneeled before Esther and begged her to save his life. Somehow he lost his balance and stumbled onto the couch where Esther was reclining. Just then Xerxes returned, saw what was happening, and accused Haman of trying to rape his queen in his own palace (vss. 5-8).

The king's servants covered Haman's head. Then Harbonah, one the king's personal servants, noted the gallows Haman had built to hang Mordecai. Xerxes ordered that Haman be hanged on the tower, and when this was done, the king's anger was appeased (vss. 9-10).

Although Haman was no longer a threat to the Jews, the king's decree against them remained in force. God used Esther and Mordecai to get Ahasuerus to issue a new set of decrees in which he permitted the Jews to defend themselves. They commemorated their victory over their enemies by establishing the Feast of Purim.

Esther 3:7 reveals that, in March or April of 474 B.C., the court astrologers and magicians cast a lot for Haman to determine when the extermination of the Jews was to take place. "Pur" was the Babylonian word for lot, and "purim" is the plural form. Chapter 9:18-32 reveals that the Feast of Purim became one of the traditional Jewish feasts established by God's people. The Jews normally observed this sacred holiday between February and March (that is, the month of Adar). The festival involved a day of joyous celebration, feasting, and giving of presents. It was intended to remind the Jews of their remarkable deliverance as a people during the time of Esther.

According to 8:1-2, the king gave Esther all that had belonged to Haman. Xerxes also made Mordecai one of his highest officials and gave him the ring Haman had worn. Esther then put Mordecai in charge of Haman's property. After that, Esther entered the king's chambers and fell at his feet, weeping and pleading with him on behalf of her people, the Jews, who were still under the death sentence (vs. 3).

Moved by Esther's display of concern for her people, the king held out his golden scepter to her (vs. 4). The situation now was different from the previous time the king had extended his scepter to Esther (5:2). On that occasion, Esther risked her life to come into the king's presence uninvited. This time she had already made her emotional appeal before the king. His gesture in extending his scepter was an indication that Esther should rise from her prostrate position and continue to speak to him.

B. Esther's Case: vss. 5-6

"If it pleases the king," she said, "and if he regards me with favor and thinks it the right thing to do, and if he is pleased with me, let an order be written overruling the dispatches that Haman son of Hammedatha, the Agagite, devised and wrote to destroy the Jews in all the king's provinces. For how can I bear to see disaster fall on my people? How can I bear to see the destruction of my family?"

Esther based her case on her relationship with Xerxes and on his judgment to do "the right thing" (Esth. 8:5). Everything depended on what pleased the king. The queen, of course, followed the strict rules of court formality and addressed the king with the utmost respect. Esther knew that only the king's pleasure and his decision could bring about the deliverance of the Jews from their enemies.

Esther was wise to remind the king that Haman had instigated the destruction of the Jews (vs. 5). While the queen knew how the king felt about Haman, she carefully avoided blaming Xerxes for any part he may have unwittingly played in the conspiracy.

The queen, instead, appealed strongly to Xerxes' acceptance of her: "If he regards me with favor . . . if he is pleased with me." Then Esther explained how horrible it would be for her to see her people destroyed (vs. 6). Here we find Esther speaking with courage, wisdom, and passion for her people. She staked everything on the king's sense of justice and his appreciation for her as his queen.

Xerxes could hardly be moved by the extermination of a subject people, for he had built his empire by ruthless subjugation of millions from India to Ethiopia. What difference would it make to him to see the Jews die? But in this case the king saw a real Jew standing before him, not an abstract community of people. Esther's personal pain gave Xerxes something to think about on more than the bureaucratic level.

C. The King's Answer: vss. 7-8

King Xerxes replied to Queen Esther and to Mordecai the Jew, "Because Haman attacked the Jews, I have given his estate to Esther, and they have hanged him on the gallows. Now write another decree in the king's name in behalf of the Jews as seems best to you, and seal it with the king's signet ring—for no document written in the king's name and sealed with his ring can be revoked."

Xerxes summoned Esther and Mordecai and favorably accepted Esther's plea for her people. He reminded them that their enemy Haman had been executed (Esth. 8:7). Then the king told them to write a new decree "as seems best to you" (vs. 8). Xerxes would seal it and it would become law. Haman's decree would not be carried out, and the Jews were given authority to defend themselves against would-be attackers (vs. 11). The irrevocability of Haman's decree made it necessary for Mordecai to duplicate in reverse all of its provisions.

Great celebrations broke out among the Jews in Susa the capital and elsewhere throughout the empire. It included many Gentiles as well as Jews (vss. 15-17). Happiness, joy, and gladness were the orders of the day. Thus through Mordecai's irrepressible faith and Esther's courage and wisdom, the Jews were preserved.

II. THE JEWS' CELEBRATION: ESTHER 9:18-23

A. Nationwide Feasting: vss. 18-19

The Jews in Susa, however, had assembled on the thirteenth and fourteenth, and then on the fifteenth they rested and made it a day of feasting and joy. That is why rural Jews—those living in villages— observe the fourteenth of the month of Adar as a day of joy and feasting, a day for giving presents to each other.

Great victories for the Jews swept the country (Esth. 9:1-15). Then the Jews who lived in Susa, the capital city, "had assembled on the thirteenth and fourteenth, and then on the fifteenth they rested and made it a day of feasting and joy" (vs. 18). The author added these words to explain that the Jews living in the city kept the Feast of Purim on the fifteenth day of Adar.

Those living in the rural areas observed it on the fourteenth day (vs. 19). Apparently the Jews in Susa were permitted two days to kill their enemies, whereas the Jews living elsewhere had only one day to carry out their defense. Thus they celebrated the feast on the fourteenth of Adar.

This celebration reminds us of earlier times when the Jews gathered to thank God for His deliverance. The songs of Moses and Miriam are one such example (Exod. 15:1-21). Similar celebrations marked the day the ark of God came to Jerusalem (1 Chron. 13—16), the dedication of the temple (2 Chron. 5—7), Hezekiah's Passover (chaps. 30—31), and Nehemiah's reading of the Word of God (Neh. 8:1-18). Such celebrations also formed the basis for worship expressed in the Book of Psalms.

B. The Annual Celebration: vss. 20-23

Mordecai recorded these events, and he sent letters to all the Jews throughout the provinces of King Xerxes, near and far, to have them celebrate annually the fourteenth and fifteenth days of the month of Adar as the time when the Jews got relief from their enemies, and as the month when their sorrow was turned into joy and their mourning into a day of celebration. He wrote them to observe the days as days of feasting and joy and giving presents of food to one another and gifts to the poor. So the Jews agreed to continue the celebration they had begun, doing what Mordecai had written to them.

Mordecai "recorded these events, and he sent letters" (Esth. 9:20) to his fellow Jews throughout the provinces of Persia. In the letters he recorded the high points of the past days, particularly that the Jews in Susa, after overcoming their enemies, rested on the fifteenth of Adar, while the Jews in the other provinces rested on the fourteenth of the month. Those days both groups kept as times of rejoicing.

Mordecai further stated that they were to observe these days of rejoicing year by year (vs. 21). Adar was to be remembered as the month during which the Jews gained relief from their enemies (vs. 22). In addition to this, they were to send gifts of food to one another and presents to the poor. When the Jews in the provinces received Mordecai's letter instructing them to establish an annual feast of rejoicing to commemorate their deliverance from their enemies, they adopted as a custom what they had begun to do (vs. 23).

Time and again throughout the Old Testament we see the importance of keeping special times for worship, sacrifice, fasting, and feasting. The Jews had so many significant milestones in their history—beginning with their exodus from Egypt—that their calendars were filled with reminders of God's goodness and mercy. Moses had laid down the laws for regular feasts, starting with the Passover, and Purim was added much later. Purim, of course, does not have the authority of Moses behind it, but it became an important part of Jewish history and tradition.

Readers wonder why Mordecai and Esther did not mention God when they established Purim. The most likely explanation is that, since the account was written in Persia soon after the events occurred, the author did not want to risk offending the Persians by directly mentioning God.

The account reveals much about God's hand in saving His people. That's why Purim has been such a popular celebration. It encourages people in difficulties to pray for deliverance even when their situations appear to be hopeless. Also, when we celebrate God's goodness regularly—not just when we're reaping His blessings—we honor Him and confess our faith, hope, and trust in Him. Our celebrations point to God as our great Deliverer.

Discussion Questions

1. What was the difference between the gesture of the king in extending his scepter to Esther the first time and the second time?
2. Why was Esther so distressed about the edict promoted by Haman?
3. Why did the Jews of Susa celebrate victory over their enemies on the fifteenth day of Adar, while the Jews in the other provinces celebrated on the fourteenth day of the month?
4. What specific activities were to accompany the Jews' time of feasting?
5. What are some practical ways that we can show gratitude to God for our victory in Christ?

Contemporary Application

In life threatening situations, people are prone to think of themselves first and others last. Esther and Mordecai responded differently to their circumstances. They were more concerned for the welfare of their people than for their own well being. They are role models for us as we encounter terrifying situations.

Consider, for example, the life challenges believers tend to face. In the midst of difficult circumstances, it might be easy for them to feel discouraged and frustrated. You can use this week's lesson to remind your students how God enabled His people in the Old Testament to prevail in the most difficult situations.

Another area of concern relates to God's perfect timing. Believers sometimes can become impatient when they do not receive the recognition they think they deserve. Encourage your students to look at life from an eternal perspective. Even if others fail to notice all the good things they have done, God is not ignorant of their deeds. In due time, He will bestow His heavenly riches on them in Christ.

A third area for consideration deals with the matter of expressing forgiveness. The jealously and pride that brought down Haman can unexpectedly trip up even the mature Christian. It is easy to magnify real or imagined slights and to strike back at them. Instead of seeking revenge, believers are to forgive those who wrong them. Although forgiving offenses is never easy, God can give His people the strength to do what is right.

Jesus Fulfills His Mission (Passion Narratives)

Love and Betrayal

DEVOTIONAL READING

Psalm 55:12-22

DAILY BIBLE READINGS

Monday March 1
Psalm 55:12-17 The Psalmist Mourns a Friend's Betrayal

Tuesday March 2
Psalm 55:18-22 A Friend Violates a Covenant

Wednesday March 3
Psalm 69:6-14 Zeal for Your House

Thursday March 4
Matthew 26:1-13 A Woman Pours Ointment on Jesus

Friday March 5
Matthew 26:14-19 Judas Agrees to Betray Jesus

Saturday March 6
Matthew 26:20-25 Jesus Announces Upcoming Betrayal

Sunday March 7
Matthew 26:31-35 Peter Promises Not to Desert Jesus

Scripture

Background Scripture: *Matthew 26:1-75*
Scripture Lesson: *Matthew 26:3-15, 20-25*
Key Verses: *While they were eating, he said, "I tell you the truth, one of you will betray me." They were very sad and began to say to him one after the other, "Surely not I, Lord?"* Matthew 26:21-22.
Scripture Lesson for Children: *Matthew 26:6-13*
Key Verse for Children: *Love is patient, love is kind.* 1 Corinthians 13:4.

Lesson Aim

To encourage the students to put their faith in Christ and talk to others about doing so.

Lesson Setting

Time: *A.D. 30*
Place: *Jerusalem*

Lesson Outline

Love and Betrayal

  I. The Plot against Jesus: Matthew 26:3-5
 II. The Anointing at Bethany: Matthew 26:6-13
    A. *The Woman's Anointing: vss. 6-7*
    B. *The Disciples' Complaint: vss. 8-9*
    C. *The Savior's Explanation: vss. 10-13*
III. The Bargain of Judas: Matthew 26:14-15
IV. The Traitor Exposed: Matthew 26:20-25
    A. *The Announcement of Jesus: vss. 20-21*
    B. *The Despair of the Disciples: vs. 22*
    C. *The Identification of Judas: vss. 23-25*

Introduction for Adults

Topic: *Love and Betrayal*

We've all seen classic movies where the young female lead decides she doesn't want to marry her handsome young betrothed. She rips off her diamond engagement ring and hurls it into the dust. He throws himself at her and begs her to change her mind, but it's too late.

Script writers did not invent this story line. The basics have been acted out since the dawn of time, but perhaps nowhere more dramatically than in Judas' broken commitment to Jesus. Judas' was the pinnacle of betrayal because he turned his back on the Son of God. Judas threw Jesus' love into the dirt. Judas traded the Lord of glory for money.

How refreshing it is to see the brilliance of the woman who poured out her life savings on Jesus. She didn't trade Jesus for money; instead, she gave all she had to Him. That's an act of devotion we rarely see, even though opportunities abound for us to show how much we love Jesus.

Introduction for Youth

Topic: *Betraying a Friend*

Governments hang traitors for selling military secrets. Sometimes we feel like doing that to friends who betray us. We trust our friends with our personal secrets, but sometimes they cannot keep a confidence and word leaks out that some of our secrets are public knowledge. While we condemn this in others, we have to be careful we are not guilty of doing it ourselves.

Consider how close Judas was to Jesus; yet Judas could not control his desire to turn Jesus in for money. The Judas account powerfully reminds us how vulnerable we are to sin. When it comes to keeping true to our Christian promises, we must be careful lest we betray Jesus for a brief joke.

Judas' treachery looks especially dark when we compare it to the woman who anointed Jesus. She risked everything to worship and honor Him. So must we.

Concepts for Children

Topic: *A Woman Shows Love for Jesus*

1. Friends offered Jesus a meal.
2. During dinner, a woman poured precious perfume on Jesus.
3. When His disciples protested, Jesus praised the woman's sacrifice.
4. It is sometimes hard for us to honor Jesus in front of other people.
5. There are many ways for us to show our love for Jesus.
6. When we love Jesus, other people will want to love Him, too.

Lesson Commentary

I. THE PLOT AGAINST JESUS: MATTHEW 26:3-5

Then the chief priests and the elders of the people assembled in the palace of the high priest, whose name was Caiaphas, and they plotted to arrest Jesus in some sly way and kill him. "But not during the Feast," they said, "or there may be a riot among the people."

As Jesus' earthly ministry drew to a close, the Passover celebration was about to begin; also, "the Son of Man" (Matt. 26:2) was about to be betrayed and crucified. This statement points to a sobering reality, namely, that humankind did not recognize the Messiah when He came to earth (John 1:10). Perhaps even more distressing is that many of the Jewish people failed to accept Him as their Savior (vs. 11).

The plot to kill Jesus was set in motion when the leading religious authorities gathered at the residence of Caiaphas, "the high priest" (Matt. 26:3). He was the son-in-law of Annas, the previous high priest. The Roman procurator Valerius Gratius appointed Caiaphas around A.D. 18, and he was subsequently removed from office around A.D. 37.

At this nefarious meeting, the attendees discussed how they might arrest Jesus by means of stealth (vs. 4). Then, after capturing the Messiah, they wanted to "kill him." The ringleaders were afraid, however, to carry out this gruesome act during the Passover because they sensed that Jesus was too popular to openly arrest. They thus decided to wait and thereby avoid inciting a riot among the people (vs. 5).

II. THE ANOINTING AT BETHANY: MATTHEW 26:6-13

A. The Woman's Anointing: vss. 6-7

While Jesus was in Bethany in the home of a man known as Simon the Leper, a woman came to him with an alabaster jar of very expensive perfume, which she poured on his head as he was reclining at the table.

The anointing described in Matthew 26:6-13 was probably the same one mentioned in John 12:1-8. Jesus had been going through towns and villages, telling the good news about God's kingdom. Along with the Twelve, a number of women accompanied Him from time to time (Luke 8:1-3), perhaps including Mary and Martha, the sisters of Lazarus (John 11:1-3). These three were among Jesus' most devoted followers and perhaps part of an inner circle of Christ's associates.

As Jesus and His disciples were traveling along, they came to Bethany (Matt. 26:6), a village located about two miles southeast of Jerusalem on the eastern slope of the Mount of Olives. While Jesus was at Bethany, He was welcomed into the home of "Simon the leper." Some have speculated that Jesus had previously cleansed this person from leprosy and that Simon was either a member of the family of Lazarus, Mary, and Martha, or a close friend.

John 12:3 reveals that the woman of Matthew 26:7 who anointed Jesus was Mary, the sister of Martha and Lazarus. Mary wanted to show her love and respect for Jesus, and so she brought to Him one of her most valuable possessions. This was an "alabaster jar" containing a rose-colored ointment made from the roots and stems of the Indian nard plant. Mary broke the neck of the jar, which contained only one application. She then poured the ointment on Jesus' head and feet.

B. The Disciples' Complaint: vss. 8-9

When the disciples saw this, they were indignant. "Why this waste?" they asked. "This perfume could have been sold at a high price and the money given to the poor."

The disciples, perhaps at the instigation of Judas (John 12:4), objected to this apparent "waste" (Matt. 26:8). Supposedly Mary could have sold the "perfume" (vs. 9) for a sizeable sum of money, which then could have been donated to the poor; but, as John 12:6 reveals, the real concern of Judas was not to help the poor but rather to pilfer as much of the money as possible from the disciples' funds for his own use.

C. The Savior's Explanation: vss. 10-13

Aware of this, Jesus said to them, "Why are you bothering this woman? She has done a beautiful thing to me. The poor you will always have with you, but you will not always have me. When she poured this perfume on my body, she did it to prepare me for burial. I tell you the truth, wherever this gospel is preached throughout the world, what she has done will also be told, in memory of her."

Thankfully, Jesus defended Mary's action. The Savior declared that she had done a "beautiful thing" (Matt. 26:10), or a loving act of service, which was especially appropriate in light of His approaching death; also, Mary's unselfish deed shone all the more brighter because of its contrast with the way the disciples were competing for power (Mark 10:37, 41). Even more strikingly, Mary's generous act contrasted with the way Judas was about to trade Jesus to the religious leaders for money.

Jesus' remark that there will always be poor people (Matt. 26:11) should not be taken as an indication that He lacked concern for the poor. In fact, He was always the champion of the oppressed and the afflicted. By making this remark, Jesus meant that His followers would have many opportunities to help the needy; but only a short time remained for His disciples to show Him their love before He died.

Jesus declared that Mary, by pouring the ointment on the Savior, prepared His body for its "burial" (vs. 12). Mary's action also underscored the supreme value of Jesus' atoning sacrifice and the great depth of Mary's devotion to Him. It is no wonder that, as believers proclaimed the Gospel worldwide, they would talk about Mary's noble deed "in memory of her" (vs. 13).

III. THE BARGAIN OF JUDAS: MATTHEW 26:14-15

Then one of the Twelve—the one called Judas Iscariot—went to the chief priests and asked, "What are you willing to give me if I hand him over to you?" So they counted out for him thirty silver coins.

Judas decided to go to the "chief priests" (Matt. 26:14) and ask how much they would pay him to help them in their efforts to arrest Jesus. The religious leaders agreed to give Judas "thirty silver coins" (vs. 15), which was about how much a rural worker would earn over a two- or three-month period. From then on Judas began to look for a good opportunity to betray Jesus (vs. 16).

The amount Judas received for his traitorous action was the price someone was required by the law to pay for a slave who had been accidentally killed (Exod. 21:32). Centuries earlier Zechariah prophesied that the Good Shepherd would be rejected for this amount (Zech. 11:12).

Greed seems to have played a part in Judas's betrayal of the Lord; but the total motivation for his betrayal may always remain a mystery. How could someone observe Jesus' love and goodness for years, then turn around and give Him up to killers? We do not know, but it happened.

IV. THE TRAITOR EXPOSED: MATTHEW 26:20-25

A. The Announcement of Jesus: vss. 20-21

When evening came, Jesus was reclining at the table with the Twelve. And while they were eating, he said, "I tell you the truth, one of you will betray me."

To maintain his appearance of faithfulness, Judas remained in the company of "the Twelve" (Matt. 26:20). This meant, of course, that he was with them for their observance of Passover, a national religious festival celebrating the Hebrews' escape from Egypt in the time of Moses. Jesus' Passover meal with His disciples took place, by prior arrangement, in the second-story room of a house in Jerusalem.

Unlike contemporary practice, first century Middle Eastern meals were not eaten while sitting at a table, but while reclining on one's side on the floor with the head closest to the low table and the feet farthest away. At various points in the meal, informal conversation took place around the table. It was perhaps during such a moment that Jesus revealed, "one of you will betray me" (vs. 21).

B. The Despair of the Disciples: vs. 22

They were very sad and began to say to him one after the other, "Surely not I, Lord?"

Jesus phrased His comment to stress the certainty of the matter. This announcement saddened the Twelve, and each of them in turn questioned Jesus about the identity of the traitor (Matt. 26:22). Perhaps the disciples actually feared they might do or say something that would betray the Savior into the hands of His enemies; or the disciples may have feared that, in an unguarded moment, they might make a misstep that would expose Jesus to danger.

C. The Identification of Judas: vss. 23-25

Jesus replied, "The one who has dipped his hand into the bowl with me will betray me. The Son of Man will go just as it is written about him. But woe to that man who betrays the Son of Man! It would be better for him if he had not been born." Then Judas, the one who would betray him, said, "Surely not I, Rabbi?" Jesus answered, "Yes, it is you."

Christ said in Matthew 26:23 that the betrayer would dip his hand in a bowl of broth with Him. Jesus was stressing just how treacherous the betrayer was; in fact, Judas was one of Jesus' trusted friends (Pss. 41:9; 55:12-14).

Perhaps in making His declaration, Jesus wanted to warn the other disciples about what was going to happen. He also wanted to give the traitor an opportunity to reconsider and repent. Jesus wanted Judas to know that the dastardly plan was not a secret. Christ also wanted all people, after the event, to know that He was aware of the trap and willingly stepped into it.

Jesus referred to Himself as the "Son of Man" (Matt. 26:24), which was a messianic title. Isaiah 53:7-9 foretold that God's people would reject and execute the Messiah. Jesus evidently referred to this when He said He had to die in accordance with the teaching of Scripture. Despite such a horrible end, it would be nothing compared to the eternal condemnation that awaited Christ's betrayer. Jesus said it would have been better if the traitor had never been born.

Judas, realizing that Christ was referring to him, addressed Jesus as "Rabbi" (Matt. 26:25), a term that can also be rendered "Teacher." This was a title of respect used for those who were knowledgeable in the law. In His response, Christ indicated that Judas was the betrayer.

Judas need not have feared being exposed. Jesus would not betray His betrayer. He knew that Judas's treachery was part of the Father's will for Jesus' death. Oddly enough, none of the other disciples suspected Judas's guilt even when he left the supper early (John 13:28-30).

Discussion Questions

1. Why were the religious leaders so eager to capture and kill Jesus?
2. What was so noble about the woman's anointing of Jesus?
3. Why did the disciples, perhaps at the instigation of Judas, react so strongly to the woman's good deed?
4. How should we understand Jesus' comment regarding the poor?
5. What key event with respect to Jesus did the woman's kind act anticipate?
6. What may have motivated Judas to betray Jesus?
7. How did the disciples—especially Judas—respond when Jesus revealed that one of them would betray Him?

Contemporary Application

The religious leaders' decision to arrest and execute Jesus, and Judas' willingness to help them, underscores how ingrained sin is in the human heart and how much everyone needs the Savior. This is just as true for young adults as it is for older adults.

Young adults, in particular, are at a stage of life where their self-identity is still emerging and growing. Also, as they seek to overcome nagging problems, they are prompted to seek the counsel of others, whether their parents, peers, or others. It is moreover why they might be inclined to purchase self-help books that promise they will become successful if they think more positively about themselves and exert greater willpower to bring about change in their lives.

While it is commendable for believers to leave behind the faults and failures of their youth, they need to know that most of their efforts to be different will prove unsuccessful. At best they will be able to discard a bad habit or two or develop a skill to make life more enjoyable. The sobering reality is that they cannot change their sinful self, no matter how hard they try.

Believers need to know that the real problem is not with their *actions*; rather, it is with their *nature*. The actions of Judas and the religious leaders underscores the truth that all of us have sinned and fallen short of God's glory (Rom. 3:23). Some adults may not realize this, however, because the human heart is extremely devious and beyond fathoming (Jer. 17:9). Satan, too, can blind them to the truth of their spiritual condition (2 Cor. 4:4).

The good news is that God has come to our aid. By sending His Son to die for our sins (as well as that of all humanity), He offers us the opportunity for forgiveness and eternal life. Adults need to know that their responsibility is to stop depending on themselves and depend solely on God's mercy. By faith they can accept the salvation He offers them in Christ.

God not only wants us to trust in Christ for salvation but also to encourage others to do so. The Lord has made us to be His ambassadors to share the Gospel with others. It is an important responsibility that we should not ignore. God can save many of our peers through our efforts to share the good news. Regardless of the method employed, the intent is to spread the Gospel to as many people as possible.

The Lord's Supper

DEVOTIONAL READING

John 13:1-15

DAILY BIBLE READINGS

Monday March 8
Luke 22:7-13 Disciples Prepare the Passover Meal

Tuesday March 9
Luke 22:14-28 Jesus Eats with His Disciples

Wednesday March 10
Luke 22:19-23 Do This in Remembrance of Me

Thursday March 11
John 13:1-5 Jesus Washes the Disciples' Feet

Friday March 12
John 13:6-10 Peter Protests

Saturday March 13
John 13:11-15 Jesus Sets an Example

Sunday March 14
Luke 22:24-30 Jesus Teaches about Greatness

Scripture

Background Scripture: Luke 22:7-30
Scripture Lesson: Luke 22:7-23
Key Verses: *"This is my body given for you; do this in remembrance of me. . . . This cup is the new covenant in my blood, which is poured out for you."* Luke 22:19-20.
Scripture Lesson for Children: *Luke 22:14-20*
Key Verse for Children: *[Jesus] said to them, "I have eagerly desired to eat this Passover with you."* Luke 22:15.

Lesson Aim

To challenge the students to approach the Lord's Supper with a renewed sense of awe at the price Jesus paid for their sins.

Lesson Setting

Time: *A.D. 30*
Place: *Jerusalem*

Lesson Outline

The Lord's Supper
  I. Passover Preparations: Luke 22:7-13
      A. *Jesus' Orders: vs. 7*
      B. *Jesus' Instructions: vss. 8-12*
      C. *Mission Accomplished: vs. 13*
  II. Signs of the Kingdom: Luke 22:14-18
      A. *Eating: vss. 14-16*
      B. *Drinking: vss. 17-18*
  III. Christ's Body and Blood: Luke 22:19-20
      A. *The Bread: vs. 19*
      B. *The Cup: vs. 20*
  IV. The Betrayal: Luke 22:21-23

Introduction for Adults

Topic: *Celebration and Anticipation*

The Jews had much to celebrate at their Passover. Their meal spoke about God's wonderful liberation from Egypt. Yet at times in the Old Testament era they lapsed in their observance of it. Perhaps the people groaned that it was too much of a burden. Perhaps the ritual had lost its sharpness.

The same thing happens to some Christians. They are not particularly bothered about their lack of regular attendance at the Lord's Supper. Their hearts are not warmed by the event. They have lost their sense of celebration of the past and of anticipation of their future. It's not a happy time for them.

Of course, as with any event, people can fall into a meaningless routine. If we do not come to the table to meet Jesus, what's the point? If we do not come to confess and repent, what's the use? No ritual can save anyone, no matter how often it is performed. Only hearts in tune with Jesus can enjoy His supper.

Introduction for Youth

Topic: *Preparing to Remember*

Family memories mean more to us the older we get. Youth is not a time to remember but a time to look ahead to the future. Thus, history is not an exciting course for some students.

But the Lord's Supper is history with a powerful influence on our futures. Our Christian faith means nothing without the history of Jesus, His death and resurrection. We cannot grow in our knowledge and faith without constantly referring to Jesus' history.

The Lord's Supper helps us to remember because we participate in visible symbols, the bread and the cup, with other people. We eat together to symbolize our common faith. Jesus' table draws us closer to Him and to each other.

We read the account and then we imagine ourselves being there when Christ served the bread and the cup. We confess that our sins drove Jesus to the cross. And then we are thankful that we did not forget to observe the Lord's Supper.

Concepts for Children

Topic: *Having Dinner with Jesus*

1. Jesus held a special meal with His followers.
2. This was a scary time for them because of what was going to happen to Jesus.
3. Jesus explained what the bread and the cup represented.
4. Our forgiveness and salvation rest on what Jesus did at the cross.
5. When we trust in Jesus, we are saved.
6. We observe the Lord's Supper to let the world know what Jesus did for all people.

Lesson Commentary

I. PASSOVER PREPARATIONS: LUKE 22:7-13

A. Jesus' Orders: vs. 7

Then came the day of Unleavened Bread on which the Passover lamb had to be sacrificed.

The night before Jesus' crucifixion, He celebrated the Passover with His disciples in an upper room specially prepared for the occasion. Moses instituted the first Passover observance the night before God freed Israel from the nation's bondage in Egypt. God commanded that Israel continue to celebrate the Passover in remembrance of His great saving work (Exod. 12:21-28).

The elements used in the Lord's Supper are visible reminders of Christ's saving work. The bread symbolizes His body and the cup represents His blood (1 Cor. 10:16; 11:23-26). The acts of eating and drinking the elements in the supper (two of the most basic acts of life) show us our dependence upon Christ. Just as we are dependent upon food and drink for physical life, we are dependent upon Christ's death and resurrection for eternal life.

In Jesus' day, thousands of Jews from all over the known world made the pilgrimage to Jerusalem for Passover. Thus an unusually large crowd was on hand to take part in the events surrounding Jesus' entry into the city (Luke 19:37-39) and His arrest, trial, and crucifixion (23:18, 27, 35, 48). Evidently many stayed on until the Feast of Pentecost, when they heard Peter's moving sermon (Acts 2:1-41).

The celebration of the feast of "Unleavened Bread" (Luke 22:7) lasted eight days, beginning with the Passover meal. The celebrations were so close together that at times the names of both were used interchangeably. Part of the observance involved the sacrifice of the Passover lamb. As the Jews gathered for the Passover celebration in A.D. 30, little did they realize that as they sacrificed their Passover lambs, the Lamb of God was about to be sacrificed to set people free from spiritual slavery (John 1:29).

B. Jesus' Instructions: vss. 8-12

Jesus sent Peter and John, saying, "Go and make preparations for us to eat the Passover." "Where do you want us to prepare for it?" they asked. He replied, "As you enter the city, a man carrying a jar of water will meet you. Follow him to the house that he enters, and say to the owner of the house, 'The Teacher asks: Where is the guest room, where I may eat the Passover with my disciples?' He will show you a large upper room, all furnished. Make preparations there."

As the time drew near, Jesus sent Peter and John ahead into the city to prepare the Passover meal (Luke 22:8). They were to look for a man carrying a water pitcher and follow him (vss. 9-10). Since women usually carried these jars, it would have been no problem for Peter and John to recognize the man Jesus was referring to. The owner of the house to which Peter and John were led was evidently expecting them. Upon their inquiry (vs. 11), he showed them a second-floor room complete with furniture (vs. 12).

C. Mission Accomplished: vs. 13

They left and found things just as Jesus had told them. So they prepared the Passover.

Next, the disciples—who probably gained access to the upper room by stairs on the outside of the house—prepared the Passover meal (Luke 22:13). Perhaps Jesus used the question recorded in verse 11 to keep the exact location of the meal a secret from His many enemies. Some think Jesus prearranged the meeting as a way for one of His Jerusalem followers to encounter Peter and John at the city gate. Others, however, think the meeting demonstrates Jesus' supernatural knowledge.

II. Signs of the Kingdom: Luke 22:14-18

A. Eating: vss. 14-16

When the hour came, Jesus and his apostles reclined at the table. And he said to them, "I have eagerly desired to eat this Passover with you before I suffer. For I tell you, I will not eat it again until it finds fulfillment in the kingdom of God."

After the official beginning of Passover, Jesus gathered His disciples to eat the meal (Luke 22:14). He told the Twelve how much He wanted to share the celebration with them (vs. 15). This would be the last time Christ would enjoy the fellowship of His disciples in this way before His upcoming crucifixion.

Jesus looked to a celebration in the coming "kingdom of God" (vs. 16) when the Passover is fulfilled. This reference could well suggest that some type of commemorative meal will be celebrated at the Second Coming. Thus, Passover is not only a reminder of God's help in the past, but also an indication of His help that is yet to come.

The Passover meal of Jesus' day followed a traditional pattern. A family or group of friends would meet for the meal after sundown. Then the head of the group would say a prayer over a cup containing the fruit of the vine.

This was the first of four cups used in the observance (although it is debated whether the fourth cup was used in the first century A.D.). Each cup represented a promise in Exodus 6:6 and 7: "I will bring you out . . . I will free you from being slaves to them . . . I will redeem you . . . I will take you as my own people."

Next, everyone would eat bitter herbs to remind themselves of the bitter times their ancestors had endured in Egypt. Then they would pour a second cup without drinking it. They would also serve the meal, the main dish of which was a specially prepared roast of lamb.

The participants, however, would not eat the meal until they had recited the Passover liturgy, had sung Psalm 113, and had prayed over the unleavened bread. A prayer over the third cup ended the feast. Finally, they would sing Psalms 114–118 and drink the contents of a fourth cup.

We marvel at God's miracles that freed the Hebrews from Egyptian slavery; but we also marvel at the miracle that sets us free from slavery to sin. The exodus from Egypt was a spectacular event; but the future exodus of believers from this sinful world will be even more spectacular. When the "the wedding supper of the Lamb" (Rev. 19:9) is finally accomplished, then Jesus will celebrate the Passover's fulfillment in the kingdom of God.

B. Drinking: vss. 17-18

After taking the cup, he gave thanks and said, "Take this and divide it among you. For I tell you I will not drink again of the fruit of the vine until the kingdom of God comes."

Only Luke mentions two cups at this meal, whereas the other synoptic Gospels mention only one. The cup mentioned in Luke 22:17 probably refers to the first cup in the traditional Passover meal. After taking the first cup and giving thanks to God, Jesus gave it to His disciples and told them to share it "among you." The Savior declared He would not partake of the "fruit of the vine" (vs. 18) until the inauguration of the divine kingdom in all its power and blessing (see 17:20-37).

III. CHRIST'S BODY AND BLOOD: LUKE 22:19-20

A. The Bread: vs. 19

And he took bread, gave thanks and broke it, and gave it to them, saying, "This is my body given for you; do this in remembrance of me."

Jesus next took the "bread" (Luke 22:19). Then, after He had thanked God for it, Christ broke the bread in pieces and gave it to His disciples. He explained that the bread symbolized His body. The flat, hard bread reminded Jews of the haste in which their ancestors had left Egypt; it reminds us of Jesus' body that was sacrificed for us. His statement is a powerful image of what He did for us.

The command "do this in remembrance of me" indicates that Jesus was instituting a new meal. It not only memorialized His crucifixion, but also served as a time of fellowship and unity for believers. The Lord's Supper (as it came to be called) moreover is a visible proclamation and symbol of Jesus' return, which believers anticipate with eagerness.

B. The Cup: vs. 20

In the same way, after the supper he took the cup, saying, "This cup is the new covenant in my blood, which is poured out for you.

After Jesus and His disciples had eaten the meal, Christ took another cup (Luke 22:20), possibly the third (the cup of blessing) of the four cups in the Jewish Passover celebration. The contents of the cup probably reminded Jews of the blood that protected their firstborn from the angel of death; it reminds us of Jesus' blood that was poured out as a sacrifice for our sins (Acts 20:28).

The Savior, quoting Jeremiah 31:31, called the liquid in the cup "the new covenant in my blood" (Luke 22:20). This means the cup was a token of the new covenant between God and believers. Jesus' atoning sacrifice ratified the covenant, making salvation possible (Heb. 8:8, 13; 9:11-28); also, His reinterpretation of the symbolism of the Passover meal indicated the dawn of a new era. Some think Jesus refused the fourth cup until He could drink it (perhaps symbolically) in the coming fullness of the kingdom.

In establishing the Lord's Supper, Jesus made a transition from the old covenant to the new. The old covenant was based on the system of sacrifices and ceremonies that reminded people of their need for salvation. The new covenant is based on the sacrifice of Christ. In His death, He fulfilled all that was symbolized in the old covenant and provided a complete means of forgiveness.

IV. THE BETRAYAL: LUKE 22:21-23

But the hand of him who is going to betray me is with mine on the table. The Son of Man will go as it has been decreed, but woe to that man who betrays him." They began to question among themselves which of them it might be who would do this.

A comparison of Luke with the other Gospels suggests that Luke's version of the Lord's Supper is arranged topically, not chronologically. For instance, in Matthew and Mark, Jesus' warning about the betrayer occurs prior to the giving of the bread and cup, whereas Luke placed it afterward (Matt. 26:20-25; Mark 14:17-21).

John 13:30, which records the departure of Judas, suggests that he may have been gone by the time the meal was shared. It is possible, though, based on Luke's account, that Judas was present at the event. If so, the contemptible nature of his hypocrisy and crime are all the more evident.

Judas's plan to betray Christ did not catch Him by surprise. He supernaturally knew what was about to happen (Luke 22:21). Even His crucifixion was under God's sovereign control and according to His eternal plan (Acts 2:23; 4:27-28); nevertheless, "woe" (Luke 22:22), or eternal gloom, awaited Judas for his act of treachery.

The intent of Jesus' statement was not merely to identify the specific individual who would betray Him; moreover, it indicated that the traitor was close to Him, somebody whom no one would suspect. As a result of Jesus' comment, the disciples were dismayed. None of them could imagine who could do such a thing; so they began to discuss who it might be (vs. 23).

Discussion Questions

1. What instructions did Jesus give to Peter and John concerning the preparations for the Passover meal?
2. What are some possible views regarding the question recorded in Luke 22:11?
3. What does the reference in verse 16 to the Passover being fulfilled possibly suggest?
4. What did the bread that Jesus broke symbolize?
5. What did the contents of the cup Jesus shared represent?
6. Upon what is the new covenant based?
7. What awaited Judas for his act of treachery?

Contemporary Application

In the Old Testament worship, the Hebrews used symbols to remind themselves of a past important event in the national history. The same is true when believers celebrate the Lord's Supper. It provides them with a reminder to thank God for the gift of eternal life.

Jesus Himself emphasized the importance of remembering that He sacrificed His life for us. After breaking the bread, and again after raising His cup, Jesus told the disciples that each time they observed Communion they should do so in remembrance of Him (1 Cor. 11:24-25).

There is more implied in this command, however, than simply being aware of the historical facts. Believers need to remember that the bread and the cup depict the events of Jesus' death and call for a response of faith on their part. The Communion elements help them recall that Christ has initiated His new covenant with those who believe.

As Christians participate in the Lord's Supper, they should not do so thoughtlessly. While it was never intended to be a gloomy event, its message is a serious one. It points to the high price Jesus paid to redeem all people from the ravages of sin. If believers have no respect for Communion, is it reasonable to think that they care for the one it represents?

Believers should be encouraged not to treat the Lord's Supper only as an afterthought or something that must be rushed through before the congregation is dismissed; instead, they need to renew their sense of awe at the price Jesus paid for their sins.

It is not possible, of course, for believers to feel a spiritual high every time they observe Communion; but they can show their awe by displaying respect and reverence to the Lord during this sacred time. Who more than Christ should command their awe? Of course, no one, for Jesus is the one who created them, saves them from their sin, and leads them in their daily lives.

Perhaps its been a while since the adults in your church, by celebrating the Lord's Supper, felt awe at what Jesus did for them at the cross. Their conscious effort to reflect upon the meaning of Communion can be a way for them to renew their esteem and reverence.

Prayer and Arrest

Scripture

Background Scripture: *Matthew 26:36-50*
Scripture Lesson: *Matthew 26:36-50*
Key Verse: *"My Father, if it is possible, may this cup be taken from me. Yet not as I will, but as you will."* Matthew 26:39.
Scripture Lesson for Children: *Matthew 26:14-16, 36, 47-50*
Key Verse for Children: *From then on Judas watched for an opportunity to hand [Jesus] over.* Matthew 26:16.

Lesson Aim

To prompt the students to follow Jesus' example by responding to mistreatment with patience and conciliation.

Lesson Setting

Time: A.D. *30*
Place: *Jerusalem*

Lesson Outline

Prayer and Arrest

  I. Jesus' Agony: Matthew 26:36-46
      A. *Jesus' Sorrow: vss. 36-38*
      B. *Jesus' Prayer: vs. 39*
      C. *Jesus' Command: vss. 40-41*
      D. *Jesus' Second and Third Prayers: vss. 42-44*
      E. *Jesus' Rebuke: vss. 45-46*
 II. Jesus' Arrest: Matthew 26:47-50
      A. *An Armed Mob: vs. 47*
      B. *Judas' Signal: vss. 48-49*
      C. *Jesus' Surrender: vs. 50*

Introduction for Adults

Topic: *Praying during Tough Times*

Cries to God fill our television screens in times of terrible disasters. Bad news from the physicians drives us to our knees. Family breakups and troubles with children force us to pray. The risk, of course, is that when the dangers pass, we forget to pray. It's great to pray during tough times, but what about the other times?

Strong habits of prayer develop during good and bad times. Prayer is much more than crying out for God's help when the house is falling in. Prayer begins with worship, praise, and thanksgiving. Prayer helps us to know God as our Lord and Savior. We can talk to Him at any time.

When Jesus entered Gethsemane, He knew what prayer was all about. Difficult moments will come at some time in our lives. Our prayer and worship disciplines will help us weather such crises.

Introduction for Youth

Topic: *Too Tired*

We all know that we should pray, but how do you find time to pray? Prayer should be part of our weekly worship times and part of our youth group's activities. We can learn to pray for each other and to lead in group prayer.

However, that's not easy if we neglect to build strong personal prayer habits. Some people follow daily prayer and Bible reading guides. Others keep journals and write their own prayers.

There is no one style of prayer. Prayer is not a special religious language for experts. When we pray, we talk to God, thank and praise Him, and ask for His help, guidance, and intervention in our needs.

When we make our daily schedules, we should block out prayer time. We can't wait until we fall into bed. We should pray when we are alert, not exhausted.

Concepts for Children

Topic: *Jesus is Betrayed*

1. Jesus knew that Judas would turn against Him.
2. Jesus gave Judas an opportunity to change his mind.
3. Even when Judas turned against Jesus, Jesus still loved him.
4. It is tough for us to deal with those who don't like us.
5. God can use these tough times to make us trust Him more.
6. God wants us to remain faithful to Jesus even when we are with our friends.

Lesson Commentary

I. Jesus' Agony: Matthew 26:36-46

A. Jesus' Sorrow: vss. 36-38

Then Jesus went with his disciples to a place called Gethsemane, and he said to them, "Sit here while I go over there and pray." He took Peter and the two sons of Zebedee along with him, and he began to be sorrowful and troubled. Then he said to them, "My soul is overwhelmed with sorrow to the point of death. Stay here and keep watch with me."

Judas Iscariot is like a thread of deception that weaves through the first three lessons of this quarter. He is the disciple among the Twelve who agreed to betray Jesus (Matt. 26:14-16) and whom the Savior spoke about at the Passover meal (Matt. 26:25; Luke 22:21-22). Judas is also the one who identified Jesus to the religious authorities by means of a kiss (Matt. 26:47-49).

The details of Judas's life are sketchy; and, because of his betrayal of Jesus, Judas is even more of a mystery, especially his reason for becoming traitorous. Greed is one possible motivation. Others suggest Judas wanted to force Christ into asserting His true power and overthrowing the Romans. A third possibility is that Judas was upset over Jesus' apparent ambivalence to the law and His association with sinners.

Judas, of course, was not operating alone at the time of Jesus' arrest. The religious and civil authorities, along with a raucous mob, accompanied Judas (Mark 14:43). Even more tragic is the fact that, once Jesus was taken into custody, all the disciples deserted Him and fled (vs. 50); yet, even in this dark period, Christ was able to entrust Himself to "him who judges justly" (1 Pet. 2:23). The Father, in turn, eventually delivered His Son from His ordeal by raising Him from the dead (Rom. 1:4; Heb. 5:7).

With respect to the events after the Passover meal, Jesus went with His disciples to pray at "Gethsemane" (Matt. 26:36). This name is derived from a Hebrew term that means "oil press." It was probably an olive orchard or garden on the lower slopes of the Mount of Olives just east of Jerusalem, across from the Kidron Valley and opposite the temple. In the location where olives were crushed and ground, the Anointed One would be crushed with grief.

In those days it was common for wealthy people to maintain a garden outside of Jerusalem, perhaps more as an escape from the city than as a place to raise vegetables. The owner of one of these gardens evidently made his olive grove available to Jesus as a place for Him to get away for prayer, rest, and fellowship with His disciples.

Jesus was aware of the test awaiting Him. He also knew He could not draw strength for that hour from His followers. He thus returned to a familiar place where He could pray to the heavenly Father.

While the others stayed behind, Jesus took Peter, James, and John with Him further into Gethsemane. This was the third time that Christ singled out these three disciples to accompany Him for a specific purpose. The other two occasions were the Transfiguration (17:1-9) and the restoring of Jairus's daughter to life (Luke 8:49-56).

As the time of His crucifixion drew near, Jesus began to be filled with anguish and distress (Matt. 26:37). He told the three that His soul was so filled with sorrow that He felt as if He were dying. He thus asked them to remain with Him and "keep watch" (vs. 38).

B. Jesus' Prayer: vs. 39

Going a little farther, he fell with his face to the ground and prayed, "My Father, if it is possible, may this cup be taken from me. Yet not as I will, but as you will."

Jesus then went on further into the garden, knelt with His face to the ground, and prayed. He petitioned that, if it was possible, the Father might allow the "cup" (Matt. 26:39) of suffering to pass from Him (see Ps. 75:8; Isa. 51:17). It seems that Jesus' prayer was a last-minute plea for an easier way of accomplishing human redemption; though Jesus' own personal anguish weighed heavily upon Him, He surrendered His desires to the Father's will.

It would be incorrect to conclude that Christ was somehow faltering in His mission. He would go to the cross, though He recoiled from the suffering it involved. As terrible as the physical pain would be, the sinless Son of God was more concerned about bearing the guilt of all people and being cut off (even temporarily) from His Father (Matt. 27:46; 2 Cor. 5:21; Gal. 3:13; 1 Pet. 2:24).

This account of Jesus' struggle reminds us that we do not have to face suffering stoically, pretending that it does not matter. We also see that God gives grace to help us endure suffering as we remain true to Him.

C. Jesus' Command: vss. 40-41

Then he returned to his disciples and found them sleeping. "Could you men not keep watch with me for one hour?" he asked Peter. "Watch and pray so that you will not fall into temptation. The spirit is willing, but the body is weak."

When Jesus returned to the disciples, He found them sleeping. Christ asked Peter, who had claimed to be ready to die for Him (Matt. 26:35), "could you men not keep watch with me for one hour?" (vs. 40). Christ urged His followers to stay awake and pray so that, in the moment of testing, they would not falter. Otherwise, the temptation to abandon Jesus would overtake them (vs. 41).

We should not be harder on the disciples than Jesus was. Even in His agony, He understood their all-too-human struggle. They had willing spirits and wanted to do what was right; but their bodies were weak, and so they slept. The contrast between the frailty of the disciples and the fortitude of the Savior is amazing.

D. Jesus' Second and Third Prayers: vss. 42-44

He went away a second time and prayed, "My Father, if it is not possible for this cup to be taken away unless I drink it, may your will be done." When he came back, he again found them sleeping, because their eyes were heavy. So he left them and went away once more and prayed the third time, saying the same thing.

In the garden we see Jesus in what was probably His most vulnerable moment. Because He faced intense internal conflict, He again left the disciples and prayed to the Father. Despite the agony of the cross, Jesus was willing to endure it so that the will of the Lord would be accomplished (Matt. 26:42).

When Jesus returned to His disciples, He again found them sleeping. Verse 43 explains that "their eyes were heavy," which means they were extremely or excessively sleepy. According to Luke 22:45, sorrow was another reason for their exhaustion.

For a third time Jesus went off alone to pray as He had before (Matt. 26:44). We do not find here a conflict between the Persons of the Godhead; rather, Christ, in the realm of His humanity, voluntarily surrendered to the will of the Father in all things. In every way the Son's desires completely harmonized with those of the Father.

E. Jesus' Rebuke: vss. 45-46

Then he returned to the disciples and said to them, "Are you still sleeping and resting? Look, the hour is near, and the Son of Man is betrayed into the hands of sinners. Rise, let us go! Here comes my betrayer!"

As before, when Jesus returned to the disciples, He found them sleeping. He woke them and declared that the time had come for Him, the "Son of Man" (Matt. 26:45), to be delivered over to sinners. In fact, Judas, the betrayer, was at hand to set in motion a series of events leading up to Jesus' crucifixion (vs. 46).

This account instructs us in at least three ways. First, if overwhelming problems came to Jesus, then we should not be surprised to find that we sometimes have to face troubles. Second, even at our weakest moment, God can minister to our need and help us. Third, because of our human weakness, we need supernatural empowerment from God to resist temptation.

II. JESUS' ARREST: MATTHEW 26:47-50

A. An Armed Mob: vs. 47

While he was still speaking, Judas, one of the Twelve, arrived. With him was a large crowd armed with swords and clubs, sent from the chief priests and the elders of the people.

Perhaps while the disciples were still in the process of waking up, Judas, accompanied by a cast sent by the chief priests and elders, arrived at center stage (Matt. 26:47). Undoubtedly, the sounds of the approaching crowd and the rattle of weapons disturbed the quiet of the garden.

The religious leaders probably could have found a way to arrest Jesus without the help of Judas, but his cooperation made their job easier. Judas, being familiar with Jesus' habits, could guide an armed crowd to Him at a time when He could be arrested without many of His supporters on hand to observe.

B. Judas' Signal: vss. 48-49

Now the betrayer had arranged a signal with them: "The one I kiss is the man; arrest him." Going at once to Jesus, Judas said, "Greetings, Rabbi!" and kissed him.

Judas had already given the throng of temple police a sign: they should seize the one he kissed (Matt. 26:48). This signal most likely had been set, not because Jesus was unknown to the mob's leaders, but because the dimly lighted, confused setting might make identification difficult.

Judas wasted no time in approaching Jesus, addressing Him as "Rabbi" (vs. 49), which could also be rendered "Teacher," and giving Him a kiss. Judas's act of betrayal is especially sinister when it is realized that it was common in the culture of the time for a disciple to kiss his master when greeting him.

C. Jesus' Surrender: vs. 50

Jesus replied, "Friend, do what you came for." Then the men stepped forward, seized Jesus and arrested him.

Judas could have saved his theatricals, not to mention the extras and their weapons, for Jesus surrendered without a fight. He even addressed Judas as "Friend" (Matt. 26:50), despite the fact that this once trusted disciple had become a traitor. The other disciples, who had slept instead of watching and praying, were not prepared for what was happening. After Peter's futile attempt to defend Jesus, they all deserted Him (vss. 51-56).

Jesus, in contrast, faced the hostility of His enemies with God-inspired boldness and courage because He had prayed. He had given Himself to the will of God, and now Christ surrendered to the tide that would sweep Him directly to the cross. Through His ordeal, He was about to strike a savage blow to the power of sin and death.

Discussion Questions

1. For what possible purposes did Jesus use Gethsemane?
2. Why did Jesus return to this familiar place on the eve of His death?
3. What did Jesus want Peter, James, and John to do during His time of anguish?
4. What did Jesus, while in prayer, ask the Father to do?
5. What did the disciples end up doing during Jesus' time of distress in the garden and why?
6. What was Jesus willing to do, despite the agony of the cross?
7. What was especially sinister about the way Judas betrayed Christ?

Contemporary Application

Although North American believers in the twenty-first century do not suffer flogging and crucifixion as a result of their commitment to God, they should not be surprised if others occasionally treat them badly for any number of reasons. For instance, they might be excluded from a social event because they are labeled as being too "religious" or a peer might spread false rumors about them because of their devotion to Christ.

Because of sin, mistreatment is inevitable in this world; thus, believers should expect it. Those who are not for Christ are against Him; thus, as believers live for the Lord, unbelievers will oppose them. Even fellow believers will occasionally let Christians down and do something that hurts them.

This does not mean that believers should intentionally try to irritate others and invite mistreatment; but they should also not be devastated when it happens. In fact, when Christians truly seek to follow God's call for their lives, some unbelievers will disapprove of it. If adults who are Christian never encounter any opposition to their faith, it may be an indication that they are not as overt in their walk with Christ as they ought to be.

Whatever mistreatment the members of your class might experience, Jesus is the supreme example for them to follow. When He was cursed, He blessed His detractors; when He was persecuted, He patiently endured the mistreatment; and when He was slandered, He humbly entrusted His circumstances to the Father.

If believers are ostracized by their peers for being perceived as excessively "spiritual," their first reaction might be outrage; however, a more Christlike response is for them to refrain from losing their temper. By demonstrating patience, adults who are Christian might have an opportunity to share their faith with their unsaved acquaintances.

Admittedly it is not always easy to be calm in tense situations, but when believers are, they reflect the biblical example of Christ when He was mistreated. God will shower them with His kindness and grace and enable them to make it through the difficult moment.

Jesus on Trial

DEVOTIONAL READING

John 10:22-30

DAILY BIBLE READINGS

Monday March 22
Mark 14:46-52 Jesus Is Arrested, Disciples Desert Him

Tuesday March 23
Mark 14:53-59 Jesus Is Taken to the High Priest

Wednesday March 24
Mark 14:60-65 Jesus Declares He Is the Messiah

Thursday March 25
John 10:22-30 The Father and I Are One

Friday March 26
Mark 15:1-5 Jesus Goes Before Pilate

Saturday March 27
Mark 15:6-10 The Crowd Wants Barabbas Released

Sunday March 28
Mark 15:11-15 The Crowd Shouts for Jesus' Death

Scripture

Background Scripture: *Mark 14—15*
Scripture Lesson: *Mark 14:55-64; 15:1-2, 12-15*
Key Verses: *"Are you the Christ, the Son of the Blessed One?" "I am," said Jesus.* Mark 14:61-62.
Scripture Lesson for Children: *Mark 14:53-65; 15:1-2*
Key Verse for Children: *Many testified falsely against [Jesus].* Mark 14:56.

Lesson Aim

To help the students better understand how radical Jesus' claims are and strive to keep their confession of Him free from unbiblical concepts.

Lesson Setting

Time: A.D. *30*
Place: *Jerusalem*

Lesson Outline

Jesus on Trial
   I. False Accusations: Mark 14:55-59
      A. No Evidence: vss. 55-56
      B. The Charge: vss. 57-59
  II. Interrogation: Mark 14:60-64
      A. No Reply: vss. 60-61
      B. Jesus' Claim: vs. 62
      C. Condemnation: vss. 63-64
 III. Before Pilate: Mark 15:1-2
 IV. Pilate's Verdict: Mark 15:12-15
      A. The Crowd's Demand: vss. 12-14
      B. The Crowd Satisfied: vs. 15

Introduction for Adults

Topic: *Falsely Accused*

John was falsely accused of molesting a junior high school girl. He lost his teaching position at the school. It took years before his name was cleared, but he never got his job back. The girl's mother's false accusation left a permanent scar on John and his family.

Jesus' trial reminds us of the risks of following God's will. At some points our confessions of faith will be tested. We are all liable to be accused of certain things just because we are Christians.

Jesus' trial not only highlights animosity toward Jesus and the church, but also shows us how to conduct ourselves when we are under fire. Our natural propensity is to cry, "Foul!" and to defend ourselves and our rights. But revenge is not the biblical way. Paul told Christians not to take matters into their own hands, "but leave room for God's wrath" (Rom. 12:19).

Introduction for Youth

Topic: *Falsely Accused*

Bearing false witness at a trial (perjury) is a crime. But, while spreading stories about someone else is not a crime, it amounts to the same thing. How easy it is to add our remarks to the tales being told, especially if the majority seems to have already decided that the stories are true. We don't want to appear to be siding with the unpopular victim.

Too often in our own culture we act like judge and jury—just like Jesus' accusers did. If we can't find the truth, we invent something that sounds like the truth, or we flavor it to tilt the scales. Many times our fellow students suffer grievously from this kind of behavior.

The trial of Jesus tells us how not to behave and how to handle lies about ourselves. If our Lord and Savior, the King of glory, refused to attack His accusers, we can follow His example. We can also declare that, because Jesus is Lord, we will not betray Him. We will stand for truth, no matter what it costs us.

Concepts for Children

Topic: *False Witnesses Against Jesus*

1. The authorities could find no evidence of any wrongdoing against Jesus.
2. The authorities condemned Jesus to death because He claimed to be God's Son.
3. Pilate, the Roman governor, agreed to the death of Jesus.
4. When others treat us wrongly, we do not have to do the same thing.
5. Jesus showed us how to stand for truth and be kind to others.
6. Even our anger must be controlled by God's Spirit within us.

Lesson Commentary

I. FALSE ACCUSATIONS: MARK 14:55-59

A. No Evidence: vss. 55-56

The chief priests and the whole Sanhedrin were looking for evidence against Jesus so that they could put him to death, but they did not find any. Many testified falsely against him, but their statements did not agree.

Jesus had two trials, one Jewish and one Roman. Each of these trials had three parts. The Jewish trial was held at night, a time when many of Jesus' supporters would be asleep and less likely to protest His arrest. The trial began with a preliminary hearing before Annas, a former high priest (John 18:12-14, 19-23). Next, the Sanhedrin tried Jesus in the quarters of the current high priest, Caiaphas (Matt. 26:57, 59-68; Mark 14:53-65; Luke 22:66-71; John 18:24). Then at daybreak this trial ended with an official condemnation of Jesus (Matt. 27:1; Mark 15:1; Luke 23:1).

At that point, the Jews took Jesus to the Roman governor of Judea and Samaria, Pontius Pilate, who questioned Him (Matt. 27:2, 11-14; Mark 15:2-5; Luke 23:2-5; John 18:28-38). Then Pilate sent Jesus to be examined by Herod, the ruler of Jesus' home territory (Luke 23:6-12). Finally, Pilate gave a judgment against Jesus, leading to His crucifixion (Matt. 27:15-26; Mark 15:6-15; Luke 23:13-25; John 19:4-16).

In terms of the events coming after Jesus' arrest, He was immediately taken to the home of the high priest, Caiaphas, where the chief priests, the elders, and the scribes had gathered (Mark 14:53). The chief priests were members of important priestly families, and mostly Sadducees. The elders were nonpriestly aristocrats, and also mostly Sadducees. The scribes were interpreters of the law, and mostly Pharisees.

Together these three groups comprised the Sanhedrin, the highest judicial council and religious tribunal of the Jewish nation. Since Judea was an occupied area, the Sanhedrin functioned under the authority of the Roman government, deciding all issues involving religious law and acting in some civil and criminal cases.

Mark did not mention the Pharisees in his list of people who had gathered to interrogate Jesus. This omission is not because the hostility of the Pharisees toward Jesus had declined, but probably because the influence of the Pharisees on Jewish politics was much less in Jerusalem than it was in the country areas. Also, the priestly party was composed mainly of non-Pharisees.

Meanwhile, Peter and John followed and were able to get inside the courtyard of the house (Mark 14:54; John 18:15). Peter wanted to know what the outcome of Jesus' arrest and interrogation would be. While Peter's intentions were noble, his presence in the courtyard would lead to his repeated denials of the Savior (Mark 14:66-72).

The religious leaders were determined to execute Jesus. Although they did not have the right to put people to death, they could condemn Jesus and turn Him over to the Romans for execution on an appropriate charge.

In seeking to build a case against Jesus that would justify sentencing Him "to death" (Mark 14:55), the Sanhedrin questioned a number of false witnesses (vs. 56). Despite their efforts, however, the Council failed to come up with any two witnesses who agreed with one another, which was essential for a conviction.

Moses had decreed that one witness was insufficient to condemn a person of a crime; instead, a person's guilt had to be established on the testimony of at least two or three witnesses (Num. 35:30; Deut. 17:6; 19:15). If the Sanhedrin could have found two false witnesses to incriminate Jesus, they would have been satisfied.

B. The Charge: vss. 57-59

Then some stood up and gave this false testimony against him: "We heard him say, 'I will destroy this man-made temple and in three days will build another, not made by man.'" Yet even then their testimony did not agree.

Finally, two false witness accused Jesus of making an impious claim (Mark 14:57). They alleged that Jesus had said He could destroy God's temple and rebuild it in "three days" (vs. 58); nevertheless, even on this point their testimonies did not agree (vs. 59). Jesus, of course, had been talking about His body and not the structure Herod had built (John 2:19).

II. INTERROGATION: MARK 14:60-64

A. No Reply: vss. 60-61

Then the high priest stood up before them and asked Jesus, "Are you not going to answer? What is this testimony that these men are bringing against you?" But Jesus remained silent and gave no answer. Again the high priest asked him, "Are you the Christ, the Son of the Blessed One?"

Perhaps Caiaphas was angry and frustrated that his plot against Jesus was not developing in the way he had planned. In any case, he "stood up" (Mark 14:60) and demanded whether Jesus had a reply to what His accusers had said. In fulfillment of Isaiah 53:7, Jesus remained silent.

Caiaphas then commanded Jesus to answer His accusers under oath by "the living God" (Matt. 26:63). According to Jewish law, Jesus was now obliged to respond to the high priest. Caiphas wanted to know whether Jesus was "the Christ, the Son of the Blessed One" (Mark 14:61).

B. Jesus' Claim: vs. 62

"I am," said Jesus. "And you will see the Son of Man sitting at the right hand of the Mighty One and coming on the clouds of heaven."

In response, Jesus clearly affirmed "I am" (Mark 14:62). Jesus then expanded on His answer by applying Psalm 110:1 and Daniel 7:13-14 to Himself. He declared that, in the future, He, "the Son of Man" (Mark 14:62), would be seated "at the right hand of the Mighty One." Jesus meant He would occupy the place of highest honor and authority in God's kingdom. Jesus also declared that He would one day return on the "clouds of heaven" to judge His enemies.

C. Condemnation: vss. 63-64

The high priest tore his clothes. "Why do we need any more witnesses?" he asked. "You have heard the blasphemy. What do you think?" They all condemned him as worthy of death.

What Jesus had said about Himself was absolutely true; nevertheless, the religious authorities rejected His claim to be the divine Messiah. Although Jewish law forbade the high priest from tearing his garments (Lev. 21:10), Caiaphas "tore his clothes" (Mark 14:63) in order to show how furious he was with Jesus' statement.

Caiaphas accused Jesus of speaking "blasphemy" (vs. 64); that is, Jesus' words were an affront to God. Caiaphas then announced that no further witnesses were needed (Matt. 26:65), for the court had heard Jesus' blasphemy. When the high priest asked his colleagues for their verdict, they declared that Jesus deserved to die (see Lev. 24:16). By this time it was probably nearing 3:00 A.M.

III. BEFORE PILATE: MARK 15:1-2

Very early in the morning, the chief priests, with the elders, the teachers of the law and the whole Sanhedrin, reached a decision. They bound Jesus, led him away and handed him over to Pilate. "Are you the king of the Jews?" asked Pilate. "Yes, it is as you say," Jesus replied.

Jewish law stipulated that a guilty verdict in a capital crime had to be delayed until the next day. Thus, very early in the morning (perhaps between 5:00 and 6:00 A.M.), "the whole Sanhedrin" (Mark 15:1) met and decided to have Jesus bound and escorted to Pilate. He normally lived at Caesarea on the Mediterranean coast. His presence in Jerusalem at this time was probably due to the Passover holiday.

The vote of condemnation after dawn gave the appearance of legality; yet the procedures of the Sanhedrin during Jesus' trial were illegal. For one thing, Jewish law required that any trial for a capital crime begin during the daytime and adjourn by nightfall. For another thing, members of the Sanhedrin were supposed to be impartial judges. Finally, Jewish rules prohibited convicting the accused on his own testimony.

Because the Romans did not give the Jews the right of capital punishment for the charge of blasphemy, the religious leaders had to convince Pilate that their demand for Jesus' crucifixion was justified. They thus fabricated three additional charges against Jesus that would be of concern to a Roman governor.

Christ allegedly misled the people, urged them not to pay taxes, and claimed to be a king (Luke 23:2). Pilate concerned himself only with the last charge. Perhaps this is because claiming to be a king sounded like treason. In that day, the Romans knew no greater threat to stability and peace than the crime of treason.

When Pilate asked Jesus, "Are you the king of the Jews?" (Mark 15:2), He responded, "Yes, it is as you say." Perhaps Jesus used this enigmatic reply to affirm that He was Israel's rightful king, but that Pilate's concept of it was flawed. Jesus stressed that He was a king in a spiritual sense (John 18:36-37).

Pilate might have been expected to interpret Jesus' words to mean He admitted the charge of treason. The governor, nevertheless, evidently did not consider Jesus a danger to the empire; and yet, Pilate knew that if he released Jesus, he would offend Jesus' accusers.

The governor then thought he saw a way out of this dilemma. The crowd expected him to the keep the practice of releasing a prisoner at Passover. This possibly was a symbolic reenactment of the freeing of the Hebrew slaves as well as a good will gesture to maintain popular support among the Jews.

IV. PILATE'S VERDICT: MARK 15:12-15

A. The Crowd's Demand: vss. 12-14

"What shall I do, then, with the one you call the king of the Jews?" Pilate asked them. "Crucify him!" they shouted. "Why? What crime has he committed?" asked Pilate. But they shouted all the louder, "Crucify him!"

The religious leaders quickly countered Pilate's move. They incited the people to demand the death of Jesus and to call for the release of a criminal named Barabbas (Mark 15:6-11). Ironically, he was guilty of the very thing Jesus had been falsely accused of—trying to force the Romans out of Palestine.

Pilate then asked the crowd what he should do with the person whom they called "the king of the Jews" (vs. 12). The people, in turn, demanded Jesus' crucifixion (vs. 13). Despite Pilate's further attempts to release Jesus, the crowd continued to demand His crucifixion (vs. 14).

B. The Crowd Satisfied: vs. 15

Wanting to satisfy the crowd, Pilate released Barabbas to them. He had Jesus flogged, and handed him over to be crucified.

Pilate finally gave in to the pressure (Mark 15:15). He wanted the approval of the crowd more than he wanted to protect the life of an innocent man, so he handed over Jesus for scourging and execution. Jesus' tormentors used a lead-tipped whip to flail His back. It was a horrible punishment, and many died in the process of being scourged.

Scripture reveals three agents at work in Jesus' trial and condemnation. In addition to the Jewish and Roman authorities, Acts 2:23 notes that these human agents were operating according to "God's set purpose and foreknowledge." It was His will that, in fulfillment of all the prophets had declared about the Messiah, He should suffer and die (3:18). In fact, everything the religious and civil authorities did happened according to the eternal will and plan of God (Acts 4:28; 1 Pet. 1:20).

Discussion Questions

1. What were the religious leaders determined to do to Jesus?
2. Why was it important for the Sanhedrin to obtain at least two witnesses who agreed?
3. How did Jesus respond when Caiaphas commanded Him to answer His accusers

under oath?

4. What was the charge that Caiaphas brought against Jesus?
5. Why did the Sanhedrin wait until dawn to make its verdict against Jesus official?
6. Why did the religious leaders have to convince Pilate of their demand to crucify Jesus?
7. What decision did Pilate finally make concerning Jesus?

Contemporary Application

The longer adults serve Jesus, the less radical His claims about Himself might seem to them; but for those who hear His claims for the first time or who have rejected those claims, His assertions to be the Son of God, the Messiah, and the King of kings sound radical.

Even for older adults, however, who have believed in Christ for several years, His claims about Himself should still sound radical, if for no other reason than that those claims should have a radical impact on their lives. For instance, Jesus claimed to be God; thus, He should be Lord over every detail of the adults' lives. Also, His claim to be the Savior means they should live uprightly in their thoughts and behavior.

The sad truth, though, is that people today continue to reject Jesus in many ways. Some are hostile to Him and try to refute or ridicule His claims at any opportunity they get. Others reject Jesus' claims by simply ignoring them. Still others think that Jesus' claims are probably true, but reject them because they will not accept the demands that believing in those claims will place on them.

The most tragic rejection of Jesus may be those who appear to welcome Christ with fanfare. Then when things do not go their way, they close the door on Him, leaving Him standing outside their hearts (so to speak).

In the final analysis, Jesus' claims are radical because He said He was God, which no other human being past, present, or future can rightfully assert; but His claims are also radical because they are supposed to have a radical claim on us as believers.

Jesus' Crucifixion

DEVOTIONAL READING

John 10:11-18

DAILY BIBLE READINGS

Monday March 29
*Isaiah 53:1-6 Isaiah's
Prophecy of the Suffering
Servant*

Tuesday March 30
*Isaiah 53:7-12 He Bore the
Sins of Many*

Wednesday March 31
*John 19:16-20 Jesus Is
Crucified*

Thursday April 1
*John 19:21-25a The King of
the Jews*

Friday April 2
*John 19:25b-30 It Is
Finished*

Saturday April 3
*John 19:31-37 The Spear
Pierces His Side*

Sunday April 4
*John 19:38-42 Joseph and
Nicodemus Take Jesus' Body*

Scripture

Background Scripture: *John 19:16b-42*
Scripture Lesson: *John 19:16b-24, 26-30*
Key Verses: *So the soldiers took charge of Jesus. Carrying his
own cross, he went out to the place of the Skull (which in
Aramaic is called Golgotha). Here they crucified him.*
John 19:16-18.
Scripture Lesson for Children: *John 19:16b-30*
Key Verse for Children: *[Jesus] went out to the place of the
Skull. . . . Here they crucified him.* John 19:17-18.

Lesson Aim

To give the students a greater sense of appreciation for
what Jesus did for them on the cross.

Lesson Setting

Time: A.D. *30*
Place: *Jerusalem*

Lesson Outline

Jesus' Crucifixion

  I. Jesus' Crucifixion: John 19:16b-27
      A. *The Place: vss. 16b-17*
      B. *Jesus' Suffering: vs. 18*
      C. *The Sign: vss. 19-22*
      D. *The Prophecy: vss. 23-24*
      E. *Jesus' Mother: vss. 25-27*
  II. Mission Accomplished: John 19:28-30
      A. *Scripture Fulfilled: vs. 28*
      B. *The Vinegar: vs. 29*
      C. *Jesus' Last Cry: vs. 30*

Introduction for Adults

Topic: *Putting Your Life on the Line*

Jesus went to the cross and tasted death for all of us, so that we might live by believing in Him. He did more than donate a bodily organ. Jesus willingly laid down His life for the sake of others.

Only on rare occasions do people volunteer to die in someone else's place. Our lives are too precious. We prefer life to death.

Jesus did not die because He deserved His execution. He died because sin's judgment is death. All have sinned and sin's wages are death. No one escapes God's righteous judgment.

In His own body Jesus bore our sins. He took the judgment we deserve. He satisfied God's righteousness. Jesus, who knew no sin, became sin for us so that we might be declared righteous before God. That's the supreme message of the Gospel.

Introduction for Youth

Topic: *Paying the Price*

Three highly ranked high school basketball players paid the price for their academic deficiencies when they got to college. Before their careers were barely launched, they were bounced for not making satisfactory grades.

We all know similar stories about paying the price for things like drug and alcohol abuse and sexual promiscuity. Although this principle is deeply ingrained in us, we still take chances and think we can escape the consequences of our misbehaviors.

In the case of Jesus, however, He paid the price not for any sins of His own but for ours. That is why His cross is the cornerstone of our Christian faith and hope. Without the cross, we are doomed to reap the consequences, not only for the bad things we do, but also for the good things we fail to do.

We may still suffer for abusing our bodies; but the good news is that we can confess our sins and thank Jesus for dying on the cross so that we might be saved.

Concepts for Children

Topic: *Jesus Was Crucified*

1. Jesus died to take away our sins.
2. Jesus' suffering shows how much we owe Him.
3. The cross points to the price God paid to save us.
4. We grow in faith, obedience, service, and worship as we keep Jesus central in our thinking.
5. Jesus' death reminds us that God hates sin.
6. When people ask us about Jesus' death on the cross, we can tell them how to be saved by trusting in Him.

Lesson Commentary

I. JESUS' CRUCIFIXION: JOHN 19:16B-27

A. The Place: vss. 16b-17

So the soldiers took charge of Jesus. Carrying his own cross, he went out to the place of the Skull (which in Aramaic is called Golgotha).

After Jesus' flogging, the soldiers who were responsible for His crucifixion took charge of Him (Mark 15:16). This execution squad, which normally consisted of four legionnaires and a centurion, led Jesus away "to be crucified" (John 19:16). Crucifixion as a means of torture and execution was invented in the East and adopted by the Romans, who used it for slaves and lower-class persons.

As was customary practice in a Roman crucifixion, Jesus was made to carry His own cross (vs. 17). Most likely, this was only the crossbeam, since the upright beam usually remained in the ground at the place of execution. This excursion was typically a humiliating procession through crowded city streets, with the victim stripped naked and enduring the crowd's taunts.

The Roman government authorized its soldiers to commandeer horses and people whenever needed. According to Matthew 27:32 and Mark 15:21, the execution squad escorting Jesus forced a man named Simon, from the North African city of Cyrene, to take the cross; and Luke 23:26 states that the cross was placed on Simon so that it might be carried behind Jesus.

Jesus was led out to a location called "the place of the Skull" (John 19:17), for which the Hebrew name was "Golgotha." Its exact location is unknown, though it is clear from verse 20 that this was outside Jerusalem's walls. The place may have had that name because it bore a resemblance to a human skull or because of the many executions that occurred there.

Once the horizontal beam arrived at the execution site, it would be slid into a groove in vertical beams already set in the ground so they could be frequently reused. The condemned was then nailed to the cross with spikes driven through the wrists and feet.

The torso would face forward, but the feet would sometimes be nailed sideways, thus twisting the waist in an unnatural position. A rope was often tied around the victim's chest, knotted between the shoulders, and then tied to the beam behind the body to prevent the body from falling forward as muscles weakened.

B. Jesus' Suffering: vs. 18

Here they crucified him, and with him two others—one on each side and Jesus in the middle.

Isaiah had prophesied that the Messiah would be "numbered with the transgressors" (Isa. 53:12) in His suffering. In fulfillment of this, two thieves were crucified with Jesus (John 19:18). What an additional agony it must have caused the sinless Son of God to be publicly identified with criminals!

C. The Sign: vss. 19-22

Pilate had a notice prepared and fastened to the cross. It read: JESUS OF NAZARETH, THE KING OF THE JEWS. Many of the Jews read this sign, for the place where Jesus was crucified was near the city, and the sign was written in Aramaic, Latin and Greek. The chief priests of the Jews protested to Pilate, "Do not write 'The King of the Jews,' but that this man claimed to be king of the Jews." Pilate answered, "What I have written, I have written."

It was common practice for the execution squad to erect a sign stating the crime for which the victim was being crucified. This sign was either hung around the victim's neck or nailed above his head. The message and public execution were designed to deter others from committing crimes.

In Jesus' case, Pilate directed that the placard read, "JESUS OF NAZARETH, THE KING OF THE JEWS" (John 19:19). This statement was written in "Aramaic, Latin and Greek" (vs. 20) so that many residents of Jerusalem could read it. Thus, Jesus was officially executed because of His claim to be the King of the Jews (Mark 15:26). The "chief priests of the Jews" (John 19:21) complained to Pilate about the wording of the tablet; nevertheless, the governor refused to change it (vs. 22).

Crucifixion was one of the most cruel and degrading methods of punishment ever contrived. Death was excruciatingly slow and bloody, with the naked victim exposed to the withering heat of the sun by day and temperatures at night dropping to between 40 and 50 degrees Fahrenheit for a spring crucifixion in Palestine.

The crucified would sag under their own weight until their diaphragm could no longer operate. Then, with all their strength, they would lift themselves to gasp for air, only to sag once again. A crucified man could live as long as 36 hours on his cross, finally succumbing to death when his lungs filled up with fluid due to the position of his arms preventing breathing. Thus, crucifixion was really death by slow suffocation.

If the execution squad wanted the victim to last longer, they would have first outfitted the cross with a block of wood as a seat or footrest. This would give the victim support and improve circulation. If the crucifiers wanted to shorten the victim's life, they would break his legs with a club to remove his ability to support himself with his legs.

D. The Prophecy: vss. 23-24

When the soldiers crucified Jesus, they took his clothes, dividing them into four shares, one for each of them, with the undergarment remaining. This garment was seamless, woven in one piece from top to bottom. "Let's not tear it," they said to one another. "Let's decide by lot who will get it." This happened that the scripture might be fulfilled which said, "They divided my garments among them and cast lots for my clothing." So this is what the soldiers did.

It was accepted Roman practice for the soldiers who performed a crucifixion to divide among themselves the possessions of the person being executed. Thus, Jesus' execution squad divided His outer garments into "four shares" (John 19:23) so that each of them could get their own piece.

The soldiers did not do this, though, with Jesus' tunic, namely, the long garment He wore under the cloak next to His skin. This item was seamless, being woven in one piece "from top to bottom." Because of its value, the executioners decided to cast lots for it (vs. 24).

These lots probably were marked pebbles or broken pieces of pottery that were thrown like dice. By throwing the marked objects (on which were possibly written their names), the soldiers determined the winner of Jesus' tunic. In so doing, they unwittingly fulfilled the prophetic words of Psalm 22:18.

E. Jesus' Mother: vss. 25-27

Near the cross of Jesus stood his mother, his mother's sister, Mary the wife of Clopas, and Mary Magdalene. When Jesus saw his mother there, and the disciple whom he loved standing nearby, he said to his mother, "Dear woman, here is your son," and to the disciple, "Here is your mother." From that time on, this disciple took her into his home.

A number of women who had accompanied Jesus during His earthly ministry stood near the cross (John 19:25). Upon spotting His mother, Mary, and the disciple He loved (probably the apostle John), Jesus said to Mary, "Dear woman, here is your son" (vs. 26). This was Jesus' normal, polite way of addressing women. Christ then said to John, "Here is your mother" (vs. 27). From then on, John took Mary "into his home."

Someone would soon need to provide for Mary, since Jesus, her oldest son, would no longer be alive. Perhaps Jesus was distancing Himself from Mary so that John could take Jesus' place as Mary's earthly son. If so, Jesus probably used the term "woman" (vs. 26) to help establish Mary and John in a new "mother-son" relationship.

II. MISSION ACCOMPLISHED: JOHN 19:28-30

A. Scripture Fulfilled: vs. 28

Later, knowing that all was now completed, and so that the Scripture would be fulfilled, Jesus said, "I am thirsty."

By now Jesus realized that everything concerning His earthly life had been accomplished; also by now, He was severely dehydrated. Thus, so that "Scripture would be fulfilled" (John 19:28), Jesus said, "I am thirsty." John saw this statement as fulfilling the description of a godly sufferer given in Psalm 69:21 (see also Ps. 22:15).

B. The Vinegar: vs. 29

A jar of wine vinegar was there, so they soaked a sponge in it, put the sponge on a stalk of the hyssop plant, and lifted it to Jesus' lips.

Jesus' thirst was met with a sponge soaked in "wine vinegar" (John 19:29). This refers to a cheap beverage diluted heavily with water. It was the drink of slaves and soldiers, and offered to those being crucified as a momentary relief from agony.

One soldier used the stalk of a hyssop, probably three feet in length, to extend the sponge to Jesus' mouth. The plant was a small aromatic bush whose exact identification is uncertain. Based on Matthew 27:48 and Mark 15:36, some think the hyssop may have been a form of reed. A standing soldier could easily reach Jesus' mouth with the hyssop stalk, for the vertical crossbeam was generally never raised above ten feet high.

John's mention of the hyssop is significant, as it recalled the blood of lambs placed with hyssop stalks on Jewish doorposts at Passover so the angel of death would pass over them (Exod. 12:22). Now the Passover lamb was about to finish His suffering; and, through His death, He would give saving protection to those marked with His blood through faith.

C. Jesus' Last Cry: vs. 30

When he had received the drink, Jesus said, "It is finished." With that, he bowed his head and gave up his spirit.

Crucifixion was the Roman government's method of humiliating and defeating those who opposed their rule; but Jesus' cross did not defeat Him. He triumphed over every evil it represented on Golgotha.

Thus, when Jesus declared, "It is finished" (John 19:30), He meant His work of redemption was "now completed" (vs. 28). The phrase recorded in verse 30 echoes His words in His prayer to the Father the night before: "I have brought you glory on earth by completing the work you gave me to do" (17:4).

The Greek verb rendered "finished" (19:30) was often used in the first and second centuries A.D. for paying, or "fulfilling," a debt; it appeared as such on receipts. This fact helps us understand why "It is finished" can literally be rendered "paid in full."

From a theological standpoint, Jesus paid our debt of sin to God in full when He became "sin for us" (2 Cor. 5:21). To know Jesus is to securely bank on the sufficiency of His finished work at the cross for a right standing before a holy God. The cross was not where Jesus was *victimized*. It was where He was *victorious* over all that separates people from God.

Discussion Questions

1. To what locale was Jesus led to be crucified?
2. What is significant about the fact that two others were crucified with Jesus?
3. How did Pilate respond to the complaint of the Jewish chief priests?
4. What did the soldiers do with Jesus' garments?
5. What arrangement did Jesus make for Mary, His mother?
6. Why did Jesus say, "I am thirty" (John 19:28)?
7. How should we understand Jesus' declaration, "It is finished" (vs. 30)?

Contemporary Application

The physical pain Jesus endured was only part of His agony of being crucified. That is why, if adults only focus on Jesus' physical torment, they will fail to appreciate the terrible humiliation He suffered throughout His ordeal; for example, it was the height of injustice for sinners to abuse and mock the one who was dying in order to save sinful people.

Despite their study of this week's lesson text, it is impossible for adults (or any person) to fully grasp the extent of Jesus' suffering; but that should not stop them from trying to comprehend with their heart some of what Jesus went through to secure their salvation. This kind of knowledge will strengthen them when they endure hardships as Christians.

An even more fundamental truth is that God's provision of forgiveness and spiritual cleansing are made possible to adults (and all people) through Christ. He is the perfect sacrifice God offered to take away the sins of the world (John 1:29). By dying on the cross, Jesus accepted the wrath of God and paid the penalty associated with our rebellion against the Lord (1 John 2:2). This means that, if people want to be forgiven their sins, they must accept the salvation God offers in Christ (Acts 16:30-31).

Down through the centuries, people have found it impossible to reform themselves sufficiently to merit salvation. That is why they turned to the Lord in faith. When people put their trust in Christ, He inwardly recreates them. Through the sovereign action of the Spirit, they are transformed into children of God. The salvation offered by Christ brings with it spiritual renewal and a heart that is willing to obey the Lord.

When people accept the new life God makes available in Christ, they have the assurance that their misdeeds will not be held against them. They also have the confidence of knowing that Jesus' perfect sacrifice has wiped away all the divine charges of wrongdoing that pertain to them. It is as if the heavenly ledger for all their misdeeds has been completely erased. Every trace of guilt has been thoroughly removed, never to return.

When people humbly receive salvation in Christ, God not only pardons them, but also allows them to enjoy an intimate relationship with Him. His love can fill their souls, and His joy can overflow every portion of their lives.

The Empty Tomb

DEVOTIONAL READING

Luke 24:1-12

DAILY BIBLE READINGS

Scripture

Background Scripture: *Matthew 28:1-15*

Scripture Lesson: *Matthew 28:1-15*

Key Verses: *"Do not be afraid, for I know that you are looking for Jesus, who was crucified. He is not here; he has risen, just as he said. Come and see the place where he lay."* Matthew 28:5-6.

Key Verse for Children: *"Then go quickly and tell his disciples: 'He has risen from the dead.'"* Matthew 28:7.

Lesson Aim

To encourage the students to affirm their belief in Christ's resurrection and express that belief to others.

Lesson Setting

Time: A.D. *30*

Place: *Jerusalem*

Lesson Outline

The Empty Tomb

  I. The Women at the Tomb: Matthew 28:1

  II. The Angel's Work: Matthew 28:2-4

  III. The Angel's Words: Matthew 28:5-7

  IV. Jesus' Appearance: Matthew 28:8-10

  V. The Chief Priests' Deception: Matthew 28:11-15

Introduction for Adults

Topic: *Changing Defeat into Victory*

Christians celebrate the resurrection of a rejected King. His resurrection brought victorious life out of dark death and despair. This perhaps is the greatest reversal in history!

Christians do not worship a dead hero. They do not idolize a man who fought for a just cause but lost. Many others have suffered terrible ends for their ideals, but none of them ever came back from the grave.

Jesus was the only perfect human who ever lived. His contemporaries hated Him, but they could find no flaws in His life and teachings. Yet the greatest life ever lived suffered a terrible end.

Thankfully, God's love, wisdom, and power provided forgiveness, hope, and eternal life out of seeming defeat. Christ's incomparable triumph from tragedy stands as the greatest event of all time. But it is more than a historical incident. Jesus lives in the hearts of all those who trust in Him.

Introduction for Youth

Topic: *Alive!*

On student trips to Washington, D.C., I used to stand in awe before the memorials to the United States' greatest heroes—Washington, Jefferson, and Lincoln. I admired their courage and wisdom. They spoke to me in their speeches and proclamations. I owe them a great debt.

Nevertheless, these greats from the past are dead and gone. We cannot know them personally. We cannot invite them into our hearts. In contrast, we can know Jesus in an intimate and personal way.

That's because Jesus is alive in heaven. There is a real person in heaven, the same person who came to earth two thousand years ago. Jesus invites our trust, worship, hope, and obedience. We can talk to Him in prayer. He is our supreme confidant and helper.

Concepts for Children

Topic: *Jesus Lives!*

1. The angel told the women looking for Jesus that He had risen from the dead.
2. Jesus' resurrection means He has defeated sin and death.
3. Jesus wants us to trust and obey Him.
4. Easter gives us a wonderful opportunity to tell others about Jesus.
5. Because Jesus rose from the grave, our eternal life is a certainty.
6. When we are discouraged and fearful, the risen Lord can brighten our day.

Lesson Commentary

I. THE WOMEN AT THE TOMB: MATTHEW 28:1

After the Sabbath, at dawn on the first day of the week, Mary Magdalene and the other Mary went to look at the tomb.

The Sabbath ended at sundown on Saturday. Jesus' followers were free to go to His tomb now, but of course they did not want to do so at night. Thus, at first light on Sunday, Mary Magdalene and Mary the mother of James and Joses went to the burial site (Matt. 28:1). They had watched Jesus' entombment and thus knew where to go (see 27:56, 61).

II. THE ANGEL'S WORK: MATTHEW 28:2-4

There was a violent earthquake, for an angel of the Lord came down from heaven and, going to the tomb, rolled back the stone and sat on it. His appearance was like lightning, and his clothes were white as snow. The guards were so afraid of him that they shook and became like dead men.

The four Gospels have some differing details about the morning of Jesus' resurrection. One point of difference is which women went to the tomb that Sunday morning.

Matthew mentions just the two Marys (Matt. 28:1). Mark says Mary Magdalene, Mary the mother of James, and Salome went to the tomb (Mark 16:1). Luke mentions the same two Mary's but adds Joannna, not Salome, and refers to "the others with them" (Luke 24:10) as well. John identifies only Mary Magdalene as going to the tomb (John 20:1).

One likely explanation for the differences is that several women went to the tomb that morning, in different groups and at different times. John, for example, reports at least two visits of Mary Magdalene to the tomb (John 20:1, 10). Her first visit seems to have been with other women, for she told Peter and John what she thought had happened to Jesus' body (vs. 2).

Peter and John then went back with Mary to the tomb to look for themselves. John's Gospel also focuses in on Mary Magdalene's account of the events because she seems to be the spokesperson for the group of women. Matthew, Mark, and Luke all refer to her first in their reports of who was there that morning.

According to Matthew 28:1, the two Marys went to the tomb to look at it, perhaps because Jewish tradition called for loved ones of the deceased to visit a tomb for three days after the burial to be sure the person had truly died. Mark 16:1 additionally relates that the women hoped to anoint Jesus' body. This was a customary practice to mask the odor brought on by decay. It was also an act of devotion.

At some point, perhaps shortly before the women's arrival at the tomb, a severe earthquake had occurred. An angel of the Lord had descended from heaven, rolled back the stone from the entrance, and "sat on it" (Matt. 28:2). The angel did not remove the stone to enable Jesus to leave the tomb; rather, the celestial being did it to permit others to enter the sepulcher and see for themselves that Jesus' body was gone.

The angel had a glorious appearance. Verse 3 says his face beamed with the brightness of "lightning" and his clothes were brilliant like snow (perhaps to reflect his holiness). His awesome presence (after he had arrived at the tomb) caused the guards to tremble with fear. They were so terrified, in fact, that they "became as dead men" (vs. 4), which possibly means they fainted. They evidently then fled in terror.

III. THE ANGEL'S WORDS: MATTHEW 28:5-7

The angel said to the women, "Do not be afraid, for I know that you are looking for Jesus, who was crucified. He is not here; he has risen, just as he said. Come and see the place where he lay. Then go quickly and tell his disciples: 'He has risen from the dead and is going ahead of you into Galilee. There you will see him.' Now I have told you."

Because the angel's appearance also frightened the women, the angel told them, "Do not be afraid" (Matt. 28:5). He then said he was aware that the women were coming to find the crucified Jesus. Next, the angel gave them the startling news that they would not find Jesus' body because He was alive. Jesus had risen from the dead, just as He had foretold (28:6; see 16:21; 17:23; 20:19). As proof that Jesus truly was alive, the angel invited the women to examine the spot where His body had been.

After the women had taken a little time to examine the empty tomb, the angel told them to deliver an important message to Christ's disciples. The message was that Jesus "has risen from the dead" (28:7) and would be going ahead of the disciples to Galilee. They would meet Him there, in fulfillment of an earlier promise to them (26:32). The statement "Now I have told you" (28:7) implies that the message from the angel was extremely important and that the women were not to delay in reporting it.

Matthew and Mark both mention that the angel directed the women to tell Jesus' disciples that they should meet Him in Galilee (Matt. 28:7; Mark 16:7). John also mentions another appearance by Jesus in Galilee to seven disciples by the sea (John 21). That Jesus would appear to His disciples in Galilee seems appropriate when we consider His earthly ministry. For all practical purposes, Galilee was His home (Matt. 21:11), and He summoned most of the disciples there.

IV. Jesus' Appearance: Matthew 28:8-10

So the women hurried away from the tomb, afraid yet filled with joy, and ran to tell his disciples. Suddenly Jesus met them. "Greetings," he said. They came to him, clasped his feet and worshiped him. Then Jesus said to them, "Do not be afraid. Go and tell my brothers to go to Galilee; there they will see me."

The two Marys, having encountered the angel and heard the news of Jesus' resurrection, felt both fear and joy. They were afraid, for they stood in the presence of a supernatural being come from heaven; but the empty tomb and the angel's words also made them experience intense "joy" (28:8). In fact, the realization that the one they thought was gone forever had come back to life sent them running, not walking, to tell the disciples.

Another surprise still awaited the women as they hurried on their way. They met the risen Lord. His "Greetings" (vs. 9) was a common statement that expressed a wish for happiness and well-being in the recipients.

Upon seeing the risen Lord, the women approached Him, fell at His feet, and worshiped Him. Paying such homage to Christ was an entirely appropriate response. The sight of Christ was also a good reason to be filled with delight, for He had conquered death.

There evidently was a strong sense of fear in the women as they prostrated themselves in the presence of the glorified Savior. Like the angel, Jesus directed the women not to be afraid (vs. 10). In His presence, they were to be courageous. Christ also repeated the same basic message the angel had given to the women. Perhaps this was to underscore the urgency of their telling the disciples to go to Galilee, where they would see Him.

It was gracious of Jesus to call the disciples "my brothers," for just a few days earlier they had denied and abandoned Him (see 26:56). Despite what they had done, He was willing to forgive them and to allow them to serve Him. They were members of the Savior's spiritual family and would share in His inheritance.

V. The Chief Priests' Deception: Matthew 28:11-15

While the women were on their way, some of the guards went into the city and reported to the chief priests everything that had happened. When the chief priests had met with the elders and devised a plan, they gave the soldiers a large sum of money, telling them, "You are to say, 'His disciples came during the night and stole him away while we were asleep.' If this report gets to the governor, we will satisfy him and keep you out of trouble." So the soldiers took the money and did as they were instructed. And this story has been widely circulated among the Jews to this very day.

In accordance with Jesus' instructions, the women went to the rest of the disciples to report that they had seen the risen Lord. Meanwhile, some of the soldiers who had been stationed at the tomb returned to Jerusalem and reported to the chief priests "everything that had happened" (Matt. 28:11). This report probably included mention of the earthquake, the appearance of the angel, and the opening of the tomb.

If the chief priests had considered the situation in an objective and unbiased manner, they would have realized that Jesus had indeed risen from the dead. Instead of believing the obvious truth, however, the chief priests assembled with the elders and devised a scheme to explain the empty tomb (vs. 12).

The religious leaders bribed the soldiers with a large sum of money, telling them to claim that, while they were asleep, Jesus' disciples stole the body from the tomb (vs. 13). The chief priests and elders promised to intercede for the soldiers, if necessary, to prevent them from being punished for dereliction of duty. If Pilate were to hear an unfavorable report, the religious leaders would satisfy his concerns about the matter and keep the soldiers out of trouble (vs. 14).

The soldiers, being pleased with this arrangement, accepted the bribe and did as they had been instructed. Perhaps with the help of the Jewish authorities, they spread a rumor that Jesus' followers had stolen His body from the tomb to fake His resurrection. Matthew noted that this story, though false, was still being circulated at the time he wrote his Gospel (vs. 15).

All four Gospels agree that Jesus' tomb was empty the first Easter morning and that Christ later appeared to His followers to prove that He had risen from the dead (1 Cor. 15:3-8). Even the religious leaders did not deny that the tomb was empty. They just invented the story that Jesus' disciples stole His body (Matt. 28:11-15).

Perhaps the strongest evidence for the truth of Jesus' resurrection is what happened to His disciples afterward. They had seen Him after He rose from the dead and heard His instructions to tell all the world about Him. They did not need to see or hear anything else. They just went into all the world and did what He told them to do. That kind of courage and determination would not come from a deception or a myth.

Discussion Questions

1. Why did the two Mary's go to the tomb where Jesus' body had been placed?
2. Why did the angel roll away the stone from the tomb?
3. How did the guards respond upon seeing the angel?
4. What message of hope did the angel give to the women?
5. How did the women respond to the angel's directive?
6. How did the women respond when they encountered the risen Lord?
7. How did the religious leaders respond upon hearing the report of the guards?

Contemporary Application

People today find it no easier to believe in Jesus' resurrection than did the apostles when they first heard the good news. In the experience of your students, people who are dead do not come back to life. Thus, saved adults should not be surprised when their non-Christian friends view the Resurrection message as interesting but not at all convincing.

As Christians, the students need to recognize the importance of affirming that Jesus' resurrection actually took place; but how should they do this? Adults who are believers can do this by cultivating a personal relationship with the risen Lord in their daily life. When they pursue a personal relationship with the Savior, they show that they truly believe He is alive, having been raised from the dead.

Although the students cannot now see, hear, or touch Jesus physically, they can draw near to Him spiritually and devotionally. Furthermore, those who want to know Christ intimately are wise to set aside a definite time each day to spend concentrating upon the risen Lord and His Word.

For some students, Bible reading and meditation come easier. For other class members, prayer and silence in the Lord's presence come easier. Whatever they decide to do, they need to begin to do it, for when they do, they enlarge the scope and richness of their time with the risen Lord.

When the students believe in the historical reality of Jesus' resurrection, and when they daily cultivate their relationship with Him, they naturally want to express their faith in His resurrection by sharing the gospel message with others. In fact, the Gospel will burn in their hearts; and sharing the good news about Christ's resurrection will not be a burdensome obligation but a joyful privilege to them.

Expression may take the form of evangelism, but also it may take the form of song or prayer. There are many ways class members can express their faith in Christ's resurrection, but whatever way they do it, they show their trust and hope in the risen Lord.

The students thus should carry the message of Jesus' resurrection, which is rooted in historical fact and enriched by their personal relationship with their living Saviour. The good news they convey goes with all the persuasion of their firsthand experience.

Furthermore, while class members express their faith in Jesus' resurrection, they do not do it alone. Wherever they go to proclaim His glory, the risen Christ goes with them. After all, they (along with all believers) are His resurrection people.

The Thessalonians' Faith

DEVOTIONAL READING

1 Thessalonians 2:13-20

DAILY BIBLE READINGS

Monday April 12
1 Thessalonians 1:1-5 Paul Remembers the Thessalonians' Faith

Tuesday April 13
1 Thessalonians 1:6-10 You Have Become an Example

Wednesday April 14
1 Thessalonians 2:1-8 Paul's Coming Was Not in Vain

Thursday April 15
1 Thessalonians 2:9-13 You Received God's Word

Friday April 16
1 Thessalonians 2:14-20 You Have Suffered for Christ

Saturday April 17
1 Thessalonians 3:1-5 Paul Sends Timothy to Encourage

Sunday April 18
1 Thessalonians 3:6-13 Timothy Brings Back Good News

Scripture

Background Scripture: *1 Thessalonians 1—3*
Scripture Lesson: *1 Thessalonians 1:2-10; 3:6-10*
Key Verses: *We always thank God for all of you, mentioning you in our prayers. We continually remember before our God and Father your work produced by faith, your labor prompted by love, and your endurance inspired by hope in our Lord Jesus Christ.* 1 Thessalonians 1:2-3.
Scripture Lesson for Children: *1 Thessalonians 1:2-3; 3:1-10*
Key Verse for Children: *May the Lord make your love increase and overflow for each other.* 1 Thessalonians 3:12.

Lesson Aim

To help the students commit themselves to trusting God more as they do what He wants.

Lesson Setting

Time: *A.D. 51*
Place: *Written from Corinth to the church in Thessalonica*

Lesson Outline

The Thessalonians' Faith

  I. Paul's Thanksgiving: 1 Thessalonians 1:2-6
      A. *Faith, Love, and Hope: vss. 2-3*
      B. *Gospel Power: vss. 4-6*
  II. Paul's Commendation: 1 Thessalonians 1:7-10
      A. *Spreading Faith: vss. 7-9*
      B. *Anticipation: vs. 10*
  III. Timothy's Report: 1 Thessalonians 3:6-10
      A. *Mutual Love: vs. 6*
      B. *Firm Faith: vss. 7-8*
      C. *Fervent Prayer: vss. 9-10*

Introduction for Adults

Topic: *Encouraging Faith*

Jim walked into Paul's hospital room and was astonished. They both knew that Paul did not have long to live. Jim wondered what to say to him. Paul seized the opportunity and told him how God had given him great peace and joy in his pain and suffering. He saw his terminal illness as the gateway to a deeper relationship with Jesus.

The Thessalonians were suffering, but Paul could not pay them a visit. He agonized over their spiritual welfare. Finally, he received good news. They were standing firm in their faith. In fact, their faith, love, and hope encouraged and inspired Paul. They ministered to him, and he was moved to greater depths of prayer.

Introduction for Youth

Topic: *Get the Message?*

What messages do we send to others about the Christian faith? If all their knowledge and understanding depended on us, what would they know, believe, and do?

From Paul's first letter to the Thessalonians we learn that the message concerns repentance and faith. We turn from our sins and give ourselves in faith to Jesus. But we also learn that we need one another. Being a Christian links us intimately with our fellow believers.

The message is all about faith, but it is also about love, joy, and endurance. Even the great pioneering apostle of our faith needed to know that the Thessalonians loved him. He wanted to be sure of their love as well as their faith. Similarly, when we make a faith commitment to Christ, we make a love commitment to one another.

Concepts for Children

Topic: *Be Encouraged*

1. Paul prayed continually for the Christians at Thessalonica.
2. The faith, love, and hope of these believers grew strong.
3. The Thessalonians suffered for their faith.
4. Paul needed the reassurance that they were standing firm.
5. We can pray for one another to remain faithful to Jesus.
6. When we can also pray that God will encourage and help other believers.

Lesson Commentary

I. PAUL'S THANKSGIVING: 1 THESSALONIANS 1:2-6

A. Faith, Love, and Hope: vss. 2-3

We always thank God for all of you, mentioning you in our prayers. We continually remember before our God and Father your work produced by faith, your labor prompted by love, and your endurance inspired by hope in our Lord Jesus Christ.

Paul wrote 1 Thessalonians after Timothy brought back the report of his visit to Thessalonica. The apostle began his first letter by praising the Thessalonians for their steadfastness under persecution. Then he began to deal with some of the problems Timothy reported.

Paul dealt with wrongdoing among the believers, such as sexual immorality and idleness. He calmed their fears about blessings for their dead loved ones in the end times. He told them that the day of the Lord would come suddenly with wrath for unbelievers but not for believers.

The central doctrinal concern of the Thessalonian epistles is the events of the end times; however, it is important to realize that other major doctrines are taught in these two short letters. While the epistles are not doctrinal treatises like Romans and Galatians, 1 and 2 Thessalonians include a well-rounded body of important theological truths.

Paul expressed praise for the Thessalonians. In his daily prayers, he thanked God for them. Paul emphasized the fervency of his prayer by using the words translated "always" (I Thess. 1:2) and "continually" (vs. 3). Beyond that, he wanted his readers to know clearly what was his recollection of them. The apostle praised God for their faith, love, and hope.

These three Christian graces frequently appear in Paul's letters and other New Testament writings. They make up the cornerstone of the Christian life, the essentials of a vital relationship with the Savior. Paul linked them with the tough kind of life expected of believers.

Faith, love, and hope produced work, labor, and patience, respectively. In short, faith resulted in deeds of kindness, justice, and mercy; love impelled costly, toilsome effort on behalf of others; and hope fostered a certainty in Christ so that one could endure whatever life brought.

B. Gospel Power: vss. 4-6

For we know, brothers loved by God, that he has chosen you, because our gospel came to you not simply with words, but also with power, with the Holy Spirit and with deep conviction. You know how we lived among you for your sake. You became imitators of us and of the Lord; in spite of severe suffering, you welcomed the message with the joy given by the Holy Spirit.

Paul next addressed his readers as "brothers loved by God" (1 Thess. 1:4). The apostle vividly remembered how the Thessalonian believers had responded to his preaching, and it was a response that made him confident in affirming that God "has chosen you." While many people had heard Paul preach, those who believed had affirmed their choosing by their faith.

The Greeks were used to traveling teachers who presented clever philosophies that they could take or leave; but Paul had not brought another academic theory, nor had he given a classroom lecture; instead, the apostle preached in Thessalonica with "power" (vs. 5), "the Holy Spirit," and "deep conviction." Paul's passionate preaching grew out of his own encounter with Christ on the Damascus road. For Paul, the Gospel was a life-or-death matter, not an intellectual exercise.

The Thessalonians had welcomed Paul's message despite having to pay a heavy price—severe suffering. Acts 17:5-9 tell us one way in which the Thessalonian believers suffered. Some local Jews stirred up a mob, which dragged some of the believers before the city officials. The Christians were soon released, but undoubtedly the attacks did not end at that point.

Opposition did not quench the faith of the Thessalonians. They welcomed the good news with joy, despite the cost. This was possible because their joy came from "the Holy Spirit" (1 Thess. 1:6).

II. PAUL'S COMMENDATION: 1 THESSALONIANS 1:7-10

A. Spreading Faith: vss. 7-9

And so you became a model to all the believers in Macedonia and Achaia. The Lord's message rang out from you not only in Macedonia and Achaia—your faith in God has become known everywhere. Therefore we do not need to say anything about it, for they themselves report what kind of reception you gave us. They tell us how you turned to God from idols to serve the true and living God.

Paul's praise for his readers builds to a crescendo in 1 Thessalonians 1:7-8. He used two word pictures to express his admiration: they had become (1) "a model" (vs. 7) of the Christian faith, and (2) through them, the gospel "rang out" (vs. 8) throughout Greece and beyond. (The provinces of Macedonia and Achaia comprised the whole of Greece.)

The Greek word rendered "a model" (vs. 7) here probably means "pattern," rather than "imprint" or "image." In other words, the church at Thessalonica set the pace for the other congregations Paul had established in Greece. The believers' conduct rightfully deserved to be called a model in at least two ways: (1) the way they had endured suffering with joy, and (2) the way they had spread the Gospel to nearby communities. They witnessed to their faith in Christ by the way they handled persecution and by their open testimonies to the unbelievers around them.

The Thessalonians had such a ringing testimony—like the carillon of a mighty cathedral—that people everywhere heard about them. Their testimony was no doubt aided by the fact that their city stood in a strategic geographic position. Their witness pointed clearly to Christ.

As a result, the report of the successful mission to Thessalonica was on the lips of Christians everywhere. Since leaving the city, Paul had learned from others what had happened, and he was excited by the reports. He rejoiced in the good news as he wrote to them about it.

The apostle reminded the new believers of the crucial point of their evangelization; namely, because most of them were Gentiles, they had rejected their traditional "idols" (vs. 9) for the sake of following Christ. Such an act is called repentance.

At one time the Thessalonians served powerless and lifeless objects; but, as a result of their favorable response to Paul's preaching, they had become slaves of Christ. They now were serving the "living and true God."

B. Anticipation: vs. 10

And to wait for his Son from heaven, whom he raised from the dead—Jesus, who rescues us from the coming wrath.

Paul reminded his readers about the heart of the Gospel—the resurrection of Christ. The true God is not an image carved out of stone. He made Himself visible in the person of Christ, who came from heaven to earth to rescue us "from the coming wrath" (vs. 10). To certify His deity—that He truly came from heaven—Jesus conquered death and rose again.

Paul, in succinct fashion, described both the beginning of Christian faith—turning to God from idols—and its outworking: waiting for the return of the Son. Waiting is not to be confused with idleness, but rather speaks to the essence of the Christian's life direction. As believers actively serve, they wait. The certainty of Jesus' return provides stability and purpose. It also keeps them from wandering into misguided ventures and aspirations.

III. TIMOTHY'S REPORT: 1 THESSALONIANS 3:6-10

A. Mutual Love: vs. 6

But Timothy has just now come to us from you and has brought good news about your faith and love. He has told us that you always have pleasant memories of us and that you long to see us, just as we also long to see you.

The central issue for Paul was the faith of the young church at Thessalonica. These new Christians had been battered, and the apostle was not there to help. He agonized over their situation while he was in Athens and finally decided to send Timothy to them. How human Paul was to suffer through this separation! Twice he wrote that he could "stand it no longer" (1 Thess. 3:1, 5).

Paul was especially concerned about the reaction of the Thessalonians to their trials. Verses 1-5 show how the apostle was both a mother and father to them (see also 2:7, 11). Thankfully, the apostle's fears vanished when Timothy returned with good news about the "faith and love" (3:6) of the Thessalonians.

Paul learned that his beloved friends had not caved in to Satan's craftiness; and they had not succumbed to trials and persecution. The apostle especially recalled with appreciation the church's expression of love for him. They remembered him fondly and shared in his desire that they might see one another again.

B. Firm Faith: vss. 7-8

Therefore, brothers, in all our distress and persecution we were encouraged about you because of your faith. For now we really live, since you are standing firm in the Lord.

Paul had wanted to encourage the Thessalonians in their trials and now he found himself encouraged by their faith. The apostle referred to his own anguish, which was both emotional and physical. "Distress" (1 Thess. 1:7) here refers to pressing care, while "persecution" refers to crushing trouble.

Acts 17:16-34 does not refer to any outright persecution Paul may have experienced in Athens. Perhaps the apostle wrote generally about how he had been treated throughout his second missionary journey; or he may have been thinking about his separation from his readers.

In any case, Paul felt better when Timothy returned with the news that the Thessalonians were standing "firm in the Lord" (1 Thess. 3:8) despite difficulties. Timothy's report encouraged Paul because it pointed him back to God and to His faithfulness and power. In a sense, Timothy's good news put new heart in the apostle and strengthened him to continue his evangelistic work.

C. Fervent Prayer: vss. 9-10

How can we thank God enough for you in return for all the joy we have in the presence of our God because of you? Night and day we pray most earnestly that we may see you again and supply what is lacking in your faith.

As Paul contemplated his strong bond of love with the church at Thessalonica, he realized it was beyond his capacity to express in words. Thus, he resorted to praise in God's presence (1 Thess. 1:9), and then pleaded with God around the clock that he might be able to see them again (vs. 10). When the apostle prayed, his thanksgiving was insufficient for the measure of blessing he had received from them.

In addition, Paul prayed about his wish to minister God's Word to the Thessalonians. The Greek word translated "supply what is lacking" is used elsewhere for mending fishing nets, but in the New Testament it usually means to make complete, restore, or equip. The apostle used the term in verse 10 to stress his desire to strengthen the faith of his readers.

Discussion Questions

1. What did Paul praise God for with respect to the Thessalonians?
2. How had the Thessalonians responded to Paul's message?
3. In what way were the Thessalonians an example for other believers?
4. What had the Thessalonians rejected in their decision to turn to God?
5. For what were the Thessalonians waiting?
6. What eliminated the apostle Paul's fears concerning the welfare of the

Thessalonians?

7. What was Paul's constant prayer to God concerning the Thessalonians?

Contemporary Application

The Thessalonian believers were experiencing a number of trials, and their faith was being tested greatly. It was such a major concern for Paul that, for a while, he was anxious how they would respond. Likewise, the faith adults have in Christ is tested and challenged on a daily basis.

Just as the Thessalonians trusted and obeyed God, so must your students. Their obedience to Him should impact every area of their lives—from home to school to work. They do the will of God when they give their best effort in their daily routines and face difficult circumstances with an attitude of hope. They are also obedient to His will when they exercise caution about the things they read, watch, and hear.

There's a personal side to God's will worth considering. For instance, the Lord wants saved adults to share their faith. Some might do it in a large-group setting, while others might witness one-on-one. It's also God's will that your students spend time with Him in prayer. While some prefer to do it in the morning, others might opt to pray at night. Regardless of how they carry out God's will for their lives, their actions should be undergirded by faith. In fact, without faith, they cannot truly please the Lord (Heb. 1:6).

The readiness of the class members to do God's will can lead them down unexpected paths. For instance, the Lord might want them to share the Gospel with someone, when they are uncertain what the response will be; or the students might be asked to serve God in a way that is new to them, perhaps singing in the choir or leading a church group.

Adults who wholeheartedly trust God are convinced that He knows what's best for them. They are willing to wait for His timing when it comes to enjoying the blessings of faith. They realize that some of these come in this life, but most are received in eternity.

Your students might continue to struggle with doubts even after they're seasoned in their faith. Instead of allowing uncertainty to control them, they should examine it in the light of what Scripture teaches. The truth of God's Word can calm them when they're feeling anxious about something.

The faith of adults in God can also be strengthened by reflecting on their past experiences and those of other believers. God's faithfulness to the class members and others in the past can encourage them when they're going through difficult times.

Coming of the Lord

Scripture

Background Scripture: *1 Thessalonians 4—5*
Scripture Lesson: *1 Thessalonians 4:13-18; 5:2-11*
Key Verse: *God did not appoint us to suffer wrath but to receive salvation through our Lord Jesus Christ.*
1 Thessalonians 5:9.
Scripture Lesson for Children: *1 Thessalonians 4:1-2, 9-12*
Key Verse for Children: *Finally, brothers, we instructed you how to live in order to please God.*
1 Thessalonians 4:1.

Lesson Aim

To encourage the students to consider the ways God comforts them in difficult times.

Lesson Setting

Time: A.D. *51*
Place: *Written from Corinth to the church in Thessalonica.*

Lesson Outline

Coming of the Lord

  I. Christ's Return: 1 Thessalonians 4:13-18
      A. *Antidote to Despair: vs. 13*
      B. *Certainty of Resurrection: vs. 14*
      C. *Order of Resurrection: vss. 15-17*
      D. *Mutual Encouragement: vs. 18*
  II. Preparation for Christ's Return:
      1 Thessalonians 5:2-11
      A. *False Hopes: vss. 2-3*
      B. *Sons of Light: vss. 4-5*
      C. *Watchful Self-Control: vss. 6-9*
      D. *Christian Anticipation: vss. 10-11*

Introduction for Adults

Topic: *Getting Ready*

The newly married couple set up housekeeping in a ground floor apartment in an old house located on a traditional street with lawns and flowers. For some time they ignored how their place looked. But one day they got word that visitors were coming: the husband's parents, who kept their place clean and sharp inside and out.

The couple sprang into action cleaning rooms, pulling weeds, and cutting grass. It was almost like the coming of the Lord. In the nick of time they made their place sparkle and it passed inspection.

What would we do differently today if we knew that Jesus would knock on our door tomorrow? It's so easy to dismiss the coming of the Lord, because we get so deeply involved in our own concerns. Our agenda becomes more important than His.

Since we do not get advance word about Jesus' coming, we can take steps to be ready to meet Him. Thinking about that prospect helps us to shape our program more like His and less like ours.

Introduction for Youth

Topic: *It's Your Life!*

Psychologists tell us that teenagers have no sense of their own mortality. They take crazy risks because they think they are immortal. They make career choices based on the best offers, looking for satisfaction in the future based on positions and money.

However, when accidents take the lives of their friends, adolescents are forced to think about life and their future. Christians step up at times like these and offer a totally different perspective on life and its meaning.

Because Jesus died, rose from the grave, and is coming again, we can fit our goals and fears into His good and perfect will. We do not have to be nervous about our future because we know it is with Jesus. Thus, knowing Jesus makes life worthwhile.

Concepts for Children

Topic: *Live to Please God*

1. Paul gave Christians clear teaching about how to live.
2. Since the beginning of the church, people have put their faith in Christ.
3. When people come to know Jesus, their lives are changed for the better.
4. Each day we should ask God to help us live in a way that pleases Him.
5. Love, peace, and hard work are qualities we can demonstrate as Christians to others.
6. The way we live for Jesus encourages others to trust in Him.

Lesson Commentary

I. Christ's Return: 1 Thessalonians 4:13-18

A. Antidote to Despair: vs. 13

Brothers, we do not want you to be ignorant about those who fall asleep, or to grieve like the rest of men, who have no hope.

Most of Paul's letters follow a two-part pattern. The first section is mainly theological, while the second part is mainly practical. First Thessalonians basically follows this pattern. The first section of the letter is as much personal as it is theological; but the second part can certainly be characterized as practical.

Chapter 4 marks the beginning of the practical part of the epistle. Here Paul started by giving pastoral instructions on "how to live in order to please God" (vs. 1). Paul then discussed matters related to maintaining sexual purity (vss. 1-8), cultivating brotherly love (vss. 9-10), and being discrete in personal habits (vss. 11-12). Then, in verses 13-18, the apostle focused on the Lord's coming.

Since Paul had been in the midst of the Thessalonians, one or more of their number had died. This raised some questions, which Timothy evidently had carried to Paul on the Thessalonians' behalf: What happens to Christians who die before the Savior's return? Do they miss out on the blessings of that future time?

Paul wrote that he did not want his readers to be ignorant about what the future held for their deceased loved ones in Christ. Believers need not be full of sorrow, like "the rest of men, who have no hope" (vs. 13). The "rest of men," of course, are unbelievers. They had no basis to expect anything good for their departed loved ones.

B. Certainty of Resurrection: vs. 14

We believe that Jesus died and rose again and so we believe that God will bring with Jesus those who have fallen asleep in him.

Paul argued in 1 Thessalonians 4:14 that, since Christ rose from the dead, believers can be certain they, too, will be resurrected; moreover, Jesus will bring with Him all the believing dead, in their resurrected form, when He returns as He promised. Because Jesus survived death, the survival of believers beyond death was equally as certain.

C. Order of Resurrection: vss. 15-17

According to the Lord's own word, we tell you that we who are still alive, who are left till the coming of the Lord, will certainly not precede those who have fallen asleep. For the Lord himself will come down from heaven, with a loud command, with the voice of the archangel and with the trumpet call of God, and the dead in Christ will rise first. After that, we who are still alive and are left will be caught up together with them in the clouds to meet the Lord in the air. And so we will be with the Lord forever.

The Thessalonian believers evidently were concerned that their dead loved ones would be at a disadvantage when Christ returned; but that would not be the case.

In fact, Paul stated on the authority of Christ that the righteous dead will be the first to join the Savior in a resurrection existence (1 Thess. 4:15).

Paul did not try to say when the Lord's coming will happen; but the apostle did say that when it occurs, three signs will accompany it: (1) "a loud command" (vs. 16), (2) "the voice of the archangel," and (3) "the trumpet call of God." The three signs mean the same thing: an announcement of Jesus' coming.

At that time, deceased believers will be the first to be resurrected from the dead in an immortal and glorified form. Then they, along with Christians alive at the time, "will be caught up . . . in the clouds" (vs. 17). The order of events suggests that at Christ's return, deceased believers will "rise first" (vs. 16) before the events of verse 17 take place.

The Greek word translated "caught up" can also be rendered "snatched away." This verb carries the ideas of irresistible strength and total surprise. In this case, the event it describes is often called the "rapture," after a word used in the Latin translation of verse 17.

In short, a time is coming when a whole generation of believers in Christ will be privileged to miss out on death. At Jesus' return, all believers living on the earth will be caught up in the air to meet the Lord; and the bodies of raptured believers will be instantaneously glorified, so that they will be like the resurrected believers.

The believers who are "caught up" will have a double reunion. They will be reunited with Christ as well as with their deceased loved ones in the faith. The joy of this gathering is probably beyond our imagination.

This meeting will take place "in the clouds." In the Old Testament, clouds were often associated with God's special activity (see Dan. 7:13). Also, when Jesus ascended to heaven, a cloud hid Him from the apostles' sight; and He will return "in the same way" (Acts 1:11). The clouds will not be a vehicle of the Lord's return; but in some sense they will be recognized as a sign of God's glory and majesty.

The main purpose of the rapture is to meet the Lord. When a dignitary paid a visit to a Greek city in ancient times, leading citizens went out to meet him and to escort him on the final stage of the journey. Paul similarly pictured Jesus as being escorted by His own people, those newly raised from the dead and those who will have remained alive. Having met the Lord in a glorified existence, they will never have to leave Him again.

D. Mutual Encouragement: vs. 18

Therefore encourage each other with these words.

As the Thessalonians thought about the death of their loved ones or the possibility of their own death before Jesus' return, they might have become discouraged. To counteract discouragement, they needed to recall that one day Christ will come in glory and gather all His followers to His side forever. In light of that promise, they were to comfort and encourage one another (1 Thess. 4:18).

II. PREPARATION FOR CHRIST'S RETURN: 1 THESSALONIANS 5:2-11

A. False Hopes: vss. 2-3

For you know very well that the day of the Lord will come like a thief in the night. While people are saying, "Peace and safety," destruction will come on them suddenly, as labor pains on a pregnant woman, and they will not escape.

The Thessalonians wanted to know when the day of the Lord will occur. Paul, in response, reminded his readers that the timing of that future day is unknown and that they ought to keep looking forward to it with confidence. It is a time when God will execute wrath upon the ungodly and shower the righteous with blessing.

Paul reminded the Thessalonians what they knew perfectly well, namely, the day of the Lord will occur suddenly and unexpectedly "like a thief in the night" (1 Thess. 5:2). People will be lulled into false security right up to the time of the day of the Lord. They will be talking about "peace and safety" (vs. 3) when destruction suddenly strikes.

Paul made reference to a pregnant woman's going into labor. The apostle's main focus was not on the intense pain of labor, but rather on the suddenness of the onset of the experience. The unsaved, being surprised by the commencement of the day of the Lord, will not escape this future time of unprecedented travail.

B. Sons of Light: vss. 4-5

But you, brothers, are not in darkness so that this day should surprise you like a thief. You are all sons of the light and sons of the day. We do not belong to the night or to the darkness.

Paul's readers were not to be taken by surprise by the day of the Lord. While they could not predict its timing, they knew that it was coming and they could expect it (1 Thess. 5:4). After all, they were "sons of the light" (vs. 5) and "sons of the day." Moral purity and truth characterized them. In contrast, unbelievers belonged "to the night" and "to the darkness." Impurity and falsehood characterized them.

C. Watchful Self-Control: vss. 6-9

So then, let us not be like others, who are asleep, but let us be alert and self-controlled. For those who sleep, sleep at night, and those who get drunk, get drunk at night. But since we belong to the day, let us be self-controlled, putting on faith and love as a breastplate, and the hope of salvation as a helmet. For God did not appoint us to suffer wrath but to receive salvation through our Lord Jesus Christ.

In 1 Thessalonians 5:6-8, Paul further compared the saved and unsaved. Like people who sleep, unbelievers are spiritually insensitive and unaware of the coming of the day of the Lord. That they get drunk is a representation of their lack of proper self-control. In contrast, believers live in the brightness of spiritual awareness and keep themselves alert and sober.

We often think about sobriety in terms of avoiding some form of sin; but in verse 8, Paul had in mind self-control's positive virtues. It means to put on the breastplate of faith and love and to don "as a helmet" the "hope of salvation." Here the apostle was using parts of a Roman legionnaire's armor to symbolize qualities that make up the believer's spiritual armor and perhaps to stress that the Christian life involves spiritual conflict.

Paul previously mentioned the trio of faith, hope, and love in 1:3. Faith is the means by which we enter the Christian life, and day by day we trust in the Lord for our care. The love that exists between God and us prompts us to be compassionate and kind to one another. The hope of salvation means that, while divine wrath awaits unbelievers, we who are Christians will abide forever with the Lord.

The day of the Lord will indeed bring sudden destruction (5:3), but this "wrath" (vs. 9) is not meant for Christ's followers. Believers, of course, along with everyone else, deserve God's wrath because of our sin; but instead of receiving judgment for our misdeeds, we will "receive salvation" because of what Jesus has done for us.

D. Christian Anticipation: vss. 10-11

He died for us so that, whether we are awake or asleep, we may live together with him. Therefore encourage one another and build each other up, just as in fact you are doing.

In the end, it does not really matter whether we pass away before Jesus comes, for He died (and rose again from the dead) so that we can abide with Him forever. Thus, whether we are living or deceased, our eternal future will be the same: "we may live together with him" (1 Thess. 5:10).

The everlasting joy we are promised in Christ is not a dry biblical truth, but rather a wonderful source of encouragement and edification. Thus, believers are to "encourage one another" (vs. 11) and build each other up in their faith. In fact, this is to continue until Jesus returns.

Discussion Questions

1. What is the basis for the believers' hope of one day being raised from the dead?
2. What three signs will accompany the Lord's return?
3. With what promise are Christians enjoined to comfort one another?
4. What will happen to the ungodly and the righteous on the day of the Lord?
5. In what sense are believers "sons of the light" (1 Thess. 5:5) and "sons of the day"?
6. In what sense are unbelievers of the "night" and of the "darkness"?
7. What eternal future has God promised believers?

Contemporary Application

In the midst of the Thessalonians' hardships, Paul reminded them of the Lord's return and urged them to draw comfort from this truth. Even believers face moments of distress and uncertainty, and the reality of Jesus' coming can be a source of consolation for them.

The years of life are filled with change and discovery as well as with emerging talents, aptitudes, and dreams; nevertheless, the students still struggle with loneliness and depression. There undoubtedly are times when the students, out of the depths of their hearts, cry for something or someone to give them peace and comfort; but before they can experience God's help and consolation, they must first recognize their own human frailty.

Only Christ can fill the void that exists in the lives of every person. When they invite the living Lord to come into their hearts, He supplies the freeing power from the bondage of evil and sin's oppression. He also helps them deal with the loneliness, depression, and insecurity they might feel at times.

Jesus comforts believers through His presence and the promises of His Word. He also consoles them through the indwelling Spirit and the loving support of Christian friends. Such evidences of compassion and care undergird the students in their times of need.

The Lord's unfailing love is the ultimate basis for comfort in difficult times. The mystery of His compassion is that it accepts and meets believers at the point of their deepest need. When they trust God's promises, they experience His solace and blessings in their lives.

It would be wrong for the class members to think that, when God comforts them, all their troubles go away. Being consoled means they receive strength to endure trials and hope to face a potentially troubled future. In fact, the greater difficulty they face, the more God reaches out in love to comfort them.

God has never failed in His promise to console believers. They should not only acknowledge this truth but also thank the Lord for the ways He has consoled them during difficult times in the past. Unlike flowers, which are a temporary delight in their eyes, God's love and care for His spiritual children are everlasting. They thus should express their gratitude to God for being like a shepherd in His care for them, especially when life is rough.

Chosen to Obtain Glory

DEVOTIONAL READING

Ephesians 1:3-14

DAILY BIBLE READINGS

Monday April 26
*Ephesians 1:7-14 We Have
an Inheritance in Christ*

Tuesday April 27
*2 Thessalonians 1:1-5 Your
Faith is Growing*

Wednesday April 28
*2 Thessalonians 1:6-12
Christ Glorified by His
Saints*

Thursday April 29
*2 Thessalonians 2:13-17
Called to Obtain Glory*

Friday April 30
*2 Thessalonians 3:1-5 The
Lord Will Strengthen You*

Saturday May 1
*2 Thessalonians 3:6-10
Imitate Us*

Sunday May 2
*2 Thessalonians 3:11-18
Do Not Be Idle*

Scripture

Background Scripture: *2 Thessalonians 1—3*
Scripture Lesson: *2 Thessalonians 1:3-4, 11-12; 2:13—3:4*
Key Verse: *But we ought always to thank God for you, brothers loved by the Lord, because from the beginning God chose
you to be saved through the sanctifying work of the Spirit and
through belief in the truth.* 2 Thessalonians 2:13.
Scripture Lesson for Children: *2 Thessalonians 1:3,
11-12; 3:1-5*
Key Verse for Children: *We ought always to thank God.*
2 Thessalonians 2:13.

Lesson Aim

To have the students recall how God has been faithful
to them and thus be encouraged to rely on His promises.

Lesson Setting

Time: *A.D. 51*
Place: *Written from Corinth to the church in Thessalonica.*

Lesson Outline

Chosen to Obtain Glory

   I. Faithfulness and Fruitfulness Despite Persecution:
      2 Thessalonians 1:3-4, 11-12
      A. Paul's Praise: vss. 3-4
      B. Paul's Prayer: vss. 11-12
  II. Strength from God to Stand Firm:
      2 Thessalonians 2:13-17
      A. The Call of God: vss. 13-14
      B. The Commitment of Believers: vss. 15-17
 III. Prayer for Paul: 2 Thessalonians 3:1-4
      A. The Thessalonians' Prayers: vss. 1-2
      B. The Lord's Provision: vss. 3-4

Introduction for Adults

Topic: *Reflecting the Glory*

Gold medal winners in the Olympic Games reflect the glory of their flags. They proudly stand for the entire world to see because they want to bring glory to their countries.

In a much larger sense, Christians seek to reflect the glory of Jesus. He is honored in us and we in Him. Therefore, we can see purpose and hope for living. We are encouraged to stand firm in our faith because we know the glory of Jesus is at stake.

In our race of life, we pursue victory for the sake of Jesus. He has called us to eternal glory. In the meantime, although we may take some hard knocks, we want to stand firm for the sake of His glory. His name is worth all the effort we can make to grow in our faith, hope, and love.

Introduction for Youth

Topic: *Steadfast Faith*

When Ernest Shackleton, the famous British explorer, left 22 men behind on an island in the Antarctic Sea, they had to keep strong faith that he would return—despite the fact that Shackleton had to cross 800 miles of wild ocean in a lifeboat to reach a whaling station. To keep steadfast faith in Shackleton's return, every day the men packed their gear. This might be the day he comes back, they told themselves, and one day he did.

Living our Christian faith is something like that. We face rugged times and days of uncertainty. Sometimes our future appears to be hopeless. But because we are in Christ, we can trust Him to find us, as it were, and bring us through our darkest hours.

Jesus lives and encourages us to keep on hoping and believing. He also wants us to give a lift to our friends who are in the pits. Our faith gets stronger when the waves blow against us. We can reach out and find that Jesus is there when we need Him most.

Concepts for Children

Topic: *Pray for One Another*

1. Paul prayed regularly for his church friends.
2. Paul prayed for the spiritual growth and strength of his friends.
3. Sometimes our lives seem to be full of problems bigger than we are.
4. We should not only pray but also encourage one another.
5. Paul's prayers show us what is most important—our faith, love, hope, and endurance.
6. We can ask God for help in developing our prayer life.

son Commentary

1. FAITHFULNESS AND FRUITFULNESS DESPITE PERSECUTION: 2 THESSALONIANS 1:3-4, 11-12

A. Paul's Praise: vss. 3-4

We ought always to thank God for you, brothers, and rightly so, because your faith is growing more and more, and the love every one of you has for each other is increasing. Therefore, among God's churches we boast about your perseverance and faith in all the persecutions and trials you are enduring.

Some months after Paul wrote 1 Thessalonians, a report (falsely supposed to be from Paul) circulated among the believers saying that the day of the Lord had already come. This prompted the apostle to write again. This time Paul also praised the Thessalonians for their perseverance amid persecution. He moreover assured them that the day of the Lord had not come and would not come until certain conditions had been met.

Paul began his second letter to the church at Thessalonica with a traditional greeting from his missionary team, which included "Silas and Timothy" (2 Thess. 1:1). They were well known to the Thessalonian believers and thus needed no introduction. Paul then reminded the Thessalonians of their heritage and position. They were members of the church and rooted in "God our Father" and in His Son, the "Lord Jesus Christ."

Perhaps some of the Thessalonians felt somewhat unworthy of Paul's commendations in his first letter (see 1 Thess. 1:2-3). That would help explain why he repeated his commendations of them in the opening lines of his second letter (2 Thess. 1:3-4). The apostle wanted to strengthen those who were wilting under the stress of continuing persecution.

Paul's initial concern was to assure the Christians of his steadfast prayers for them (vs. 3). He did not offer them an escape plan or a promise of political relief; instead, he promised them his prayers.

One might expect a church under pressure to shrivel up and die. Persecution causes that to happen sometimes; but the Thessalonian believers refused to be overcome by persecution. These Christians were also growing in faith and increasing in love.

In verse 4, Paul claimed victory for his readers. They were enduring "persecutions and trials." Undoubtedly, some of the persecutions were physical, but more likely Paul had in mind social stigma, ridicule, the loss of status, and even the loss of their livelihood. The believers were paying a heavy price for their faithfulness to Christ.

The believers were marching boldly ahead—so much so that Paul could boast about them among the other churches. The Thessalonians' faithful perseverance in the midst of adversity was a powerful witness not only to the citizens of the city but to the Christians in other locales as well.

B. Paul's Prayer: vss. 11-12

With this in mind, we constantly pray for you, that our God may count you worthy of his calling, and that by his power he may fulfill every good purpose of yours and every act prompted by your faith. We pray this so that the name of our Lord Jesus may be glorified in you, and you in him, according to the grace of our God and the Lord Jesus Christ.

After giving a glimpse of God's judgment of unbelievers (2 Thess. 1:5-10), Paul brought his readers back to the present. The apostle again reminded the Thessalonians of his persevering prayers for them. He would continue to intercede for them, rather than forget or abandon them (vs. 11).

Paul's usage of "with this in mind" refers back to the plan of God to punish the wicked and reward the righteous. In light of this truth, the apostle prayed that God would count the Thessalonians "worthy of his calling." Paul was referring to the high and holy calling of living and suffering for Christ.

The apostle also prayed that God would fulfill "every good purpose" in the Thessalonians; also, Paul petitioned the Lord to bring about "every act prompted by . . . faith" in the lives of his readers. This is a case where God used the faith of the Thessalonians to motivate them to serve Him. Likewise, the Lord would enable them to accomplish their Christ-honoring intentions.

Here we find a promising, hopeful outlook for Paul's readers. They were enduring hardships, but God's power was still available to them. His power applied to their plans could liberate them from depression, and from feelings of uselessness or despair. He could enable them to maintain a bold, powerful witness; and sometime in the future, their faith in Christ would be vindicated.

Paul wanted to see "the name of our Lord Jesus" (vs. 12) glorified through the Thessalonians' success and faithfulness; and as they exalted and glorified the Savior, they were glorified in Him. The two go hand in hand. When the church flourishes in boldness, in faith, in worship, in service, and in witnessing, Jesus is exalted in the community.

II. STRENGTH FROM GOD TO STAND FIRM: 2 THESSALONIANS 2:13-17

A. The Call of God: vss. 13-14

But we ought always to thank God for you, brothers loved by the Lord, because from the beginning God chose you to be saved through the sanctifying work of the Spirit and through belief in the truth. He called you to this through our gospel, that you might share in the glory of our Lord Jesus Christ.

Paul foresaw a time when Christ will judge the lawless one, along with all who will follow this satanic deceiver (2 Thess. 2:1-12); but Paul hastened to assure his readers that they would not be among those judged. Their eternal future included blessing by God (vss. 13-15).

The apostle thanked God for the Thessalonian believers—not so much because of who they were in themselves as because of who they had become through God's grace to them. Paul called his readers people who were "brothers loved by the Lord" (vs. 13). God had especially shown His love for the Thessalonians by choosing them for salvation.

Christians understand this verse in different ways. Some think that God long ago foreordained some individuals (but not others) for receiving His salvation. Others say that God formed His plan of salvation long ago but that the matter of who receives salvation is determined by the exercise of free human will.

In either case, we read that the Thessalonians' salvation came "through the sanctifying work of the Spirit and through belief in the truth." In other words, God the Spirit had made unholy people holy, and the people themselves had put their faith in the gospel truth.

It is instructive to compare the Thessalonian believers and the future followers of the lawless one. Those who will be judged rejected "the truth" (vs. 12). In contrast, the Thessalonians were saved "through belief of the truth" (vs. 13).

On a practical, historical level, Paul's preaching of the Gospel had been the means by which God had called the Thessalonians to salvation (vs. 14). One reason for this was so that they might share in the "glory of our Lord Jesus Christ." This was a far different end than that awaiting the followers of the man of sin.

B. The Commitment of Believers: vss. 15-17

So then, brothers, stand firm and hold to the teachings we passed on to you, whether by word of mouth or by letter. May our Lord Jesus Christ himself and God our Father, who loved us and by his grace gave us eternal encouragement and good hope, encourage your hearts and strengthen you in every good deed and word.

Paul urged his readers to "stand firm" (2 Thess. 2:15) in their faith and hold on to the gospel teachings they received from him. In order for them to do this, they would need divine help; thus, at this point in his letter, Paul prayed that God would encourage and strengthen them.

In the apostle's prayer, he invoked both the "Lord Jesus Christ" (vs. 16)—God the Son—and God the Father. Paul reminded his readers that God loved them. The apostle may have had in mind the sacrifice of Christ. Surely no greater evidence of divine love could be imagined.

God also gave the Thessalonians "eternal encouragement and good hope" through grace. "Eternal encouragement" probably refers to the effects of salvation. Because the Thessalonians had been saved, they had received a permanent change of attitude. "Good hope" probably was their anticipation of future blessings. They had reason to expect kindness from the Lord at His return.

Paul prayed that God would comfort the hearts of his readers and strengthen them "in every good deed and word" (vs. 17). Despite the persecution and false teaching in Thessalonica, God could give believers there the spiritual uplift they required. He could also refresh their hearts and give them the fortitude to go on believing and obeying the truth.

III. PRAYER FOR PAUL: 2 THESSALONIANS 3:1-4

A. The Thessalonians' Prayers: vss. 1-2

Finally, brothers, pray for us that the message of the Lord may spread rapidly and be honored, just as it was with you. And pray that we may be delivered from wicked and evil men, for not everyone has faith.

In Paul's first prayer request, he desired that "the message of the Lord" (2 Thess. 3:1) spread rapidly and be "honored" wherever the apostle proclaimed it. At the time Paul wrote this letter, he was probably in Corinth; thus, he was thinking especially about the future of Christianity in that major city and in the surrounding territory of Achaia.

The Gospel would be honored as people came to believe in it. It deserved to be recognized as the only complete truth about how people can find peace with God. That is what had happened in Thessalonica, and it could happen in Corinth and elsewhere.

Paul's second prayer request was for deliverance "from wicked and evil men" (vs. 2). The apostle was doing spiritual battle in Corinth with people who opposed what he was preaching (Acts 18:6, 12-17). Thus, the prayer support of fellow believers was essential.

The reason the apostle gave for the opposition he faced is that "not everyone has faith" (2 Thess. 3:2). The Thessalonians knew how bigoted, wicked people in their own city had abused Paul (Acts 17:5-9). Thus, his desire for deliverance from enemies of the Gospel in other places was something his readers could understand.

B. The Lord's Provision: vss. 3-4

But the Lord is faithful, and he will strengthen and protect you from the evil one. We have confidence in the Lord that you are doing and will continue to do the things we command.

Paul again assured the Thessalonians of God's ability to take care of them. That "the Lord is faithful" (2 Thess. 3:3) means He can be depended on completely by all who believe in Him. The Thessalonians could depend on Him to give them strength and protection against "evil" (in general) and the "evil one," Satan (in particular).

Because God would be faithful to the Thessalonians, Paul had "confidence in the Lord" (vs. 4) that they were obeying and would continue to obey his teachings. Evidently, then, the apostle associated his commands with effective opposition to the evil one. By believing and living as Paul taught, the Thessalonians could frustrate the plans of Satan.

Discussion Questions

1. Why did Paul pray for the believers in Thessalonica?
2. How were Paul's readers responding to persecution?
3. What was the nature of Paul's petition in 2 Thessalonians 1:11?

4. How had God especially shown His love for the Thessalonians?
5. What was the means by which God had called the Thessalonians to salvation?
6. What was the nature of Paul's first prayer request?
7. What was the reason Paul gave for the opposition he faced?

Contemporary Application

Paul put the Thessalonians' persecution in the right perspective. He told them to endure it with perseverance and faith, to trust in God's judgment, to be confident in His purposes, and to hope in His power. These admonitions are just as relevant today in the lives of believers as they were in the early church.

Consider, for example, the fact that the students live in a time when life's challenges can seem overwhelming, especially when they carry a high risk factor. There are occasions when they try to figure out the best course of action to take and are not sure what to do. This situation, in turn, can leave them feeling discouraged and defeated.

At such times, it helps for believers to reflect on how God has been with them in past situations. Rehearsing previous events and circumstances will reinforce their confidence in God's loving care. They will discover that He can use even unpleasant happenings to shape their lives and strengthen their faith.

Both the students' personal experiences and the testimony of Scripture reinforce the truth that God keeps His promises to His people. His faithfulness takes a variety of forms, and all of them are designed to strengthen believers in their daily walk with Him.

The promises of God are dependable, and they are meant for all believers. For instance, the Lord promises to walk with them through the darkest valleys of life (Ps. 23:4). He pledges to give them His incomprehensible peace (Phil. 4:6-7). He even vows to never forsake them in their time of need (Heb. 13:5).

Often when the students need to trust God's promises, they instead focus on their fears. Doing this, though, restrains their spiritual growth. It can also steer them away from potentially interesting challenges that are high-risk. There are times when God wants believers to set aside their fears and rely on His promises.

In those moments when fear rears its ugly head, the students can find encouragement in the many promises of God's Word. They can examine the ones that relate to their fears and problems, and trust in them. When believers focus their attention on God's promises (rather than their fears), they will be filled with hope, peace, strength, and understanding to get them through their difficulties.

Worthy Is the Lamb

Scripture

Background Scripture: *Revelation 4—5*
Scripture Lesson: *Revelation 5:1-10*
Key Verse: *"Worthy is the Lamb, who was slain, to receive power and wealth and wisdom and strength and honor and glory and praise!"* Revelation 5:12.
Scripture Lesson for Children: *Luke 4:16-21*
Key Verse for Children: *"The Spirit of the Lord is on me, because he has anointed me to preach good news to the poor."* Luke 4:18.

Lesson Aim

To prompt the students to consider ways they can thank God for His help during difficult times.

Lesson Setting

Time: A.D. *95*
Place: *The island of Patmos*

Lesson Outline

Worthy Is the Lamb
  I. Who Is Worthy? Revelation 5:1-4
    A. *The Seven-Sealed Scroll: vs. 1*
    B. *The Angel's Plea: vss. 2-3*
    C. *John's Despair: vss. 4*
  II. Worthy Is the Lamb: Revelation 5:5-10
    A. *The Lion's Triumph: vs. 5*
    B. *The Lamb's Death: vss. 6-7*
    C. *The Lamb's Worship: vss. 8-10*

Introduction for Adults

Topic: *Who Is Worthy?*

"Worthy" is not a word that crops up in our ordinary conversations. Sometimes we feel that certain individuals are not worthy to be our leaders because of their moral failures or incompetence. But rarely do we think of worthiness as it relates to God's dealings with us.

Many people think they will be worthy of God's favor because of their good deeds and accomplishments. In fact, all of the world's religions except Christianity are based on that bogus idea. It is false because no one will ever win God's favor. Our sins rule out that possibility.

So we have to look to someone who is worthy to get us to heaven and spare us the judgment we deserve. Only Christ fills the bill. One overwhelming fact emerges from Revelation. Jesus is our only hope of heaven. Therefore, we honor, praise, and serve Him.

Introduction for Youth

Topic: *Worthy of What?*

"I don't deserve this honor," said the captain of the football team after he was named Player of the Year. Then he went on to thank his coach, his teammates, and his parents. We all appreciate what others have done to make our accomplishments possible.

The Bible tells us that only Christ deserves our worship. He is supremely worthy of all that we can do to bring Him glory. How do we show others that Jesus is worthy? We do so by being faithful in prayer and worship, by thinking about His teachings, and obeying what He commands.

Jesus is so great that it is a dishonor to His name when we fall into poor worship habits. Going to church once a week is better than not going at all, but it is far from the best we can do to honor Jesus. He is so great that He deserves our thoughts, our desires, and our hopes all of the time.

Concepts for Children

Topic: *Jesus Cares for the Poor*

1. Jesus reached out to people who had been rejected by others.
2. Jesus offered people hope, forgiveness, and a new life.
3. People are poor in spirit because they have not put their faith in Jesus.
4. God blesses us with many things so that we can share them with others.
5. We can help our church assist the poor in our communities.
6. Jesus can help us to reach out to others in need.

Lesson Commentary

I. WHO IS WORTHY? REVELATION 5:1-4

A. The Seven-Sealed Scroll: vs. 1

Then I saw in the right hand of him who sat on the throne a scroll with writing on both sides and sealed with seven seals.

Revelation begins and ends with Christ. Though filled with magnificent visions and symbols that may be difficult to understand, first and foremost the book is about Jesus—His character, His mission, and His final goal of bringing all things into subjection to His Father's perfect will. Thus, despite the mystery surrounding Revelation, this book is primarily characterized by hope. John declared that Christ will one day return to vindicate the righteous and judge the wicked and unbelieving.

At the start of Revelation, we learn about John's encounter with the glorious Son of Man (1:1-20). Then, in chapters 2 and 3, Christ urged seven congregations to remain loyal to Him despite the oppression they were suffering. This material brings to light the temptations and hardships that Christians of John's day faced. Some broke under pressure and compromised their faith, while others refused to waver in their commitment to the Lord. Throughout Christ's messages to the seven churches of Asia Minor, He declared that He would vindicate the upright and one day bring them to a place of eternal rest.

Chapters 4 and 5 of Revelation form a gateway to the rest of the book. In chapter 4, the Father appears in a scene of worship as the King of heaven and earth. Then, in chapter 5, innumerable angels sing hymns of praise to Christ.

As John looked, he saw that God held a "scroll" (vs. 1) in His right hand. This roll of papyrus or leather had writing on the inside and outside, and it was sealed in seven different places. This made the document absolutely inaccessible and virtually impossible for an unauthorized person to open.

In ancient times, scrolls usually had writing on only one side and were sealed in one place. The writing on the front and back indicates that the decrees of God recorded on the scroll were extensive. The number seven, perhaps representing completion or perfection, indicates how thoroughly the contents of the scroll were sealed for secrecy.

There are varying views about the contents of this sealed scroll, including God's covenant, His law, His promises, and a legal will; however, the close parallel with Daniel 12:4 suggests the scroll of Revelation 5:1 contained God's end-time plan for the future.

The idea is that, unless the seals of the scroll were broken, God's purposes would not be accomplished, including the Messiah's judgment of the wicked and vindication of the upright. In John's vision, these seals are opened in chapter 6.

B. The Angel's Plea: vss. 2-3

And I saw a mighty angel proclaiming in a loud voice, "Who is worthy to break the seals and open the scroll?" But no one in heaven or on earth or under the earth could open the scroll or even look inside it.

John saw a "mighty angel" (Rev. 5:2) issue a call for someone to come forward and break the seals, revealing the scroll's contents. Interestingly, the angel did not ask who was able, influential, or powerful enough; instead, he asked who was "worthy to . . . open the scroll."

The Greek term rendered "worthy" refers to that which is "fit" or "deserving." In this context, it denotes both the ability and the authorization to execute God's plans. Only someone who was morally perfect could "break the seals." Amazingly, no one in all of God's creation responded to the angel's summons (vs. 3).

C. John's Despair: vs. 4

I wept and wept because no one was found who was worthy to open the scroll or look inside.

John was so caught up in the unfolding drama that he wept repeatedly when no could be found who was sufficiently "worthy to open" (Rev. 5:4) the scroll and read it contents. Apparently John sensed the urgent significance of the document.

II. WORTHY IS THE LAMB: REVELATION 5:5-10

A. The Lion's Triumph: vs. 5

Then one of the elders said to me, "Do not weep! See, the Lion of the tribe of Judah, the Root of David, has triumphed. He is able to open the scroll and its seven seals."

In the midst of John's anguish, one of the 24 elders seated about the throne told him to stop weeping (Rev. 5:5). These celestial beings were previously mentioned in 4:4 and 10. In John's vision, he saw 24 thrones surrounding God's royal seat, and 24 elders were on these thrones. They wore white clothes, which represent purity and uprightness. They also wore gold crowns, which symbolize honor, splendor, and victory.

Some think these elders are exalted angels who served God in His heavenly court. Others think they are glorified saints in heaven. Still others think the number 24 is a symbolic reference to the 12 tribes of Israel in the Old Testament and the 12 apostles in the New Testament. In this case, all the redeemed of all time (both before and after Christ's death and resurrection) are represented before God's throne and worship Him in His heavenly sanctuary.

Verse 10 says the 24 elders prostrated themselves before God's throne and placed their crowns at the base of His royal seat. These were fitting acts of worship to give the one who controls all time and all people (vs. 11).

In 5:5, one of these elders revealed the person who was worthy to take the scroll from God's hand and open its seals—"the Lion of the tribe of Judah, the Root of David." Both of these metaphors are familiar Old Testament titles, and together summed up Israel's hope for the coming Messiah (see Gen. 49:9-10; Isa. 11:1, 10; Jer. 23:5).

God's people had called Judah—the founder of the tribe—a lion, and now the elder applied the name to the greatest of all the members of Judah. The lion represented power and victory, and these were typified in the risen Christ. In contrast, the Greek word translated "Root" (Rev. 5:5) describes a humble shoot or sprout out of the main stem. As the "Root of David," Jesus is identified as the Messiah who sprang from the house and lineage of David.

John learned that Christ "has triumphed." The Greek term means "to win a victory" or "to overcome." Jesus triumphed over Satan, sin, and death through His atoning sacrifice and resurrection. Christ alone had the virtue and authority to consummate God's end-time plan.

B. The Lamb's Death: vss. 6-7

Then I saw a Lamb, looking as if it had been slain, standing in the center of the throne, encircled by the four living creatures and the elders. He had seven horns and seven eyes, which are the seven spirits of God sent out into all the earth. He came and took the scroll from the right hand of him who sat on the throne.

John next fixed his gaze on the entity appearing "in the center of the throne, encircled by the four living creatures and the elders" (Rev. 5:6). The four beasts are first mentioned in 4:6-9. There they were in the center around God's throne. The eyes covering the front and back of each creature may symbolize their unceasing watchfulness.

The four beasts probably were angels, perhaps similar to the cherubim of Ezekiel 1 and 10 or the seraphim of Isaiah 6. They guarded the throne of God, proclaimed His holiness, and led others in worship. The four beasts may have portrayed various aspects of divine majesty, represented God's attributes, or symbolized the natural order of creation.

As John continued watching, he did not see a mighty lion, but instead a Lamb that looked as if it had once been killed (Rev. 5:6). This unexpected image portrays sacrificial death, thus linking the Messiah to the Old Testament Passover lamb (see Exod. 12:5-6; Isa. 53:7).

This Lamb, who bore the marks of death, also possessed the symbols of divine power and the abundance of knowledge. The "seven horns" (Rev. 5:6) may represent perfect power, and the "seven eyes" may indicate the Lamb's perfect knowledge. John explained further that the seven eyes were "the seven spirits of God." This is a reference to the perfection of the Spirit. His basic ministry is to exalt Christ and make His presence known to all who trust in Him.

John watched as the Lamb came forward and took the scroll from God's "right hand" (vs. 7). By allowing this action, the Father authorized His Son to carry out His plan for the world.

C. The Lamb's Worship: vss. 8-10

And when he had taken it, the four living creatures and the twenty-four elders fell down before the Lamb. Each one had a harp and they were holding golden bowls full of incense, which are the prayers of the saints. And they sang a new song: "You are worthy to take the scroll and to open its seals, because you were slain, and with your blood you purchased men for God from every tribe and language and people and nation. You have made them to be a kingdom and priests to serve our God, and they will reign on the earth."

When the Lamb took the scroll, the "four living creatures and the twenty-four elders" (Rev. 5:8) around the throne fell down in worship before Him. They played harps, or lyres, the instruments used to accompany the singing of psalms. Their "golden bowls" full of incense were symbolic of the prayers of the Lord's holy people. The saints may have petitioned Him to bring about the full and final realization of His kingdom.

The worshipers began to sing a "new song" (vs. 9), for the Lord was about to inaugurate the new redeemed order of His kingdom. The participants sang this hymn to the Lamb as Redeemer. They praised His worthiness to take the scroll and "open the seals." The fact that Christ died for the sins of the whole world is reflected in the declaration that the redeemed will come from "every tribe and language and people and nation."

The result of Christ's sacrificial death is that He made His people "a kingdom and priests" (vs. 10) to serve their God. Christ will be the rightful King, and His people will compose His kingdom. They will "reign on the earth" with Him at the consummation of history.

John next heard the singing of countless numbers of angels around "the throne" (vs. 11), along with the voices of the "the living creatures and the elders." The heavenly choir praised the Lamb for His worthiness (vs. 12). It was fitting for Christ to receive glory, power, and praise for who He is and what He has done. He is the Son of God, the one who died on the cross so that those who trust in Him might become His servants in His kingdom.

Discussion Questions

1. What characterized the scroll in God's right hand?
2. What are the various views concerning the contents of the scroll?
3. What caused John to weep repeatedly?
4. What is the significance of the names used in Revelation 5:5 to describe the Messiah?
5. How was Jesus able to triumph over Satan, sin, and death?
6. Why was the Lamb worthy to take the scroll?
7. What was the result of Christ's sacrificial death?

Contemporary Application

The churches of John's day were experiencing a time of suffering; and while your students may not be oppressed in this way, they still encounter times of distress. These moments of anguish can affect them spiritually, emotionally, and physically; and at times adverse circumstances can make them feel overwhelmed.

Interestingly, jewelers place diamonds on black velvet so that the sparkle of the gems is enhanced by the contrast of the dark background. When the class members explore the depths of the tight places God has delivered them from, they will understand more about the magnificence of His rescue.

God wants Christians to be honest enough with themselves and others to admit their own inabilities in the face of devastating situations. There are plenty of everyday irritations and problems He expects them to handle; but they cannot trust Him as they need to unless they know when to admit they are unable to cope.

Gratitude is a helpful starting point in enabling the students to handle the difficulties of life. They can begin by thanking the Lord for the gift of His Son. As the slain Lamb, He has prevailed, and His victory is the basis for the students' ability to triumph in hard circumstances.

Believers can also thank the Father for the abiding presence of His Son in their lives. He redeemed them from a potential life of sin and shame so that they can faithfully worship and serve Him. This does not mean the class members will avoid problems in life; but it does mean their lives will have enduring significance.

The devil likes to keep Christians so busy that they do not have time to reflect on all the Lord is doing on their behalf. The students should not fall into the trap of thinking that spirituality is defined by how busy they are in church activities. While these have their place, they are no substitute for praising and thanking God for His help in difficult times.

The class members can express gratitude to the Lord in several ways. They can do so directly as well as in the presence of others; also, the students can encourage others to become grateful praise-givers. Such people of praise readily discover that the Lamb is present to walk with them through life's toughest moments.

Salvation Belongs to God

Scripture

Background Scripture: *Revelation 7*

Scripture Lesson: *Revelation 7:1-3, 9-10, 14b-17*

Key Verse: *"The Lamb at the center of the throne will be their shepherd; he will lead them to springs of living water. And God will wipe away every tear from their eyes."* Revelation 7:17.

Scripture Lesson for Children: *Acts 16:25-32, 35-36*

Key Verse for Children: *"The magistrates have ordered that you and Silas be released. Now you can leave. Go in peace."* Acts 16:36.

Lesson Aim

To encourage the students to rejoice because Jesus knows them intimately and cares for them.

Lesson Setting

Time: A.D. *95*

Place: *The island of Patmos*

Lesson Outline

Salvation Belongs to God

   I. Salvation of God's Servants: Revelation 7:1-3

  II. Worship of the Redeemed: Revelation 7:9-10

      A. *Universal Participation: vs. 9*

      B. *Universal Praise: vs. 10*

 III. God's Salvation Promises: Revelation 7:14b-17

      A. *Suffering and Service: vss. 14b-15*

      B. *Preservation and Provision: vss. 16-17*

Introduction for Adults

Topic: *The Faithful Are Rewarded*

Faithfulness to God and His commands is a major theme of Scripture. Moses and Joshua enjoined Israel to be faithful. The prophets preached faithfulness. Jesus asked whether He would find faith when He returns. The apostles pursued and taught lives of faithfulness.

What a joy it is then to look at a preview of what God has in store for those who love and obey Him. Of course, faithfulness comes at a high price, as we shall see in John's vision. Terrible things befall God's people because they hold to His name.

John's vision, however, gives us a glimpse of God rewarding our faithfulness. Because we are washed in Jesus' blood, we are entitled to join the multitudes singing God's praises before His throne. Is this what we really are looking for? Does the prospect of worshiping the Lamb excite us and encourage us?

Introduction for Youth

Topic: *Try a New Life!*

Rags to riches is a common theme of books and movies. We love stories about people who make it to the top despite horrendous obstacles. We admire our friends who succeed despite huge handicaps.

In a much larger sense, John's vision of heaven is a rags to riches story. Sin makes us helpless, condemned beggars before God. We can offer Him nothing to earn His favors. How then can we ever hope to gain heaven's riches? It is only by putting our faith in Christ.

Concepts for Children

Topic: *Jesus Cares for Prisoners*

1. Paul and Silas were put in a prison for telling people about Jesus.
2. Paul and Silas did not give up their faith, but sang hymns to God.
3. When we face tough times, we can trust God to give us the strength we need to make it through the experience.
4. God caused an earthquake to free the prisoners.
5. God also sent Paul to tell the jailer how to be saved.
6. We can offer hope and peace to those who are upset and fearful.

Lesson Commentary

I. SALVATION OF GOD'S SERVANTS: REVELATION 7:1-3

After this I saw four angels standing at the four corners of the earth, holding back the four winds of the earth to prevent any wind from blowing on the land or on the sea or on any tree. Then I saw another angel coming up from the east, having the seal of the living God. He called out in a loud voice to the four angels who had been given power to harm the land and the sea: "Do not harm the land or the sea or the trees until we put a seal on the foreheads of the servants of our God."

John wrote the Book of Revelation during a period of exile and suffering on the island of Patmos (1:9). At this time, Rome persecuted Christians, demanded that they renounce their faith, and pressured them to worship the emperor. It is quite possible that the aging apostle was sentenced to hard labor in the rock quarries on this island for refusing to deny the Lord. (John was the only apostle not executed as a martyr.)

The book is addressed to seven churches in the Roman province of Asia (1:4, 11), which is now part of western Turkey. The cities in which these churches were located were Ephesus, Smyrna, Pergamum, Thyatira, Sardis, Philadelphia, and Laodicea. Some experts think the apostle wrote the book during the persecution that occurred under the reign of Nero (A.D. 64–68), while other experts maintain John wrote Revelation during the reign of Vespasian (A.D. 69–79).

Though there are symbolic images in Revelation that may refer to either Nero or Vespasian, the evidence suggests that the apostle wrote the book later, during the reign of Domitian (A.D. 81–96). Throughout this period, emperor worship was prevalent all over the empire—a problem that was addressed in Revelation. For this reason many scholars think John wrote Revelation around A.D. 95, a date the early church fathers also favored.

In terms of the book's sixth chapter, it mentions a series of seal judgments. The chapter ends with the opening of the sixth seal and the people of the earth trying to hide themselves from "the wrath of the Lamb" (vs. 16). The opening of the seventh seal is dramatically delayed while Christ reassures His followers that He has not forgotten them.

In John's unfolding vision, he saw "four angels" (7:1), and each one was standing on one of the earth's four corners. The angels' identity is not clear. Some say they are the four living creatures mentioned in chapters 4 through 6, while others think they are four previously unidentified celestial beings. In either case, they function as God's agents of destruction.

The angels held back the four winds of judgment from blowing across "the earth." Thus, not a leaf rustled in the trees and the sea became as smooth as glass. The mention of the four winds is reminiscent of similar expressions found in the Old Testament (Jer. 49:36; Ezek. 37:9; Dan. 8:8).

John saw another angel "coming up from the east" (Rev. 7:2), and he held "the seal of the living God." In ancient times, people would fold documents and tie a cord around them. They would then press a lump of clay over the knot and stamp the clay with a seal. This was their way of identifying and protecting the document's contents.

People in John's day would use signet rings and cylinders as their seals for a variety of purposes. Rulers would authenticate official documents with seals, and they would represent offices inside their government with seals. Merchants also attached seals to goods during transportation to indicate ownership and ensure protection. When the Lord placed His seal on His servants, He identified them as His own and guaranteed their protection as the time of distress continued.

God gave the four angels power to harm the lands and seas of the earth; but He prevented them from doing so until His angels had placed a seal on "the foreheads" (vs. 3) of His servants. The Lord's ability to bring the judgments to a halt tells us that He is ultimately in control.

II. WORSHIP OF THE REDEEMED: REVELATION 7:9-10

A. Universal Participation: vs. 9

After this I looked and there before me was a great multitude that no one could count, from every nation, tribe, people and language, standing before the throne and in front of the Lamb. They were wearing white robes and were holding palm branches in their hands.

According to Revelation 7:4-8, God placed His seal on the foreheads of 144,000 people from all the tribes of Israel. The Lord choose 12,000 people from each tribe. In Ezekiel 9:4, it is suggested that God's mark of ownership and protection is the Hebrew letter *taw*, which looks like the English letter "X." Revelation 3:12, 14:1, and 22:4 suggest that God's name is the imprint He places on the foreheads of His servants.

The identity of the 144,000 saints mentioned in 7:4-8 is debated. They could be a select group of people from the literal 12 tribes of Israel; or they could be a specific number of believers whom God will in some way shield during a final period of distress. It could be that 144,000 (calculated using 12 as a multiple of 12) is a symbolic number for the fullness of the people of God. In other words, the Lord will bring all His followers safely to Himself. He could protect them either by removing them from the earth (this is called the Rapture) or by giving them the strength they need to endure persecution and remain loyal to Him.

We can only imagine how stirred John was as he saw in heaven "a great multitude" (vs. 9) that was too large to count. Certainly the depth of their unity far exceeded any earthly counterpart. This throng was made up of people from every nation, tribe, people, and language, and they stood before the throne of God and before the Lamb. Many ideas have been suggested regarding the identity of this host of believers. They could be the saved of all ages, only Gentile believers, or martyrs killed during a final period of great distress, to name three common views.

One remarkable aspect of the scene John saw in heaven is the position of the believers before God. While earth is about to feel the full force of the Lamb's wrath, these saints are standing before God's throne, a place of safety and security. The Lord has accepted and honored them as His true servants.

The early readers of Revelation might have associated "white robes" with the garb of Roman generals, who dressed in this fashion when celebrating their triumphs. The clothing worn by the saints in heaven represent the purity, righteousness, and glory of Christ.

People in ancient times used "palm branches" in a variety of ways. For instance, returning Roman conquerors wore garlands fashioned from palm leaves, and Greek athletes received palm branches for winning important races. The Jewish people used palms to build shelters during the Feast of Tabernacles, an occasion expressing their joy at God's deliverance and preservation. The palm branches in John's vision represented total victory and unending joy.

B. Universal Praise: vs. 10

And they cried out in a loud voice: "Salvation belongs to our God, who sits on the throne, and to the Lamb."

Everything about the scene points to the acceptance of these believers before God. They are celebrating triumph in a place of honor before the Lord and the Lamb. This truth is reflected in the chorus the multitude in heaven shouted before the throne. They acknowledged that salvation comes only from God the Father, and the Lamb, His Son (Rev. 7:10).

III. GOD'S SALVATION PROMISES: REVELATION 7:14B-17

A. Suffering and Service: vss. 14b-15

And he said, "These are they who have come out of the great tribulation; they have washed their robes and made them white in the blood of the Lamb." Therefore, "they are before the throne of God and serve him day and night in his temple and he who sits on the throne will spread his tent over them."

John may have been curious about the identity and origin of the vast number of people who were clothed in white robes and standing before God's throne. If so, one of the elders discerned this and rhetorically asked the apostle about the multitude (Rev. 7:13).

In light of John's response, the elder explained that the worshipers had "come out of the great tribulation" (vs. 14). Based on the elder's response, some identify this with a period of persecution shortly before the return of Christ. Others, however, note that believers have endured affliction and grief throughout history, so that the entire church age can be seen as a time of tribulation (2 Thess. 1:5-6; 2 Tim. 3:1, 12).

Perhaps John intended to comfort both first-century Christians as well as God's people living during a period of final crisis. Thus, the disputed identity of this group does not alter the hope John sought to convey to believers. Through faith in Christ we, too, can find acceptance before the Father and will someday experience His glory.

Because the worshipers in John's vision had "washed their robes" (Rev. 7:14) in "the blood of the Lamb," their garments had been made white. This vast throng, like all believers, have been saved on the basis of Christ's sacrifice.

The elder revealed that the glorified state will include service for God in His heavenly sanctuary; but labor for the Lord will be a delight, performed without the fatigue and boredom that so often mark activities in this life. Scripture does not tell us what that service will entail, but surely it will involve worship, adoration, and continuous praise.

The term rendered "spread his tent over" (vs. 15) refers to God sheltering and protecting His people with His presence. In eternity, the Lord's glorious presence will always remain like a canopy or tent over His people.

B. Preservation and Provision: vss. 16-17

"Never again will they hunger; never again will they thirst. The sun will not beat upon them, nor any scorching heat. For the Lamb at the center of the throne will be their shepherd; he will lead them to springs of living water. And God will wipe away every tear from their eyes."

Revelation 7:16-17 presents a dramatic contrast to the death, famine, war, and sorrow of chapter 6. The believers who have endured hardship will find rest and relief from their pain. For all believers, heaven will be a blessed contrast to the suffering felt on earth. In the Lord's presence, they will experience joy, blessing, and comfort.

As seen in Genesis 3:22-24, God expelled Adam and Eve from the Garden of Eden so they would not eat fruit from the tree of life. God did not want them to live forever in their sinful state. In Revelation 7:17, however, Christ leads the redeemed to the waters of life. The imagery is that of a shepherd guiding his sheep to a freshwater spring in the desert. Salvation from the death that sin brought into the world will be complete. In heaven, the righteous will enjoy unending life.

In Bible times shepherds performed numerous duties as they cared for their flocks. In addition to finding adequate shelter for sheep, shepherds also had to lead them to good pasturelands and ample supplies of water. Knowing that their flocks were easy prey, shepherds spent part of their time warding off attacks from savage animals. If necessary, shepherds were willing to risk their own lives to ensure the safety of the flock.

At night several shepherds might bring their flocks into a protected area called a sheepfold. This was a cave, shed, pen, or courtyard that had one entrance and was enclosed by branches or stone walls. In addition to providing some protection from the weather, the wall also prevented the flock from getting out and wild animals from getting in and preying on the sheep.

The elder told John that God will wipe away all tears from the eyes of His people. They will never experience pain, suffering, sickness, grief, and death. In some way, the Lord will cause their past never to bring them remorse in the coming age.

Discussion Questions

1. What were the four angels doing?
2. For how long were these angels prevented from harming the lands and seas of the earth?
3. What did the great multitude declare concerning God and the Lamb?
4. According to the elder, who were the vast number of worshipers?
5. What will the glorified state include for believers?

Contemporary Application

The shepherding imagery of Revelation 7:17 reminds believers that the Lord is always with them and knows them better than they understand themselves. It can be encouraging for them to know that Jesus is their constant companion.

This means that those who are saved need never feel lonely, even when human friends have been removed. The imagery also implies that the class members do not need to give into feelings of inadequacy when called to undertake a significant task. Jesus is near to give wisdom and offer courage when they are venturing into the unknown.

One way for the students to think about Christ's abiding presence is to compare this attribute to radio waves. Although these impulses cannot be seen or felt, they are around believers at all times. With these radio waves they are surrounded by a tremendous wealth of information; however, access is not automatic. God's people must tune in to receive the benefits.

The Shepherd, who gives courage to the fearful and promises to be the companion of the lonely, is ever-present. By turning to Him in prayer, believers may draw on His power, especially as they face the challenges of each day.

A Call for Endurance

DEVOTIONAL READING

2 Timothy 2:3-13

DAILY BIBLE READINGS

Monday May 17
*John 16:29-33 In the World
You Face Persecution*

Tuesday May 18
*Matthew 10:16-22 Endure
to the End*

Wednesday May 19
*Matthew 24:9-14 Many Will
Fall Away*

Thursday May 20
*Matthew 24:45-50 Be
Faithful to the Task*

Friday May 21
*1 Corinthians 15:12-20 Our
Hope in the Risen Lord*

Saturday May 22
*1 Corinthians 15:54-58 We
Have Victory Through
Christ*

Sunday May 23
*Revelation 4:6-13 A Call for
Endurance*

Scripture

Background Scripture: *Revelation 14*
Scripture Lesson: *Revelation 14:6-13*
Key Verse: *This calls for patient endurance on the part of the
saints who obey God's commandments and remain faithful to
Jesus.* Revelation 14:12.
Scripture Lesson for Children: *Mark 8:22-26*
Key Verse for Children: *"One thing I do know. I was blind
but now I see!"* John 9:25.

Lesson Aim

To help the students recognize why it is important for
them to renew their relationship with God.

Lesson Setting

Time: A.D. 95
Place: *The island of Patmos*

Lesson Outline

A Call for Endurance
    I. God's Eternal Gospel: Revelation 14:6-7
        A. *Universal Proclamation: vs. 6*
        B. *Universal Worship: vs. 7*
   II. God's Eternal Judgment: Revelation 14:8-12
        A. *Babylon's Downfall: vs. 8*
        B. *False Worship: vss. 9-10*
        C. *Horrific Torment: vs. 11*
        D. *Saintly Endurance: vs. 12*
  III. Blessed Rest: Revelation 14:13

Introduction for Adults

Topic: *A Call for Endurance*

Steel hardens under intense heat. The finest sword blades in the world are made out of steel that stands the most severe tests. Our spiritual steel hardens in combat. In John's vision he saw combat with the beasts and with Babylon. Whatever they stand for, we know they used powerful attractions to draw people away from the Lord.

When we engage the enemy, we toughen our spiritual fibers. We grow stronger in faith and in resistance to sin. We know better how to resist the devil. God wants us to grow; thus He puts us through the fire, so to speak, so that our faith will come forth refined like pure gold (1 Pet. 1:7).

Introduction for Youth

Topic: *Where Do I Belong?*

The standing invitation of the United States Marine Corps is for a "few good men." The Marines are an elite group and they take great pride in their traditions and in their training. Only the fittest survive and are entitled to belong to the Marines.

When God's eternal judgments take place, we know that only the fittest will be entitled to spend eternity with Him. What we go through now is like Marine Corps basic training. We are hit with the worst kinds of obstacles and temptations—anything that can derail us and cause us to quit and deny Jesus.

God, of course, saves us by His grace. All He requires is our faith in His Son. But that is just the entrance to His kingdom. Our decision to follow Christ puts us into mortal combat with sin, temptation, and the devil. To win this battle we need spiritual hardness and toughness. We need to be as tough in our spiritual battles as the Marines are in their wartime conflicts.

Concepts for Children

Topic: *Jesus Gives Sight to the Blind*

1. Jesus responded to requests to heal the blind man.
2. People came to Jesus because they knew His love and power.
3. When we walk with Jesus, others will come to us for help with their needs.
4. We have many opportunities to serve those who suffer from various physical ills.
5. Many people are also spiritually blind, so they do not know that Jesus is their Savior.
6. Jesus wants to shine in the lives of others through us.

Lesson Commentary

I. GOD'S ETERNAL GOSPEL: REVELATION 14:6-7

A. Universal Proclamation: vs. 6

Then I saw another angel flying in midair, and he had the eternal gospel to proclaim to those who live on the earth—to every nation, tribe, language and people.

The Book of Revelation contains three series of seven judgments: the seal judgments of chapter 6, the trumpet judgments of chapters 8 and 9, and the bowl judgments of chapter 16. There are three primary views regarding the interrelationship of these judgments.

According to some experts, the judgments occur simultaneously, and the repetition signifies the intensification of each judgment. In this case, the later series of judgments repeat the earlier ones. Others think the judgments unfold in successive fashion. In this case, the judgments are consecutive, with one calamity following the preceding one for a total of 21 judgments. Still others think one series of judgments contains the next series in a telescopic fashion. For example, the seventh seal judgment introduces and contains the seventh trumpet judgments. And the seventh trumpet judgment introduces and contains the seven bowl judgments.

Up until this point in John's unfolding vision, he had been recounting the various seal and trumpet judgments being unleashed on humankind. After the blowing of the seventh trumpet, the apostle presented such key symbolic characters as the woman, the dragon, the beast, the false prophet, and the 144,000.

Then, as John watched, he saw an angel flying "in midair" (14:6). God gave this celestial being "the eternal gospel" to proclaim to all the people of the earth. Some think this is the saving message of Jesus' death and resurrection. More likely the announcement recorded in verse 7 denotes the content of the good news the angel proclaimed.

B. Universal Worship: vs. 7

He said in a loud voice, "Fear God and give him glory, because the hour of his judgment has come. Worship him who made the heavens, the earth, the sea and the springs of water."

The angel directed all earth's inhabitants to "fear God and give him glory" (Rev. 14:7). This emphasis on revering and honoring the Lord was made in light of the fact that the time for Him to judge the wicked had come. The angel also urged humanity to worship the Creator of heaven and earth. This has been God's will for earth's inhabitants throughout history.

Some think the angel's message is only a declaration that judgment is about to fall, with no appeal being made for the wicked to repent. The context, however, suggests that the Lord was making a final call for the people of the world to abandon their sin and acknowledge Him as their God.

II. God's Eternal Judgment: Revelation 14:8-12

A. Babylon's Downfall: vs. 8

A second angel followed and said, "Fallen! Fallen is Babylon the Great, which made all the nations drink the maddening wine of her adulteries."

John next saw another angel following the first one across the sky and announcing that the great city of Babylon had fallen (Rev. 14:8). In Revelation, "Babylon" probably represents an entire world system, as well as a city, in rebellion against God. It thus is a suitable image of a society that persecutes believers but which God will ultimately destroy.

The celestial being explained that Babylon had seduced the nations of the world like a prostitute and made them drunk on "the maddening wine of her adulteries." The reference to Babylon echoes terminology found in Daniel 4:30. In fact, there are numerous similar literary correspondences between Daniel and Revelation. This suggests that what is anticipated in Daniel concerning the end times comes to final fulfillment in Revelation.

The identity of Babylon in Revelation is disputed. Some think it is a code name for Rome, which in John's day was the epitome of opposition to God and His people. Others maintain that some notorious ancient city—such Babylon, Rome, Tyre, or Jerusalem—will be rebuilt in the end times as the capital of a great world empire headed up by Antichrist. Still others think Babylon represents the corrupt political, commercial, social, and religious systems of the world.

B. False Worship: vss. 9-10

A third angel followed them and said in a loud voice: "If anyone worships the beast and his image and receives his mark on the forehead or on the hand, he, too, will drink of the wine of God's fury, which has been poured full strength into the cup of his wrath. He will be tormented with burning sulfur in the presence of the holy angels and of the Lamb."

John next saw a "third angel" (Rev. 14:9) following the first two across the sky. This creature announced that those who worshiped the beast that came out of the sea or the "image" made to represent it will experience God's judgment. The same end was true for those who are branded on their forehead or hand with the distinctive "mark" of the beast.

The sea beast is first mentioned in 13:1. This grotesque creature has "ten horns and seven heads." On each horn there is a crown, and on each head there is a pretentious name that is an insult to God. The sea beast represents an evil entity that, in the end times, will spread wickedness, persecute believers, and gather the world in rebellion against the Lord (Dan. 7:19-25; 2 Thess. 2:1-10; Rev. 19:19). John explained that the dragon gives the beast its great power, rule, and authority (Rev. 13:2). Hence, the sea beast is the deputy of Satan and exists to do the devil's bidding.

Verse 11 mentions a second beast "coming out of the earth." This evil entity is the lieutenant of the first beast, and uses it s authority to compel the world to worship this creature (vs. 12). In some ways, the beast from the land is a mock imitation of the Holy Spirit. Together, Satan, the sea beast, and the land beast form an unholy trio as a counterfeit to the triune God (see 16:13).

The land beast performs astonishing miracles—like making "fire to come down from heaven" (13:13)—to dupe the world into worshiping the sea beast. The land beast even talks people into making "an image" (vs. 14) of the sea beast. The land beast also pressures them to "worship the image" (vs. 15).

The land beast will force people to have "a mark" (vs. 16) placed on their forehead, perhaps in mock imitation of the seal that God places on the foreheads of His servants (see 7:3). Whatever the exact nature of the land beast's brand or tattoo, it will signify that those having it are controlled by the sea beast and loyal to it.

In light of this background information, we can understand more clearly why God will judge those mentioned in 14:9. John used the phrases "the wine of God's fury" (vs. 10) and "the cup of his wrath" to refer to the Lord's judgment. This is reminiscent of Old Testament passages that depicted God's wrath as a cup of wine that the wicked drank (Ps. 75:8; Isa. 51:17; Jer. 25:15-17). In Bible times people considered undiluted wine to be extremely potent. It thus became a symbol for severe judgment; for example, Revelation 14:10 says that the "the wine" of God's wrath is "poured full strength."

Such a horrible end is justified, for the wicked rejected "the Lamb." The Greek noun *arnion*, which is rendered "Lamb," appears throughout the Book of Revelation, especially in worship passages, as a title for Christ. This designation is the central messianic image in the book. It underscores the importance of Christ's redeeming work and helps to shed light on other major themes in Revelation.

Some experts even go so far as to say that the Lamb motif in Revelation is a starting point for understanding what the book teaches about the Messiah. The idea is that John used the name "Lamb" in a comprehensive way to describe Christ in the fullness of His person and work. In fact, this image so dominates the canvas of John's literary masterpiece that the Lamb is present throughout Revelation, whether explicitly or implicitly.

Verse 10 states that divine judgment took place in the presence of the holy angels and the Lamb. Does this mean that, as some have accused, the Lord was gloating over the demise of the wicked? Such a conclusion is unlikely; instead, the emphasis is on their eternal condemnation, which vindicated the faith and devotion of the saints to the Lamb. The latter are those who abandoned, rather than embraced, the ways of the world.

The presence of pain, suffering, and evil in the world causes some people to wonder whether a good God exists, and if He does, why He does not put an end to it if He can. John's vision, as recorded in Revelation, does not explain why there is evil; but it does spotlight an important and encouraging truth. God has placed restraints on evil, and He will one day judge the wicked for their heinous deeds against the upright.

C. Horrific Torment: vs. 11

"And the smoke of their torment rises for ever and ever. There is no rest day or night for those who worship the beast and his image, or for anyone who receives the mark of his name."

Revelation 14:11 contains a chilling reminder about the eternal future of the wicked. Those who persecuted and killed believers will be tormented in the lake of fire while the holy angels and the Lamb watch (vs. 10). The smoke from the torment of the wicked will go up throughout eternity, and they will have no relief from their anguish (vs. 11).

D. Saintly Endurance: vs. 12

This calls for patient endurance on the part of the saints who obey God's commandments and remain faithful to Jesus.

John was well aware of the sorrows his fellow believers had to endure for Christ. The apostle also knew they were tempted to compromise their faith. John thus urged them to patiently bear their trials, "obey God's commandments" (Rev. 14:12), and "remain faithful to Jesus."

III. BLESSED REST: REVELATION 14:13

Then I heard a voice from heaven say, "Write: Blessed are the dead who die in the Lord from now on." *"Yes," says the Spirit, "they will rest from their labor, for their deeds will follow them."*

Revelation 14:13 contains encouraging promises. A "voice from heaven" announced that the Lord will eternally bless all who remain faithful to Him to the end of their lives. The Spirit also announced that the righteous (in contrast to the wicked) will one day rest from their hard work of serving God. The Lord will reward them for faithfully doing His will, despite the toil and anguish they may have to experience.

Verse 13 contains the second of seven beatitudes appearing in the book (see 1:3; 16:15; 19:9; 20:6; 22:7, 14). These passages use the Greek word *makários*, which is rendered "blessed." The term underscores the hope that believers have in the midst of their distressing experiences.

Since the present is a time of suffering and the kingdom a period of future blessedness, believers are encouraged during the interim period to exercise that kind of patient endurance that was exemplified by Jesus. Such encouragement is counterbalanced by the apostolic exhortation to obey the prophetic words being conveyed to them in Revelation.

John wrote this book to disclose God's ultimate goal of history, namely, the victory of Christ at His coming. The Messiah will return as the triumphant ruler and conqueror of the world. Jesus, in power and glory, will defeat Satan's hosts, condemn those who reject Him, and bring His redeemed into glory.

Discussion Questions

1. What did the first angel declare?
2. What was the announcement made by the second angel?
3. What declaration did the third angel make?
4. What does "the wine of God's fury" (Rev. 14:10) refer to?
5. What encouraging promises are found in verse 13?

Contemporary Application

When people first become Christians, their relationship with God feels strong. They are eager to do whatever He asks and they desire to conform their lives to His will. Over time, however, their devotion may wane. This common situation underscores the importance of believers renewing their relationship with God.

If the students' relationship with God has weakened to a certain extent, it will take some time for them to renew it. At first, the task might seem daunting; but rather than give up, the class members need to cultivate the "patient endurance" referred to in Revelation 14:13.

This implies taking gradual and realistic steps in renewing one's relationship with the Lord. At times the process will be difficult and costly in terms of what God leads the students to do or stop doing. Regardless of the steps that are taken, they can rest assured that it will be well worth their time, effort, and sacrifice.

Perhaps a starting point for class members would be to examine their inner spiritual lives. What is their attitude toward "God's commandments"? How "faithful to Jesus" are they? The students should next examine the external aspects of their spiritual lives, especially in terms of their relationships with others.

Self-evaluation will be painful at times. As part of the renewal process, the Lord will bring to mind areas of the class members' lives He wants to change. It might be the way they think, the words they use, or the activities they do. Regardless of how God brings about change, His ultimate goal will be to draw them closer to Him.

A New Heaven and Earth

DEVOTIONAL READING

Revelation 22:1-5

DAILY BIBLE READINGS

Monday May 24
*Revelation 19:6-10 The
Lord Almighty Reigns*

Tuesday May 25
*Revelation 21:1-7 A New
Heaven and Earth*

Wednesday May 26
*Revelation 21:9-14 John Sees
the Holy City*

Thursday May 27
*Revelation 21:22-27 God's
Glory Is Its Light*

Friday May 28
*Revelation 22:1-5 There Will
Be No More Night*

Saturday May 29
*Revelation 22:6-10 I Am
Coming Soon!*

Sunday May 30
*Revelation 22:12-17 I Am
the Alpha and Omega*

Scripture

Background Scripture: *Revelation 21:1—22:5*
Scripture Lesson: *Revelation 21:1-7, 22-27*
Key Verse: *"Now the dwelling of God is with men, and he
will live with them. They will be his people, and God himself
will be with them and be their God."* Revelation 21:3.
Scripture Lesson for Children: *John 16:16-20, 22*
Key Verse for Children: *[Jesus said,] "I will see you again
and you will rejoice."* John 16:22.

Lesson Aim

To encourage students to strengthen their trust in God
by testifying to His work in their lives.

Lesson Setting

Time: *A.D. 95*
Place: *The island of Patmos*

Lesson Outline

A New Heaven and Earth

I. Intimate Communion with God: Revelation 21:1-7
    A. *The New Jerusalem: vss. 1-2*
    B. *The Lord Among His People: vss. 3-4*
    C. *The Renewal of All Things: vss. 5-7*
II. The Glory of God and the Lamb:
    Revelation 21:22-27
    A. *The Divine Presence: vss. 22-23*
    B. *The Presence of the Nations: vss. 24-26*
    C. *The Elimination of All Evil: vs. 27*

Introduction for Adults

Topic: *A New Homecoming*

"We've found the perfect house," some people say when they succeed in finding the home of their dreams. However, year after year they discover that what seemed like a perfect house needs repairs, upkeep, and even remodeling. They work hard to keep it livable and enjoyable.

Our journeys through life are something like that. We launch our relationship to God and then we find that discipleship is hard work. We can't fall behind in our worship and service. We need constant renewal and stimulation to keep walking with God.

For our sakes, God tells us that one day our struggles will be over. At the end of the age, the Father and Son will abide with us. We, in turn, will experience unimagined joy in their presence.

Introduction for Youth

Topic: *A New World Coming!*

Space missions no longer excite us like they once did. But among today's students could be those who someday will inhabit a new world in deep space. Something in human beings drives them to push back the old frontiers.

Jesus told us about a new world, that is, an entirely new creation. Our universe will be replaced by a new one—not just with new physical attributes, but also with moral and spiritual qualities, including freedom from sin, fear, sickness, and death.

God's picture of the future far surpasses anything we could ever imagine or achieve. We must listen to what He says, so that we will not miss the greatest adventure of all time.

Concepts for Children

Topic: *Jesus Brings Joy!*

1. Jesus' followers were sad because He told them about His upcoming death.
2. Jesus promised to give His followers a joy that would be greater than their fears and sorrows.
3. Jesus can give us joy even in hard times.
4. Our friends must know about the joy that comes from trusting Jesus for salvation.
5. We can experience joy in Christ during our times of prayer, worship, and service.

Lesson Commentary

I. INTIMATE COMMUNION WITH GOD: REVELATION 21:1-7

A. The New Jerusalem: vss. 1-2

Then I saw a new heaven and a new earth, for the first heaven and the first earth had passed away, and there was no longer any sea. I saw the Holy City, the new Jerusalem, coming down out of heaven from God, prepared as a bride beautifully dressed for her husband.

In John's unfolding vision, the condemnation of the wicked (Rev. 20:11-15) is followed by the new creation that awaits believers. The apostle related that he saw "a new heaven and a new earth" (21:1). These are total replacements for their old counterparts, "the first heaven and the first earth," which God had destroyed. He evidently did this to eliminate any corrupting presence or influence of sin (2 Pet. 3:7, 10-13).

God will also eliminate the vast and mysterious seas. In the Old Testament, the sea was a symbol for the agitation and restlessness associated with evil (Isa. 57:20; Jer. 49:23). In the Book of Revelation, the sea is the source of the satanic beast and a burial site for the wicked dead (Rev. 13:1; 20:13). In the eternal state, there can be no physical and symbolic place for this seething cauldron of wickedness.

What John saw is consistent with Isaiah's reference to the "new heavens and a new earth" (Isa. 65:17). The apostle, however, was not thinking of merely a world free of sin and hardness of heart. John's vision was of a creation new in all its qualities.

The apostle's attention quickly passed from the creation to the new heaven and earth and to "the Holy City, the New Jerusalem" (Rev. 21:2), which God sent down out of heaven. The Lord magnificently adorned the new Jerusalem (the bride) for her husband (the groom). The implication here is that the city surpassed the beauty of everything else God had made.

In the ancient Near East, the wedding ceremony usually took place after dark at the bride's house. Prior to the wedding ceremony, the groom and his friends would form a procession and walk to the home of the bride. After the couple was officially married, the procession would return to the home of the groom or his father.

As the procession journeyed along a planned route, friends of the groom would join the group and participate in singing, playing musical instruments, and dancing. The bride would wear an ornate dress, expensive jewelry (if she could afford it), and a veil over her face. The groom typically hung a garland of flowers around his neck.

Once the procession arrived at its destination, a lavish feast, lasting up to seven days, would begin. Friends would sing love ballads for the couple and share stories about them. Everyone would consume food and drink in generous quantities. At the end of the first day's festivities, the bride and groom would be escorted to their private wedding chamber.

Some think the new Jerusalem in the Book of Revelation is a symbol of the Christian community in heaven; however, based on the detailed information recorded in 21:10-21, others maintain the new Jerusalem will be a literal city where God's people dwell for all eternity. In either case, the main point is that a new world is coming, and it will be glorious beyond imagination.

B. The Lord Among His People: vss. 3-4

And I heard a loud voice from the throne saying, "Now the dwelling of God is with men, and he will live with them. They will be his people, and God himself will be with them and be their God. He will wipe every tear from their eyes. There will be no more death or mourning or crying or pain, for the old order of things has passed away."

A loud voice from the heavenly throne declared that "the dwelling of God is with men" (Rev. 21:3); in other words, in the eternal state God will permanently dwell among the redeemed of all ages. They will be His people, and He will be their God. The voice also disclosed that five scourges of human existence will not exist in the eternal state—tears, death, sorrow, crying, and pain. The new order will eliminate all these forms of sadness (vs. 4).

C. The Renewal of All Things: vss. 5-7

He who was seated on the throne said, "I am making everything new!" Then he said, "Write this down, for these words are trustworthy and true." He said to me: "It is done. I am the Alpha and the Omega, the Beginning and the End. To him who is thirsty I will give to drink without cost from the spring of the water of life. He who overcomes will inherit all this, and I will be his God and he will be my son."

God declared that He was doing away with the old order and making "everything new" (Rev. 21:5). God told John to write down what He had said, for His words were "trustworthy and true." Believers could stake their hopes for eternity on the divine promise because it was accurate and reliable.

This verse is one of several places in Revelation where "the throne" of God is mentioned. In ancient times thrones were symbols of power, sovereignty, and majesty. The throne in heaven serves as a reminder of the just reign of God over the course of history. Also, the Lamb's constant presence near, around, and on the throne makes it the focal point for His exercise of power.

God's presence blazes forth from the celestial throne. In 4:2-3, for example, the image is one of a transparent jewel radiating the splendor of the divine. It is interesting to note that throughout Revelation John did not describe the details of God's appearance. This reminds us that the Lord's greatness and glory are beyond our ability to comprehend.

In 21:6, the phrase "It is done" could also be rendered "It has happened." The idea is that everything the Lord declared was finished and absolutely certain to occur. This was possible because God is "the Alpha and the Omega" as well as "the Beginning and the End."

God's declaration of Himself as "the Alpha and the Omega"—drawing upon the first and last letters of the Greek alphabet—is emphatic in the original. It's as if the divine were saying, "I and no other." It is similar in meaning to the expressions "the Beginning and the End" and "the First and the Last" (1:17; 22:13).

The idea behind these statements—which are applied interchangeably to both the Father and the Son—is one of *totality*. In other words, the Lord is the beginning and ending of all things. Also, His rule encompasses the past, the present, and the future. Furthermore, He is sovereign over all that takes place in human history and is directing its course to a final and proper conclusion (Col. 1:17; Heb. 1:3).

In John's unfolding vision, God promised to give water from the life-giving fountain to everyone who was thirsty (Rev. 21:6). This pledge is a vivid reminder of the refreshment and satisfaction believers will enjoy in heaven. In the eternal state, God will satisfy the yearnings of the soul.

This assurance is grounded in the Lord's own nature. Those who overcome in this life will receive an eternal inheritance and an eternal relationship. They will be the eternal people of the eternal God (vs. 7). Virtue and purity will characterize life for the redeemed in heaven; and the Lord will ban from heaven all who are characterized by the vices listed in verse 8.

II. THE GLORY OF GOD AND THE LAMB: REVELATION 21:22-27

A. The Divine Presence: vss. 22-23

I did not see a temple in the city, because the Lord God Almighty and the Lamb are its temple. The city does not need the sun or the moon to shine on it, for the glory of God gives it light, and the Lamb is its lamp.

In Revelation 21:9-21, John gave a stunning description of the new Jerusalem, which is the final dwelling place for God's people. The city sparkles like a precious gem and radiates the majesty of the Lord. The city is a gigantic cube and the same shape as the Most Holy Place in the tabernacle and temple.

In ancient Israel, both the tabernacle and the temple were set apart for God and became the place where He manifested His presence among His people. Every detail of their exterior construction and interior contents were to correspond exactly with God's definitive instructions. Unlike the Jerusalem of Bible times, the new Jerusalem will have no temple within it (vs. 22). The reason is that "the Lord God Almighty and the Lamb" are the city's temple. Similarly, the new Jerusalem will have no need for the sun or the moon, for "the glory of God" (vs. 23) illuminates the city and "the Lamb" is the city's source of light.

John's reference to the Lord God as the "Almighty" (vs. 22) renders the Greek noun *pantokrator*, which means "all-powerful" or "omnipotent." Outside Revelation this term is found only once in the New Testament (2 Cor. 6:18), but here it occurs nine times. The word conveys the sense of God being invincible. The idea is that no matter how fierce and wicked Satan may be, he cannot defeat God. In the Lord's time and in His way He fulfills His promises and accomplishes His sovereign purpose in history. Thus, though human rulers might claim total dominion over the world and have themselves celebrated as rulers of history, in reality it is God alone to whom dominion over the world and history belongs.

B. The Presence of the Nations: vss. 24-26

The nations will walk by its light, and the kings of the earth will bring their splendor into it. On no day will its gates ever be shut, for there will be no night there. The glory and honor of the nations will be brought into it.

All "the nations" (Rev. 21:24) will walk in the light of the new Jerusalem. Likewise, "the kings of the earth" will bring their glory and honor to the city. The new Jerusalem will truly be the center of life for the redeemed in eternity. It will be such a safe and secure haven that during the day its gates will never "be shut" (vs. 25). Even night, with all the fears and uncertainties connected with it, will be eliminated.

In the new Jerusalem, God will be worshiped face-to-face. The city will be a cosmopolitan place, where redeemed humanity in all its cultural diversity will live together in peace. In fact, the "glory and honor of the nations" (vs. 26) will stream into the new Jerusalem.

C. The Elimination of All Evil: vs. 27

Nothing impure will ever enter it, nor will anyone who does what is shameful or deceitful, but only those whose names are written in the Lamb's book of life.

God will vindicate the faith of the redeemed by not permitting any immoral or wicked people to enter the holy city. The inhabitants of the new Jerusalem will only be those whose names are recorded in "the Lamb's book of life" (Rev. 21:27). The book of life is mentioned several times in Revelation, beginning in 3:5. There Jesus assured the believers in Sardis that He would never erase from this heavenly list the names of those who had remained loyal to Him.

The next occurrence is in 13:8, where it is disclosed that those who revere the beast will have their names omitted from the divine list of God's people. This book belongs to Christ the Lamb, whom God in His eternal plan allowed to be sacrificed to atone for the sins of the world. Verse 8 could also mean that God placed the names of the redeemed in the book of life before He created the world.

In 17:8, it is disclosed that those who belong to this evil world system do not have their names recorded in the book of life. The significance of this omission is brought out in 20:12. At the great white throne judgment, God will open the book of life and deliver from condemnation only those whose names appear therein (vs. 15). These are the ones who trusted in Christ for salvation and correspondingly have a place in the new Jerusalem (21:27).

Discussion Questions

1. What will replace "the first heaven and the first earth" (Rev. 21:1)?
2. In what way will the new Jerusalem be prepared?
3. What statements did God make about Himself to assure believers that His

promises will be fulfilled?

4. Why will the new Jerusalem not need any temple or source of light?

5. What kind of place will the new Jerusalem be?

Contemporary Application

Trust for believers is acquired one experience at a time. They often place their faith in people and confidence in circumstances, only to be let down or disappointed. God, however, will never fail His people. As "the Alpha and the Omega" (Rev. 21:6), He has the ability to do what He says; and as "the Beginning and the End," He has power to fulfill all His promises.

Three kinds of evidence prove that the students can trust God. First, they have the witness of Scripture. Second, they have the testimony of others concerning what God has done for them. Third, class members learn to trust God through personal experience. Each time they experience His strength, love, and goodness, their trust has an opportunity to grow like a flourishing plant.

God repeatedly told His people to remember what He had done for them (see, for example, Deut. 6:12). Also, Jeremiah said that God's mercies "are new every morning" (Lam. 3:23). Moreover, Israel failed spiritually because the nation had a limited spiritual memory bank (see Isa. 17:10). These truths underscore how important it is for believers to strengthen their trust in God.

Through prayer and Bible study, the class members can plant their feet daily on Christ the Rock. They can also strengthen their trust in God by testifying to His work in their lives. Doing this brings to the students' conscious level of awareness just how involved the Lord is in their daily matters. Moreover, testifying to others will not only strengthen the faith of the students but also those who listen to what they have to say.

Hold Fast to the Faith

The Reason to Be Faithful

DEVOTIONAL READING

Colossians 1:15-20

DAILY BIBLE READINGS

Monday May 31
Acts 4:5-12 Christ Is the Cornerstone

Tuesday June 1
Colossians 1:15-20 Christ Is the Image of God

Wednesday June 2
Colossians 1:21-27 Christ in You, the Hope of Glory

Thursday June 3
Colossians 2:1-6 In Christ Are Treasures of Wisdom

Friday June 4
Hebrews 1:1-5 Christ, the Reflection of God's Glory

Saturday June 5
Hebrews 1:6-13 You Established the Universe

Sunday June 6
Hebrews 1:14—2:4 Salvation Declared through Christ

Scripture

Background Scripture: *Hebrews 1:1—2:4*
Scripture Lesson: *Hebrews 1:1-9; 2:1-4*
Key Verse: *The Son is the radiance of God's glory and the exact representation of his being.* Hebrews 1:3.
Scripture Lesson for Children: *Genesis 6:9-18; 7:1-5*
Key Verse for Children: *Noah did all that the LORD commanded him.* Genesis 7:5.

Lesson Aim

To reinforce our confidence that Jesus is able to meet all our needs.

Lesson Setting

Time: *Before A.D. 70*
Place: *Possibly from Rome*

Lesson Outline

The Reason to Be Faithful

  I. God's Revelation: Hebrews 1:1-3
     A. *By the Prophets: vs. 1*
     B. *By the Son: vs. 2*
     C. *The Son's Nature and Work: vs. 3*
  II. The Son's Superiority to Angels: Hebrews 1:4-9
     A. *In Relationship: vss. 4-5*
     B. *In Worship: vs. 6*
     C. *In Ministry: vss. 7-9*
  III. Warning to Believers: Hebrews 2:1-4
     A. *The Exhortation: vs. 1*
     B. *The Reason to Remain Faithful: vss. 2-4*

Introduction for Adults

Topic: *The Reason to Be Faithful*

When we marry, we show that we have more than enough reasons to be faithful to our spouses. And the longer we are married, the stronger those reasons become, simply because we get to know one another better. Love is the best reason to be faithful.

The Letter to the Hebrews gives us a host of reasons to be faithful to Jesus. The writer of this epistle did not tell us to grow in our love for Jesus. Instead, the author told us to look at how great Jesus is. The more that we fill our minds with His greatness, the more we will love Him and be faithful to Him.

Introduction for Youth

Topic: *Why Be Faithful?*

If we had to pick one reason to be faithful to Christ, what would it be? Would we choose His sovereign power and glory, His upholding the universe, or His being better than the angels? Probably not. We would declare our loyalty to Him because He "provided purification for sins" (Heb. 1:3).

Behind this truth is the fact that Jesus died on the cross for us. Of course, we also see our wickedness and our desires to have things our own way. How could Jesus love us that much? He did and therefore we do not ever want to betray Him. He paid too much for us to turn our backs on Him.

Concepts for Children

Topic: *By Faith: Noah Built an Ark*

1. Because of all the bad things people were doing, God sent a flood on the earth.
2. God, however, was pleased with the way Noah lived for Him.
3. God told Noah to build a large boat called an ark.
4. God used the ark to rescue Noah, his family, and the creatures of the earth from the Flood.
5. God does not like sin.
6. By trusting in Jesus, we can receive God's forgiveness.

The Lesson Commentary

I. GOD'S REVELATION: HEBREWS 1:1-3

A. By the Prophets: vs. 1

In the past God spoke to our forefathers through the prophets at many times and in various ways.

Ironically, despite what can be inferred about the writer of Hebrews, his identity remains a mystery. Some have argued for Pauline authorship; yet the letter's vocabulary, style, and theology differ noticeably from Paul's letters. Unlike the author of Hebrews, however, Paul always identified himself in his writings.

The language of Hebrews is polished, deliberate, and without outbursts of emotion so characteristic of Paul. The apostle used Greek, Hebrew, and other sources in his Old Testament quotations, while the author of Hebrews used only the Greek translation of the Old Testament. Hebrews 2:3 seems to say that the author did not hear the word of salvation directly from the Lord, whereas Paul did. If the apostle wrote Hebrews, he left none of the usual clues.

Others have suggested that the writer of the epistle was Barnabas, or Apollos, or Epaphras, or Silas, or even Priscilla. The last option is most unlikely, for in 11:32 the author referred to himself with a masculine gender participle.

In the end, it seems clear that this book won its place in the New Testament by its merit, not by the esteem of its author—*and rightly so.* The letter has theological affinities with Paul. Also, John's lofty description of Christ as the divine "Word" is detectable. Moreover, there is the portrayal of Jesus' suffering, as described in the three Synoptic Gospels.

In the opening of his Letter to the Hebrews, the author emphasized the superiority of Christ, who, as God's only Son, died on the cross to provide salvation for all people. To underscore Christ's superiority, the author compared the incompleteness of the Old Testament prophets with the completeness of His revelation through His Son.

Four prepositional phrases in 1:1 reveal some of the characteristics of God's communication. The occasions were "at many times" and the methods were "in various ways." The recipients were "the forefathers" and the medium was through "the prophets." The idea is that God had been active throughout the history of His people.

The basis for God choosing to reveal Himself in progressive stages rests on the fact that He works with us according to the level of our understanding. At first, He revealed Himself only in shadows and symbols; but as people came to know more about Him and the way He works, He became more explicit in His dealings and revelations.

B. By the Son: vs. 2

But in these last days he has spoken to us by his Son, whom he appointed heir of all things, and through whom he made the universe.

The Lord spoke through the prophets and in various ways. On those occasions when God communicated His word to people of faith, they passed on this message to others. While acknowledging these ancient revelations for what they taught people about God, the author implied that they were fragmentary and incomplete. At most they pointed to a time when God would reveal Himself more fully and finally in "his Son" (Heb. 1:2).

The candid statements appearing in verse 1 were not meant to lessen the value of God's revelation through the Hebrew prophets. The fact that He considered them the transmitters of divine revelation is evidence of just how much respect He held for these faithful servants of the Lord; but the same God who had partially revealed Himself in times past now had revealed Himself completely in His Son.

In Old Testament times, the prophets who spoke had their distinctive personalities and mannerisms. But now, with the advent of the Son, things are different. Everything is localized in Him. He in turn gives full and final expression to all that was previously revealed, and He does so in a way that is focused, clear, and eternally relevant.

"In these last days" (vs. 2) would carry a special significance for the readers, who probably interpreted the phrase as meaning that Jesus, as the Savior, had ushered in the messianic age. He is not merely the end of a long line of Old Testament prophets, but also the one for whom the Hebrews had waited for centuries. He is the complete and distinct revelation of God.

Even with the coming of the Savior, the inspired nature of God's communication has not changed. The messages He conveyed through the prophets to the community of faith were graced by His power and love; and this remains true now that Jesus has revealed the Father to us. In fact, what Christ has unveiled is harmony with all that appears in the Old Testament, for what the prophets foretold finds its fulfillment in the Messiah.

In what follows, the writer made seven statements to show the superiority of Christ's revelation. First, God appointed Jesus "heir of all things," that is, the creation. Second, it was through Christ that God "made the universe." In fact, the Son was with the Father at the dawn of time.

C. The Son's Nature and Work: vs. 3

The Son is the radiance of God's glory and the exact representation of his being, sustaining all things by his powerful word. After he had provided purification for sins, he sat down at the right hand of the Majesty in heaven.

Third on the writer's list is the fact that Jesus is "the radiance of God's glory" (Heb. 1:3). In essence, Christ is the revelation of the majesty of God. Fourth, Jesus is "the exact representation of His being." This means everything about the Son represents God exactly and the Son is like the Father in every way.

Fifth, Christ upholds "all things." This means He is carrying the universe toward the fulfillment of His divine plan. Sixth, Jesus "provided purification for sins."

Through His redeeming work on the cross, Christ dealt with humanity's problem with sin. In fact, His sacrifice brought about complete redemption for humanity's transgressions. Seventh, Christ was granted the place of highest honor, at the "right hand of the Majesty in heaven."

II. THE SON'S SUPERIORITY TO ANGELS: HEBREWS 1:4-9

A. In Relationship: vss. 4-5

So he became as much superior to the angels as the name he has inherited is superior to theirs. For to which of the angels did God ever say, "You are my Son; today I have become your Father"? Or again, "I will be his Father, and he will be my Son"?

For the various reasons given by the writer of Hebrews, the Son is to be considered superior to all things, including "the angels" (1:4). The Hebrew people had long held angels in high esteem because these heavenly beings were instrumental in the giving of the law at Mount Sinai. The author told the Hebrews that God's Son is absolutely above all angels.

Both the Old and New Testaments affirm the existence of angels (2 Kings 6:8-23; Heb. 13:2). They are spirits (Heb. 1:14) who dwell in heaven (Matt. 22:30) and are sent to earth as messengers of God. They are mighty (Ps. 103:20) and powerful (2 Thess. 1:7) and possess great wisdom (2 Sam. 14:20). Ordinarily angels are invisible to us (2 Kings 6:17), though they have appeared as humans (Luke 24:4). Angels serve God by serving us (Heb. 1:14), providing us protection (Dan. 6:22), guarding us (Ps. 91:11), guiding us (Acts 8:26), and helping us (Dan. 10:13). In addition to good angels, there are also fallen ones who serve the purposes of Satan (Rev. 12:7-9). Contrary to popular belief and artistic portrayal, few angels in the Bible are explicitly stated to have wings. In fact, Isaiah 6:2 may be the sole instance. On the other hand, angels are said to have the ability to fly (Dan. 9:21).

To emphasize Jesus' superiority, the writer of Hebrews said Christ's name is superior to that of the angels (Heb. 1:4). The idea is that Jesus' character and work—which were summed up in His name—were far superior even to those of the heavenly beings. The author of Hebrews then quoted a number of Old Testament passages to show how and why Christ is superior to the angels. In 1:5, the writer first quoted Psalm 2:7 and then 2 Samuel 7:14 to indicate that God had never singled out an angel and applied to that being the status He had accorded His Son.

It is clarifying to note that the Jewish readership of Hebrews highly regarded the Hebrew Scriptures. There was no better way to substantiate the superiority of Christ than by citing pertinent verses from the Old Testament. Those reading Hebrews would have to admit that even their sacred writings affirmed that Jesus was better than anyone else.

B. In Worship: vs. 6

And again, when God brings his firstborn into the world, he says, "Let all God's angels worship him."

Hebrews 1:6 refers to Jesus as "the firstborn." These words depict the Son's unique relationship as an heir to the Father. The source of the quotation in this verse might be from either Deuteronomy 32:43 or Psalm 97:7. The intent was to show that Christ is worthy of the angels' worship in the same way that God is worthy of such. Jesus' deity is also affirmed.

C. In Ministry: vss. 7-9

In speaking of the angels he says, "He makes his angels winds, his servants flames of fire." But about the Son he says, "Your throne, O God, will last for ever and ever, and righteousness will be the scepter of your kingdom. You have loved righteousness and hated wickedness; therefore God, your God, has set you above your companions by anointing you with the oil of joy."

Hebrews 1:7, which quotes Psalm 104:4, stresses that, while the angels are God's servants, Jesus is the divine Son and King. Hebrews 1:8-9, which quotes Psalm 45:6-7, underscores Jesus' divinity, royal status, and supremacy over creation. Because Christ loves righteousness and hates wickedness, God set His Son above all other people and beings, and anointed Him to carry out the most sacred function of all time—to bring people to salvation.

Because the writer of Hebrews knew that many of the Jews had a high regard for angels, he wanted to make it clear that Christ was far above any celestial being, both in terms of who He is (namely, the God-man) and what He accomplished (namely, redemption for the lost). In stressing these truths, the author of the epistle hoped to encourage his readers to remain faithful to Christ.

III. WARNING TO BELIEVERS: HEBREWS 2:1-4

A. The Exhortation: vs. 1

We must pay more careful attention, therefore, to what we have heard, so that we do not drift away.

Hebrews 2:1-4 explains why the first two chapters of the letter discuss at length angels in relation to the Son. The readers evidently were in danger of drifting away from the basic teachings of Christianity. In the place of biblical teaching, they were considering adapting strict Jewish teaching, including the reverence of angels, whom they believed were instrumental in delivering God's law to Moses at Mount Sinai.

Verse 1 urged believers to consider carefully the message of the Gospel. Because the Son is superior to the angels, Christians should give heed to what He had said. This would prevent them from slipping away from God's greater revelation through Christ.

B. The Reason to Be Faithful: vss. 2-4

For if the message spoken by angels was binding, and every violation and disobedience received its just punishment, how shall we escape if we ignore such a great salvation? This salvation, which was first announced by the Lord, was confirmed to us by those who heard him. God also testified to it by signs, wonders and various miracles, and gifts of the Holy Spirit distributed according to his will.

Hebrews 2:2-3 is the hinge of the writer's argument. In essence, if the Hebrews had seriously considered the message of the law that had come through the angels, then how much more so should they consider the message of salvation that had come through the Son. Also, if the law administered by angels had attached to it severe penalties for neglecting it, how much more seriously will people be penalized for neglecting the message conveyed by God's Son?

The Lord Himself had announced this salvation. It was then confirmed by those who had first heard the Gospel and had passed the message on to others. According to verse 4, God's own testimony of supernatural acts confirmed the reality and truth of this salvation.

Discussion Questions

1. Why do you think some believers might have given too high a priority to the Old Testament and angels?
2. What were the dangers of drifting away from the true faith?
3. By what reasoning did the writer try to argue that Jesus is superior?
4. What are some of God's good gifts that Christians might be tempted to overvalue?
5. By what means can we catch ourselves when, in our loyalties, one of God's gifts is rivaling God Himself?

Contemporary Application

We can never talk too much about Jesus. We learn the good news and believe it so that we can receive forgiveness and eternal life. But how much do we learn about Jesus after that? How much time do we give to studying the four Gospels and the application of the salvation narrative in the epistles?

It has often been said that cults thrive on poorly educated Christians. Without a growing knowledge of Jesus, people can easily drift away and be sucked in by false teachers. That danger is real and the best prevention is continual study of and reflection on the glories of Christ.

To ignore Jesus is to expose ourselves to mortal danger. Diligent study, praise, and testimony keep us fresh in our walk with Jesus. We need to depend on Him every day just as much as we need our daily swim, hike, or stint on the treadmill.

Jesus Fulfills the Plan of Salvation

DEVOTIONAL READING

Philippians 2:5-11

DAILY BIBLE READINGS

Monday June 7
Acts 2:32-36 God Has Made Jesus Messiah

Tuesday June 8
Acts 2:37-41 Forgiveness of Sins through Christ

Wednesday June 9
Colossians 2:8-12 Raised with Christ through Faith

Thursday June 10
Philippians 2:5-11 Jesus Christ Is Lord

Friday June 11
Hebrews 2:5-9 Jesus Tasted Death for Everyone

Saturday June 12
Hebrews 2:10-18 Jesus Is the Pioneer of Salvation

Sunday June 13
Hebrews 3:1-6 Christ, the Son, Was Faithful

Scripture

Background Scripture: *Hebrews 2:5-18*
Scripture Lesson: *Hebrews 2:5-18*
Key Verse: *For this reason [Jesus] had to be made like his brothers in every way, in order that he might . . . make atonement for the sins of the people.* Hebrews 2:17.
Scripture Lesson for Children: *Genesis 12:1-9*
Key Verse for Children: *So Abram left, as the LORD had told him.* Genesis 12:4.

Lesson Aim

To appreciate more and more what Jesus has done for us.

Lesson Setting

Time: *Before A.D. 70*
Place: *Possibly from Rome*

Lesson Outline

Jesus Fulfills the Plan of Salvation

   I. Christ's Reign and Suffering: Hebrews 2:5-9
      A. *Jesus' Reign: vss. 5-8*
      B. *Jesus' Suffering: vs. 9*
  II. Christ's Incarnation: Hebrews 2:10-13
      A. *God's Plan: vs. 10*
      B. *Our Oneness: vss. 11-13*
 III. Christ's Priestly Work: Hebrews 2:14-18
      A. *Jesus' Victory Over Satan and Death: vss. 14-15*
      C. *Jesus' Victory Over Sin and Temptation: vss. 16-18*

Introduction for Adults

Topic: *Partners in Suffering*

Stan had successfully recovered from a serious surgery. Less than two years later his wife was diagnosed with cancer. Then Stan realized how much caregivers suffer the pain of those who face threatening illnesses.

Husbands and wives are partners "in sickness and in health," as some marriage vows say. In a similar way, we share suffering with our Lord Jesus. It may be hard for us to appreciate His leaving heaven's glory to become one with us; nevertheless, we can praise Him because He gave us eternal life. By His suffering and death we gain our forgiveness.

In fact, Jesus' suffering was so important that it fully qualified Him to be our Savior. Now, having died for our sins and risen from the dead, Jesus reaches out from heaven to help us. He partners with us in our sufferings.

Introduction for Youth

Topic: *Help with Suffering*

Someone has observed that youths take risks because they think they are immortal. Yet our schools send another message. There are adolescents who suffer serious disabilities, many of which are holdovers from birth and early childhood. The presence of these young people tests our willingness to identify with them. Do we reach out to them or do we pass by on the other side?

Jesus did not refuse to become one with the human race. Jesus entered our sphere of life, wicked and sinful though we are and with multitudes of character flaws. And, although we do disgusting things and think disgusting thoughts, Jesus did not turn aside in disgust.

Christ came to our rescue, died for our sins, and forever lives to stand by us in our suffering and temptation. He is the source of our salvation. Happy are we when we entrust our lives to His care!

Concepts for Children

Topic: *By Faith: Abraham Obeyed God*

1. Abraham obeyed God's command to leave his home.
2. Abraham acted in faith, even though he did not know where he was to go.
3. Abraham's faith took him through uncertain times.
4. God is always with us, even when our way seems unclear.
5. God's presence and blessing are more important than what we own.
6. God will give us the strength and courage to obey Him.

The Lesson Commentary

I. CHRIST'S REIGN AND SUFFERING: HEBREWS 2:5-9

A. Jesus' Reign: vss. 5-8

It is not to angels that he has subjected the world to come, about which we are speaking. But there is a place where someone has testified: "What is man that you are mindful of him, the son of man that you care for him? You made him a little lower than the angels; you crowned him with glory and honor and put everything under his feet." In putting everything under him, God left nothing that is not subject to him. Yet at present we do not see everything subject to him.

Oddly enough, there is included in the Letter to the Hebrews no description of the recipient church, and only a few clues vaguely identifying the epistle's readers. For instance, some scholars point to the author's greeting from "those from Italy" (13:24) as evidence that the letter's recipients were Italians, perhaps living in Rome. Using the same phrase, however, other scholars say the greeting is evidence that the letter was written *from* Italy. There is no way of verifying either interpretation.

Despite such uncertainties, the epistle contains a fair amount of information about the original recipients and their situation. For example, they spoke Greek and used the Greek translation of the Old Testament. They could follow arguments drawn from the Hebrew sacred writings, and were interested in the Old Testament sanctuary, sacrificial system, and priesthood.

The original readers had not heard the Gospel directly from Jesus, but from apostles (2:3), had faced previous persecution (10:32-34), and were facing present persecution, including expulsion from Jewish institutions (13:12-13). They were in danger of falling away, perhaps fearing death (2:14-18), though their faith had not yet led to martyrdom (12:4). In addition, they may have been undergoing a transition in church leadership (13:7, 17), and were therefore concerned about security and permanence (6:19; 11:10; 13:8, 14).

With respect to this week's lesson text, the writer of Hebrews had previously commented on the great salvation announced by the Lord, confirmed by the apostles, and testified to by miracles (2:1-4). The author then revealed that angels will not control "the world to come" (vs. 5). This refers to the messianic age, which will reach its final and most complete stage when Christ returns.

The Father has made His Son the King of the future world. To explain this point, the author showed how Jesus, the perfect man, fulfilled the ideal for humans to be rulers; for instance, in verses 6-8, the writer quoted Psalm 8:4-6. This part of the Davidic psalm presents the paradox of people being insignificant yet highly honored.

David wondered why God loves and cares for humans, who seem so unimportant against the backdrop of the universe. After all, in the present era, God has made people, who are mortal, lower in rank to the angels, who are immortal; nevertheless, God has also crowned humans, like a monarch, with glory and honor. And, like a conqueror, they have the world put under their feet.

In Hebrews 2:7, the phrase "a little lower" could also be rendered "for a little while lower." In that case, the phrase would refer to the fact that people are inferior to the immortal angels only for the present because we are mortal. Adam and Eve were immortal until their sin; and human beings will be immortal again after the resurrection.

The author of Hebrews picked up on the last phrase of the quote in verse 7 to reaffirm that "everything" (2:8) in the world was subjected to people (see Gen. 1:28); but then the author pointed out the obvious fact that, as we look about us, we see that humans are not in complete control of the world.

B. Jesus' Suffering: vs. 9

But we see Jesus, who was made a little lower than the angels, now crowned with glory and honor because he suffered death, so that by the grace of God he might taste death for everyone.

The writer of Hebrews explained that, when Adam introduced sin into the human race, he impaired our ability to be the rulers God intended; but, just as we observe that not everything is subject to us, so we "see Jesus" (2:9), who fulfilled the ideal David described. All things are subject to Christ, including the world to come.

To fulfill the ideal, Jesus had to become a true human being. Like other people, He was made "a little lower than the angels." Thus, though Jesus is fully God, He also became fully human; of course, as a man, Christ was without sin and He obeyed the Father even to the point of dying for the sins of humanity. For the Son's obedience, the Father crowned Him "with glory and honor." He now sits on the throne in heaven at the right hand of the Father.

II. CHRIST'S INCARNATION: HEBREWS 2:10-13

A. God's Plan: vs. 10

In bringing many sons to glory, it was fitting that God, for whom and through whom everything exists, should make the author of their salvation perfect through suffering.

It was God's desire that those who trusted in Christ (and thus became members of His spiritual family) would share in Jesus' "glory" (Heb. 2:10). Only the Lord could make this happen, for He created all things and all things exist for His glory.

Jesus is the "author" of our salvation, for it originates with Him. As our leader, He first went down the path of suffering, opening up the way of salvation so that others could enter it. Though the perfect Son of God, Jesus needed to become fully qualified as our human representative. He was made "perfect" by successfully resisting temptations and enduring many trials, including death. In this way, He earned the right to be our Savior.

By saying that God made Jesus perfect, the writer did not intend to imply that Christ was ever morally or spiritually imperfect; rather, he meant that through suffering, Jesus was altogether able to carry out the task God had given Him. Because Christ so thoroughly identified with us, He became qualified to be sacrificed on our behalf.

Thus, by suffering on the cross, Jesus fulfilled—or perfected—the plan of God. By subjecting Himself to the law, Jesus fulfilled it, thus satisfying God. It is not that the Son somehow improved through suffering, but He showed His perfect concern for humanity by tasting its bitterness. He therefore filled every qualification to be our Savior.

B. Our Oneness: vss. 11-13

Both the one who makes men holy and those who are made holy are of the same family. So Jesus is not ashamed to call them brothers. He says, "I will declare your name to my brothers; in the presence of the congregation I will sing your praises." And again, "I will put my trust in him." And again he says, "Here am I, and the children God has given me."

Christ is the one who restores believing sinners to a place of holiness with God. In fact, both Jesus and His followers belong to the same heavenly Father. That is the reason He is not "ashamed to call them brothers" (Heb. 2:11).

The author of Hebrews was trying to dissuade his readers from turning back to Judaism. One way he could change their minds was by emphasizing the familial bond they had with Christ. He wasn't just their Savior and Lord. He was also proud to call them His spiritual brothers and sisters. This truth would encourage them to remain loyal to Christ even in the midst of their darkest trials.

In verse 12, the writer quoted from Psalm 22:22 (which concerns the sufferings and triumphs of God's righteous servant) to explain that the Messiah proclaimed God's character to His brothers, namely, those who believe in Him. Furthermore, the Messiah would sing God's praises in the midst of His people, showing them that He is one with them.

Hebrews 2:13 quotes Isaiah 8:17-18 to express how the Messiah put His trust in God to see Him through His earthly ministry; additionally, believers are the spiritual children whom God has given to Christ. The idea is that, if Jesus is our brother, then God is our Father. Ultimately, of course, Jesus joined humanity to become our Savior.

III. CHRIST'S PRIESTLY WORK: HEBREWS 2:14-18

A. Jesus' Victory Over Satan and Death: vss. 14-15

Since the children have flesh and blood, he too shared in their humanity so that by his death he might destroy him who holds the power of death—that is, the devil—and free those who all their lives were held in slavery by their fear of death.

In order to redeem the lost, it was necessary for the Son to become incarnate. He then died on the cross to atone for humanity's sins. In this way, Jesus destroyed the devil's power to kill, for his accusations against believers were now groundless (Heb. 2:14).

It would be incorrect to conclude from this verse that that Jesus somehow caused the devil to no longer exist. Rather, Christ devastated Satan's ability to wield the power of death. Jesus did this so that the devil would no longer exploit people through their tendency to sin and their fear of death.

Verse 15 reveals that people are gripped by the "fear of death." The devil, in turn, exploits this fear to enslave people; but Jesus, through His redemptive work at Calvary, freed believing sinners from the fear of death.

B. Jesus' Victory Over Sin and Temptation: vss. 16-18

For surely it is not angels he helps, but Abraham's descendants. For this reason he had to be made like his brothers in every way, in order that he might become a merciful and faithful high priest in service to God, and that he might make atonement for the sins of the people. Because he himself suffered when he was tempted, he is able to help those who are being tempted.

The incarnation of Christ points to the fact that He came to earth to help Abraham's descendants, not "angels" (Heb. 2:16). It may be best to see the writer of Hebrews referring to both Jews and Gentiles in his mention of "Abraham's descendants" (see also Gal. 3:29).

In order for Christ to represent human beings before God, He had to become fully human Himself. Only by being tested in every way as people are and by triumphing over every temptation He encountered could Jesus be the merciful "high priest" (Heb. 2:17) of those who trusted in Him.

Though Christ was without sin, He died on the cross for the sins of others; and He demonstrated His faithfulness by bearing God's wrath. The idea is that Jesus, at the cross, dealt with our sin in such a way that it no longer stands as a barrier to our open fellowship with God. This, in turn, implies the restoration of the once broken relationship between God and us (Rom. 3:25; 1 John 2:2; 4:10). The Father's love for us is the reason the Son sacrificed Himself on our behalf (John 3:16; 1 John 4:9-10).

Hebrews 2:18 reveals that Jesus shared all the facets of human experience, including hunger, fatigue, temptation, and pain. This assures us that we can look to Him for help in our time of testing, confident that He has experienced similar trials and is the helper we need.

What did the writer of Hebrews seek to accomplish in emphasizing the fullness of Christ's humanity? The author wanted to underscore that Christ is the believers' merciful and faithful High Priest. The only way Christ could qualify as such was by becoming completely human and entering fully into the human experience. By becoming one with us, Christ alone could atone for our sins and represent us before God.

Discussion Questions

1. What are some of the ways that human beings compare to and contrast with angels?
2. In order to bring salvation to people, why did Jesus become one of us (as opposed to becoming an angel)?
3. What did Jesus give up in becoming a human being?

4. How did Jesus' life and death result in victory over Satan, sin, and death?
5. Is belief in the fact of Jesus' victory enough to save us or does God want us to make a more personal response?

Contemporary Application

Part of our task as Christians is to learn the facts of Scripture and pass them on to others. If we say that we must learn and teach theology, that scares off most people. But Hebrews is heavy-duty theology. What we have studied in this week's lesson cuts to the heart of what we believe.

The lesson text is filled with eternally relevant truths. If we do not understand, believe, and teach them, we consign ourselves to spiritual mediocrity and an anemic relationship with God. The writer of Hebrews was so passionate about this issue that he piled on one significant truth after another. He taught about Christ's coming to earth, His becoming one of us, His suffering for our sins, and His victories over sin, death, the devil, and temptation.

It is imperative for all Christians to grasp fully how these truths affect their lives. We cannot push these facts off on the so-called "professional theologians." We must apply them to our hearts and minds. Thus, the only satisfying answer to spiritual malnutrition is a full course meal of truths about Christ. Feasting on what is taught in Hebrews can begin to satisfy our needs.

Be Faithful: Obey!

DEVOTIONAL READING

2 Corinthians 5:16—6:2

DAILY BIBLE READINGS

Monday June 14
Psalm 95:6-11 Do Not Harden Your Hearts

Tuesday June 15
Deuteronomy 1:22-33 The Israelites Rebelled in the Wilderness

Wednesday June 16
Deuteronomy 11:22-32 Obedience to God Brings Blessing

Thursday June 17
2 Corinthians 5:16—6:2 We Are Ambassadors for Christ

Friday June 18
Hebrews 3:12-19 Hold Your Confidence Firm

Saturday June 19
Hebrews 4:1-5 We Who Believe Enter God's Rest

Sunday June 20
Hebrews 4:6-13 Make Efforts to Enter that Rest

Scripture

Background Scripture: *Hebrews 3:12—4:13*
Scripture Lesson: *Hebrews 3:12-4:2, 9-13*
Key Verse: *We have come to share in Christ if we hold firmly till the end the confidence we had at first.* Hebrews 3:14.
Scripture Lesson for Children: *Genesis 17:15-21; 21:1-7*
Key Verse for Children: *Sarah became pregnant and bore a son to Abraham in his old age.* Genesis 21:2.

Lesson Aim

To fully embrace and experience the promise of God's rest.

Lesson Setting

Time: *Before A.D. 70*
Place: *Possibly from Rome*

Lesson Outline

Be Faithful: Obey

I. The Failed Attempt to Enter God's Rest: Hebrews 3:12-19
   A. *Warning One Another: vss. 12-13*
   B. *Remembering the Scriptural Exhortation: vss. 14-15*
   C. *Understanding the Reason for the Israelites' Failure: vss. 16-19*

II. The Standing Promise of God's Rest: Hebrews 4:1-2

III. The Exhortation to Enter God's Rest: Hebrews 4:9-13
   A. *The Sabbath Rest of God: vss. 9-10*
   B. *The Believers' Desire to Enter God's Rest: vs. 11*
   C. *The Power of God's Word: vss. 12-13*

Introduction for Adults

Topic: *Be Faithful: Obey!*

Heart disease exacts a terrible toll. Medical science continues to help us to find the causes and offers new treatments almost annually. What we used to call hardening of the arteries is blamed on diet, smoking, alcohol, and so on. Now we can repair and bypass those bad arteries.

This week's lesson text could well be called the diagnosis and treatment of blocked spiritual arteries. Unbelief and disobedience cause the problem. God tells us clearly in His Word that, by our faithful obedience to Him, we can stay healthy and strong spiritually.

Some people with heart disease refuse to change their habits and they suffer and die. People who turn their backs on God's offer of forgiveness, peace, and rest in Christ face a gloomy spiritual end. Their hard hearts will bring them down, just as surely as the Israelites fell during 40 years in the desert.

Introduction for Youth

Topic: *Stay Faithful*

Faithfulness, loyalty, and commitment are the bedrock of community, family, and church life. When we encounter social and spiritual disasters, invariably we can trace the causes to failures in faithfulness, loyalty, and commitment.

Long ago the Israelites learned this lesson. Despite their professions of allegiance to the Lord, once they gained their freedom, the Israelites turned against Him. They lost the goal of their liberation.

The professions of faith we make when we are young will be tested in many ways. We might ask ourselves whether it is really worth staying faithful to Jesus. Isn't it more fun to do what we want to do, rather then keeping God's rules? One fact will never change—staying faithful to God provides the only solid foundation for a worthwhile life. Nothing else comes close.

Concepts for Children

Topic: *By Faith: Sarah Had a Baby*

1. God had promised a baby to Abraham and Sarah, even when they were very old.
2. At first, Sarah laughed at this promise and thought it was impossible.
3. Nevertheless, Sarah grew in her confidence in the Lord.
4. On some occasions we find it hard to accept God's promises.
5. We grow in faith by obeying what God tells us to do.
6. Everything God has promised in the Bible He will do.

The Lesson Commentary

I. THE FAILED ATTEMPT TO ENTER GOD'S REST: HEBREWS 3:12-19

A. Warning One Another: vss. 12-13

See to it, brothers, that none of you has a sinful, unbelieving heart that turns away from the living God. But encourage one another daily, as long as it is called Today, so that none of you may be hardened by sin's deceitfulness.

Just as the authorship and readership of the Letter to the Hebrews is debated, so too is the date when the epistle was written. While it is impossible to fix a date with absolute certainty, all the evidence strongly suggests that the letter was penned between A.D. 60 and 70. There are several passages in this epistle that help us make this determination.

In particular, Hebrews 10:11 may indicate that animal sacrifices were still being offered at the temple in Jerusalem—a ritual that ceased after A.D. 70, when the temple was destroyed. In fact, the writer said the old covenant "is obsolete and aging [and] will soon disappear" (8:13), perhaps implying that this letter was written shortly before the destruction of Jerusalem.

Also, the epistle's conclusion tells about Timothy's release from prison (13:23), perhaps indicating that the letter likely was written sometime after A.D. 60. Some even conjecture that, because the church community had not yet suffered death for their faith, the epistle should be dated before Nero's persecution of Christians in A.D. 64. If so, then the suffering mentioned in 10:32-34 would have been caused by the edict of Claudius, a decree that expelled Jews from Rome in A.D. 49 (Acts 18:2).

With respect to this week's lesson, the writer of Hebrews, having compared Christ and Moses in 3:1-6, then compared Christians to the Israelites who wandered in the wilderness for 40 years before reaching the promised land (vss. 7-11). The author reminded his readers that God had promised them rest in Christ just as He had promised the Israelites rest in the promised land.

The writer made his point in 3:7-11 by quoting Psalm 95:7-11. He then appealed to his audience to enter God's rest. The author implied that if his readers strayed from faith in Christ, a punishment just as severe as what happened to the wilderness generation of Israelites might happen to them.

Psalm 95 places particular emphasis on the worship of God, which makes it a worship psalm. This portion of Scripture is also a royal psalm because of the way it acknowledges God as the great King (vs. 3). Furthermore, the psalm has three movements, with each reflecting a mood of the worshiping community: the worship of God in a mood of celebration (vss. 1-5); the worship of God in a mood of contemplation (vss. 6-7); and the worship of God in a mood of obedience (vss. 8-11). Ultimately, the psalm is a call for obedience in worship and a reminder of God's judgments in times past on people who did not take Him seriously.

In Hebrews 3:12, the writer urged his readers to be alert spiritually so that they could not be led astray into rebelling against "the living God." To strengthen their resolve against permitting "a sinful, unbelieving heart" from festering, the author advocated that they encourage and support each other on a regular basis (vs. 13). Without regular Christian fellowship, the Hebrews would have to face on their own the hardening of sins' deceitfulness.

B. Remembering the Scriptural Exhortation: vss. 14-15

We have come to share in Christ if we hold firmly till the end the confidence we had at first. As has just been said: "Today, if you hear his voice, do not harden your hearts as you did in the rebellion."

The solution, then, was for the Hebrews to "share in Christ" (Heb. 3:14); and to do so, they would have to persevere in their initial confidence in Him. Here we see that the believers' faith is evidenced by their faithfulness.

To emphasize the urgency of the need for perseverance, the writer, in verse 15, again quoted Psalm 95:7-8. By telling his readers to guard themselves against hardened hearts, the author of Hebrews meant for them to restrain themselves from both disobeying God and following their own whims and desires. Acting according to their own will was what the Israelites had done in the wilderness.

C. Understanding the Reason for the Israelites' Failure: vss. 16-19

Who were they who heard and rebelled? Were they not all those Moses led out of Egypt? And with whom was he angry for forty years? Was it not with those who sinned, whose bodies fell in the desert? And to whom did God swear that they would never enter his rest if not to those who disobeyed? So we see that they were not able to enter, because of their unbelief.

Hebrews 3:16-18 contains a number of rhetorical questions. The writer's point was to show how a generation of Israelites had died while wandering in the wilderness. It was because they had refused to believe God's promise that they would not possess the land of Canaan.

When God told the Israelites, whom Moses had led out of Egypt (vs. 16), to enter the land, they balked. Believing that they would be slaughtered if they fought against the land's inhabitants, they went so far as to begin the process of choosing a leader to guide them back to Egypt and slavery. Such an act was rebellion, sin, and disobedience (vss. 17-18).

The author pointedly said that the Israelites' "unbelief" (vs. 19) prompted them to turn away from the promised land. This rebellious act, in turn, cut them off from receiving an inheritance in that land. Similarly, for the readers to turn away from Christ meant that they would be kept from receiving the rest promised to believers.

II. THE STANDING PROMISE OF GOD'S REST: HEBREWS 4:1-2

Therefore, since the promise of entering his rest still stands, let us be careful that none of you be found to have fallen short of it. For we also have had the gospel preached to us, just as they did; but the message they heard was of no value to them, because those who heard did not combine it with faith.

In Hebrews 4, the author referred to several different kinds of rest. *Creation rest* (vss. 3-4) concerns God resting after Creation. Similarly, God has prepared a rest that

His people may enter. *Canaan rest* (vs. 8) relates to Joshua leading the Israelites into the promised land, where they entered into God's rest. In fact, Deuteronomy 12:9 refers to the land of Canaan as the Israelites' "resting place."

Continuing rest (vss. 9-11) concerns the fact that David wrote about God's rest (see Ps. 95) around 400 years after the Israelites had entered the promised land. For the author of Hebrews this meant that God's rest is continuously offered to those who have faith in the Lord. *Christian rest* reminds us that, when people become believers, they enter into God's rest. In *consecration rest,* people enter into God's rest at some point after conversion when they fully surrender their lives to the Lord and allow Him to work through them. Finally, the concept of *celestial rest* reminds us that people cannot enter God's rest completely until they go to heaven.

The good news is that Christians can possess the promise of entering God's rest. This "rest" (Heb. 4:1) is both spiritual and eternal. The rest that had been offered to the Israelites centuries earlier symbolized the spiritual rest that culminated in the salvation offered by Christ.

The rebellious Israelites had missed out on entering God's rest because of their unbelief. Their lack of "faith" (vs. 2) rendered God's promise of no value to them. The Hebrews were warned not to make the same mistake. To actually become recipients of God's rest, believers had to combine hearing God's promise—"the gospel preached"—with having faith in that promise. Thus, firmly trusting God was the key to the door of His rest. The outgrowth of such faith was obedience.

III. THE EXHORTATION TO ENTER GOD'S REST 4:9-13

A. The Sabbath Rest of God: vss. 9-10

There remains, then, a Sabbath-rest for the people of God; for anyone who enters God's rest also rests from his own work, just as God did from his.

The author continued to use the Israelites' rebellion against entering the promised land and their later entrance under Joshua as symbolic of entering God's rest. The author moved from descriptions of creation rest (Heb. 4:4) to Canaan rest (vss. 6, 8) to continuing rest (vs. 7) to contemporary rest for his readers (vss. 9-11). The writer realized that the Israelites had eventually entered the promised land (vs. 8); and though they had dwelt in the land and had even experienced periods of peace and independence, the promise of God's rest remained unfilled.

In verse 9, the writer referred to "a Sabbath-rest for the people of God." The author here made reference to the Jews' weekly day of rest to stress that, in Christ, a special kind of rest had come. For those who trusted in Him, He provided spiritual and eternal rest.

Those who enter "God's rest" (vs. 10) also cease from their own labor in the same way the Lord ceased from His labor after the Creation. Some say Christians live in this rest here and now. Others say believers receive it as a heritage, but will reap the full benefits of this rest in the hereafter.

In either case, the main point is that believers can rest from any attempt to work for or earn their own salvation. When we place our faith in Christ, we can rest assured in God's grace, realizing that His work in Christ was completed at the cross.

B. The Believers' Desire to Enter God's Rest: vs. 11

Let us, therefore, make every effort to enter that rest, so that no one will fall by following their example of disobedience.

There is a bit of irony in the way Hebrews 4:11 is worded: "Let us, therefore, make every effort to enter that rest." The idea is that believers were to be diligent about entering God's rest, which He offered through faith in Christ. If they failed to do this, their end would be as fatal as that of the rebellious Israelites, who lived unfulfilled lives and died in the wilderness.

Ultimately, entering God's rest is a matter of faith. We must take God at His Word, especially His assurance that we can find true and enduring rest in Christ. We must also resist the temptation to doubt God and disobey His injunctions to respond to Him in faith. When we choose to believe the Lord, He showers us with His undying love and eternal blessings.

C. The Power of God's Word: vss. 12-13

For the word of God is living and active. Sharper than any double-edged sword, it penetrates even to dividing soul and spirit, joints and marrow; it judges the thoughts and attitudes of the heart. Nothing in all creation is hidden from God's sight. Everything is uncovered and laid bare before the eyes of him to whom we must give account.

The writer of Hebrews warned about the dangers of a hardened, unbelieving, and disobedient heart. The good news is that it can be penetrated by "the word of God" (4:12). The author especially had in mind the Hebrew Scriptures and the teachings of Christ.

God's Word, like a double-edged sword, is sharp. It is also living and powerful, reaching to the innermost recesses of our being and judging our souls. Because the Word of God can penetrate the hardest human heart, the God of that Word can see into the deepest secrets of our thoughts, feelings, and desires. The writer used comprehensive language in verse 13 to underscore this assertion. In short, everything is exposed before God, to whom we are responsible to give an account.

A superficial view of Scripture might lead one to conclude that it is antiquated and irrelevant; but we know that God's Word is the exact opposite of this. The Bible is spiritually potent and dynamic. In fact, it is like a high-tech surgical instrument that can cut deep into our hidden aspirations and desires. Despite all our pretenses and fabrications, Scripture is able to disclose who we really are inside.

Discussion Questions

1. What factors might have hindered first century Jews from becoming Christians or remaining devoted to the Savior?
2. By what means did the writer of Hebrews argue that Christians should remain

faithful to Jesus?

3. What would have been the benefits of the Jewish Christians encouraging one another in their faith?

4. What do you feel the writer meant by the "rest" (Heb. 4:1) he encouraged his hearers to enter?

5. Which of these four—hearing, believing, obeying, or sharing God's Word—causes you greatest struggle? Why?

Contemporary Application

Some professing Jewish Christians, who were the recipients of the Letter to the Hebrews, may have been on the brink of relinquishing their commitment to the Lord. They had begun to consider leaving the church and reintegrating into the Jewish synagogue worship of the day. In response to their circumstances, the writer of Hebrews encouraged them to remain firm in their faith in Christ.

From the text of the epistle, we can surmise that these Hebrew people were confronting a choice. Should they persist in Christianity, or should they renounce their Christian beliefs and settle into a more conventional lifestyle? The writer of the letter advised them to make the best decision and stressed the importance of persevering by keeping their faith in God's Son.

The author of the epistle noted that Christ is the supreme and sufficient revealer and mediator of God's grace. He is the "great high priest" (4:14), who came to earth to offer the once-for-all, perfect sacrifice for the sins of the world (9:27-28). Though these Hebrew believers were no doubt steeped in Jewish traditions, the writer reminded them that Christ is God's full and final revelation (1:1-3).

The author—citing the covenant Jesus established as replacing and as better than the covenant God established with the Israelites at Mount Sinai—said God could now be approached through His Son. Through the sacrifice of Christ, we can be forgiven of our sins and have an everlasting relationship with the Lord.

Jesus: The High Priest

DEVOTIONAL READING

Hebrews 7:21-28

DAILY BIBLE READINGS

Monday June 21
*Genesis 14:11-20
Melchizedek Blessed
Abraham*

Tuesday June 22
*Psalm 110:1-7 The Lord Is
a Priest Forever*

Wednesday June 23
*Hebrews 4:14—5:4 Our
High Priest Knows Our
Weaknesses*

Thursday June 24
*Hebrews 5:5-10 Jesus
Learned Obedience through
Suffering*

Friday June 25
*Hebrews 7:11-17 A Priest
Not through Physical Descent*

Saturday June 26
*Hebrews 7:18-22 The
Guarantee of a Better
Covenant*

Sunday June 27
*Hebrews 7:23-28 Jesus Holds
a Permanent Priesthood*

Scripture

Background Scripture: *Hebrews 4:14—5:10*
Scripture Lesson: *Hebrews 4:14—5:10*
Key Verse: *Therefore, since we have a great high priest who
has gone through the heavens, Jesus the Son of God, let us
hold firmly to the faith we profess.* Hebrews 4:14.
Scripture Lesson for Children: *Exodus 2:1-10*
Key Verse for Children: *[Levi's wife] got a papyrus basket
for [Moses], . . . placed the child in it and put it among the
reeds along the bank of the Nile.* Exodus 2:3.

Lesson Aim

To find consolation in Christ as our great High Priest.

Lesson Setting

Time: *Before A.D. 70*
Place: *Possibly from Rome*

Lesson Outline

Jesus: The High Priest

  I. Our Compassionate High Priest: Hebrews 4:14-16
      A. *The Exhortation: vs. 14*
      B. *The Basis for the Exhortation: vss. 15-16*

 II. Qualifications for High Priesthood: Hebrews 5:1-4
      A. *Divinely Appointed: vs. 1*
      B. *Empathetic with Others: vss. 2-3*
      C. *Called by God: vs. 4*

III. Christ's Qualifications for High Priesthood:
      Hebrews 5:5-10
      A. *Divinely Appointed and Called: vss. 5-6*
      B. *Characterized by Reverence and Piety: vs. 7*
      C. *Designated in the Line of Melchizedek: vss. 8-10*

Introduction for Adults

Topic: *Approach in Boldness*

To approach God boldly is not to approach Him flippantly. Some people are so casual with God that they take His name in vain. In contrast, some people are so unfamiliar with God that they find it hard to pray to Him.

Christians enjoy confidence before the Father because they know the Son has opened the door to fellowship with Him. God is holy; yet He gave His Son to save us from judgment and death. The only way we can approach the Father without fear is through His Son. In fact, no one comes to the Father except through His Son (John 14:6).

We can pray and worship with boldness because Jesus sits at the Father's right hand. Christ intercedes for us as our merciful and faithful High Priest. Because He is our heavenly representative, we are freed to worship God with joy.

Introduction for Youth

Topic: *Who Cares for Me?*

Brian's case was fairly typical. His parents divorced and he lived with his dad, who had a hard time building a good relationship with him. Brian got into trouble at school. He developed emotional problems and was hospitalized. To put it simply, Brian could not fill the vacuum in his life caused by a broken family.

Many adolescents rightly ask, "Who cares for me?" They lack strong family ties. They don't have any good friends. They wander fruitlessly from one activity to another and often get into deep trouble.

Without sounding sanctimonious, we should try to introduce teens like Brian to Jesus. In order to do so, we must enjoy a valid faith ourselves. We must be able to explain how Jesus makes a difference, even when no one else seems to care.

Concepts for Children

Topic: *By Faith: Jochebed Saved Her Son*

1. The Egyptians were determined to reduce the number of Hebrew people.
2. Among the Hebrews living in Egypt were those who chose to obey God.
3. For example, a woman named Jochebed risked her life when she put Moses in a basket in the river among the reeds.
4. God honored the courage of Jochebed, and Moses later became Israel's leader.
5. When we live by faith, Jesus calls us to obey Him courageously.
6. If events make us afraid, we can seek God in prayer and talk to other Christians about our fears.

The Lesson Commentary

I. OUR COMPASSIONATE HIGH PRIEST: HEBREWS 4:14-16

A. The Exhortation: vs. 14

Therefore, since we have a great high priest who has gone through the heavens, Jesus the Son of God, let us hold firmly to the faith we profess.

The Letter to the Hebrews is directed to Christians who had faced adverse circumstances and challenges to their faith. They evidently had lost their initial enthusiasm for the Christian faith, failed to progress in spiritual understanding and discernment, and seemed to be growing more slothful and discouraged. They even had begun to question whether they should remain professing Christians or revert to their old ways and traditions.

To help his readers make the right choice, the author of Hebrews pointed to Christ as the perfect revelation of God. In essence, the writer encouraged his readers to make the better choice—to choose the eternal salvation of the Lord, even if it has trials and tribulations, rather than to renounce what is true.

The exhortation to persevere in the pilgrimage of faith is grounded in the writer's argument. He maintained that the Old Testament itself testified to the imperfection of the covenant at Sinai and its sacrificial system. This, in turn, pointed ahead to a new High Priest—Jesus Christ. The Messiah is better than the mediators, sanctuary, and sacrifices of the old order. In association with Christ, there is greater grace and glory. And He is the guarantee of this better covenant bond, for He links believers inseparably with the Lord of grace.

With respect to this week's lesson, the writer of Hebrews had previously finished stressing that everything we think, say, and do is completely exposed to God (4:12-13). This sobering truth underscores our need for a sympathetic High Priest, one who can meet our deepest spiritual desires. That Person is Jesus.

As one who lived through trials and tribulations, Christ is able to understand what His people are experiencing. His ability to comprehend us, His proximity to the Father, and His reconciling act on the cross give us the confidence that we can find help at the throne of grace in our time of need.

Hebrews 4:14 may be regarded as the thesis statement of the epistle. There is no other strong and straightforward declaration about Christ's priesthood in the rest of Scripture. The author had touched on Jesus as our High Priest in 2:17 and 3:1, but at this point in his letter, the topic becomes a controlling concept. By calling Christ a "great high priest" (4:14), the writer implied Jesus' superiority to all the generations of Jewish high priests.

Though the high priests were the only ones permitted to pass beyond the final curtain of the tabernacle or temple into the most holy place, Jesus "has gone through the heavens" (or, alternately, "gone into heaven") and taken His rightful place at the right hand of the Father. Many think this is a reference to Jesus' ascension into heaven.

The Hebrews were beginning to lack spiritual steadfastness. The writer thus urged them to embrace unyieldingly their faith in "the Son of God" (Heb. 4:14). This is a significant biblical title for Jesus and underscores the special and intimate relationship that exists between the first and second persons of the Trinity (Matt. 16:16; Luke 1:35). "Son of God" indicates that Jesus is to be identified with the Father and considered fully and absolutely equal to Him (John 5:18; 10:30, 36).

B. The Basis for the Exhortation: vss. 15-16

For we do not have a high priest who is unable to sympathize with our weaknesses, but we have one who has been tempted in every way, just as we are—yet was without sin. Let us then approach the throne of grace with confidence, so that we may receive mercy and find grace to help us in our time of need.

A key reason we, as believers, can put our trust in Christ is that He can "sympathize with our weaknesses" (Heb. 4:15). He became one of us and experienced life just as we do. Jesus, in fact, faced all the sorts of temptations we do; but unlike us, our High Priest remained "without sin."

The sinless one, rather than turning haughtily away from sinners, invites such people to His Father's "throne of grace" (vs. 16). They should do so with confidence, not in what they had achieved, but in what Christ has achieved. They especially are to draw near in their time of need to "receive mercy and find grace to help."

In this verse, the Greek word translated "help" is *boetheian*, and a form of this word is found in only one other place in the New Testament—Acts 27:17. The context of the Acts passage is a storm at sea in which Paul's party was caught. As one last measure to hold together the shaken ship, the sailors used *boetheiais*, or "helps"(KJV), to undergird the vessel. Technically, this procedure is called "frapping." Cables were passed underneath the ship and tied around the hull in an attempt to hold the vessel together.

This information suggests the intent behind the author of Hebrews use of "help" in Hebrews 4:16. He sought to encourage his readers to seek God's undergirding in their time of need.

II. QUALIFICATIONS FOR HIGH PRIESTHOOD: HEBREWS 5:1-4

A. Divinely Appointed: vs. 1

Every high priest is selected from among men and is appointed to represent them in matters related to God, to offer gifts and sacrifices for sins.

The writer of Hebrews next discussed the nature of the high-priestly office in ancient Israel. He noted that the nation's religious leaders chose a high priest from a pool of qualified men (namely, the descendants of Aaron) and appointed him to that office (5:1). This means that no person could lobby to be a priest. The eligibility for priestly service was already settled by God's choosing (vs. 4).

The high priest represented his fellow Israelites in matters pertaining to God. Specifically, he offered "gifts" (vs. 1; which were voluntary) and "sacrifices" (which were required) for their sins.

B. Empathetic with Others: vss. 2-3

He is able to deal gently with those who are ignorant and are going astray, since he himself is subject to weakness. This is why he has to offer sacrifices for his own sins, as well as for the sins of the people.

The author of Hebrews noted that the priests had weaknesses of their own. For this reason, they could understand the frailty of the ones they were representing, offer kindly direction to the ignorant, and gently admonish the wayward (5:2); and a priest's sinful nature required him to offer sacrifices to atone for his own misdeeds as well as for those of the people he represented (vs. 3).

C. Called by God: vs. 4

No one takes this honor upon himself; he must be called by God, just as Aaron was.

Hebrews 5:4 underscores that the high-priestly office was sacred, and it was an honor to serve in it. To seize control of this office would be a sign of disrespect for God, who had graciously instituted it. The Bible records several instances in which disaster occurred when someone tried to perform high priestly duties without authorization.

The need for a priesthood is rooted in people's consciousness of sin. Those whose hearts and lives have been stained by sin could not enter the presence of a holy God. They needed a mediator, a go-between, a representative—someone who could approach God with sacrifices and prayers on their behalf. The priest was authorized to come before God and intercede in behalf of the people.

The priests were to be from among Aaron's descendants and were to be free of physical defects. Priests were required to dress in designated attire and to live in strict obedience to the law. Besides upholding the civil and religious codes that applied to all Israelites, they had to execute those laws applying to their vocation as priests.

The high priest was at the top of this religious hierarchy. While priests in general represented the people before God, the high priest was their supreme representative. He was uniquely consecrated to God through the anointing of his head with sacred oil (Lev. 8:12; 21:10; Ps. 133:2). Other priests had oil sprinkled on their garments only, but the high priest became the "anointed priest."

II. CHRIST'S QUALIFICATIONS FOR HIGH PRIESTHOOD: HEBREWS 5:5-10

A. Divinely Appointed and Called: vss. 5-6

So Christ also did not take upon himself the glory of becoming a high priest. But God said to him, "You are my Son; today I have become your Father." And he says in another place, "You are a priest forever, in the order of Melchizedek."

Christ did not take it upon Himself to assume the high priesthood, but rather was called to the office by God (Heb. 5:5). To illustrate this point, the author of the epistle first quoted Psalm 2:7. The idea is that the Father declared Jesus to be His

Son when He raised Him from the dead (Acts 13:30; Rom. 1:4). Thus only the Son has a right to minister as High Priest in heaven.

The writer of Hebrews then quoted from Psalm 110:4 to stress that the Father appointed His Son to a unique high-priestly office. Jesus' priesthood was not in the Aaronic line. He is a High Priest forever in "the order of Melchizedek" (Heb. 5:6). Melchizedek is a type of Christ.

The historical circumstances involving Melchizedek are recorded in Genesis 14:17-20. The imperial powers of Mesopotamia had attacked five city-states in the Transjordan and Negev. The enemy carried off a large number of captives, including Abraham's nephew Lot. As soon as Abraham heard the news, he gathered a force of 318 armed men and pursed the invaders north to Damascus. The patriarch took the eastern kings by surprise and achieved a stunning victory. He not only rescued Lot but also everything else the enemy had stolen.

The grateful king of Sodom was about to suggest to Abraham that he keep all the plunder and return only the captives; but, before the king could make this proposition, Melchizedek—the ruler of Salem (later Jerusalem)—met Abraham and blessed him. The patriarch then gave him a tenth of the items he had rescued.

B. Characterized by Reverence and Piety: vs. 7

During the days of Jesus' life on earth, he offered up prayers and petitions with loud cries and tears to the one who could save him from death, and he was heard because of his reverent submission.

In Hebrews 5:7, the writer directed his readers' attention to the time in the Garden of Gethesemane when Christ anguished over the prospect of having to die on the cross (Luke 22:39-44). With loud cries and tears, Jesus appealed to the one who could save Him from death. Because Christ honored and obeyed the Lord, God the Father answered His request by raising Him from the dead.

C. Designated in the Line of Melchizedek: vss. 8-10

Although he was a son, he learned obedience from what he suffered and, once made perfect, he became the source of eternal salvation for all who obey him and was designated by God to be high priest in the order of Melchizedek.

The author, in Hebrews 5:8, may have been alluding to Jesus' temptation in the desert as well as to the Crucifixion when he wrote about Jesus' afflictions. In the process of His suffering, Jesus "learned obedience." This does not mean Christ turned from disobedience to obedience; rather, it means that He obeyed God in a way that He had never done before. The Son obeyed the Father as a human being.

Verse 9 says that Jesus was "made perfect." This does not mean that Christ was ever imperfect. The writer was stressing that Jesus' human experience entered a new dimension of fullness and completion as a result of overcoming temptations and dying on the cross.

Whereas Aaron and his successors offered many sacrifices that could never really atone for sin, Christ offered one perfect sacrifice—Himself—to atone for sins forever; and, whereas the Aaronic priests served for a limited time, Christ's priesthood abides forever (7:23-28).

Jesus' life of learned obedience and His victory over sin offset the disobedience of Adam (Rom. 5:19). That is why Christ could become the source of "eternal salvation" (Heb. 5:9) for all who "obey him." Stated another way, Jesus lives forever to intercede as the believer's "high priest" (vs. 10).

Discussion Questions

1. What qualifies Jesus to be our high priest?
2. How do these qualities encourage us to hold firmly to our faith?
3. In what matters do we especially need His mercy and grace?
4. What do Christ's reverent submission and obedience suggest with regard to our walk with God when we suffer?
5. What steps can we take to improve our relation with our heavenly High Priest?
6. What is there about Jesus that we can offer to someone else?

Contemporary Application

Does Jesus really care? This is a question that frequently crosses our minds when we face tough times. The devil immediately sows seeds of doubt, suggesting that, if Jesus really loved us, we would not be going through a difficult experience.

Intellectually, we know Jesus cares, but it is difficult to allow that fact to override our emotional pain, doubts, and fears. That's one reason why the teaching about Jesus as our High Priest is so important and valuable.

When we're down, we can tell Jesus how we feel and that we know He experienced what we are called to endure. Because He suffered as one of us in His humanity, we know we are not alone. He has gone before us and He wants us to come to His Father's heavenly throne for help.

We find great encouragement for ourselves and others when we ask Jesus to show us what it means to obey in the midst of suffering. And we have a significant message of hope to those who have never known Jesus as their High Priest.

Be Faithful to Teaching

DEVOTIONAL READING

Psalm 119:97-106

DAILY BIBLE READINGS

Monday June 28
*Galatians 1:6-12 There Is
No Other Gospel*

Tuesday June 29
*Galatians 5:1-10 Stand
Firm in Christ's Freedom*

Wednesday June 30
*Hebrews 10:32-39 Don't
Abandon Your Confidence*

Thursday July 1
*Psalm 119:97-101 Your
Decrees Are My Meditation*

Friday July 2
*Psalm 119:102-106 Your
Word Is a Light*

Saturday July 3
*Hebrews 5:11-6:3 Move on
to Solid Food*

Sunday July 4
*Hebrews 6:4-12 Do Not
Become Sluggish*

Scripture

Background Scripture: *Hebrews 5:11—6:12*
Scripture Lesson: *Hebrews 5:11—6:12*
Key Verse: *Therefore let us leave the elementary teachings
about Christ and go on to maturity.* Hebrews 6:1.
Scripture Lesson for Children: *Joshua 2:1-4,8-9, 11b-14;
6:20, 23*
Key Verse for Children: *"The LORD your God is God in
heaven above and on earth below."* Joshua 2:11.

Lesson Aim

To encourage students to remain faithful to Christ and
grow in spiritual maturity.

Lesson Setting

Time: *Before A.D. 70*
Place: *Possibly from Rome*

Lesson Outline

Be Faithful to Teaching

    I. No Longer Babes: Hebrews 5:11-14
        A. *Slowness to Learn: vs. 11*
        B. *Slowness to Mature: vs. 12*
        C. *Maturity and Immaturity Contrasted: vss. 13-14*
    II. A Call to Spiritual Growth: Hebrews 6:1-12
        A. *Moving Forward in Understanding: vss. 1-3*
        B. *Refusing to Forsake Christ: vss. 4-8*
        C. *Remaining Confident of Better Things: vss. 9-12*

Introduction for Adults

Topic: *A Call to Higher Faith*

Our churches include people of weak and strong faith, people who know virtually nothing about the Bible and people who have been studying and living the Bible for many years. In such circumstances it is hard to know how to stress the importance of possessing a growing, mature faith. After all, what difference does it make?

Many people are comfortable with the spiritual level they have attained. They lack the desire to learn and grow. They do not believe the warning that without growth they are in danger of spiritual drift and decay.

We must show the values of a strong, mature faith. We can help one another in worship, Bible study, and service. Above all, we must make sure that our own faith is an attractive advertisement to others of the value of Christian growth.

Introduction for Youth

Topic: *Growing Stronger*

Jim broke his wrist in a fall, and when his cast was removed he was amazed by how much strength he had lost. Physicians told him that our muscles start to atrophy within 48 hours if we cannot use them. Therefore, it takes considerable therapy to regain our strength.

Spiritual atrophy sets in just as quickly and with the same results. When we break fellowship with God by disobeying Him, we lose spiritual strength and vitality.

The Hebrew Christians were in danger of losing their spiritual grip. The writer recommended a good diet and told them to push up their learning skills. With good exercises, they would grow stronger in Christ.

There are no secrets. Faithful worship, prayer, fellowship, and obeying what God tells us to do will keep us on the road to spiritual strength.

Concepts for Children

Topic: *Rahab's Faith Saved Her Family*

1. The Israelites needed help to conquer Jericho.
2. God gave them help in the person of Rahab.
3. Rahab's faith in God led her to hide the spies and claim a promise of their protection.
4. God took care of Rahab and her family when Jericho fell.
5. Rahab is a strong example of how we can trust God in times of risk and danger.
6. When we believe God's love and power, we can do what He asks us to do.

The Lesson Commentary

I. No Longer Babes: Hebrews 5:11-14

A. Slowness to Learn: vs. 11

We have much to say about this, but it is hard to explain because you are slow to learn.

The author of Hebrews had compared Jesus to the angels and to Moses. The writer had also called Christ our King and High Priest. Although the author would later in his epistle continue to establish both Jesus' purpose and superiority, he interrupted his theological argument to warn his readers against slipping into a denial of the Christian faith.

The writer had been explaining that Jesus fulfilled His role as God's appointed High Priest when He offered His body as a sacrifice for our sins. The author sensed, though, that his readers had become spiritually sluggish and mentally lazy; and, because they had not pursued maturity in the faith, they had not reached their full spiritual potential. Consequently, they were not astute enough to follow his teaching (5:11).

B. Slowness to Mature: vs. 12

In fact, though by this time you ought to be teachers, you need someone to teach you the elementary truths of God's word all over again. You need milk, not solid food!

The writer pointed out that a span of time had elapsed since the Hebrews had originally received the Christian message. Their knowledge of the faith should have advanced, but instead it was stagnant. Rather than function as teachers, they needed to be reminded of some of the doctrinal basics; and instead of being able to devour spiritually "solid food" (vs. 12), they were still in need of spiritual "milk."

C. Maturity and Immaturity Contrasted: vss. 13-14

Anyone who lives on milk, being still an infant, is not acquainted with the teaching about righteousness. But solid food is for the mature, who by constant use have trained themselves to distinguish good from evil.

The author of Hebrews wrote that spiritual infants have not advanced enough in their growth to understand teaching about "righteousness" (5:13). The point is that the recipients of the epistle had not yet learned through instruction and experience how to discern right from wrong. In contrast, the mature are ready for spiritually "solid food" (vs. 14). Because they exercise themselves in spiritual perception, they gain sound judgment to "distinguish good and evil."

Training and competition in athletic events form the backdrop of the metaphor behind this verse. In fact, the English word "gymnasium" is derived from the Greek term rendered "trained." In essence, just as one gets a physical workout in a gymnasium, so we build up our moral and mental muscles by training our senses to discern good and evil.

II. A CALL TO SPIRITUAL GROWTH: HEBREWS 6:1-12

A. Moving Forward in Understanding: vss. 1-3

Therefore let us leave the elementary teachings about Christ and go on to maturity, not laying again the foundation of repentance from acts that lead to death, and of faith in God, instruction about baptisms, the laying on of hands, the resurrection of the dead, and eternal judgment. And God permitting, we will do so.

After admonishing his readers for their lack of moral and spiritual development, the author of Hebrews encouraged them to advance from their knowledge of "elementary teachings" (6:1) of the Christian faith to a more mature understanding of doctrinal truths. It would be incorrect to think he wanted them to depart from these teachings; rather, he wanted them to hold firmly to these basic truths of the faith while acquiring a more substantive knowledge about the Lord.

The Greek term rendered "maturity" could also be translated "completeness." The writer of Hebrews contrasted being at the stage of spiritual maturity to that of elementary knowledge. In order to advance from the latter to the former, one needed to actively pursue full growth in Christ.

After one has laid the foundation of a building, the action is not repeated; instead, one goes on to add the walls and the rest of structure. Similarly, the readers of the epistle should have built on the foundational teachings of the Christian faith they had learned.

The items listed in verses 1-2 would have been familiar to members of an orthodox Jewish community. If modern Christians were asked to develop a list of six elementary teachings, they might not include all those in the writer's list, and they might include some the author left out. Thus, it is important to note that some of the items in the Hebrews list are teachings carried over from Judaism.

For instance, the Greek word for "baptisms" (vs. 2) is not the one typically used for Christian baptism, but the one referring to Jewish washings or purification rites. And Jews practiced the laying on of hands for commissioning someone to public office or as part of the sacrificial ritual long before Christians practiced it in imparting the Holy Spirit. Apparently, the readers of the epistle figured they could relax or even regress to their former Jewish teachings and forget the distinctions between Jewish beliefs and Christian beliefs.

The author, realizing that his readers were toying with the idea of slipping back into Judaism, stressed the importance of going forward to Christian maturity. God's help, of course, would be needed in learning and heeding Christian doctrine (vs. 3). Perhaps the writer was reminding his readers that full credit for any spiritual growth ultimately went to God.

B. Refusing to Forsake Christ: vss. 4-8

It is impossible for those who have once been enlightened, who have tasted the heavenly gift, who have shared in the Holy Spirit, who have tasted the goodness of the word of God and the powers of the coming age, if they fall away, to be brought back to repentance, because to their loss they are crucifying the Son of God all over again and subjecting him to public disgrace. Land that drinks in the rain often falling on it and that produces a crop useful to those for whom it is farmed receives the blessing of God. But land that produces thorns and thistles is worthless and is in danger of being cursed. In the end it will be burned.

The author of Hebrews felt the need to warn his readers that there was a danger greater even than immaturity. That grave danger was apostasy. The writer denied the possibility of "repentance" (6:6) to a certain group of people once they have fallen away. This group is made up of people who have benefited from five experiences, most of which can be interpreted in at least two ways.

First, these people "have . . . been enlightened" (vs. 4). By this the author may have meant they have come to understand the full implications of the Gospel. Or he may have meant they have been baptized. Second, these people "have tasted the heavenly gift." This may mean they have accepted God's gift of grace for salvation. Or it may mean they have participated in the Lord's Supper. Third, these people "have shared in the Holy Spirit." This perhaps means they have been endowed by the Holy Spirit and have exercised His gifts. Or perhaps it means they have experienced the laying on of hands.

Fourth, these people "have tasted the goodness of the word of God" (vs. 5). Does this mean they have accepted the Gospel by faith, or does it merely mean they have heard Scripture readings and Christian preaching? The experts are undecided. Fifth, these people "have tasted . . . the powers of the coming age." This means they have observed and perhaps personally benefited from the miracles of the messianic age, which began with Christ's advent.

Interpreters for centuries have approached these verses with caution. In fact, Bible scholars today remain divided over whether the people who have participated in the five experiences cited in verses 4 and 5 are authentic Christians. The pivotal phrase is in the next verse: "if they fall away" (vs. 6).

Some Christians claim the people cited in verses 4 and 5 are individuals who merely profess to be believers, not genuine ones who later defect. In contrast, other Christians maintain the people cited in these verses are genuine believers who later lost their faith. Yet another view is that the people cited in these verses are genuine believers who backslide but don't lose faith.

Regardless of which viewed is preferred, it's clear the writer was dealing with a serious issue. He warned that there is no way for those who fall away "to be brought back to repentance" (vs. 6). Here again, different scholars have understood the Greek word rendered "impossible" in varying ways.

Some say the writer meant that repentance in such cases is impossible for humans, but not for God. Others say the writer meant that repentance is impossible as long as the defector continues in defiant insurrection. Still others say the author meant literally what he said—it is an absolute impossibility to repent again after having enjoyed experiences like the five listed. In that way these scholars equate falling away with blasphemy against the Holy Spirit (see Mark 3:29).

In any of these views the eternal gravity of falling away remains uncontested. Those who apostasize crucify the Son of God all over again and subject Him to public disgrace (Heb. 6:6). In essence, the person who does this demonstrates that he or she has come to despise the fact that the Son of God died for his or her sins.

The author resorted to an agricultural analogy to help explain his warning in verses 4-6. He described two fields, both of which receive rain. One field is cultivated and produces a crop. This field "receives the blessing of God" (vs. 7). The other field grows and therefore will eventually be cleared by burning. This field "is in danger of being cursed" (vs. 8).

The writer's point is clear. The Hebrews were like a field. The five experiences noted in verses 4 and 5 were blessings of God like rain. If a person remained faithful, he or she would be like the first field: spiritually fruitful and divinely blessed. But if a person fell away, he or she would be like the second field: spiritually barren and divinely cursed.

C. Remaining Confident of Better Things: vss. 9-12

Even though we speak like this, dear friends, we are confident of better things in your case—things that accompany salvation. God is not unjust; he will not forget your work and the love you have shown him as you have helped his people and continue to help them. We want each of you to show this same diligence to the very end, in order to make your hope sure. We do not want you to become lazy, but to imitate those who through faith and patience inherit what has been promised.

Addressing his readers as "dear friends" (Heb. 6:9), the author told them that, despite his warnings, he was "confident" they would continue to grow in Christian maturity. This, in turn, would be an evidence of their regenerate status. The writer assured his readers that the Lord would always remember how they had served and loved Him and His people (vs. 10). Indeed, they were continuing to serve God by assisting their fellow believers; also, He would one day reward those believers who show kindness to His people.

This truth would help the readers to see that God cared for them and had not ignored them. As they labored for Him and helped their fellow believers, these Christians would be energized in their faith; and, as they encountered hard times, they would be less likely to get discouraged. In fact, despite the hardships, the Lord's awareness and approval of their good deeds would strengthen their faith in and devotion to Him.

After commending these Christians for their work, the author encouraged them to "show this same diligence to the very end" (vs. 11). The idea is that, by continuing to show Christlike love to the end of their lives, the Hebrews would make certain the reality of their hope for salvation.

The writer, cautioning against being "lazy" (vs. 12), stated his desire that his readers would imitate believers characterized by "faith and patience." He did not want them to simply observe these people of faith; rather, he wanted them to actively perform the same task that the faithful had performed. If his readers would do this, they would be sure to possess what God promised, as had the faithful.

Discussion Questions

1. How might the fact that the original readers were living under the threat of persecution affect the way we interpret the Letter to the Hebrews?
2. To what degree were the readers of this epistle responsible for their own spiritual dullness?
3. How do you think the writer intended for his readers to be trained by practice to "distinguish good from evil" (5:14)?
4. How do you think the writer would have defined the word "maturity" (6:1)?
5. What specific steps can we take to move us in the direction of spiritual maturity?

Contemporary Application

It is our sinful human tendency to be lazy and undisciplined; and it takes a lot of motivation and effort to move forward to Christian maturity. We must say *no* to worldly desires and sinful impulses and *yes* to the things of God. We must train ourselves to be faithful in our walk with Christ and in doing what God desires. If we decide it is not worth the effort, we will become spiritually lethargic and too debilitated to be of any use to God.

One way of broadening and deepening our faith in Christ is through an in-depth study of the Bible. God's Word not only teaches the basic doctrines of the Christian faith, but also provides the principles we need for daily living.

A popular saying is applicable here: "What makes the difference is not how many times you have been through the Bible, but how many times and how thoroughly the Bible has been through you." In other words, it is not enough for us to study the Bible—no matter how long we have been in the faith. We must also apply its teachings to our lives.

Another way for us to press on to spiritual maturity is by accepting and fulfilling responsibilities available to us in the church or with regard to some other Christian activity. For example, we could become mentors, a role that involves teaching and discipling others. This demands that we not only study God's Word more seriously during our preparations than we otherwise would on our own, but also that we use the spiritual knowledge we have learned from our walk with the Lord.

Jesus Brings a New Covenant

DEVOTIONAL READING

Hebrews 10:10-18

DAILY BIBLE READINGS

Monday July 5
*Jeremiah 31:31-37 I Will
Make a New Covenant*

Tuesday July 6
*Hebrews 8:1-6 Jesus,
Mediator of a Better
Covenant*

Wednesday July 7
*Hebrews 8:7-13 God's Laws
Written on Our Hearts*

Thursday July 8
*Hebrews 9:1-12 The Blood of
Christ Secured Redemption*

Friday July 9
*Hebrews 9:13-18 The Blood
of Christ Purifies Us*

Saturday July 10
*Hebrews 9:23-28 Christ's
Sacrifice Removes Sin*

Sunday July 11
*Hebrews 10:10-18 Christ's
Single Offering Perfects Us*

Scripture

Background Scripture: *Hebrews 8—9*

Scripture Lesson: *Hebrews 8:6-12*

Key Verse: *The ministry Jesus has received is as superior to
theirs as the covenant of which he is mediator is superior to the
old one, and it is founded on better promises.* Hebrews 8:6.

Scripture Lesson for Children: *Judges 7:2-5, 7, 16-18, 20-21*

Key Verse for Children: *[Gideon] worshiped God . . . and
called out, "Get up! The LORD has given the Midianite camp
into your hands."* Judges 7:15

Lesson Aim

To encourage the students to rejoice in the provisions
of the new covenant.

Lesson Setting

Time: *Before A.D. 70*

Place: *Possibly from Rome*

Lesson Outline

Jesus Brings a New Covenant

   I. A Priest in the Heavenly Sanctuary: Hebrews 8:6

  II. A Declaration of the New Covenant:
     Hebrews 8:7-12

     A. *The Need for a New Covenant: vs. 7*

     B. *The Nature of the Old Covenant: vss. 8-9*

     C. *The Nature of the New Covenant: vss. 10-12*

Introduction for Adults

Topic: *Call to Perfection*

When two people are in love, they try their best to make each other happy. Then they make a commitment to mutual love, trust, and respect. This is called the marriage vow or covenant. Then, in the following years, if theirs is a mutually satisfying relationship, they try to please each other, not because there is a law dictating them to do so, but because of their mutual love.

Our relationship with Christ is something like that. We want to please Him, not because we are mandated to do so, but because He lives in a new covenant relationship with us. In our relationship of love with Him, we want to bring Him joy, honor, and glory.

When we commit ourselves to Christ by faith, we start to carry out a lifelong journey of trust and obedience. We realize that we are His people and that we belong to Him. The wonderful blessings and privileges of salvation under Jesus' new covenant motivate us to grow in our knowledge of Him.

Introduction for Youth

Topic: *A Spiritual Pact*

People are constantly entering into agreements, and some of these are better than others. Regardless of the inferiority and limitations of all humanly devised arrangements, the new covenant between God and His people is flawless. Those who trust in Christ can rest assured that God will one day fulfill everything He has pledged to do for them in this agreement.

The sacrifice of Christ on the cross is the basis for this last statement. His atonement enables our relationship with God to be profoundly transformed. By trusting in the Son, we are no longer outsiders looking in on the family of God. We have become His spiritual children, enjoying all the blessings and responsibilities that come with family membership. Let us rejoice in these wonderful truths.

Concepts for Children

Topic: *Gideon's Faith Delivered Israel*

1. God gave Gideon a plan to reduce the number of his troops.
2. God promised Gideon victory over the Midianites with only 300 troops.
3. Gideon's soldiers blew their trumpets, broke their jars, and help up their torches as they shouted in praise to God.
4. Each of Gideon's soldiers stood in his place around the camp, and the Midianites cried out and fled.
5. God can use our faith in Him to do great things for Him.

The Lesson Commentary

I. A PRIEST IN THE HEAVENLY SANCTUARY: HEBREWS 8:6

But the ministry Jesus has received is as superior to theirs as the covenant of which he is mediator is superior to the old one, and it is founded on better promises.

In Hebrews 7, the author explained that Christ's priesthood is according to the order of Melchizedek. By describing Jesus' high-priestly ministry in this way, the writer of the epistle established a basis by which he could emphasize how much better that ministry was to the Levitical priesthood. Hebrews 8 continues this line of reasoning regarding the superiority of Christ's priesthood.

Unlike other priests, our High Priest is so great that He has now taken His rightful place in heaven, God's dwelling place, at the right hand of the Father (vs. 1). That Jesus sat down implies that He has completed His work of salvation. And to have sat down at the right hand of the Father implies that Christ has earned and deserves to be in the place of highest honor.

The writer, by making a slight adjustment in his presentation of the imagery of heaven, wrote that Jesus is a servant "in the sanctuary, the true tabernacle set up by the Lord, not by man" (vs. 2). At Mount Sinai, God had instructed Moses to construct a tabernacle, a tent that was to be set up in the center of the Israelites' encampments as they traveled toward the promised land. It was to be the center of the Israelites' worship. The writer said that the sanctuary of that earthly tent was modeled after the sanctuary in heaven, at which Christ serves as our High Priest. In fact, the author called the earthly tabernacle "a copy and shadow of what is in heaven" (vs. 5).

God Himself set up the sanctuary in heaven, and He gave Moses specific details as to how to set up its earthly counterpart. God wanted the earthly tabernacle to reflect heavenly reality. That is why He warned Moses, "See to it that you make everything according to the pattern shown you on the mountain" (vs. 5; see Exod. 25:40). Even so, because humans constructed the earthly tabernacle, it was defective and temporary. Because God established the heavenly sanctuary, it is perfect and permanent.

The author reminded his readers that the high priest offers sacrifices for the sins of the people. Therefore, he reasoned, our High Priest must also have something to offer as a sacrifice for our sins (Heb. 8:3). This is true even though Christ does not carry out the ongoing duties of His priesthood here on earth—even though His sacrifice of Himself did take place here. The writer said that earthly priests perform their duties in earthly sanctuaries. Their priesthood is on the earth. Christ is the heavenly counterpart of that priesthood in a far greater sense.

Christ could not become an earthly priest and carry out priestly functions in the temple because by birth He belonged to the tribe of Judah. On earth the tribe of Levi was prescribed by the Mosaic law to perform those functions (vs. 4). Because Jesus' ministry is heavenly and unlimited, it is superior to that of the Levitical priests. Jesus, as the mediator between God and humanity, has established a new and better covenant than the old one based on the Mosaic law. The new covenant is better precisely because it is "founded on better promises" (vs. 6). The author would spell out those "better promises" in verses 10-12.

II. A DECLARATION OF THE NEW COVENANT: HEBREWS 8:7-12

A. The Need for a New Covenant: vs. 7

For if there had been nothing wrong with that first covenant, no place would have been sought for another.

Some Bible scholars hold that the idea of the covenant is the determining or controlling concept of Old Testament thought. The author of Hebrews mentioned the concept of covenant by name in 8:6. In verses 7-13, he demonstrated where he got his notion of a new covenant.

The author resorted here to an argument parallel to one he had used earlier (see 7:11-28). He had already maintained that, if the Levitical priesthood had been sufficient, there would have been no need for God to talk about another order of priesthood (see Ps. 110:4). Similarly, the writer of Hebrews argued, if the first covenant had sufficiently met the needs of people and had adequately provided for their salvation, then there would have been no need for a new covenant to replace it (8:7). But the old covenant was insufficient and inadequate. It was not adequate to bring people to God, and therefore a new covenant had to be established.

B. The Nature of the Old Covenant: vss. 8-9

But God found fault with the people and said: "The time is coming, declares the Lord, when I will make a new covenant with the house of Israel and with the house of Judah. It will not be like the covenant I made with their forefathers when I took them by the hand to lead them out of Egypt, because they did not remain faithful to my covenant, and I turned away from them, declares the Lord.

The author of Hebrews next explained that God, through the Old Testament prophets, foretold the coming of the new covenant. But before beginning the quotation from Jeremiah 31:31-34, the writer of Hebrews said that God had found fault with the people under the old covenant (vs. 8), primarily because they did not continue in that covenant. Although God initiated the old covenant with the Israelites, the people agreed to it. Thus the covenant was a mutual obligation between God and the people. But the people often failed to live up to their part of the obligation. As a result human failure rendered the old covenant inoperative.

At this juncture the author employed the longest Old Testament quotation used in the New Testament—Jeremiah 31:31-34. This prophecy, quoted in Hebrews 8:8-12, is most completely treated here in the New Testament. Although Ezekiel had written about God's establishing an "everlasting covenant" (Ezek. 16:60), only Jeremiah had spoken about a "new covenant" (Jer. 31:31).

Jeremiah did not say that the covenant God made with the Israelites would be renewed. Rather, the prophet said that a completely new covenant would be established (Heb. 8:8). Thus it would not even be "like" (vs. 9) the old covenant. Jeremiah also explained why the old covenant was a failure: "because [the houses of Israel and Judah] did not remain faithful to [the Lord's] covenant, and [He] turned away from them."

C. The Nature of the New Covenant: vss. 10-12

This is the covenant I will make with the house of Israel after that time, declares the Lord. I will put my laws in their minds and write them on their hearts. I will be their God, and they will be my people. No longer will a man teach his neighbor, or a man his brother, saying, 'Know the Lord,' because they will all know me, from the least of them to the greatest. For I will forgive their wickedness and will remember their sins no more."

The prophet Jeremiah, turning from the failure of the past covenant to the promise of the new covenant, described at least four ways in which the new covenant would be better than the old. First, the new covenant would be inward and dynamic (Heb. 8:10). God's Word would actually have a place inside the minds and hearts of His people. The old covenant had been inscribed on tablets of stone and was external; but in regard to the new covenant, His people would internalize His teachings.

Second, the new covenant would provide a way for believers to have an intimate relationship with God. Here Jeremiah echoed several Old Testament promises (see Gen. 17:7; Exod. 6:7; Lev. 26:12); but the life, death, and resurrection of Christ opened a new avenue for people to relate to their heavenly Father. Because of the salvation Jesus provided, all believers can enter into God's presence.

Third, the new covenant would enable believers to have a deeper knowledge of God (Heb. 8:11). An inclusiveness about knowing and learning about God will exist under the new covenant that was foreign to the people under the old. No longer will this knowledge be limited to some people. All believers will have a personal knowledge of the Lord.

Fourth, through the new covenant, the forgiveness of sins is an eternal reality (vs. 12). The all-knowing God will not only pardon our sins, but also never again remember them. Through Christ's sacrifice, our sins have been dealt with once for all.

After concluding the quotation from Jeremiah, the author of Hebrews wrote a sentence that was pivotal to his entire argument, for it makes a clear demarcation between the old covenant and the new. The establishment of a new covenant naturally implies that the old covenant is obsolete. And what is obsolete needs to be replaced; what is replaced becomes useless; and what is useless will eventually disappear from the scene altogether (vs. 13).

Discussion Questions

1. What weaknesses do you see in the old covenant?
2. Under the old covenant, did the greater problem lie with the covenant or the people who did not keep it? Why?

3. Within the new covenant, what laws has God placed in His people's minds and hearts?

4. In what sense do new covenant Christians not need teachers (Heb. 8:11)?

5. What greater responsibilities do we, as new covenant Christians, bear?

Contemporary Application

Some people are startled to think that God chooses to have a relationship with human beings. They figure instead that He just wants to boss people around. This week's lesson text makes God's will clear. He wants all people to know Him intimately.

This heart-to-heart relationship with God is cultivated through several key factors. Believers need to have an accurate understanding of God and how He deals with people. Christians must also trust the Lord completely. This requires them to believe that He has their best interests at heart.

Such an intimate relationship will thrive when believers communicate openly with God through prayer. They are willing to venture out and express to Him their hidden doubts, negative feelings, and inappropriate desires. Such prayers allow them to receive God's forgiveness and find help from Him.

Finally, a heart-to-heart relationship with God is built on hope. The Lord understands the believers' need for assurance about what the future holds. He thus offers them unceasing fellowship with Him in the present and the promise of a joyful eternity to come.

Roll Call of the Faithful

Scripture

Background Scripture: *Hebrews 11*

Scripture Lesson: *Hebrews 11:1-2, 4-13*

Key Verse: *Without faith it is impossible to please God, because anyone who comes to him must believe that he exists and that he rewards those who earnestly seek him.* Hebrews 11:6.

Scripture Lesson for Children: *1 Samuel 17:12-14, 20, 38-40, 45, 48-49*

Key Verse for Children: *"This day the LORD will hand you over to me, . . . and the whole world will know that there is a God in Israel."* 1 Samuel 17:46.

Lesson Aim

To encourage the students to be strong in their faith.

Lesson Setting

Time: *Before A.D. 70*
Place: *Possibly from Rome*

Lesson Outline

Roll Call of the Faithful

   I. Faith Described: Hebrews 11:1-2
      A. *Hope and Certainty: vs. 1*
      B. *Ancient Testimonies: vs. 2*

  II. Faith Exemplified: Hebrews 11:4-13
      A. *Abel: vs. 4*
      B. *Enoch: vs. 5*
      C. *All Who Believe: vs. 6*
      D. *Noah: vs. 7*
      E. *Abraham: vss. 8-12*
      F. *Faith's Endurance: vs. 13*

Introduction for Adults

Topic: *Living Faith*

How much faith is enough faith? Biblical insight into this matter can be found in Hebrews 11. Faith is never described as the lever to demand things from God; rather, faith is exemplified as enduring trust in God's promises, which transcend the here and now.

Faith drives us to believe that eternal values are the most important. We keep looking for "the city with foundations" and for a "heavenly country." While that city and country are our eternal reward, we live by faith now according to God's standards of justice and holiness.

This means that our faith moves us out from the proclamation of the Gospel to help people in need. We bring help in the here and now because our hope is firm in God's promises. Faith prompts obedience, hope, love, and hard work.

Introduction for Youth

Topic: *Faith Alive*

In his novel, *A Walk to Remember,* Nicholas Sparks vividly tells how Jamie, a high school senior, brings an entirely new perspective into the life of her boyfriend. She does this, not with high-pressure religion, but by living out her own faith in God.

Eventually, not only Landon but also his family and his pals come to a new appreciation of the power of faith in the rough and tumble of high school life in a small town. Jamie moved them, not by her preaching, but by her living faith.

The possibilities of similar responses to faith arise almost every day. If our faith means anything, we will put it on the line in front of our friends. We need to talk with one another about how to do this tactfully and lovingly. We need to talk about how to handle ridicule and possible loss of friends.

When our faith permeates our values and our conduct, others will see the difference. Some will be changed, and some will not. But we are called to be faithful at all times and in all places.

Concepts for Children

Topic: *David's Faith Delivered a Nation*

1. David was the youngest of Jesse's eight sons.
2. David followed Jesse's orders to go to his older brothers' encampment.
3. Just as David got there, the army of Israel was going into battle.
4. King Saul dressed David in armor to fight Goliath.
5. David took off the armor and faced Goliath with just his sling and five smooth stones he had chosen.
6. Just as God gave David the strength to face Goliath, so too God can give us the strength to obey Him.

The Lesson Commentary

I. FAITH DESCRIBED: HEBREWS 11:1-2

A. Hope and Certainty: vs. 1

Now faith is being sure of what we hope for and certain of what we do not see.

In Hebrews 10:38, the writer quoted Habakkuk 2:4 to stress that the righteous person lives by faith. Based on that statement, Hebrews 11 is devoted to portraying the lives of Old Testament heroes who lived by faith. As result, chapter 11 is probably the best-loved portion in Hebrews and is often called "The Honor Roll of Faith." It furnishes us with brief biographies of belief and encourages us to fortify our faith in God as many who have gone before us have done.

The original readers of Hebrews may have wondered if it would be easier simply to fade back into their former Jewish traditions and religious practices. To them the author gave a description of biblical faith. He said that faith is a present and continuing reality. It is the confident assurance that gives substance to what we "hope for" (vs. 1). Faith is also the evidence for our conviction of the certainty of "what we do not see."

In this discussion, "faith" is a key theological term. In one sense, it refers to a person's trust in God. In another sense, it is used in the New Testament to refer to the body of truths held by followers of Christ. Belief, or faith, can be understood as having four recognizable elements. First is *cognition*, an awareness of the facts; second is *comprehension*, an understanding of the facts; third is *conviction*, an acceptance of the facts; and fourth is *commitment*, trust in a trustworthy object.

Popular opinion sees faith as irrational. It is supposedly believing in something even when your mind tells you not to. In contrast, the biblical concept of faith includes both reason and experience. Such faith, however, is not limited to what we can see. It makes unseen spiritual realities perceivable, not by willing them into existence, but by a settled conviction that what God has said about them is true.

B. Ancient Testimonies: vs. 2

This is what the ancients were commended for.

The writer implied by his remarks that there are realities for which there is no visible evidence; and yet those realities are no less true. It is through faith that we know those realities exist, especially God's promise of salvation, which cannot be physically seen or felt. How, then, can one recognize the presence of faith in the life of a believer? The author appealed to a long list of biblical examples to answer this question. God commended them precisely because of their faith in Him (Heb. 11:2).

There are two problems some people have with the past. They either disregard it or forget it. Hebrews 11 stresses the importance of remembering the past and living by faith. We discover from the testimony of other believers who have gone before us that we can remain faithful to the Lord—despite the hardships we might be experiencing—because He will remain faithful to us.

The writer said it was the faith of the Old Testament saints that made them pleasing to God. Their trust in the Lord was well founded, for He is the Creator and Ruler of the universe. We perceive with the mind that the physical universe was equipped by the spoken command of God. Biblical faith enables us to perceive and accept the truth that what is seen was made out of what cannot be seen (vs. 3). Despite all appearances to the contrary and despite all of the naturalistic explanations about the origin of the universe, God gave existence to the cosmos. We have nothing but the written Word of God to explain how life first began, and we believe what it has revealed to us.

II. FAITH EXEMPLIFIED: HEBREWS 11:4-13

A. Abel: vs. 4

By faith Abel offered God a better sacrifice than Cain did. By faith he was commended as a righteous man, when God spoke well of his offerings. And by faith he still speaks, even though he is dead.

The author began his list of those who lived by faith with the example of Abel (Heb. 11:4). Both Abel and his brother Cain brought sacrifices to the Lord; but because of Abel's faith, his sacrifice was more pleasing to God than Cain's. The Lord thus commended Abel for being a righteous person (see Gen. 4:1-16).

Righteousness by faith becomes a key theme in Hebrews 11. Though the upright actions of faithful people are referred to time and again, the author implied that faith was the wellspring of their righteous acts and that God commended them for their faith (see Gen. 15:6).

Numerous conjectures have been recorded as to why Abel's sacrifice was superior to Cain's. Some think God accepted Abel's sacrifice because, as an animal offering, it involved blood, whereas Cain's, as a type of grain offering, did not. Others note that Abel's sacrifice was living and Cain's was lifeless, or that Abel's grew spontaneously and Cain's grew by human ingenuity.

Perhaps the strongest reason Abel's offering was accepted and Cain's was rejected lies in the attitude of both brothers. Abel offered his sacrifice willingly, and thus his was a demonstration of faith. Hebrew 11:4 reveals that, though Abel is dead, his faith speaks to all the generations that follow him.

B. Enoch: vs. 5

By faith Enoch was taken from this life, so that he did not experience death; he could not be found, because God had taken him away. For before he was taken, he was commended as one who pleased God.

Hebrews 11:5 next mentions Enoch, about whom Scripture says little. Because of his faith, Enoch did "not experience death." Instead, God took him away (see Gen. 5:24). The reason is that Enoch's life "pleased God" (Heb. 11:5).

C. All Who Believe: vs. 6

And without faith it is impossible to please God, because anyone who comes to him must believe that he exists and that he rewards those who earnestly seek him.

The author stressed that it is impossible to please God "without faith" (Heb. 11:6). Those who approach Him must first believe that He exists. Moreover, they must believe that He rewards those who "earnestly seek him." Expressed differently, we must believe that God both exists and cares for us. Here we see that faith is so foundational to the Christian life that one cannot be in a relationship with God apart from it.

D. Noah: vs. 7

By faith Noah, when warned about things not yet seen, in holy fear built an ark to save his family. By his faith he condemned the world and became heir of the righteousness that comes by faith.

The writer next touched on the faith of Noah (Heb. 11:6). God warned him about something that was yet to happen. Because Noah had faith, he responded to God in reverence and obedience. In particular, Noah built an ark to preserve his family and some of the earth's living creatures. Moreover, he warned an ungodly generation about the coming catastrophe. Here we see that true faith results in good works.

Because Noah took God at His word, the Lord rescued him and his family from the destruction of the Flood. Noah became an "heir of the righteousness that comes by faith." The unbelieving world, however, was condemned for its preoccupation with the present.

E. Abraham: vss. 8-12

By faith Abraham, when called to go to a place he would later receive as his inheritance, obeyed and went, even though he did not know where he was going. By faith he made his home in the promised land like a stranger in a foreign country; he lived in tents, as did Isaac and Jacob, who were heirs with him of the same promise. For he was looking forward to the city with foundations, whose architect and builder is God. By faith Abraham, even though he was past age—and Sarah herself was barren—was enabled to become a father because he considered him faithful who had made the promise. And so from this one man, and he as good as dead, came descendants as numerous as the stars in the sky and as countless as the sand on the seashore.

Abraham, like Noah, made important life choices based upon the promises of God. While the patriarch lived in Ur of the Chaldees, the Lord commanded him to leave his country and move his family to a place God would later make known (Heb. 11:8). This meant departing from relatives, friends, and familiar surroundings to travel to an unknown location.

Abraham, in faith, obeyed God's command. The patriarch's response shows how obedience and faith are related to one another in the believer's life. In short, faith is expressed through obedience.

Though Abraham knew he was going to a place he would one day inherit, he was unacquainted with the land. He had no maps or travel guides to help him know what his ultimate destination would be. He had only God's command and promise. This suggests that the implications of faith and obedience are not always obvious.

Abraham continued to live by faith even after he had reached his destination. While in Canaan, he adopted the lifestyle of a sojourner or temporary resident (vs. 9). Though God had promised to give the patriarch the land as an inheritance, he and his son Isaac and grandson Jacob lived in tents and moved from place to place. Abraham trusted that God would fulfill His promise in His own time and in His own way.

Though a pilgrim, Abraham did not live aimlessly. He was seeking a "city with foundations" (vs. 10). This refers to the heavenly Jerusalem, the dwelling place of God and His people (12:22). The Lord is the one who designed and constructed this everlasting city. It is a fitting dwelling place for those who have trusted in God (Rev. 21:2-4).

It was by faith that Abraham and Sarah were enabled to become parents at a late age (Heb. 11:11; see Gen. 15:1-6; 21:1-7). God's promise to the patriarch was that he would have countless descendants (Heb. 11:12; see Gen. 22:17); and yet Abraham and Sarah were well past the normal parenting age when their son, Isaac, was conceived. Abraham, nevertheless, kept faith in God and His promise, and eventually that promise was realized.

F.   Faith's Endurance: vs. 13

All these people were still living by faith when they died. They did not receive the things promised; they only saw them and welcomed them from a distance.

The people mentioned in Hebrews 11:8-12 were still living by faith when they died; yet not one of them had seen the ultimate fulfillment of God's promise (vs. 13). They had accepted God's promise by faith, even though His promise was not clearly visible; and they had recognized that the complete fulfillment of God's promise was heavenly, not earthly. They saw themselves as earthly pilgrims whose ultimate citizenship was in God's hands.

Here we see that the will of God is not some mysterious destiny that must somehow be pried from the hidden counsels of heaven. Its broad outlines are plainly revealed in Scripture. For instance, it is God's will that we live holy lives and seek His guidance in every circumstance. Regardless of how many options lie before us, it is always God's desire that what we do is in harmony with His Word.

Discussion Questions

1. What for you is the significance of the description of faith recorded in Hebrews 11:1?
2. Why do you think our faith in Christ so pleases God?
3. Why do you think God preferred Abel's sacrifice over Cain's?
4. What enabled various Old Testament examples of faith to maintain strong trust in and obedience to the Lord?
5. To what step of faith might God be calling you?

Contemporary Application

Faith and action are inseparably linked. This is evident from the lives of the saints discussed in Hebrews 11. Just as the Old Testament heroes of faith trusted and obeyed God, so must we. Our obedience to the will of God should impact every area of our lives—from the office to the home.

Stepping out in faith requires our readiness to obey God's will. This, in turn, can lead us down unexpected paths. At first this might seem scary to us; but then we come to see that God knows what is best for us. We learn through life experiences to wait on His timing when it comes to enjoying the blessings of faith. Some of these come in this life, but most are received in eternity.

One example of the clarity of God's will for us is His desire that we live holy lives and seek His guidance in every circumstance. Regardless of how many options lay before us, it is always God's will that we act in harmony with His Word.

Like the saints who are mentioned in the Old Testament, we might struggle from time to time with doubts. Instead of allowing uncertainty to control us, we should examine our fears in the light of what Scripture teaches. The truth of God's Word can calm us when we are feeling anxious about something; and the Lord's faithfulness to us and others can encourage us when we are going through difficult times.

Faithfulness and Discipline

DEVOTIONAL READING

1 Peter 4:12-19

DAILY BIBLE READINGS

Monday July 19
Psalm 94:8-15 Happy Are Those God Disciplines

Tuesday July 20
Deuteronomy 8:1-5 The Lord Your God Disciplines

Wednesday July 21
Hebrews 12:1-6 Run with Perseverance

Thursday July 22
Hebrews 12:7-11 Discipline Yields the Fruit of Righteousness

Friday July 23
Hebrews 12:12-17 Make Straight Paths for Your Feet

Saturday July 24
Hebrews 12:18-24 Watch How You Treat God's Grace

Sunday July 25
Hebrews 12:25-29 Offer God an Acceptable Worship

Scripture

Background Scripture: *Hebrews 12*
Scripture Lesson: *Hebrews 12:1-13*
Key Verse: *Endure hardship as discipline.* Hebrews 12:7.
Scripture Lesson for Children: *2 Kings 5:1-4, 9-16*
Key Verse for Children: *"If only my master would see the prophet who is in Samaria! He would cure him of his leprosy."* 2 Kings 5:3.

Lesson Aim

To encourage the students to seek to become more holy as they experience God's discipline.

Lesson Setting

Time: *Before A.D. 70*
Place: *Possibly from Rome*

Lesson Outline

Faithfulness and Discipline

  I. Run Your Race: Hebrews 12:1-3
     A. *Determining to Do So: vs. 1*
     B. *Focusing on Jesus: vss. 2-3*

  II. Accept Your Discipline: Hebrews 12:4-6
     A. *The Struggle against Sin: vs. 4*
     B. *The Value of Heavenly Discipline: vss. 5-6*

  III. Trust Your Heavenly Father: Hebrews 12:7-13
     A. *Sharing in God's Holiness: vss. 7-10*
     B. *Reaping Righteousness and Peace: vs. 11*
     C. *Reaching Out to the Discouraged: vss. 12-13*

Introduction for Adults

Topic: *Maturing in Faith Through Discipline*

We would all agree that disciplines of various kinds have shaped our lives in significant ways in our families, homes, and careers. But we struggle with the fact that God disciplines us for our good.

Perhaps discipline as a word scares us, for it too often carries the idea of punishment rather than the concepts of correction, training, and growth. We believe that babies and children need discipline; but as God's people, too often we rebel when He tries to teach us something.

The writer of Hebrews focused more on the results than on the process of God's discipline, and he was very concrete about the positive outcomes: holiness and fruitfulness. As we fix our eyes on Jesus in our walk of faith, we can be confident that He will bring us through—not only to cross the finish line, but also to cross it with honor and glory for the Lord.

Introduction for Youth

Topic: *Accepting Discipline*

"This is going to hurt me more than it does you." How often my father said that before he disciplined me. We may cry out to God in the midst of some trial, only to realize that He is allowing the difficulty to occur for our eternal good. We discover that this is true when we yield to God's discipline and mature spiritually.

This week's lesson stresses the importance of becoming more holy as we experience God's discipline. All of us have a need to become more holy—more fully set apart for God and His service. This can only take place as we wholeheartedly commit ourselves to following Christ.

Concepts for Children

Topic: *A Girl's Faith Helped a Leper*

1. Naaman's disease created an opportunity for loving service.
2. A young servant girl demonstrated both love and faith.
3. The girl believed the reports about a prophet named Elisha.
4. Other servants persuaded the army officer to change his mind, and God healed him.
5. God gives us many opportunities to help people, some of whom may not be too eager to accept God's love.
6. With courage and faith we can tell people about Jesus.

The Lesson Commentary

I. RUN YOUR RACE: HEBREWS 12:1-3

A. Determining to Do So: vs. 1

Therefore, since we are surrounded by such a great cloud of witnesses, let us throw off everything that hinders and the sin that so easily entangles, and let us run with perseverance the race marked out for us.

Hebrews 12 begins with the author's describing the Christian life in terms of a footrace, a popular sporting event in his day. The writer's comparison shows us that from the day we come to faith in Christ until the day we die, our life is one long contest against everything that would prevent us from achieving holiness and fulfilling the Lord's will for our lives.

Chapter divisions, which were placed in the Bible centuries after it was written and compiled, can prove misleading. For instance, Hebrews 12:1-3 piggybacks perfectly onto chapter 11. In fact, the first word in 12:1 ("Therefore") alerts us to the fact that what we are reading proceeds directly from what comes before it. The writer said, "Therefore, since we are surrounded by such a great cloud of witnesses." Presumably the witnesses were people of faith mentioned in chapter 11.

From the perspective of runners in a stadium, the spectators all around them in the stands might look something like a cloud of people. In a sense Christians also have a cloud of people watching us: the saints in heaven. As "witnesses" (12:1), they watch us and cheer us on in our race. They are also motivating examples of faithfulness.

With the departed saints as our examples, we should "throw off everything that hinders and the sin that so easily entangles." Runners in the ancient world raced unclothed. So like throwing off cumbersome clothing, we should throw off everything that might impede our spiritual progress. In mentioning "the sin that so easily entangles" us, the writer may have had in mind particularly the danger of defection resulting from discouragement—in other words, apostasy.

We are to "run with perseverance the race marked out for us." This goes to show that our spiritual race is more like a marathon than a sprint. We must have the determination and the fortitude to keep running a long time and not quit.

B. Focusing on Jesus: vss. 2-3

Let us fix our eyes on Jesus, the author and perfecter of our faith, who for the joy set before him endured the cross, scorning its shame, and sat down at the right hand of the throne of God. Consider him who endured such opposition from sinful men, so that you will not grow weary and lose heart.

Every race has a definite goal, a tape to break. The wise runner is one who keeps his or her eyes on the finish line and doesn't look back. As Christians, we too have a goal; we are heading for Jesus. And so the writer of Hebrews urged, "Let us fix our eyes on Jesus" (12:2). After all, Christ is "the author and perfecter of our faith." While we must persevere in our running, it is Jesus who enables us to both begin and complete the race.

One way Jesus helps us to finish our race is by being an example. He is the champion runner of the ages. As we struggle in our race, we can know that He has already been there and has shown that the race can be won. Just as we are to keep our eyes fixed on Jesus, so He kept His eyes fixed on the joy of completing the mission the Father had given to Him. And just as we are to persevere in the race marked out for us, so Jesus "endured the cross, scorning its shame." The cross brought great suffering and disgrace, but Christ kept in mind that the glory of enduring the cross would be much greater.

Despite facing the highest hurdle anybody has ever had—the Cross—Jesus successfully completed His race. And instead of receiving the wreath of leaves awarded to a victorious runner in the ancient world, Christ was rewarded with supreme authority. He took His seat in the place of highest honor beside His Father's throne in heaven.

The writer of Hebrews, knowing that his readers would sometimes feel weary and lose heart because of opposition, urged them to consider Jesus (vs. 3). The Lord had to endure terrible opposition from sinners, and yet He persevered until He won the victory. Taking inspiration from Christ, we can persevere in our race no matter what obstacles wicked people may place in our way. Christ is our supreme example.

II. ACCEPT YOUR DISCIPLINE: HEBREWS 12:4-6

A. The Struggle against Sin: vs. 4

In your struggle against sin, you have not yet resisted to the point of shedding your blood.

> A schoolmaster was once asked what would be the ideal curriculum for children. He answered, "Any program of worthwhile studies, so long as all of it is hard and some of it is unpleasant." The original readers of Hebrews had been experiencing what was hard and unpleasant in their "struggle against sin" (12:4). Thankfully, however, none of them had so far "resisted to the point of shedding . . . blood." This probably means none of them had been martyred.

B. The Value of Heavenly Discipline: vss. 5-6

And you have forgotten that word of encouragement that addresses you as sons: "My son, do not make light of the Lord's discipline, and do not lose heart when he rebukes you, because the Lord disciplines those he loves, and he punishes everyone he accepts as a son."

> Despite the fact that their struggle was not as bad as it could be, the Hebrews were being tempted to look on their suffering in the wrong way. Once more the author brought in some Old Testament Scripture to hammer home his point. This time he zeroed in on Proverbs 3:11-12.
>
> This passage teaches those being disciplined by the Lord to respond properly. We are not to err by making light of it. Neither are we to err by losing heart, taking it *too* seriously. We should recognize that discipline from the Lord is a sign that

He loves us and considers us His spiritual children (Heb. 12:5-6). And therefore, we should accept His discipline and pay attention to what He's trying to teach us through it.

III. Trust Your Heavenly Father: Hebrews 12:7-13

A. Sharing in God's Holiness: vss. 7-10

Endure hardship as discipline; God is treating you as sons. For what son is not disciplined by his father? If you are not disciplined (and everyone undergoes discipline), then you are illegitimate children and not true sons. Moreover, we have all had human fathers who disciplined us and we respected them for it. How much more should we submit to the Father of our spirits and live! Our fathers disciplined us for a little while as they thought best; but God disciplines us for our good, that we may share in his holiness.

The author's aim was to make his audience aware of suffering as a teaching tool used by God; in other words, discipline is pedagogical. Therefore, the writer's punch line plummets out of the first part of Hebrews 12:7—"Endure hardship as discipline; God is treating you as sons."

Normally good parents discipline their children. Likewise, God disciplines all His spiritual children. When He does so, we should not think He no longer cares about us. Rather, we should recognize that the discipline demonstrates we are members of His heavenly family (vss. 7-8).

Furthermore, the writer argued from the lesser to the greater ("how much more")—from human parents upward to the heavenly Father (vs. 9). If we respect our earthly parents when they discipline us, we should much more "submit to the Father of our spirits and live!" Discipline by God should not cause us to think worse of Him, but rather to respect Him all the more.

In human discipline there is always the element of imperfection, even though our parents disciplined us as well as they knew how (vs. 10). By an upgraded contrast, divine discipline is always "for our good, that we may share in his holiness." God's discipline is always wise, and we can be sure it is needed and contributes to our spiritual growth.

B. Reaping Righteousness and Peace: vs. 11

No discipline seems pleasant at the time, but painful. Later on, however, it produces a harvest of righteousness and peace for those who have been trained by it.

The author admitted that no discipline is pleasant while it's occurring; in fact, it's downright painful. The benefit appears only later, when it "produces a harvest of righteousness and peace for those who have been trained by it" (Heb. 12:11). The Greek word rendered "trained" is based on the word from which we get *gymnasium.* We could say discipline gives us a tough workout, but helps us get into shape. As the saying goes, "No pain, no gain."

Because God is our loving heavenly Father, He never disciplines us for sadistic reasons. And He does not enjoy seeing us experience pain. When God disciplines us, His intent is to help us grow and succeed in our walk with Christ. When we try to avoid God's discipline, we sacrifice long term spiritual maturity for short term ease. The real joys and victories of the Christian life will elude us, unless we yield to God's loving hand of discipline in our lives.

C. Reaching Out to the Discouraged: vss. 12-13

Therefore, strengthen your feeble arms and weak knees. "Make level paths for your feet," so that the lame may not be disabled, but rather healed.

The writer of Hebrews, perhaps returning to the running imagery, exhorted his readers to strengthen their limp hands and enfeebled knees (12:12). Verse 13 extends the imagery by quoting from Proverbs 4:26. The Hebrews were to smooth out the racetrack so that even the lame could get around it without falling and hurting themselves.

The idea is that, as we are running our own race, we should look out for our fellow believers and try to help them succeed in their races as well. By God's grace the Christian life is one in which we all can eventually wear the wreath of victory—no matter what disabilities we start with.

Here we see that a holy response to God's discipline is realistic, not naive, about life. We should not minimize the pain and loss we or others are experiencing. Instead, we should remain confident that God will bring good out of evil and that He will not forsake us. We become more holy when we remain calm after being terminated from work. And we grow in holiness when we respond with kind words to those who hurl abusive comments at us. Furthermore, when we show love, not hatred, after being harassed by others, we become more holy.

Discussion Questions

1   In your opinion, what is the relationship between Hebrews 11 and 12?
2. What kind of weight do you think prevents believers from running their race well?
3. Why is it appropriate for God to discipline us as His spiritual children?
4. In what ways has God disciplined you? How have you responded?
5. What can you do to help other believers run their race of faith better?

Contemporary Application

You have probably heard sermons in which the speaker defined holiness as being set apart to God for His use. The basic idea is that we belong to God and exist to do His will. Because we are His children, He disciplines us so that we might become more holy in our thinking, in our acting, and in our witness for Him.

The way we respond to God's discipline can shape our view of life. For instance, we become more worldly in our thinking if we respond to God's discipline with bitterness and anger. In contrast, we become more holy in our thinking when we respond to His discipline with humility and trust.

Our growth in holiness can enhance our witness to others; for instance, imagine a friend at church who gets angry with you over something you said. If you lash out in anger, you could worsen the situation. By remaining calm and respectful, you give God the opportunity to enhance your witness and move you along to spiritual maturity.

As we run the race of Christian living with perseverance, we leave an example for others to follow. We encourage them to break with sinful habits and become more Christlike in their behavior. We also spur them on to spiritual maturity. As an outcome of our marathon of faith, we not only possess the fruit of an upright life, but also assist those who are coming after us to grow in godliness.

Select Good Leaders

DEVOTIONAL READING

Acts 20:17-28

DAILY BIBLE READINGS

Monday July 26
Acts 6:1-7 Select Those Full of the Spirit

Tuesday July 27
Acts 20:17-24 Paul Didn't Shrink from His Ministry

Wednesday July 28
Acts 20:25-31 Keep Watch over the Flock

Thursday July 29
Hebrews 13:7-17 Remember Your Leaders

Friday July 30
1 Timothy 3:1-7 A Bishop Must Be above Reproach

Saturday July 31
1 Timothy 3:8-13 Deacons Must Be Serious

Sunday August 1
1 Timothy 5:17-22 Good Leaders—Worthy of Double Honor

Scripture

Background Scripture: *1 Timothy 3:1-13; 5:17-19*
Scripture Lesson: *1 Timothy 3:1-13; 5:17-19*
Key Verse: *Keep hold of the deep truths of the faith with a clear conscience.* 1 Timothy 3:9.
Scripture Lesson for Children: *Acts 6:8-9, 13-15*
Key Verse for Children: *Stephen, a man full of God's grace and power, did great wonders and miraculous signs among the people.* Acts 6:8.

Lesson Aim

To accept and apply God's principles of church leadership.

Lesson Setting

Time: A.D. *62–64*
Place: *Macedonia*

Lesson Outline

Select Good Leaders

   I. Qualifications for Overseers: 1 Timothy 3:1-7
      A. An Honorable Responsibility: vs. 1
      B. Personal Background: vss. 2-5
      C. Spiritual Background: vss. 6-7
  II. Qualifications for Deacons: 1 Timothy 3:8-13
      A. Personal and Spiritual Background: vss. 8-10
      B. Wives and Deaconesses: vs. 11
      C. Faithful Service: vss. 12-13
 III. Double Honor for Elders: 1 Timothy 5:17-19
      A. Receiving Respect and Support: vss. 17-18
      B. Screening Complaints: vs. 19

Introduction for Adults

Topic: *Foundations for Effective Leadership*

From its earliest days the church was an organized body of believers, not a collection of individuals doing as they pleased. Therefore, congregational leadership is critical. Godly, effective leaders are needed because, without them, there could be anarchy in which everyone does what is right in their own eyes.

Clearly, then, congregations need responsible leaders to carry out their missions. Also, churches need qualified leaders to facilitate their spiritual ministries. A well-organized congregation lacking spiritual vitality is just another organization. We must be certain that our churches are not cut off from the life of Christ.

Introduction for Youth

Topic: *Who Me, Lead?*

After one glance at Paul's high standards for Christian leaders, our first response might be that we are not qualified for the task. Of course, it is good to be humble rather than cocky. But the Bible tells about great leaders—Moses and Jeremiah, for example—who felt unqualified for their tasks.

When we feel that way, we open the doors for God to exercise His love, wisdom, and power in our lives. Jesus sent the Holy Spirit to be our teacher and helper. He gives us all the wisdom and strength we need. In fact, Christ's power can be magnified in our weaknesses.

The Holy Spirit gifts the church with leaders. When we open ourselves to the Spirit, He uses us to help others come to saving faith in Christ. This is what it means to be a true a spiritual leader!

Concepts for Children

Topic: *Stephen Shared His Faith*

1. Stephen was part of a small group given the job of serving widows in the church.
2. Stephen was gifted with powerful spiritual qualifications.
3. Stephen was also a bold, skillful witness for Jesus.
4. Many of our friends are looking for spiritual guidance and help.
5. Many times God calls us to do things in order to prepare us for leadership.
6. Through Bible study, prayer, and worship, we can prepare ourselves to serve others.

The Lesson Commentary

I. QUALIFICATIONS FOR OVERSEERS: 1 TIMOTHY 3:1-7

A. An Honorable Responsibility: vs. 1

Here is a trustworthy saying: If anyone sets his heart on being an overseer, he desires a noble task.

Paul wrote 1 Timothy after he had left Timothy in Ephesus to deal with problems in that church. For some reason, Paul could not stay to handle the situation himself, but left Timothy there as his representative as he journeyed on to Macedonia. Paul probably wrote to Timothy shortly after arriving in Macedonia, to give him further instruction regarding his supervision of the churches in the area of Ephesus.

During Paul's first imprisonment in Rome, Ephesus had become a center of false teaching. Several years earlier Paul had foretold that spiritual wolves would enter the Ephesian church, distort the Gospel, and seek to lead people away from the truth (Acts 20:29-30). Because that prediction had come true, Paul needed Timothy to deal with these false teachers while the apostle ministered elsewhere.

Besides dealing with the false teachers, Timothy also needed to give the authoritative instructions on church order that he had received from Paul. In addition, Timothy needed encouragement and written authority to carry out the difficult assignment given to him.

First Timothy was meant to be shared with the church (4:6, 11; 6:2, 17). This epistle would let the members of the congregation know that Timothy had the authority to act, as well as give him a firm basis for the truths he taught. Paul's command for Timothy not to let anyone look down on his youth seems to have been directed beyond him to anyone in the church who might think Timothy was too young to be in a prominent leadership position (4:12).

In summary, Paul's concern in the epistle lies with Timothy, those exposed to the false teaching, and the preservation of the Gospel. Timothy had to stand on his own in the midst of the storm in the Ephesian church and help appoint leaders, as well as confront and refute the false teachers. For this he needed Paul's encouragement to be strong and remain true to the sound doctrines of the faith as well as the biblical authority to carry out his task.

In chapter 3 of his letter, Paul turned his attention to the subject of leadership in the church. It is interesting to note that he did not discuss the duties of pastors and deacons; rather, he devoted his attention to the personal qualities of those who serve in these positions. The apostle was concerned about selecting the right people because the false teachers at Ephesus were seeking positions of leadership in the church.

The statement "here is a trustworthy saying" underscores the importance Paul placed on the office of "overseer." Those who wanted to become an overseer had noble aspirations. In the New Testament the terms "overseer" and "elder" are used interchangeably and refer to the person who had general supervision and care of the church (for example, a pastor).

B. Personal Background: vss. 2-5

Now the overseer must be above reproach, the husband of but one wife, temperate, self-controlled, respectable, hospitable, able to teach, not given to drunkenness, not violent but gentle, not quarrelsome, not a lover of money. He must manage his own family well and see that his children obey him with proper respect. (If anyone does not know how to manage his own family, how can he take care of God's church?)

There were certain preconditions that had to be met before a believer could serve as a pastor of a congregation. Overseers first of all had to be blameless (1 Tim. 3:2). Paul was not referring to those who were completely sinless; rather, he meant believers who were above reproach among non-Christians.

Those who pastored also had to be faithful to their spouse. This was important in a culture where polygamy and adultery were rampant. Moreover, overseers had to be vigilant, or temperate, and sober, or earnest. These qualifications indicate that ministers must exercise wisdom, caution, and sensibility as they carried out their duties. They must be well-behaved or respectable in conduct to others. The pastor should also be hospitable, that is, willing to provide food, lodging, and fellowship to needy Christians.

Overseers had to be able to teach—in other words, skilled in communicating the Word of God. This qualification was especially noteworthy in light of the problem with the false teachers at Ephesus. It is the minister's responsibility to diligently study the Bible and teach it with clarity and conviction to his or her audience.

Pastors were not to be addicted to wine, for they needed a clear mind and a well-disciplined life (vs. 3). They were to be operating under the influence of the Spirit, not alcohol. Overseers were to be gentle people, not violent and argumentative. Their affections were to be on God, not money. They were to be characterized by patience, not belligerence and covetousness. Reasonableness and approachability, not a contentious and greedy disposition, were the qualities of a good minister.

The overseers had to do a good job of managing their family (vs. 4). For example, their children were to be well-behaved, respectful, and obedient, not rebellious and unruly. Paul reasoned that if a minister could not maintain an orderly home, how could he or she possibly succeed in providing for the spiritual needs of God's people (vs. 5).

C. Spiritual Background: vss. 6-7

He must not be a recent convert, or he may become conceited and fall under the same judgment as the devil. He must also have a good reputation with outsiders, so that he will not fall into disgrace and into the devil's trap.

There are many accounts of immature and inexperienced believers being thrust too quickly into positions of church leadership. Paul said those who were newly converted to the faith should not be made pastors, for there is a strong possibility they could become inflated with pride. They then would invite the kind of judgment God imposed on Satan when he became conceited (1 Tim. 3:6).

Finally, Paul stated that those who were chosen as overseers should have the respect of the unsaved people in the community; otherwise, they would fall under heavy criticism and be disgraced by the devil (vs. 7). If the townspeople knew about unsavory traits or activities associated with a believer who wanted to be pastor, the church had to consider him or her unqualified. Satan is never too busy to spring a trap for a minister whose life breeds scandal in the community.

II. QUALIFICATIONS FOR DEACONS: 1 TIMOTHY 3:8-13

A. Personal and Spiritual Background: vss. 8-10

Deacons, likewise, are to be men worthy of respect, sincere, not indulging in much wine, and not pursuing dishonest gain. They must keep hold of the deep truths of the faith with a clear conscience. They must first be tested; and then if there is nothing against them, let them serve as deacons.

The basic meaning of "deacons" (1 Tim. 3:8) is "servant." In the early church, they performed essential duties that complemented the overseers' activities. For this reason, the church had to exercise care in choosing deacons.

"Worthy of respect" refers to dignity, whereas "sincere" underscores the danger of giving conflicting statements. Integrity is the central idea. Such overseers invested their time in ministry, not in getting drunk or amassing wealth. Thus, piety, not greed, was the deacons' concern. Such a disposition was based on a sound understanding of apostolic doctrine. To possess a "clear conscience" (vs. 9) meant that deacons not only embraced the truth but also obeyed it.

The deacons' life was to be examined prior to selection to see whether they had the listed characteristics (vs. 10). When they had proven they were serious about their faith and found to be above reproach, they were then to be considered for church leadership.

B. Wives and Deaconesses: vs. 11

In the same way, their wives are to be women worthy of respect, not malicious talkers but temperate and trustworthy in everything.

There are two ways of understanding 1 Timothy 3:11. Some think Paul was referring to the wives of deacons, while others think he was talking about women who held the office of deaconess. Regardless of which view is taken, it is clear that women in the church at Ephesus had been a prime target of the false teachers.

Paul stressed that the women needed to be reverent and dignified, rather than given to slanderous or malicious gossip. They likewise were to exercise self-control and be worthy of trust, regardless of the situation. There is no end to the blessings such women can impart by their faithfulness to the Gospel, their virtuous testimony, and their charitable deeds.

C. Faithful Service: vss. 12-13

A deacon must be the husband of but one wife and must manage his children and his household well. Those who have served well gain an excellent standing and great assurance in their faith in Christ Jesus.

The requirements of faithfulness in marriage and well-managed households applied to deacons as well as overseers (1 Tim. 3:12). Those who served well in their leadership positions would win the respect of their fellow believers and experience "great assurance" (vs. 13) in their Christian faith.

III. DOUBLE HONOR FOR ELDERS: 1 TIMOTHY 5:17-19

A. Receiving Respect and Support: vss. 17-18

The elders who direct the affairs of the church well are worthy of double honor, especially those whose work is preaching and teaching. For the Scripture says, "Do not muzzle the ox while it is treading out the grain," and "The worker deserves his wages."

In 1 Timothy 5:17, Paul dealt with the support of elders. While some think "honor" should be used exclusively in the sense of respect, most think the context also supports financial reimbursement for church leaders who excelled at preaching and teaching. Those who preached and taught would need to spend considerable time in preparation for those activities. It was only fair that they receive some compensation for their labor.

In verse 18, Paul quoted from Deuteronomy 25:4 and Luke 10:7 to support his contention of reimbursement for church leaders. Both the Old and New Testaments uphold the right of ministers to be financially supported by those who benefit from their ministry. It is interesting to note that Paul referred to both Luke 10:7 and Deuteronomy 25:4 as divinely inspired Scripture. This implies that some Christian writings were soon placed on the same level of inspiration and authority as the Old Testament Scriptures.

B. Screening Complaints: vs. 19

Do not entertain an accusation against an elder unless it is brought by two or three witnesses.

There might be times when an elder had to endure the opposite of honor. In these cases, believers were not to consider any accusation against an elder unless it was substantiated by "two or three witnesses" (1 Tim. 5:19; see Deut. 19:15). The idea is that any action taken had to be based on established fact, not gossip or the careless slander of an adversary.

In situations where church leaders were found to be sinning (for example, the false teachers at Ephesus), Timothy was to rebuke them in the presence of the entire church. This public form of censure would serve as a warning to the rest of the congregation about the negative consequences associated with sin (1 Tim. 5:20).

Discussion Questions

1. Why do you think Paul saw quality church leadership as being so important?
2. In what way is a person's relationship with his or her family a good test of his or her potential for church leadership?
3. Do you feel the standards for church leaders should be higher than those of

other church members? Why or why not?

4. Why did Paul recommend giving even an otherwise highly qualified new Christian a time of testing before being given a leadership position?

5. What other virtues do you think are essential for quality church leadership?

Contemporary Application

The world defines leadership as the ability to direct the thoughts, plans, and actions of others. People supposedly are good leaders if they can command the obedience, confidence, respect, and loyal cooperation of their subordinates. The emphasis is on the followers doing exactly what the leader wants.

The biblical model for leadership is exactly the opposite of this. If people want to be great leaders in the eyes of God, they must unsparingly serve others. They also must humbly set aside their desires and minister to the needs of others. Their goal is to shepherd the flock of God willingly, not because they are forced to do so. Devout Christian leaders make the Bible their guidebook and the holiness of God their life aim. They seek to be an example to those whom they are spiritually leading and feeding. Their ultimate goal is to please the Chief Shepherd of their soul, not themselves.

If a survey was taken of what churches thought about their leaders, one would get a wide range of responses. A few believers would say they were satisfied with those running their church. Others, however, would complain about the leaders being too lax or too rigid, too detached or too meddling. Many would lament the lack of integrity and godliness among their leaders.

The scandals that have rocked some congregations over the improprieties of their leaders underscore the need for selecting quality individuals to serve in the church. Believers not only want godly leaders but also deserve it. Christians know that, when their church leaders are weak or lacking in credibility, the congregation suffers. Paul's teaching reminds us about the need for choosing seasoned believers for leadership positions in the church.

Be Ministers of Godliness

DEVOTIONAL READING

2 Peter 1:3-11

DAILY BIBLE READINGS

Monday August 2
*Romans 6:19-23 Become
Slaves to Righteousness*

Tuesday August 3
*2 Corinthians 6:14—7:1
Pursue Holiness*

Wednesday August 4
*1 Timothy 4:6-10 Train
Yourself in Godliness*

Thursday August 5
*1 Timothy 4:11-16 Be an
Example to Believers*

Friday August 6
*1 Timothy 5:1-8 Honor
Widows, Older Persons*

Saturday August 7
*1 Timothy 6:11-16 Pursue
Righteousness, Godliness*

Sunday August 8
*1 Timothy 6:17-21 Do Good,
Store Up Treasure*

Scripture

Background Scripture: *1 Timothy 4:7-16; 5:1-8*
Scripture Lesson: *1 Timothy 4:7-16; 5:1-8*
Key Verse: *Godliness has value for all things, holding
promise for both the present life and the life to come.*
1 Timothy 4:8.
Scripture Lesson for Children: *Acts 8:4-13*
Key Verse for Children: *Philip went down to a city in
Samaria and proclaimed the Christ there.* Acts 8:5.

Lesson Aim

To foster love and mutual respect in the church.

Lesson Setting

Time: A.D. *62–64*
Place: *Macedonia*

Lesson Outline

Be Ministers of Godliness
  I. A Good Minister of Jesus Christ:
      1 Timothy 4:7-10
      A. *The Value of Godliness: vss. 7-8*
      B. *The Hope of Salvation in God: vss. 9-10*
  II. A Godly Example: 1 Timothy 4:11-16
      A. *Setting an Example: vss. 11-13*
      B. *Remaining Diligent in Ministry: vss. 14-16*
  III. Respect for All, Honor for Widows:
      1 Timothy 5:1-8
      A. *Dealing with Different Kinds of People: vss. 1-2*
      B. *Meeting the Needs of Destitute Widows: vss. 3-8*

Introduction for Adults

Topic: *Exercise and Sacrifice*

Jean decided to start a program in weight lifting to increase her bone density and head off the inroads of osteoporosis. Her regular routine meant that some other things had to go undone. She established priorities and decided that her long-term health was most important.

In Jean's case, exercise and sacrifice went hand in hand. And so it does with our spiritual disciplines. We will not increase in godliness unless we let go of some other time-consuming activities. Those activities may not be undesirable in themselves, but if they keep us from growing in holiness, then we must get rid of them.

Paul understood the value of strict discipline in church growth and development. He called on Timothy to set the pace so that he would be known for godly conduct in everything he did. Our faith likewise calls us to be serious about our godliness. Only then will our churches flourish.

Introduction for Youth

Topic: *Faith Training*

Faith training is much harder than physical training, for the former deals with intangibles. We cannot weigh our faith or measure it against a stopwatch. But when our faith is well developed, it will show in everything we do.

The Bible does not divide life into compartments. Our faith must touch how we respond to people, how we do our work, how we talk, and how we help those in need. In that sense, our faith is very tangible.

In fact, Paul said that, if we do not provide for our families, we don't have saving faith. That's just one way we demonstrate our faith. When we are young, God gives us many opportunities to train and grow our faith. Each time we say *yes* to Him, we grow a notch in our faith.

Concepts for Children

Topic: *Philip Preached His Faith*

1. Philip became one of the first church leaders.
2. The early Christians in Jerusalem were mistreated and left the city.
3. Philip preached in Samaria the good news about Jesus.
4. Later Philip told the good news to an official from a place called Ethiopia.
5. Because Philip obeyed God, many people trusted in Jesus for salvation.
6. God wants us to tell others about Jesus.

The Lesson Commentary

I. A GOOD MINISTER OF JESUS CHRIST: 1 TIMOTHY 4:7-10

A. The Value of Godliness: vss. 7-8

Have nothing to do with godless myths and old wives' tales; rather, train yourself to be godly. For physical training is of some value, but godliness has value for all things, holding promise for both the present life and the life to come.

There were many worldly myths and old wives' tales being spread by the false teachers at Ephesus. Paul told Timothy to have nothing to do with them; instead, he was to "train [himself] to be godly" (1 Tim. 4:7). The word rendered "train" conveys the idea of discipling oneself for a particular task. In this case, Timothy was to make godliness the pursuit of his life. We are godly if our life is characterized by holiness and an abiding reverence for God.

Paul noted that bodily exercise was slightly beneficial for a short while. The apostle might have been alluding to the asceticism of the false teachers, although the image of an athlete in physical training was common in ancient times. In contrast, training oneself to be godly was eternally profitable in all areas of life. The person was spiritually blessed not only in the present but also in the future (vs. 8). For instance, a disciplined life of godly pursuits brought peace, joy, and a sense of accomplishment now and eternal riches in heaven.

In the ancient world athletes followed a strict regimen of exercise, diet, and rest in order to champion their sport. If they emerged victorious in competition, they would receive a perishable wreath. In contrast, believers spiritually disciplined themselves to bring glory to the Lord. They faced stiffer challenges with far more at stake than winning or losing an earthly trophy. The salvation of many depended on God's people faithfully proclaiming the Gospel. It is a great responsibility that should not be taken lightly.

B. The Hope of Salvation in God: vss. 9-10

This is a trustworthy saying that deserves full acceptance (and for this we labor and strive), that we have put our hope in the living God, who is the Savior of all men, and especially of those who believe.

Paul's emphasis on pursuing godliness was reliable and worthy of complete "acceptance" (1 Tim. 4:9). In fact, the promotion of spiritual and eternal values motivated believers such as Paul to serve the Lord to the fullest degree. He was willing to labor to the point of exhaustion and endure the reproach of antagonists for the cause of Christ (vs. 10).

Despite the sacrifices that were made, those who faithfully proclaimed the Gospel were trusting in the living God. They refused to make themselves or others the basis for their hope. They knew that only the Lord could save people from their sin. Although God has made salvation through Christ available to all people, only those who believe in the Son are actually redeemed.

II. A Godly Example: 1 Timothy 4:11-16

A. Setting an Example: vss. 11-13

Command and teach these things. Don't let anyone look down on you because you are young, but set an example for the believers in speech, in life, in love, in faith and in purity. Until I come, devote yourself to the public reading of Scripture, to preaching and to teaching.

As a pastor, Timothy was under obligation to command and teach the doctrinal truths Paul had laid before him. It also was Timothy's duty to continue instructing the believers at Ephesus to heed these truths (1 Tim. 4:11). Of course, the congregation needed a godly example to follow as well as sound doctrine to obey. That is why Paul urged his child in the faith to be an example of godliness to others.

Timothy was a relatively young man when Paul wrote to him. Some of the false teachers at Ephesus were putting Timothy down because he was not as old as them (vs. 12). Paul made it clear, however, that one's age was not the only factor to consider when it came to being godly. The example a minister set for others also had to be taken into account.

Spiritual maturity did not necessarily belong to elderly Christians. It also could characterize younger believers. That is why Paul urged Timothy to be a godly example to the Christians at Ephesus in what he said and did. He was to be a role model for them in the compassion he showed, the attitude he displayed, the faith he demonstrated, and the virtuous way he lived. Such a godly lifestyle would undercut the efforts of some who called his leadership into question.

Timothy was not to establish his authority by flaunting it; rather, he was to do so by being faithful to his ministerial duties. Until Paul had the opportunity to visit him at Ephesus, Timothy was to devote himself fully to the public reading, preaching, and teaching of Scripture (vs. 13).

B. Remaining Diligent in Ministry: vss. 14-16

Do not neglect your gift, which was given you through a prophetic message when the body of elders laid their hands on you. Be diligent in these matters; give yourself wholly to them, so that everyone may see your progress. Watch your life and doctrine closely. Persevere in them, because if you do, you will save both yourself and your hearers.

God blessed Timothy with the ability to do an effective job of pastoring. This was recognized and declared by various elders at the time they laid hands on him for ordination (1 Tim. 4:14). He was not to ignore or take lightly the significant leadership role he was to have in the church. Timothy was to devote personal time and energy to cultivating his pastoral gift. He also was to exercise it effectively in shepherding God's people.

Paul directed Timothy to give serious attention to his pastoral ministry. He was to diligently fulfill his ministerial call; in fact, he was to devote himself entirely to the preaching of the Word and the shepherding of the flock at Ephesus. If he faithfully discharged his duty, the growth of his spiritual life and the advancement of his ministry would be evident to everyone in the church (vs. 15).

As Timothy progressed in his pastoral duties, he was to pay close attention to how he behaved and what he believed. He was to remain true to the Gospel and loyal to the truths Paul had taught (vs. 16). Paul was convinced that Timothy's love for the Lord and His Word would be contagious among the believers he pastored.

As Timothy diligently pursued his pastoral duties, he would save both himself and those who heard him preach. We know from Scripture that God saves a person; nevertheless, He graciously uses devout believers to lead people to trust in Christ. It would be wrong to conclude, however, that God is finished working with someone the moment he or she believes the Gospel. The progressive sanctification of the believer continues until he or she is finally glorified in heaven.

III. Respect for All, Honor for Widows: 1 Timothy 5:1-8

A. Dealing with Different Kinds of People: vss. 1-2

Do not rebuke an older man harshly, but exhort him as if he were your father. Treat younger men as brothers, older women as mothers, and younger women as sisters, with absolute purity.

Paul had told Timothy not to let anyone look down on him because he was relatively young (1 Tim. 4:12). The apostle balanced out this directive by telling his spiritual child not to rebuke an "older man" (5:1). This means Timothy was not to treat the older members in a harsh or impatient manner. Instead, he was to speak to them as he would address his own father; in other words, he was to be respectful, considerate, and tactful in his choice of words.

Paul was urging Timothy not to abuse the authority he possessed as a pastor. Thus, the advice Paul gave also applied to other age groups. Timothy was to treat younger men like brothers, older women like mothers, and younger women like sisters. Regardless of what he said or did, Timothy's behavior was to be characterized by absolute purity (vs. 2). If he remembered that the Ephesian church was his spiritual family, Timothy would avoid neglecting, bullying, or taking advantage of anyone.

B. Meeting the Needs of Destitute Widows: vss. 3-8

Give proper recognition to those widows who are really in need. But if a widow has children or grandchildren, these should learn first of all to put their religion into practice by caring for their own family and so repaying their parents and grandparents, for this is pleasing to God. The widow who is really in need and left all alone puts her hope in God and continues night and day to pray and to ask God for help. But the widow who lives for pleasure is dead even while she lives. Give the people these instructions, too, so that no one may be open to blame. If anyone does not provide for his relatives, and especially for his immediate family, he has denied the faith and is worse than an unbeliever.

In 1 Timothy 5:3-16, Paul gave many guidelines regarding the treatment of widows. In the early church, the death of a woman's husband could leave her in an abandoned and helpless state. Widowhood was also viewed with reproach by many in Greco-Roman society. Thus, a widow without legal protection was often vulnerable to neglect or exploitation. Sadly, it was far too common for greedy and unscrupulous agents to defraud a destitute widow of whatever property she owned.

Paul told Timothy it was the church's responsibility to "give proper recognition to those widows who are really in need" (vs. 3). By this the apostle meant that truly destitute widows were to be materially cared for by God's people. Since widows who were homeless and penniless could not rely on support we might take for granted (for example, pensions, life insurance, and government assistance), they had to rely on Christians for financial help.

Not every widow in the Ephesian church was destitute, however. There were some who had children and grandchildren who could supply their material needs. Paul said the widow's immediate family should prove the sincerity of their devotion to Christ by financially helping out their needy parents and grandparents. This was to be done willingly and with gratitude, not grudgingly. Such a charitable response was immensely pleasing in God's sight (vs. 4).

Paul said the church had a special obligation to meet the needs of godly widows who were destitute and all alone. Although materially impoverished, they led exemplary lives of prayer and devotion to the Lord (vs. 5). What a testimony it would be for God to use the Ephesian church to answer the prayers for help made by poverty-stricken widows!

Not every widow deserved help, however. Some indulged themselves in the pleasures of the world. Although they enjoyed the ecstasies of life, they were spiritually "dead" (vs. 6). These widows were not eligible for the support of the church. Timothy was to urge them, and the whole church as well, that living for the moment was senseless and displeasing to God. He was to exhort those who focused on enjoying temporal pleasures to abandon their sinful ways and conduct themselves in a manner that was blameless or above reproach (vs. 7).

Paul again targeted believers whose parents and grandparents were struggling to financially survive. He sternly rebuked the unwillingness of some in the Ephesian church to provide for the material needs of their loved ones. The apostle said these ingrates, by their selfish and uncaring actions, had practically denied the faith. They were behaving in a way that was worse than unbelievers (vs. 8).

Discussion Questions

1. What does it mean to have one's "hope in the living God" (1 Tim. 4:10)?
2. For what reasons might Paul have been so insistent on "the public reading of Scripture" (4:13)?
3. What do you think would have happened in Timothy's ministry if he had allowed people to despise his youth?
4. Why did Paul give Timothy instructions for dealing with specific age and gender groups (5:1-2)?
5. If you were to become a quality Christian leader among your peers, which of Paul's instructions to Timothy would be most relevant in your situation? Why?

Contemporary Application

The church is filled with all sorts of people. There are men and women, large families and single people, widows and widowers, young couples and retired couples. Each of these groups represents a variety of perspectives, desires, and needs.

With such a diverse mix all worshiping, fellowshipping, and growing together as a congregation, it is easy for conflicts to arise and for divisions to occur. Misunderstandings and arguments can be avoided if everyone treats their fellow Christians with sensitivity and due regard. That is why Paul stressed the responsibility that God's people have to foster love and mutual respect in the church. This emphasis can go a long way to enhancing the unity of a congregation.

As believers we want to know what doctrines to embrace and which ones to reject. We also want to know the best way to live for God. If we look to the unsaved for answers, we will be swayed into thinking that being powerful, rich, and influential are most important. This week's lesson makes it clear that our goals in life should be based on the teachings of God's Word. We see that all false doctrines are to be rejected and that ungodly behavior is to be shunned. We also learn that our ministries for Christ should be given a high priority.

Handle God's Word Rightly

Scripture

Background Scripture: *2 Timothy 2*
Scripture Lesson: *2 Timothy 2:1-15*
Key Verse: *Do your best to present yourself to God as one approved, a workman who does not need to be ashamed and who correctly handles the word of truth.* 2 Timothy 2:15.
Scripture Lesson for Children: *Acts 16:11-15*
Key Verse for Children: *The Lord opened [Lydia's] heart to respond to Paul's message.* Acts 16:14.

Lesson Aim

To underscore the need to courageously suffer and diligently labor for Christ.

Lesson Setting

Time: A.D. *66–67*
Place: *Rome*

Lesson Outline

Handle God's Word Rightly

  I. The Value of Commitment: 2 Timothy 2:1-7
       A. *Teaching Others: vss. 1-2*
       B. *Laboring Diligently for Christ: vss. 3-7*
 II. Suffering for the Elect: 2 Timothy 2:8-13
       A. *The Suffering of Jesus and Paul: vss. 8-10*
       B. *The Faithfulness of the Lord: vss. 11-13*
III. An Approved Worker: 2 Timothy 2:14-15
       A. *Warn against Quarreling: vs. 14*
       B. *Correctly Handle Scripture: vs. 15*

Introduction for Adults

Topic: *Grace for God's Workers*

When we prepare our list of qualifications for church leaders, we often begin with their education and experience. These are important factors to consider. We can put our degrees and our positions on paper for inspection.

It's much harder, though, to evaluate the qualifications Paul had in mind for success in ministry. He upheld virtues like commitment to the Gospel and endurance in the face of persecution. Of course, professional training such as we know it was not available in his day. We can profit from such training.

At the same time, all of us—not just our leaders—must always put our devotion to Jesus above everything else. We may have many other recommendations, but without those qualities we will not count for much in God's sight.

Introduction for Youth

Topic: *Working for God*

Career options have changed dramatically in recent years. Young people can anticipate exciting work using computer technology, for example. New discoveries mean new opportunities in business and professional life.

It's hard for church leaders to compete with business and education when it comes to attracting young people to Christian ministry and service. Reading what Paul said to Timothy leaves us cold, because he said nothing about stock options and retirement benefits.

However, when we open our dreams and ambitions to God, He gives us the intense satisfaction of serving people in ministry. Like Timothy, we are called to think about what we can do for Jesus, not just professionally but with all of our interests and skills.

Concepts for Children

Topic: *Lydia Was Faithful*

1. Lydia put her faith in Jesus.
2. Lydia encouraged many people to trust in Christ.
3. As a businesswoman, Lydia had many opportunities to tell people about Jesus.
4. Jesus wants us to be faithful to Him at school and in our play activities.
5. Making friendships for Jesus requires us to reach out to people who do not know about Him.
6. When we give what we have to Jesus, He will bless many people through us.

The Lesson Commentary

I. The Value of Commitment: 2 Timothy 2:1-7

A. Teaching Others: vss. 1-2

You then, my son, be strong in the grace that is in Christ Jesus. And the things you have heard me say in the presence of many witnesses entrust to reliable men who will also be qualified to teach others.

The second time Paul wrote to Timothy, the apostle continued several themes begun in his first epistle. For instance, he wanted Timothy not to be discouraged or intimidated by those who did not respect him as the leader of the church. Paul also wanted Timothy to know how to confront and correct the false teachers who were causing confusion and dissension in the congregation and be courageous enough to stand against them (2 Tim. 2:25; 3:12-14; 4:3-5).

Paul was writing from a Roman prison and seemed to know that the end of his life was near. This was not the first time Paul had been detained by the authorities. He had been held in prison in a number of places. Earlier in Rome he had been kept under house arrest. Paul had always eventually been released. This time, however, he sensed that the outcome would be different. He spoke about how he had finished his work and completed the race. However, he did not intend that this letter to Timothy would be his last contact with him. Instead, the apostle hoped Timothy would be able to come visit him in Rome.

Church tradition states that Paul was executed by the emperor Nero near the end of his reign of terror. Nero committed suicide in A.D. 68, so Paul probably wrote this last epistle around A.D. 67.

Second Timothy reveals some of Paul's personal concerns. In it he opened his heart to his younger colleague in the faith, expressing sorrow and anger about those who had turned their backs on the apostle and left the truth of the Gospel. In some ways Paul felt completely abandoned (1:15; 4:10). The apostle thus poured out his heart to Timothy. The bleak prison walls had cut Paul off from those he longed to be with. The lonely echoes of the dungeon heightened the intensity of his desire to see Timothy as soon as possible (1:8; 2:3; 4:9).

Despite Paul's hardships, the Holy Spirit used him to minister greatly to others. The apostle's words are now part of Scripture and have continued to strengthen and encourage church leaders throughout the centuries. Pastors and lay leaders who have struggled against opposition—either from within the church or from without—have found comfort in Paul's words to Timothy as he ministered at Ephesus.

Concerning Timothy, his father was Greek, and his mother—Eunice—was a devout Jewish Christian. Timothy's mother and grandmother—Lois—diligently instructed Timothy in the Hebrew Scriptures from his earliest childhood. Luke wrote that the young man had a good reputation in both Lystra and Iconium (Acts 16:1-2).

Paul met Timothy while in Lystra on his first missionary journey. Apparently Timothy made a good impression on the apostle, for he selected him for service right away. Timothy must have been quite young when he first joined Paul on his second missionary journey—especially considering Paul's exhortation in 1 Timothy 4:12, which was written at least 10 years after Timothy began itinerating with the apostle.

Timothy accompanied Paul on numerous segments of his missionary journeys. Eventually the young man became one of the apostle's most devoted companions. This might explain why Paul planned to send Timothy to Corinth during a time of great tension and division. The breaks in his accompanying the apostle occurred when Timothy was instructed to minister at churches in such areas as Ephesus and Corinth. The testimony of Scripture is that Paul's co-worker enjoyed a long and fruitful ministry in evangelism and teaching.

With respect to the first chapter of 2 Timothy, four important truths are stressed related to Paul's overall purpose. First, he was confident that Timothy would devotedly serve the Lord at Ephesus. Second, God had given Timothy all he needed to be an effective minister. Third, Timothy was to rekindle the spiritual gift he originally received from the Lord. Fourth and finally, Timothy had excellent examples to follow in remaining loyal to Christ.

Timothy seemed to have a hesitant, reserved personality. In the face of stiff opposition from antagonists to the Gospel, it would be hard for him to remain a courageous witness. Realizing this, Paul urged his child in the faith to be spiritually strong in the grace of God that was available to all who trusted in Christ (2:1).

Timothy was not just to take a stand for the Gospel. He was also to spread the good news to other believers. Over the years as Timothy accompanied Paul on his missionary journeys, he heard the apostle teach a number of things to many people. Paul told his close friend to commit, or entrust, these truths to dependable and reliable believers who would also be qualified to teach others the same things (vs. 2). Paul's exhortation to Timothy was prompted by the fact that false teachers were constantly trying to distort the apostolic doctrines of the faith.

B. Laboring Diligently for Christ: vss. 3-7

Endure hardship with us like a good soldier of Christ Jesus. No one serving as a soldier gets involved in civilian affairs—he wants to please his commanding officer. Similarly, if anyone competes as an athlete, he does not receive the victor's crown unless he competes according to the rules. The hardworking farmer should be the first to receive a share of the crops. Reflect on what I am saying, for the Lord will give you insight into all this.

It was only a matter of time before Timothy would be persecuted for his faith. As Paul sat in a Roman prison and awaited execution, he urged his friend to patiently endure the hardship of suffering as a "good soldier of Christ Jesus" (2 Tim. 2:3).

Rather than flinch and falter when the situation became unpleasant, Paul wanted his co-worker to put up with adverse circumstances. Of course, Timothy could not fight alone against stiff opposition. He needed to rely on the grace of God made available in Christ. Timothy also had to work with other believers in battling the forces of darkness. Presumably some of these would be individuals he led to Christ and taught to be knowledgeable and loyal followers of the Savior.

Paul used three analogies from everyday life to stress how important it was for

Timothy to remain wholeheartedly devoted to the task of serving the Lord. First, soldiers on active duty would not entangle themselves in everyday matters; rather, they would remain focused on pleasing their commanding officer (vs. 4). Second, champion athletes did not win the event unless they obeyed the rules, for violations lead to disqualification (vs. 5). Third, it was the hardworking farmer who was entitled to the first share of the crops (vs. 6).

The soldier analogy stressed the importance of prolonged dedication while the athlete and farmer analogies moreover emphasized the promise of future reward. Paul was not saying that loyal servants of Christ would reap monetary riches; rather, they would be eternally blessed by God. In addition, they would have the joy of seeing lives transformed through the proclamation of the Gospel. Paul urged Timothy to seriously consider what he said. The apostle was convinced the Lord would enable his beloved friend to grasp the significance of these important truths (vs. 7).

II. SUFFERING FOR THE ELECT: 2 TIMOTHY 2:8-13

A. The Suffering of Jesus and Paul: vss. 8-10

Remember Jesus Christ, raised from the dead, descended from David. This is my gospel, for which I am suffering even to the point of being chained like a criminal. But God's word is not chained. Therefore I endure everything for the sake of the elect, that they too may obtain the salvation that is in Christ Jesus, with eternal glory.

Paul directed Timothy's attention to their Savior, Jesus Christ. He was fully human, as His ancestry from King David testified. (The Redeemer fulfilled God's promise to grant to one of David's descendants an everlasting kingship.) Jesus was also fully divine, as His resurrection from the dead confirmed (2 Tim. 2:8). Because Jesus is human, He can serve as a substitutionary sacrifice for the lost. And because He is divine, His atonement is infinite in its saving value.

The incarnation, death, and resurrection of Christ were the essential truths of the Gospel that Paul declared. We can see that he did nothing wrong in telling others about the Savior; nevertheless, the Roman authorities locked the apostle up and treated him like a criminal. Although Paul was chained, the Gospel remained unshackled (vs. 9).

For this reason, the apostle was willing to endure all sorts of suffering. His desire was that God's special people—the elect—might be saved and receive eternal glory in Christ (vs. 10). Paul was referring to the believer's final and complete salvation in which God bestowed a resurrection body and a completely transformed human nature. Through Christ, the people of God would triumph over sin and death and experience the fullness of unending joy in the Lord's presence.

B. The Faithfulness of the Lord: vss. 11-13

Here is a trustworthy saying: If we died with him, we will also live with him; if we endure, we will also reign with him. If we disown him, he will also disown us; if we are faithless, he will remain faithful, for he cannot disown himself.

Many Bible scholars think 2 Timothy 2:11-13 was part of an early Christian hymn. These verses stress the faithful and certain truth that eternal glory will follow a relatively short time of suffering for Christ. As Paul said, if we are spiritually united with Christ in His death on the cross, we likewise now have eternal life. (It is also true that we will be resurrected from the dead when Jesus returns for His church.) If we presently endure suffering for the sake of the Gospel, we will also reign with Christ in His kingdom.

Verse 12 contains a solemn warning against apostasy. If anyone denies that they ever knew Christ, He in turn will deny that He knows, or acknowledges, them as His own. On a positive note, if we are not as faithful as we ought to be, the Lord will still remain faithful to us. Our salvation does not rest on our ability to endure; rather, it depends on the faithfulness of God. After all, the Redeemer cannot deny who He is or what He pledged to do for His own (vs. 13).

III. An Approved Worker: 2 Timothy 2:14-15

A. Warn against Quarreling: vs. 14

Keep reminding them of these things. Warn them before God against quarreling about words; it is of no value, and only ruins those who listen.

Timothy was to remind the believers at Ephesus about the truths of the Gospel. This was imperative because some were teaching false doctrines. Paul's coworker was to call on God as his witness as he solemnly warned the troublemakers not to argue about inane philosophical matters that helped no one. In fact, those who listened were spiritually harmed by what was said (2 Tim. 2:14).

B. Correctly Handle Scripture: vs. 15

Do your best to present yourself to God as one approved, a workman who does not need to be ashamed and who correctly handles the word of truth.

Unlike the religious frauds at Ephesus, Timothy was to make every effort to present himself to God as one approved by Him. Timothy would have no cause for shame as long as he taught the message of truth, namely, the Gospel. He was to diligently study and accurately expound the Word so that others might know sound doctrine (2 Tim. 2:15).

Proficient use of the Scripture involves correctly handling it. In ancient Greece, the word translated "correctly handles" was used to describe a father's cutting meat into the exact proportions his family needed at mealtime. The term also was used to refer to a farmer's plowing straight furrows. Finally, the word was used to describe the careful slicing of animal hides into square sections so that a tentmaker could exactly fit and sew them together. From these illustrations we can see how important it is to precisely interpret and apply Scripture.

Discussion Questions

1. In what ways does grace make a Christian strong?
2. Why would Timothy need to "reflect on" (2 Tim. 2:7) what Paul had written?
3. In what sense could Paul believe that the Word of God was "not chained" (vs. 9)?
4. Over what types of words might Timothy and his congregation be tempted to wrangle?
5. Which of Paul's analogies seems most appropriate for you? Why?

Contemporary Application

As believers, we also cannot ignore the suffering that Christ went through for us. We moreover cannot disregard the trials. His apostles and disciples of the early church endured for our ultimate benefit. As your class members discuss the material in this week's lesson, be sure to stress that God summons believers to courageously suffer and labor for Christ.

None of us, of course, looks forward to the prospect of suffering for the cause of Christ; and yet all who want to live a godly life as a follower of Jesus will be persecuted by others. Believers also know they will suffer many things before they finally enter the kingdom of God.

So, what should be our attitude toward suffering? Some greet agony and sorrow with a detached, cold frame of mind, while others react with bitterness and rage. God's Word teaches, however, that we should face suffering with an attitude of joy, for we know that God is maturing us, making us more Christlike, and helping us to become more holy; and, as this week's lesson teaches, we should face the prospect of suffering with courage and zeal.

Remain Faithful

Scripture

Background Scripture: *2 Timothy 3:1—4:8*
Scripture Lesson: *2 Timothy 3:1-5, 12—4:5*
Key Verse: *[Timothy], keep your head in all situations, endure hardship, do the work of an evangelist, discharge all the duties of your ministry.* 2 Timothy 4:5.
Scripture Lesson for Children: *2 Timothy 1:2-7*
Key Verse for Children: *I have been reminded of your sincere faith, which first lived in your grandmother Lois and in your mother Eunice and, I am persuaded, now lives in you.* 2 Timothy 1:5.

Lesson Aim

To stress that believers should heed the truth of God's Word.

Lesson Setting

Time: A.D. *66–67*
Place: *Rome*

Lesson Outline

Remain Faithful

   I. The Rise of Godlessness: 2 Timothy 3:1-5
      A. *The Warning about the Last Days: vs. 1*
      B. *The Presence of Impiety: vss. 2-5*
  II. The Equipped Believer: 2 Timothy 3:12-17
      A. *Suffering Persecution: vs. 12-13*
      B. *Remaining Faithful: vss. 14-15*
      C. *Heeding Scripture: vss. 16-17*
 III. The Proclamation of the Word: 2 Timothy 4:1-5
      A. *Faithfully Ministering Scripture: vss. 1-2*
      B. *Taking Note of the Irreverent: vss. 3-4*
      C. *Keeping a Clear Mind: vs. 5*

Introduction for Adults

Topic: *Remaining Steadfast*

The Bible itself is our best defense against evildoers, impostors, and deceivers. Therefore, it's our duty to keep on studying, proclaiming, and obeying God's Word. At the same time, we must gear our families and churches for instruction in Scripture, both for salvation and for remaining steadfast in the face of various opponents of the Gospel.

Our Christian education programs must center on teaching salvation through faith in Christ. We dare not assume that just because people attend Sunday school and church—even those who come from Christian homes—they have necessarily come to personal faith in Christ.

Every child must respond as Timothy did when he heard the good news. Parents, teachers, and pastors working together can help to bring salvation and faith to our children.

Introduction for Youth

Topic: *Facing Hard Times*

We only mislead people when we offer the joys and blessings of the Gospel without the hardships. In our culture, however, hardships are not so easy to define. We might face some ridicule, or lose some friends, but we still have many other choices.

Perhaps we look in the wrong place for the battle for our souls. Paul warned Timothy not just about physical but also spiritual hardships. These arise when people choose contemporary myths and reject God's Word.

In today's culture, hardships could easily consist of rejecting ungodly, unwholesome elements in entertainment, literature, and sports. Satan uses music, television, radio, the Internet, books, and magazines to lure us away from God's truth. For some youths, it's a hardship to let go of these things for the sake of following Jesus.

Concepts for Children

Topic: *A Faithful Mother and Daughter*

1. Paul remembered Timothy as one of his children in the faith.
2. Paul also remembered the faith of Timothy's mother and grandmother.
3. Paul reminded Timothy to make full use of the special abilities he had from God.
4. Paul reminded Timothy that the Spirit would give him love and self-control.
5. God wants us to grow in the right ways so that we bring joy to ourselves and to others.

The Lesson Commentary

I. THE RISE OF GODLESSNESS: 2 TIMOTHY 3:1-5

A. The Warning about the Last Days: vs. 1

But mark this: There will be terrible times in the last days.

Throughout the first two chapters of 2 Timothy, Paul encouraged his younger protégé to be unwavering in his commitment to the Gospel. In the third chapter, Paul shifted his focus. Looking beyond the current situation in Ephesus, he acknowledged that in the future the church would face greater challenges and opposition.

In 3:1, Paul referred to "the last days." This is the era inaugurated by Christ at His first advent and it extends to His second coming for His people. The apostle wanted Timothy to understand that as the church age drew to a close, horrible times would come. The presence of false teachers at Ephesus represented how real the threat was.

B. The Presence of Impiety: vss. 2-5

People will be lovers of themselves, lovers of money, boastful, proud, abusive, disobedient to their parents, ungrateful, unholy, without love, unforgiving, slanderous, without self-control, brutal, not lovers of the good, treacherous, rash, conceited, lovers of pleasure rather than lovers of God—having a form of godliness but denying its power. Have nothing to do with them.

The list of vices in 2 Timothy 3:2-5 covers a broad but comprehensive range of ungodly characteristics. As the end of the age nears, people will increasingly set their affections on themselves and feed their greedy desire to amass more material goods. They will be self-congratulating and arrogant. They will slander God and revile people, rebel against parental authority, be ungrateful, and practice impiety (vs. 2).

In the last days, the wicked will be compassionless, irreconcilable, maligning and denigrating, easily led into sin, cruel and abusive, and haters of all that is good (vs. 3). They will be unfaithful and untrustworthy, reckless, bloated with conceit, and lovers of sensual pleasures rather than lovers of God (vs. 4).

These frauds will look like godly Christians; however, they will deny the power of Christ that is the basis for all true piety and devotion. Paul warned Timothy and the rest at Ephesus not to have anything to do with such people, for they could bring confusion and harm to the church (vs. 5).

II. THE EQUIPPED BELIEVER: 2 TIMOTHY 3:12-17

A. Suffering Persecution: vs. 12-13

In fact, everyone who wants to live a godly life in Christ Jesus will be persecuted, while evil men and impostors will go from bad to worse, deceiving and being deceived.

Paul was not the only one who would have to suffer for the cause of Christ. The apostle related that anyone who was united to the Savior by faith and wanted to live in a godly manner as His follower would be persecuted by opponents of the Gospel

(2 Tim. 3:12). In fact, believers should come to expect trouble from others as they witnessed for Christ.

Paul said that as the end of the church age drew near, wicked people and those who pretended to be what they were not would become worse than ever before in history. This would be especially true as they tried to deceive others and also were themselves deceived by spiritual frauds (vs. 13). It is clear that once the truth of the Gospel is abandoned, all forms of evil and subterfuge are possible. This is the terrible price that is paid for rejecting God's saving message.

B. Remaining Faithful: vss. 14-15

But as for you, continue in what you have learned and have become convinced of, because you know those from whom you learned it, and how from infancy you have known the holy Scriptures, which are able to make you wise for salvation through faith in Christ Jesus.

Over the years Paul taught Timothy a number of important things. The apostle urged his dear friend to remain faithful to what he learned, believed, and knew were absolutely true. Since these teachings came from such a trustworthy and dependable minister as Paul, Timothy could have the utmost confidence in their reliability (2 Tim. 3:14).

Paul said the message he proclaimed was consistent with the truths Timothy's Jewish mother and grandmother taught him from the holy scriptures during his childhood. The apostle's comment suggests the false teachers were improperly interpreting the Old Testament. When correctly understood, it pointed the learner to Christ, who occupied a central role in God's overall plan of redemption. The Bible gave Timothy the wisdom that would eventually lead to salvation through faith in Christ (2 Tim. 3:15).

C. Heeding Scripture: vss. 16-17

All Scripture is God-breathed. And is useful for teaching, rebuking, correcting and training in righteousness, so that the man of God may be thoroughly equipped for every good work.

When Paul wrote 2 Timothy, the books of the Old Testament were the Scriptures used by the church. At that time, the New Testament did not exist as an authoritative and finalized collection of sacred writings. In fact, some of the New Testament books were probably not yet penned. Even though this is the case, what the apostle said about the origin and accuracy of the Old Testament would equally apply to the New Testament. In other words, both Old and New Testaments are the inspired and infallible Word of God.

Paul declared that all Scripture is given by inspiration of God (2 Tim. 3:16). The apostle used a Greek term that means "God-breathed"; in other words, the Lord is the origin and ultimate author of Scripture. Although He supernaturally directed the biblical writers, He did not override their intelligence, individuality, literary style, personal feelings, or any other human factor. Nevertheless, God's own complete and coherent message to humankind was recorded with perfect accuracy.

Inspiration extends equally and absolutely to all portions of Scripture. All the books of the Bible are error-free in what they teach. This involves every aspect of them. It is not restricted to moral and religious truths but even extends to the statement of facts. This includes information of a scientific, historic, or geographic nature. The doctrine of inspiration not only encompasses details of vital importance to Christian belief, but also anything that the sacred writers affirmed to be true.

As Paul talked about the origin and authority of Scripture, he stated that the study and application of it was eternally beneficial. For example, it was immeasurably useful for teaching sound doctrine and for showing people where they had strayed from the truth. The Bible was also useful for correcting sinful behavior and for training people how to live in an upright manner.

From verse 16 we learn that God's Word is supremely authoritative. This means it possesses the absolute right to define what we should believe and how we should behave. When Scripture is consistently heeded, God's servants will be thoroughly prepared and equipped to do every kind of good work for His glory (vs. 17).

Thus, there is no substitute for Scripture when it comes to combatting false teaching, learning the ways of the Lord, and ministering for Him. We insult God, deceive ourselves, and cheat others when we fail to study the Bible diligently and obey it wholeheartedly. If each of us fills our life to overflowing with God's Word, the spiritual benefits from this act will spill over to a world that needs the knowledge of salvation. There is no other infallible beacon to guide people to an eternally safe harbor.

III. THE PROCLAMATION OF THE WORD: 2 TIMOTHY 4:1-5

A. Faithfully Ministering Scripture: vss. 1-2

In the presence of God and of Christ Jesus, who will judge the living and the dead, and in view of his appearing and his kingdom, I give you this charge: Preach the Word; be prepared in season and out of season; correct, rebuke and encourage—with great patience and careful instruction.

In 2 Timothy 1:6, Paul urged his co-worker to reinvigorate the spiritual gift God had given him. The series of appeals that followed were brought to a conclusion in the first part of chapter 4. In the midst of the opposition, Timothy would face from various antagonists to the Gospel. Paul thus urged him to never give up, but to remain faithful to his calling and ministry.

Paul began by summoning God the Father and the Lord Jesus as his witnesses. The apostle briefly noted that Christ would one day judge the living and the dead. The Savior, of course, would first return to earth and establish His kingdom (vs. 1). The comments Paul made would help Timothy to view the command he was about to receive with the utmost solemnity.

Among the many things Paul's longtime friend could do, none was more important than his dedication to proclaim the Gospel of Christ. Timothy was to be ready and willing at all times, regardless of whether it was the popular or unpopular thing to do. He was to use the Word to correct and censure the transgressor and exhort and encourage the wayward to do what was right. Paul's co-worker was also to exercise great patience as he carefully taught others the truths of righteousness (vs. 2).

B. Taking Note of the Irreverent: vss. 3-4

For the time will come when men will not put up with sound doctrine. Instead, to suit their own desires, they will gather around them a great number of teachers to say what their itching ears want to hear. They will turn their ears away from the truth and turn aside to myths.

Paul said there were some associated with the church at Ephesus who would eventually become intolerant of solid Bible preaching. Instead of welcoming the teaching of the apostles, these heretics would direct their attention to demon-inspired doctrines. The figurative expression "itching ears" (2 Tim. 4:3) means the apostates had a restless desire to learn anything but the truth. They would search for so-called religious experts who would cater to their insatiable appetite for falsehoods and lies.

These individuals would exchange the eternally lifesaving message of the Gospel for godless fables (vs. 4). Paul may have been referring to mythical Jewish stories and fabricated Old Testament genealogies, all of which were unscriptural. Those who abandoned the good news to embrace doctrinal error were misleading themselves and others. Only a return to sound doctrine could reverse the spiritual harm and confusion they created.

C. Keeping a Clear Mind: vs. 5

But you, keep your head in all situations, endure hardship, do the work of an evangelist, discharge all the duties of your ministry.

Timothy faced several different challenges to his faith and ministry. On the one hand, there were antagonists to the Gospel who would use violence to prevent the good news from spreading any further. On the other hand, there were false teachers who subverted the truth with their godless chatter.

The apostle urged Timothy to be sober-minded and mentally alert for any possible sign of attack. When trials came, Paul's co-worker was to remain calm and patiently endure the affliction. Instead of getting sidetracked like others, Timothy was to focus on his calling, namely, to proclaim the Gospel and lead people to Christ. As long as he did the work of an evangelist, he would fulfill his God-given ministerial duties (2 Tim. 4:5).

Discussion Questions

1. What happens to society when authority is ignored and people treat each other brutally?
2. Why are some people easily led astray by spiritual frauds?
3. How can our example of godliness and devotion make a difference in the lives of other Christians?

4. Why is proclaiming the Gospel so important?

5. How can we use God's Word to teach others the right way to live?

Contemporary Application

As Christians, we want our lives to count for something. If we drink heavily at the well of worldly philosophy, however, we will be led to think that everything in life is relative and fleeting. We supposedly should live it up, knowing that there is no life after death. Such notions stand opposed to the teachings of God's Word and thus are to be rejected. There is life after death, and the decisions we make now will have eternal ramifications.

If we want our lives to have eternal significance, we must commit ourselves wholeheartedly to the cause of Christ. This includes not only trusting in Him for salvation, but also willingly serving Him regardless of the circumstances. As this week's lesson indicates, faithful service to the Lord brings rich and everlasting blessings.

Thus, as we grow in our walk with Christ, we should become increasingly desirous to serve and please the Lord. We should also become more and more aware of our own sin and be shocked by the rampant violence and impiety that exists in society. Of course, a sober look at the way things are might leave us feeling mentally numb and disoriented.

That is why we need to hear and heed what is contained in this week's lesson. We learn that troubling times and terrible people are coming, and we should be prepared for the eventuality. We also discover that, despite the injustice and hardships we might endure at the hands of others, God and His Word never change. We can look to Him for strength and gain reassurance from the Bible. As we abide by the truth of Scripture, our lives will rest on a foundation that cannot be shaken by the raging forces of darkness all around us.

Do Good Works

DEVOTIONAL READING

James 1:19-25

DAILY BIBLE READINGS

Monday August 23
  2 Corinthians 9:10-15
  Generosity Glorifies God

Tuesday August 24
  *Matthew 5:11-16 Let Your
  Light Shine before Others*

Wednesday August 25
  *Titus 2:1-5 Elders Should
  Teach the Younger*

Thursday August 26
  *Titus 2:6-10 Be a Model of
  Good Works*

Friday August 27
  *Titus 2:11-15 Be Zealous for
  Good Deeds*

Saturday August 28
  *Titus 3:1-6 Be Ready for
  Every Good Work*

Sunday August 29
  *Titus 3:7-11 Good Works
  Are Excellent and Profitable*

Scripture

Background Scripture: *Titus 2:1—3:11*
Scripture Lesson: *Titus 2:7-8, 11-14; 3:1-10*
Key Verse: *In everything set them an example by doing what
is good. In your teaching show integrity.* Titus 2:7.
Scripture Lesson for Children: *Matthew 8:5-13*
Key Verse for Children: *Jesus said to the centurion, "Go! It
will be done just as you believed it would." And his servant
was healed at that very hour.* Matthew 8:13.

Lesson Aim

To underscore how vital it is for believers to make
every effort to perform good deeds.

Lesson Setting

Time: A.D. *63–65*
Place: *Macedonia*

Lesson Outline

Do Good Works
  I.   The Right Example: Titus 2:7-8
  II. The Blessed Hope: Titus 2:11-14
       A. *The Revealing of God's Grace: vs. 11*
       B. *The Implications of God's Grace: vss. 12-14*
  III. The Kindness of God: Titus 3:1-8
       A. *Doing What Is Good: vss. 1-2*
       B. *Remembering Our Sinful Past: vs. 3*
       C. *Recognizing Our Salvation in Christ: vss. 4-7*
       D. *Devoting Ourselves to What Is Beneficial: vs. 8*
       E. *Shunning Strife: vss. 9-10*

Introduction for Adults

Topic: Do the Right Thing

Over the years adults have several role models to follow and imitate. Some influence them to be good and upstanding citizens while others seem to advocate a sinful and unwholesome lifestyle. Eventually people can feel trapped in their patterns of ungodly behavior. A sense of hopelessness and despair can overwhelm them as they reflect on what their life has become.

This week's lesson teaches that people do not have to remain enslaved to sinful habits. The grace of God, which is made available through faith in Christ, can set them free. They are saved, however, to worship and serve the Lord, not their unspiritual nature. As you teach the material in the lesson, be sure to emphasize that biblical truth should lead to godly conduct among all believers, regardless of their age, gender, or social status.

Introduction for Youth

Topic: Do the Right Thing

Most of us are familiar with Ephesians 2:8-9; but how many of us know what verse 10 says? Paul wrote, "For we are God's workmanship, created in Christ Jesus to do good works." This means God gave us new life in Christ so that we might devote our time and energy to perform wholesome and beneficial deeds.

The implication is both profound and sobering. Unless we, as Christians, are actively performing good deeds, we are not existing as the Lord originally intended. In other words, we have a God-given capacity and desire to reach out to others in tangible and practical ways with the love of Christ. We will discover in this week's lesson that part of our new redemptive character includes a strong yearning to perform acts of kindness and compassion, especially for those in great need.

Concepts for Children

Topic: The Centurion Who Had Faith

1. When a Roman soldier asked Jesus to come and heal his servant, Jesus agreed to do so.
2. The soldier said that Jesus could use His authority to heal the servant from a distance.
3. Jesus said the soldier's faith was strong and told him to return home.
4. Jesus healed the servant because of the faith of the soldier.
5. Jesus is pleased when we trust in Him for our daily needs.

The Lesson Commentary

I. THE RIGHT EXAMPLE: TITUS 2:7-8

In everything set them an example by doing what is good. In your teaching show integrity, seriousness and soundness of speech that cannot be condemned, so that those who oppose you may be ashamed because they have nothing bad to say about us.

Titus was a Gentile believer who often served as Paul's emissary. For instance, at some point during Paul's ministry, he and Titus traveled to Crete. Finding that the church needed to be organized, Paul left Titus behind to "straighten out what was left unfinished and appoint elders in every town" (Titus 1:5).

Paul's letter was prompted both by the need to appoint suitable leaders in Crete and by the encroachment of false teaching there. The content of the letter indicates that false teachers had been dwelling on fables instead of on the Scriptures. False teaching had corrupted the morals of Cretan believers, who were also in danger of being influenced by their unbelieving neighbors. In addition, legalism threatened to distort the saving message of grace as the unmerited gift of God.

Paul's letter to Titus is grouped with the apostle's two letters to Timothy under the category of Pastoral Epistles because of its emphasis on the local church. Its similarity in content with Paul's First Letter to Timothy suggests that Titus was probably written about the same time, while Paul was still at liberty, between A.D. 63–65.

Paul encouraged Titus to be an example of good works to the young men in the churches of Crete. Every area of his life was to be a pattern of the kind of behavior he was to instill in others. For example, the ministry of Titus was to be free from tainted motives, one of which was the desire to become materially affluent. As he reached out to others, he was to be earnest and dignified, not indifferent and crass. Sincerity, not duplicity, was to characterize his teaching (Titus 2:7).

Titus was to remain virtuous in what he said and did. He thus would reinforce the truths of the Gospel and give them greater impact. He was to offer doctrinally correct and spiritually uplifting instruction. His teaching was to be so wholesome and pure that no one would be able to justly criticize or censure it. Despite their efforts to discredit the Gospel, the opponents of Titus would be unable to do so and ashamed for even trying (Titus 2:8).

II. THE BLESSED HOPE: TITUS 2:11-14

A. The Revealing of God's Grace: vs. 11

For the grace of God that brings salvation has appeared to all men.

In the initial part of Paul's letter, he focused on the kind of things Titus ought to teach. The apostle next provided the theological basis for the practical instructions he gave, namely, the grace of the Lord and the work of Christ. As the believers on Crete drew upon these two resources, their lives would be spiritually transformed.

In particular, Titus was to teach and encourage the believers on Crete to live in a godly manner. The grace of God—His undeserved love and mercy—was the basis for such exhortation. The light of God's grace suddenly appeared on the scene of history when Christ became a human being. Through Jesus' death and resurrection, God's grace displaced the darkness of sin and made redemption possible for everyone who believes. All people regardless of gender, race, or social status could be saved through faith in Christ (Titus 2:11).

B. The Implications of God's Grace: vss. 12-14

It teaches us to say "No" to ungodliness and worldly passions, and to live self-controlled, upright and godly lives in this present age, while we wait for the blessed hope—the glorious appearing of our great God and Savior, Jesus Christ, who gave himself for us to redeem us from all wickedness and to purify for himself a people that are his very own, eager to do what is good.

The grace of God was meant to have a transforming effect on the lives of believers on Crete. Through the proclamation of the Gospel, Titus exhorted them to renounce all forms of irreverence and impiety and to reject the wanton and forbidden desires of their past (Titus 2:12).

Titus also urged the believers on the island to cultivate three virtues in their walk with the Lord. First, they were to be self-controlled, in other words, temperate and discreet in their personal lives. Second, they were to be upright, that is, virtuous and honest in their dealings with others. Third and finally, they were to be godly—in other words, devoted to the Lord and obedient to His commands.

The period of time in which the Cretan believers lived was characterized by wickedness and rebellion. This epitomized the present evil age of world history. The coming age of the Messiah's rule stood in sharp contrast, for it would be characterized by goodness and righteousness. Titus was to urge his fellow Christians to live for the Lord. It would not be easy to obey God, especially when so many of their peers behaved in an unruly and uncivilized manner. God's grace would always be present to help His struggling people maintain a solid witness for Christ.

The believers on Crete were to lead holy lives and eagerly wait for the joyous fulfillment of their hope—the glorious return of Jesus Christ. Their hope was not something they merely wished for. It was absolutely certain to happen (Titus 2:13). Jesus' second coming would be an awesome display of His majesty and splendor. This was to be expected since He is the great God and Savior of the world.

When God the Son came to earth as a human being, He voluntarily died on the cross to redeem us. This means He paid the price to free us from the guilt and condemnation of sin. He also cleansed us from all forms of iniquity and lawlessness so that we might be His blameless and holy people. Out of gratitude, we enthusiastically search for ways to help others in need and demonstrate the truth of the Gospel (Titus 2:14).

There were three outstanding facts Titus was teach the believers on Crete. First, God saved them from their sin. Second, their redemption in Christ was intended to produce lives of virtue and godliness. Third, they were to joyously look forward to the return of their Savior.

III. The Kindness of God: Titus 3:1-8

A. Doing What Is Good: vss. 1-2

Remind the people to be subject to rulers and authorities, to be obedient, to be ready to do whatever is good, to slander no one, to be peaceable and considerate, and to show true humility toward all men.

Paul stressed the importance of submitting to every form of human government. Believers were to willingly, not grudgingly, obey their earthly rulers (Titus 3:1). Being ready to do good at all times meant that believers refused to slander and brawl with others; instead, they were to be considerate, gentle, and humble (vs. 2).

B. Remembering Our Sinful Past: vs. 3

At one time we too were foolish, disobedient, deceived and enslaved by all kinds of passions and plea-sures. We lived in malice and envy, being hated and hating one another.

Paul noted that all believers had once been disobedient, dishonest, and resentful. They needed to recognize that the way they once lived—namely, in sin—got them nowhere. It led to bickering and dissension, rather than love and unity (Titus 3:3). Paul, of course, included himself here. The specific acts may have differed, but the sinful spirit was the same.

C. Recognizing Our Salvation in Christ: vss. 4-7

He saved us, not because of righteous things we had done, but because of his mercy. He saved us through the washing of rebirth and renewal by the Holy Spirit, whom he poured out on us generously through Jesus Christ our Savior, so that, having been justified by his grace, we might become heirs hav-ing the hope of eternal life.

Perhaps the most remarkable aspect of salvation is that God redeemed us despite our sinful condition. We certainly did not deserve to be saved; yet, despite our dis-obedience, malice, and envy, He reached out to us in kindness and love by sending His Son (Titus 3:4).

Paul noted that our salvation does not rest on any good works we have done (vs. 5). Deliverance depends on God's free grace. This, in turn, results in "the washing of rebirth" (our spiritual regeneration) and the "renewal by the Holy Spirit" (our spiritual refurbishing). Christ, of course, makes the outpouring of the Spirit possi-ble (vs. 6). Having been made right with God, we look forward to the sure hope of eternal life (vs. 7).

D. Devoting Ourselves to What Is Beneficial: vs. 8

This is a trustworthy saying. And I want you to stress these things, so that those who have trusted in God may be careful to devote themselves to doing what is good. These things are excellent and profitable for everyone.

Paul noted that his instructions to Titus were true and trustworthy. The apostle thus wanted Titus to stress these teachings, which were useful and helpful to believers (Titus 3:8). Those heeding these instructions would be more inclined to do "what is good."

E.   Shunning Strife: vss. 9-10

But avoid foolish controversies and genealogies and arguments and quarrels about the law, because these are unprofitable and useless. Warn a divisive person once, and then warn him a second time. After that, have nothing to do with him.

Earlier in his letter Paul had warned Titus about the false teachers in Crete (Titus 1:10). In 3:9, Paul again alerted Titus to the excesses of these frauds. They may have held to mythical Jewish stories and fabricated Old Testament genealogies, all of which were unscriptural. The charlatans also may have been disseminating an early form of Gnosticism.

Such speculations, Paul noted, were useless and pointless, for they resulted in confusion and division. That is why Titus was to warn the troublemakers once or twice. After that, he was to have nothing to do with them (vs. 10). The apostle knew that those who refused to listen to correction were bent on living in sin. Paul declared that their actions revealed how condemned they were before God (vs. 11).

Although there is no way to be certain, some have conjectured that Titus was slightly older than Timothy and less timid in nature. In any case, we have seen from Paul's letter that Titus was capable of handling difficult assignments, perhaps because of his affection for those to whom he ministered. His ministry record was one of faithful and unselfish service. Titus is a prime example of the New Testament ideal of servant leadership. He was as capable of leading as he was following.

Discussion Questions

1. How do salvation and good works relate to each other?
2. Why are the experience of salvation and the subsequent transformed life both so important?
3. In the transformed life, why are good *words* and good *works* both so important?
4. In the church, which controversies are worth discussing?
5. What are some of the unprofitable and worthless controversies that have caused unnecessary division in local churches?

Contemporary Application

What do Mohandas Gandhi and Mother Theresa have in common? The world thinks of them as individuals who have done much good for humanity. To illustrate, both are known as social reformers with a genuine concern for the plight of the disadvantaged and homeless. Undoubtedly, there are many areas of disagreement that evangelical Christians have with these two prominent figures; nevertheless, for all their flawed beliefs and actions, the world admires the good they tried to accomplish during their lives.

How will our unsaved acquaintances remember us? Will they think about all the money we made, the prestigious jobs we had, or the vast possessions we owned? If so, our legacy will be short-lived. However, the memory of us will endure a long time if others recall us as being individuals who both loved the Lord and were eager to perform good deeds. It is sobering to realize that people remember us more for what we do than for what we say. As you teach this week's lesson, be sure to stress how vital it is for believers to make every effort to perform good deeds.

You should also note to your students that we are creatures of habit. For example, we usually follow a set routine as we get ready for each day's responsibilities. We even follow an established pattern on Sunday morning. We might drive the same route to church, attend the same Sunday school class we did a year ago, and sit in "our spot" during the worship service.

It should not be surprising to learn that we have ingrained sinful habits. These cannot be changed, however, apart from the power of God. The Spirit uses His Word to gradually but surely transform our thoughts and actions. As we submit to the teachings of Scripture, our lives begin to reflect the beauty of Christ. And as we have learned in this week's lesson, the entire process is due to the grace of God.

Notes

Notes

Notes